MODERN GREECE:

A NARRATIVE

OF A

RESIDENCE AND TRAVELS IN THAT COUNTRY;

WITH

OBSERVATIONS ON ITS ANTIQUITIES, LITERATURE, LANGUAGE, POLITICS, AND RELIGION.

BY HENRY M. BAIRD, M.A.

ILLUSTRATED BY ABOUT SIXTY ENGRAVINGS.

NEW YORK:
HARPER & BROTHERS, PUBLISHERS,
FRANKLIN SQUARE.
1856.

PREFACE.

THE author of this volume spent a year at Athens, for the prosecution of special studies, and traveled extensively, both in Peloponnesus and in Northern Greece. During repeated tours, nearly every site famous in the ancient history of the country was visited, together with those places which have figured prominently in more recent transactions. The following pages are the result of observations noted at the time, although, for various reasons, the form of a diary has not been retained throughout.

Several chapters have been devoted to the literature of Modern Greece—a subject to which little attention has been given, out of that country itself. The manners and customs, politics, religion and religious festivals, and the state of popular education, have been made the topics of separate examination. The author has taken great satisfaction in chronicling the unexampled progress of the Greek race in civilization and intelligence; and, while advocating no particular theory as to its origin, has felt that sufficient interest and sympathy have not been entertained in Christian Europe and America for the struggles of that race to free itself from the trammels of tyranny—political, religious, and intellectual—with which so many centuries of barbarism had invested it.

About forty of the illustrations in this volume have been executed after original sketches from nature.

The author can not abstain from expressing in this place his obligations to the Rev. Jonas King, D.D., and his estimable lady, whose house was his home for so many months, and whose suggestions were so useful to him in the prosecution of his plans. Nor would he fail to mention the Rev. Dr. Hill, and the Rev. Messrs. Arnold and Buel, who did all in their power to render his sojourn at Athens so fruitful of pleasant reminiscences. He would do injustice to his feelings were he to leave unnoticed the open cordiality that characterizes the Athenian men of letters, whether professors or students, and their readiness to facilitate the researches of the stranger.

CONTENTS.

CHAPTER V.

WALKS ABOUT ATHENS.

CHAPTER VI.

STUDENT LIFE IN ATHENS.

CHAPTER VII.

MODERN GREEK CUSTOMS.

CHAPTER VIII.

THE COURT AND POLITICS OF GREECE.

CHAPTER IX.

THE GREEK CHURCH.

CHAPTER X.

CHURCH FESTIVALS AT ATHENS.

CHAPTER XI.

THREE DAYS IN ARGOLIS.

CHAPTER XII.

ÆGINA AND EPIDAURUS.

CHAPTER XIII.

MANTINEA—TRIPOLITZA—SPARTA.

CHAPTER XIV.

MEGALOPOLIS AND MESSENE.

CHAPTER XV.

PHIGALEA, OLYMPIA, AND ARCADIA.

CHAPTER XVI.

STYX, MEGASPELION, AND VOSTITZA.

CHAPTER XVII.

DELPHI—PARNASSUS—CHÆRONEA.

CHAPTER XVIII.

THERMOPYLÆ AND EUBŒA.

CHAPTER XIX.

THEBES AND ELEUSIS.

CHAPTER XX.

RAMBLES IN ATTICA.

CHAPTER XXI.

THE MODERN GREEK LANGUAGE.

CHAPTER XXII.

THE MODERN GREEK LITERATURE.

ILLUSTRATIONS.

MODERN GREECE
Author's Route
IONIAN SEA
AEGEAN SEA
CORINTHIAN G.
G. OF PATRAS
SARONIC GULF
ARGOLIC GULF
LACONIAN GULF
MESSENIAN GULF
ARCADIA
ACHAIA
MEGARIS
PHTHIOTIS
THESSALY
Lamia
Larissa Cremaste
Xerochori
Achmet Aga
Vanitza
Karavanserai
Lepotina
Vrachori
Missolonghi
Thermus
Calydon
Naupactus
Galaxidi
Elatea
Hyampolis
Orchomenus
Chalcis
Eretria
Aulis
Delium
Thebes
Tanagra
Thespia
Plataea
Leuctra
Marathon
Phyle
Eleusis
Cephisia
ATHENS
Piraeus
Keratea
Thoricus
C. and T. of Sunium
Patras
Vostitza or Aegium
Monastery of Megaspelion
Kalavryta
Basilico
Kalamaki
Corinth
Nemea
Epidaurus
Mycenae
Argos
Tiryns
Nauplia
Clarenza
C. Clarenza
Elis
Sophis
Olympia
Mantinea
Tripolitza
Tegea
Andritzena
Apollo
Phigalea
Megalopolis
Stilo
Sparta
Marathonisi
Navarino
Modon or Methone
Coron
C. Gallo
SPHACTERIA
Pylus
C. Taenarum or Metapan
Napoli de Malvasia
Malea Pr.
Troezen
Hermione
Hydra
HYDRA
CALAURIA
SPEZZIA
CEOS
CYTHNUS
SERIPHUS
CIMOLOS
MELOS
SCYROS
C. Mandili
MACRIS
S. MAURA
ITHACA
Bathi
CEPHALONIA
Samos
ZANTE
Zante
CYTHERA
J. WELLS

GATE OF HADRIAN AT ATHENS.

MODERN GREECE.

CHAPTER I.

APPROACH TO ATHENS.

"Whoever does not wish to see Athens, is foolish; he who sees it and is not pleased with it, is more foolish; but the climax of folly is to have seen it, to be pleased with it, and yet to leave it."—*Ancient Author.*

On a beautiful morning toward the end of September, I found myself on board the French steam-ship *Lycurge*, off the eastern coast of Lacedæmonia. For the last three days, since leaving Valetta, we had been sailing slowly and quietly over a motionless sea in a direct course for Cape Matapan. Only at noon, on the previous day, had the faint outline of distant mountains become perceptible; and at dusk we approached the shores of Messenia. We were not yet near enough, however, to view with any distinctness the island of Sphacteria, behind which was fought the Battle of Navarino.

The wind had been contrary all night, and we made but little progress after doubling Cape Matapan. When I came on deck in the morning, the first objects visible on shore were the high mountains, not very distant, that skirt this side of Peloponnesus. So barren did they seem, that scarce a patch of verdure relieved their rugged uniformity. Below this rocky chain could be descried, as though rising out of the waves, the sea-girt walls and towers of Monembasia, a locality which finds no record in ancient history, but has appeared conspicuous in recent wars. Built, not unlike Gibraltar, on the end of a small peninsula, it is so strongly fortified both by nature and by art as to be nearly impregnable.

The sea was calm and unruffled. Not a ripple could be seen disturbing its placid surface. The sky was cloudless, and the day one of the fairest of autumn. The clear atmosphere gave to all around a deceptive appearance, which was quite new to me. The most distant objects seemed close at hand, and I could scarcely credit the assertion of the captain that we were at least five or six miles from shore. The steamer plowed its way as over the dark blue waters of some small inland lake.

We were not many hours in crossing the mouth of the Argolic Gulf, and approaching the group of islands that lie off the extremity of the northeastern peninsula of the Morea. The pretty town of Spetzia appeared on our left, built upon the side of a hill and running down to the water's edge. In half an hour more we were opposite the picturesque town of Hydra, where were born most of the distinguished naval commanders in the Revolution. At length, about noon, we entered the Saronic Gulf, and Attica itself came into sight. The passengers collected on the bows, and watched with eager eyes the shore, which seemed rather to recede as we advanced. The only unconcerned spectators were a group of Frenchmen, who, seated on a pile of luggage on the forecastle, were diverting themselves with a game of cards. Running by the island of Ægina, on whose height we could easily distinguish with a glass the ruined columns of the temple of Jupiter, in the midst of a wild and desolate district, we made toward the port of Piræus. For miles far out on the Saronic Gulf, a white building served as a beacon to indicate the site of Athens itself. It was the palace of King Otho. The rest of the town was hidden from our sight by the hill of the Acropolis. Presently we could see the high signal-pole standing on the promontory Munychium. At about four o'clock we had rounded it, and were entering Piræus through a narrow opening, guarded on both sides by the ruins of ancient moles.

The paddle-wheels had scarcely ceased to move before we were surrounded by a multitude of row-boats, each manned by a Greek in the native costume, wearing the bright red *fezi* slouched on his head, and a long blue tassel fluttering in the wind. All were loud in their appeals; but as the quarantine officers had not yet made us their visit, they kept a respectful distance. "*Have a boat, sir?*" "*Voulez-vous un bâteau?*" resounded from all quarters; while the less favored linguists, relying mainly on the strength of their lungs to make themselves understood, poured forth a volley of unintelligible Greek. Though I had been schooling myself to the native pronunciation under the friendly direction of a pleasant Sciote, whose lessons had relieved the tedium of the passage from Marseilles, their volubility was too much for my small practice. Rather than resign myself to the tender mercies of the boatmen, I resolved to make common cause with my companion, the Greek merchant. After a short delay, leave was given us to land, and this served as a signal for the simultaneous onset of half a score of couriers and runners for the hotels, each eager to get custom. We soon found the one we wanted, and, having secured our luggage, embarked in one of the boats for shore. We left the motley group of watermen, expecting every moment to see them fall from brawling to fighting; but their disputes never result in any thing more serious than the success of one in supplanting the rest.

The harbor of Piræus is less than three-fourths of a mile in length, and opens toward the west; where, between the piers that project from either side, a heavy chain was stretched during the earlier ages. The modern town lines the eastern side with a continuous row of neat white houses, generally two stories in height. A number of sloops and caïques were drawn up to the wharves, but the brigs and larger vessels stood out at anchor in deeper water.

A custom-house officer and a dozen idlers awaited our arrival on Grecian soil. The examination of our effects was brief, owing, perhaps, partly to the happy influence of a silver coin or two, which my companion managed to slip dexterously into the hand of the inspecting officer. We were in no mood after our long sea-voyage to remain longer than necessary at Piræus. My friend and myself were equally intent upon reaching our journey's end, and enjoying a respite from the fatigue and vexation of travel. I am wrong, however, in representing our eagerness as equal. I had before me only the prospect of a long, though, it is true, far from uninteresting course of study, on classic ground. The Sciote who stood beside me, an intelligent man of five-and-forty, had accumulated a handsome fortune in foreign parts, and was connected with the extensive mercantile house of A. and Co.* He had come hither, as I subsequently learned, on an errand of love.

* Mr. A., from his extensive business connections, was able to give me much valuable information respecting the Greek mercantile houses, which are every year increasing in number and in importance. I was astonished to learn how numerous they are. They already abound in England. Manchester may be styled their head-quarters, for there are no fewer than *sixty* Greek establishments in that city. London possesses *forty* more, and Liverpool seven. Trieste boasts of *seventy*, and Marseilles, Odessa, and Leghorn, each of more than twenty. How many are to be found in Constantinople it is quite impossible to state: certainly one hundred would be a very small estimate. Such were the statements of a merchant, than whom no one could be found with better means of acquiring accurate information. The wonderful success of these commercial houses he attributed to their unity of action more than to any other single cause. Prudence in all their investments, combined with rare sagacity, has insured them against loss of capital and reputation. The great houses of Rallis, Argentis, and others, have branches all over the globe, each to a certain degree independent, and yet each reposing an implicit confidence in the others. In this way, by their tact and by their union, the Greek houses have begun to exercise an important influence on the trade of the East, which is little by little falling into their hands. Through their instrumentality, Manchester fabrics are distributed over Asia Minor in exchange for native produce. The Eastern war has doubtless augmented their influence upon the grain market of the world, and the number of Greek merchants at Liverpool must now be far greater than in 1851. Mr. A.'s statements are confirmed in almost every particular by the writer of an able article on this subject in the *New York Daily Times* of October 20, 1855.

Having well-nigh, if not quite, attained the age of an old bachelor, he had bethought himself of matrimony; and, casting about for a wife, had fixed his choice upon a certain damsel whose good looks and good qualities he had taken upon trust. The negotiations between the parents and himself (for it is not customary to attach much weight to the young lady's choice in such matters) had proved mutually satisfactory. The happy man was now on his way to Athens for the first time to find his betrothed, of whose personal appearance, except by means of a portrait and descriptions, he knew about as much as I did. The lady in question was also a native of Scio, whose children rarely marry into families of foreign extraction.

Our courier had provided a carriage, one of the best the place could boast of, and we jumped in; the Greek official touched his cap, and we rattled off through the streets of Piræus. We noticed, in passing, that the streets along the wharves were well paved, and all the thoroughfares laid out with strict regard to symmetry and a regular plan. The better class of houses, too, were built of stone, neatly stuccoed. It was not long ere we emerged from the town, and entered upon the road which leads in a nearly direct line to Athens, a distance of about five miles. Nothing was requisite to beguile our attention as we rode toward "the city," as the Athenian of the olden time was wont to style it by pre-eminence. We sat watching with no common emotion the various objects that successively presented themselves to the eye. For the first time I began to realize that I was at length in Greece, and that the curtain was soon to rise upon the scene of so many triumphs of art and eloquence. As we issued from the streets of Piræus, the heights back of the town intercepted the whole prospect; but presently the plain of Athens unfolded itself before us in all its loveliness. On the right, but a few hundred yards distant, was the bay of Phalerum, running parallel to the road, and afterward making a gradual bend where the sea is nearest to Athens. Beyond it stretched the long ridge of Mount Hymettus, barren of trees and uncultivated. To the left, in the distance, rose the more pointed summit of Pentelicus, whose marble rock, exposed by the quarryings weighed down under the heavy load of the dark-blue clusters. of past centuries, reflected the rays of the sun like new-fallen snow. Then came Mount Parnes, and a chain of lower hills running down from it to the sea-shore opposite the Straits of Salamis, whose rugged isle, cleft with many a deep ravine, terminated the panorama. In the midst of the plain could be descried, far on before us, the city of Athens itself, or rather a portion of it; for the greater part lay concealed behind the Acropolis, on whose summit could barely be distinguished the columns of the Parthenon, so discolored by time as to have assumed a sober autumnal tint.

For two or three miles the dusty road along which we drove has been built on the foundations of one of the "Long Walls" connecting Athens with its port. Adjoining it is a low, marshy meadow, in the middle of which stands a lonely monument, small and plain, marking the grave of Kariskakis, who fell here in a conflict with the Turks during the Revolution. The ground about it is strewn with the bones of his brave comrades, and ever and anon, as the plough or some accident reveals to the sight a skull or a solitary bone, the peasant adds it to the heap which has accumulated within a neighboring inclosure, where the remains of so many heroes lie bleaching in the sun.

Passing this spot, the road crossed the scanty bed of the Cephissus, and entered the olive-grove which clothes either bank of the river with its dark-green foliage. The trunks of the olive-trees were thick, and occasionally assumed fantastic shapes like the willows that grow in some parts of Switzerland. Emerging from the grove, which only flourishes where the trees can be constantly supplied with water, we came to vineyards, each surrounded with its low wall of sun-dried clay, and protected from the effects of sunshine and rain by a sort of thatch of straw or brush. The vines, like all surrounding vegetation, had a dry and dusty aspect. Not a green patch of grass was any where to be seen. The distant fields were brown, as if parched by the prevailing heat; for since April or May no rain had fallen, with the exception, perhaps, of one or two transient showers. The vines were kept trimmed within a short distance of the ground, and the branches were

The vintage had begun some weeks previous, but was not yet half over.

At length, winding about the base of the hill of the Observatory, we found ourselves at the very portal of Athens. The various objects that struck the eye were already familiar to me through descriptions and delineations. The Greek merchant was astonished to see a stranger from the New World pointing out with readiness the ruins which he had never before surveyed. The Parthenon, with its brown columns towering above the town on the lofty Acropolis, was not to be mistaken. The Pnyx, witness to the eloquence of Demosthenes, and the Hill of Mars, where St. Paul addressed the men of ancient Athens, were both on the right; while the Temple of Theseus, the oldest, yet the best preserved monument of Greece, stood but a few steps from the entrance to the modern town.

I had been much interested in speculating upon the probable aspect of the modern town, and the condition of its inhabitants. From the desponding accounts of former travelers, I had formed rather low conceptions of Greek civilization and intelligence. The descriptions of the people, their appearance and manners, had left me in doubt whether they were not to be classed among semi-barbarous nations of the earth. Yet there lurked a secret hope that I might find that some prejudice had inclined those travelers to look with too little sympathy upon the struggles of a nation shaking off the chains of twenty centuries of servitude. Their foibles, I imagined, ought to be viewed rather with the eye of a Democritus than with that of an Heraclitus. Whether my anticipations were correct or not will be gathered from the sequel. I, at least, looked with delight upon every symptom of refinement, and congratulated myself upon the prospect of comfort in my future sojourn.

We had arrived on Sunday. The day being universally kept rather as a period of recreation than as one sacred to religious purposes, the streets were thronged with people engaged either in promenading or in visiting their friends. Their striking costumes, so different from any thing to be seen in western cities, gave peculiar animation to the scene. A characteristic, however, which could not but force itself on the observation, was the fact that so few well-dressed women were to be seen in the crowd; and on closer investigation I learned that they were never allowed to walk out alone or unaccompanied by husband or father. Such is still the strength of Eastern habits and notions of propriety, notwithstanding the increased communication with the rest of Europe.

We drove through a number of winding streets to the Hotel d'Orient, an old and inelegant edifice fronting on a neglected square in the immediate vicinity of the Royal Mint. The building had formerly served as the palace of the young King Otho, on occasion of his first coming to Greece; and I was, I am credibly informed, so fortunate as to occupy his majesty's bedchamber, in which I spent my first night at Athens. The only other lodgers at the hotel were a couple of Irishmen, with whom my Sciote companion and I partook gayly of a good dinner at the table d'hôte, ending off with a dessert of delicious grapes and figs, and a taste of the famous Hymettus honey. The younger Irishman was the correspondent of a London journal, but stood in daily expectation of a post under the Greek government. He considered himself secure of a professorship of English in the royal gymnasium of Patras, to which he conceived himself entitled by reason of services rendered during the late difficulties between Great Britain and this country. His rather unpatriotic effusions in defence of the Greek ministry attracted considerable notice at the time of their publication in England.

ACROPOLIS FROM THE PNYX.

CHAPTER II.

FIRST IMPRESSIONS.

THE hours were too fashionable at the Hotel d'Orient. I was impatient to sally forth; but breakfast could not be served before nine o'clock. Instead, therefore, of undertaking to explore the labyrinth of alleys we had passed through the night before, I received from my good friend the Sciote a parting lesson in pronunciation, with which I graduated from his school. Fortified with a good meal and a store of Greek phrases, I set out to find the individuals for whom I brought letters of introduction. I had too little confidence in my own proficiency to trust myself alone, and mine host committed me to a guide, who should conduct me first to the house of Dr. King. Avoiding the principal thoroughfares, he led me by the nearest route, which happened to be through a maze of crooked lanes branching off at every possible angle. Their average breadth could scarcely exceed twenty feet, and they were often lined with blank walls, or houses without a single window opening on the street. More frequently the heavy iron bars with which the latter were provided conveyed the impression that the inmates lived in hourly apprehension of a burglar's attack. We issued from one of these alleys into a wider street, paved with stone, and dignified by the name of Hadrian. The garden attached to Dr. King's house fronts upon this street; but, to reach the gate, we had to go through a narrow lane which runs along its side. Here my conductor left me engaged in a mental discussion whether I should ever be able alone to retrace my steps to my hotel.

On pushing open the heavy door, I found myself in a moderate-sized garden, the end of which is bounded by a long two-story stone house, with a broad flight of steps in front leading to the upper floor. Dr. King himself was walking in the garden. He courteously invited me to enter the house, and introduced me to his wife, who received me with equal cordiality. Mrs. King is a native Greek, born at Smyrna, and had never visited the United States; but she speaks English with fluency and grace. Mrs. King wore, like most of the Greek ladies, the dress of her native city. The most characteristic portion of this costume is the head-dress, consisting of a small red *fezi*, or skull-cap, around which the braided hair is wound. Dr. King is a man of some sixty years, rather below the medium stature, and apparently of a weak constitution. His head is large and intellectual. His face is a fair index of his character, in which suavity of manner and warmth of heart are associated with an unusual measure of determination and energy. In its well-defined lineaments one may read the man "whom no contumely, no violence, no danger can move from the cause he has undertaken, and the opinions he has espoused."* Principle has been weighed in him, and has not been found wanting.

Dr. King had already been acquainted by letter with the objects of my coming to Greece. He entered into them with warmth, and expressed his desire to assist in their furtherance to the extent of his power. He concluded by kindly insisting on my spending at least the first months of my sojourn under his roof, where the Greek is almost exclusively spoken, until I should become more familiar with the manners and customs of the country. I felt no disposition to decline an invitation so cordially extended, and that very afternoon I found myself domiciled at his house.

* Cicero pro Ligario, c. 9.

Besides his duties as missionary of the American Board, Dr. King was then also discharging the functions of consul of the United States. The latter office, though not one of his own seeking, and, indeed, forced upon him by circumstances beyond his control, had lately been of considerable service. One Sabbath morning, not many months before my arrival, his Greek service was attended by an uncommonly large number of persons. Among the rest came some beardless youths, as it soon became evident, for the express purpose of creating a disturbance. At the close of the discourse, one of them arose, and taking up the theme of the day, commenced a violent harangue. In answer, the missionary stated that he would willingly enter into a discussion with him on any day that might be appointed, with the exception of Sunday. But the people would not hear of such a thing as putting it off to another time, and filled the air with their outcries. "This is my private house," said Dr. King, "and I do not wish this uproar; but furthermore it is the Consulate of the United States, and I will not have it." "We know it is the Consulate of the United States, but we mean to have the discussion now," cried the mob, in reply. They went so far as to threaten the servants for interfering, and turned some of the family quite out of the room. It so happened, by a singular coincidence, that Dr. King had only the day previous received from Washington a tin box containing an American flag, sent under seal of the Department of State. A happy thought struck him. With the assistance of his old man-servant, *Barba* Constantine, he hoisted the flag on one of the columns of the porch. The wind filled its ample folds, and displayed every star and stripe to the wondering gaze of the crowd below. Instantly the tumult of voices was stilled. They had dared to insult the consul of the United States, but they were afraid of his flag. No sooner did they catch a glimpse of it, than the chief aim of each seemed to be to reach the gate before the others. In half a minute not a man of them was to be seen upon the premises.

This part of Athens is the old town, if that appellation can be given to the portion which is only a quarter of a century old. Looking from my window, I have the northeastern corner of the Acropolis before me at the distance of a few hundred feet, crowned by the old Turkish and Frank walls which tower far above. On this side their base can scarcely be reached, by reason of the steep ledges of rock that occupy most of the acclivity. In one or two places, however, a slope of grass stretches up to the very foot of the wall, which, on account of this facility of approach, has been built stronger and higher. Wherever a patch of grass exists, flocks of goats and black sheep are to be seen clambering over the rocks and browsing on points apparently the most inaccessible. From the veranda on the opposite side of the house the eye glances over a collection of houses standing in a slight depression. Beyond the more remote of these, the little white chapel of St. George, on the summit of Mount Lycabettus, just appears. The trees that are scattered about stand in gardens; for there are not a dozen in the streets of the old town. All of them look strange to an American. The cypress is, perhaps, the most striking. Its spire-like form, so regular and tapering, is associated in the traveler's mind with Eastern cemeteries; but here it is also a favorite in the vicinity of houses. We have one near us which waves most gracefully, and creaks most lugubriously at the lightest breeze. In an adjoining inclosure there is a fine old laurel which has attained a size rare in Western Europe, and a mulberry-tree of only twenty years' growth overshadows nearly the whole garden. The greatest curiosity of this kind in Athens is the palm-tree that stands in the "Hodos Hermou," very near the western entrance, where it constitutes one of the first objects that greet the stranger's eye. It is a date-palm, introduced, doubtless, by the Turks, but in too high a latitude to yield fruit.

My anxiety for letters led me first to the post-office, where, as the French mail had been distributed, I hoped to find a package of them from America. But I was disappointed, not having made due allowance for the increased time demanded for communication. A month is the average time a letter takes in coming from New York to Athens; though I remember once to have opened one precisely three weeks after date. The post-office is a low wooden house with a rickety portico. All the business of the establishment is transacted by half a dozen clerks. Like the employés of some other post-office departments, they are not above the suspicion of occasionally violating the sacredness of epistolary correspondence. And whenever trouble of any kind is brewing, the Government frequently finds it very convenient to ignore that provision of the constitution which forbids all tampering with the mails.

From the post-office I strolled through the market-place—the *agora* or *bazari*, as it is indifferently called. On the way thither I walked by the common prison, a one-story building without a window opening on the street. But through the grated door I saw a crowd of miserable looking creatures, wandering aimlessly about an open space. A motley crew they were. Men and women and children, the condemned and the accused as yet untried, the petty thief and the murderer, the hardened villain and the neophyte in vice, all huddled together to the number of one hundred and fifty in a court fifty feet square. The building was erected years ago, and used to serve as a *Medresé* or school; it still bears that Turkish appellation. But I doubt if the instruction once given in letters was half so complete as the lessons of crime and wickedness imbibed by those who are confined for a fortnight within its walls.

The market-place was nearly empty of purchasers, albeit the traders still sat cross-legged in their booths, which nestle about the old gray walls of Hadrian's porticoes. Though now near the end of September, the sun continues to pour down his rays with scorching power, and the air is insufferably hot, even in the shade. Every body keeps to the house during five or six hours of the day; and at noon the streets are almost as deserted as at night. Strangers are warned by residents not to deviate from this practice, unless they are willing to pay for the imprudence by a dangerous and often fatal disease. An hour or two of exposure in the sun is pretty sure to bring on an attack of the Greek fever, which is the curse of Athens at the present day. Although late in the season, fruits of every sort are yet in their prime. Those that belong to southern climates peculiarly are to be found here in the greatest profusion, and at what would seem to us a ridiculously small price. On the other hand, apples are a rarity, and those for sale are small and inferior; nor will the peaches compare with those of our American orchards. But the apricots, pomegranates, and melons of all kinds are excellent. The *francosyca* are a puzzle to the stranger till he recognizes them as the fruit of the common prickly-pear, whose curiously-jointed stems grow here to an astonishing size. The Greeks I meet will not credit my assertion that this plant is a native of the American continent originally, for they say that it grows wild in the remotest parts of Mani. The Greek grapes are decidedly the best I have ever tasted. The choicest *Fontainebleau* or *Muscat* can not approach the luscious flavor of the Smyrniote. Some of these varieties resemble the Malaga grapes of our shops. Another species, from Tenos I believe, is peculiar, the fruit not showing a vestige of a seed within. It is very sweet, and smaller than the rest. There is a large black grape, one of which from curiosity I measured, and found it over four inches in circumference. The produce of the vineyards around Athens, though not of such choice kinds, is excellent and plentiful. An *oke* (nearly three pounds) of the black grape, is sold for a copper coin answering to one cent and two-thirds of the American currency, and the price of the white is but just double. As the vintage has been in progress for some time, the *must*, or unfermented juice of the grape, can be procured. It enters into the composition of a number of national dishes. Mixed with flour it forms the *mustalevria*, a refreshing food of about the consistency of the "apple-butter" of our Western States, which it resembles in color also. In its perfection the mustalevria has a sprinkling of almonds, and is ornamented with the red pomegranate seeds. It is also dried in sticks that are as hard as stone.

On the other side of the narrow alley that runs along one side of the Consulate, lives Sir Richard Church, whose acquaintance I had the pleasure of making on the third day after my arrival. Upon introduction he adverted at once to the friendship he had formed five years before with my father, and asked what news I brought with me from America, a country in which he takes a lively interest. Conversation naturally turned on the thrilling scenes in which General Church himself had been an actor, and the combats of the patriots whom he had come from England to head. He expressed his regret at the fact that Greece has to so great an extent failed to answer the expectations, perhaps too sanguine, of her well-wishers. This failure he attributed, not to the people themselves, but to the weak and injudicious government under which they live. A government that squanders on frivolous objects the revenue which should be expended on the improvement of the roads and the education of the masses, can not merit the esteem and affection of those who are true friends of the national welfare. The expenditures, he informed me, exceed the revenue by several million drachms annually; and this deficit is every year helping to swell the public debt.

General Church is at present one of the most prominent members of the opposition. He is regarded by King Otho, it is to be presumed, with the personal dislike which that monarch continues to cherish toward all, without exception, who took an active part in the formation of the Constitution of 1843. Callerges, who was its prime-mover, and who sat upon one of the cannon that were pointed at the palace, ready to be fired in case the king should refuse to ratify that document, was at first treated with marks of the highest favor. But when the storm was past, the first opportunity was seized to send him away from the royal presence, in a sort of banishment, to Argos. General Church, who occupied a high post in the army, resigned in consequence of some slight shown him by the ministry, and the latter were only too glad to rid themselves of a man too upright and inflexible for the doing of their behests. He retains a seat for life in the Greek senate, where, rather by his private influence and his vote than by public speeches, he seeks to promote pure and patriotic legislation. Unfortunately the country needs something more than good laws—it needs their faithful execution.

General Church expressed the lively interest he had taken in reading the newspaper accounts of the brilliant engagements of our Mexican campaigns. He spoke with the warmest admiration of the conduct of the war by Generals Scott and Taylor, and made particular inquiries whether any reliable history of the whole conflict had recently appeared in the United States. Few men living, probably, have had a better opportunity to become thoroughly acquainted with the history of the Greek revolution. I was pleased to learn from his own lips that he had collected all the materials for such a record of it as the world demands, and that he himself either had commenced, or intended soon to commence reducing them to the shape of a systematic narrative. Sir Richard's previous career in Italy and elsewhere, during which he earned in the British service his present rank of Lieutenant General, was varied and thrilling. I had subsequently the pleasure of perusing a manuscript account of some of his adventures in ridding the kingdom of Naples of the banditti who infested it. They were so full of romantic interest, that I regretted the limitation of a perusal of them to a very small circle of friends. Were it proper, I would gladly transcribe one or two of them upon these pages.

Among the most distinguished English residents in Athens there was none I more desired to see than Mr. George Finlay, the historian. He had been upon a visit to his native land, from which he returned not long after I reached Greece. One day Dr. King proposed a call upon him. His name was already familiar to me from the various works he has recently published on the modern history of Greece, as well as from his connection with the recent difficulties between the Greek and English governments. The most eligible spot in the city was chosen for the site of the king's palace, and some lands of Mr. Finlay were among those that were absorbed by the garden attached to it. But the ministry refused to make to the owners any adequate indemnification for the loss of the ground they had appropriated. Mr. Finlay having little faith in the power or inclination of the law-courts to grant him redress, appealed to his own government, who enforced his claims by a powerful fleet which for one hundred days blockaded the ports of Greece.

We entered Mr. Finlay's house, situated in the old quarter of the city, through a garden well stocked with flowers, and were received in his study. The walls, besides being stored with perhaps the choicest private library in the capital, were further ornamented with a valuable collection of antiquities found in this country, and a candelabrum and a curious brazen mirror graced the mantle. Mr. Finlay is a tall and somewhat slender man, about fifty years of age. His face is one of those which inspire confidence and respect, and his eye is bright and intellectual. I have seldom met one whose conversation is more entertaining. No subject can be started with which he does not seem perfectly familiar, and, where you least expect it, he is able to rectify your misapprehensions, or unravel what before seemed an enigma. History, however, is his favorite topic. With the Mediæval history of Greece no man living is better acquainted; and few, besides the Frenchman Buchon, have made it so careful a study. Mr. Finlay told me that he was still engaged upon his work, which is to contain in four independent volumes the vicissitudes of Greece, from the fall of Corinth to the conquest by the Turks. This is a portion of history which should have been treated by Gibbon, but to which that writer never deigned to devote more than a stray paragraph. Those who have read Mr. Finlay's able productions must, I think, acquiesce in the greater number of his conclusions. On the great controverted point of the origin of the modern Greeks, he adopts a middle course between those who declare them of Sclavonic ancestry, and those who affirm them to be scions of the noble stock of the Hellenes. As a natural consequence, he displeases the advocates of both theories. I only regret that, in delineating the mutations of the Greeks under the Frank domination, he has chosen to look at them from the foreign rather than the native point of view, and given us the chronicles of the conquerors instead of those of the vanquished.

To my countrymen, the Rev. Dr. Hill of the Protestant Episcopal Mission, and the Rev. Messrs. Arnold and Buel of the Baptist Mission, I shall have opportunity to refer in another connection. The kindly offices of these gentlemen contributed essentially to the attainment of the ends for which I visited Greece. Of the more private evidences of friendship received by me, in common with so many wayfarers, at their hospitable homes, I can, of course, make no adequate mention in these pages.

THE PROPYLÆA.

CHAPTER III.

THE ACROPOLIS.

MUCH as I desired to see the Acropolis and its classic contents, I was obliged to defer my first visit until late in the afternoon. The hill was already casting its long shadows over the eastern quarter of the town when, with a party of friends, I sallied forth. The heat was yet oppressive, and many of those whom we met were, like ourselves, provided with white cotton umbrellas, and wore white shoes, so pleasant for the feet in this sultry season. Two or three steep lanes, interrupted by an occasional stairway, led us to the clear ground at the foot of the Acropolis; but without a guide we would indubitably have lost our way, and come to a stand in some filthy court. It is a consolation to know that, if modern Athens can boast of an intricate maze of streets, ancient Athens would seem to have been but little better off in this respect. The father of Greek verse must have used some poetic license when he spoke of the wide streets of Athens. For a writer, who flourished some three centuries before the Christian era, and had traveled in foreign parts, expresses his regret at their narrowness and irregularity. He contrasts the capital with its port, Piræus, and states that the former was badly laid out as to its streets and squares, on account of its antiquity. "If a stranger," adds he, "were to be suddenly set down in the midst of the town, so small, inconvenient, and ill-situated are the houses, that he would doubt whether he were actually in famous Athens. But of this he would be speedily convinced, if, looking up in some more open spot, he should catch a glimpse of the Odeum, the most handsome in the world; the theatre, magnificent, great, and wonderful; the sumptuous, conspicuous, and admirable temple of Minerva, called the Parthenon, rising aloft, and striking the beholder with admiration."*

We, however, had reached a point whence we could survey the whole city, while we obtained a good view of the Acropolis itself. It is an oblong height, perhaps three quarters of a mile in circuit at the base, with a barrier of steep rocks rising on every side to prevent the approach of invaders. Above these tower the grim old walls, to whose foot, even, it is in most places all but impossible to ascend. On this side they are said to have been raised by the Pelasgians, when the Athenian state was yet in its infancy; but these original works have probably been destroyed to the very foundation. Much of those which now exist, were built by the Athenians when they regained their city after the retreat of Xerxes. In such haste were the citizens to restore the crumbling fortress, that they are said to have seized whatever first came to hand, and converted it to use. It is interesting to notice, to this very day, stones evidently drawn from some more ancient, and perhaps ruined edifice, deeply imbedded in the midst of other masonry. At one place there is a conspicuous row of drums of marble columns, which probably belonged to the old Parthenon, a temple burned by the Persians when they ravaged Attica with fire and sword. The rest of the wall is a singular medley of works of every age. Here a bit of Roman brick-work, there a Frankish bastion or Turkish parapet, all mixed in in-

* *Dicæarchus Vit. Græc.*, p. 8.

extricable confusion. Every conqueror has left some traces of his power, while Time, the greatest conqueror of all, has been undoing their boasted work.

But we must now approach the entrance, and to reach it we were obliged to make half the circuit of the hill. On the way we passed a small portal, in what was once a Turkish defence. One jamb was formed of an old marble slab that had once graced some sacred inclosure, as the following imprecation against all sacrilegious trespassers indicates. The similarity it bears to those curses which the monks of the Middle Ages used to insert on the fly-leaves of their books, is striking, to say the least.

"I intrust the guardianship of this Chapel to the Infernal Gods, to Pluto, and to Ceres, and to Proserpine, and to the Furies, and to all the Infernal Gods. If any one shall deface this Chapel, or mutilate it, or remove any thing from it, either himself or by means of another, to him may not the land be passable, nor the sea navigable, but may he be utterly uprooted. May he experience all evils, fever and ague, and quartan ague, and leprosy. And as many ills as man is liable to, may they befall that man who dares to move any thing from this Chapel."

We reached the entrance of the Acropolis at the western end, where it connects with the lower height of the Areopagus, or Hill of Mars, the scene of St. Paul's masterly defence. Here the slope was originally more gradual, and offered the easiest, or, in fact, the only approach. Formerly there stood here a splendid gateway, strongly defended by walls and overlooking towers on either side, and a broad flight of steps led directly up behind it. More recently this was found too difficult to protect, and now the visitor passes through no fewer than three portals before he can say that he is fairly within. Over the outermost of these a Turkish inscription is to be seen. I understand that its import is the boast that the Christian *giaour* shall never again hold possession of this citadel. If so, it stands there a sufficient refutation of its own falsehood. I was unable to vouch for the correctness of the interpretation; and having no Turkish dragoman at hand, we went on to the second gate, which was closed. A loud rap brought to the door a soldier dressed in rather rusty European uniform, who, on our presenting a printed permit good for the whole season, opened the gate, and admitted us into a small court. Here was a lodge, before which half a dozen guards were lounging and smoking their *chebouks*. A classic air was given to their abode by a promiscuous collection of fragments of statuary; while a number of marble cannon-balls, made during the recent wars out of the pillars of the Parthenon or Propylæa, lay scattered about. Some were evidently intended for guns of large calibre.

One of the guards now opened a third gate, and passing through we found ourselves at the base of an acclivity, above which rose the Propylæa. A series of marble steps, some of which were discovered beneath the rubbish of a Turkish battery that formerly encumbered the spot, and others in their original places, have been partially restored under the direction of the Archæological Society. The centre is paved with large slabs of stone, and served in old times as a carriage-way. The pavement was grooved to give a foothold to the yoke of oxen that annually drew the car of Minerva up to the temple of the goddess. In these Panathenaic festivals a vast concourse of people were accustomed to attend the solemn convoy, the men carrying offerings, or baskets containing the sacred utensils, the women shouldering jars of pure water, while comely virgins brought the most pleasant flowers to bedeck the virgin goddess, and form a fragrant bed around her statue. Most conspicuous in the throng was said to be the new *peplus* with which the figure of Minerva was to be clothed or screened. It was a magnificent robe woven by the maidens of the noblest families, who disputed the right of having a part in the honorable task. The conflicts of Minerva with the giants were the subject of the embroidery, which was fastened, as a sort of sail, to the mast of a boat laid upon the sacred car.

We stood upon the threshold of the wonderful inclosure, with somewhat of the same awe and reverence that inspired the ancient pilgrim as he entered the precincts of the gorgeous temple. If he was filled with superstitious dread of the august deities whom he imagined the tenants of the spacious fabric, we were overwhelmed with wonder and admiration of the genius that planned the graceful architecture, and the liberal statesman who shrank from no expense to decorate his native city and render it the gem of Greece. The *Propylæa*, which we had now reached, was a fit introduction to the host of temples, statues, and altars within. Less famous now than in former times, it was placed by the ancients on a level with the Parthenon, so far as beauty of design and exquisite finish were concerned. While yet entire, it stood directly in view of the people assembled for deliberation on the Pnyx; and Demosthenes and Æschines often took occasion, from the sight of its magnificence, to exhort a declining age to emulate the glory and renown of their forefathers. It is said that Epaminondas was heard to exclaim, that he would never rest satisfied until he had transported the Propylæa, and set it down at the entrance of the Cadmean hill in Thebes.

The object of the edifice seems to have been two-fold. It was designed to be ornamental, and at the same time a strong military fortification, commanding the sole access to the citadel. The combination was difficult, but seems to have been admirably attained. Let me attempt to give an idea of the arrangement. The main structure consists of a massive marble wall pierced by five portals, of which the central one is much the largest. With its bronze gates, it might easily withstand the assaults of the enemy who should succeed in bursting through the lower walls, while exposed to the galling arrows of the troops from the heights on either side of the ascent, which afforded them every advantage of situation. This is the defensive part. The ornamental consists of wide porticoes on either front. That which faces the steps is the deeper. It is, I think, a circumstance worthy of note, that wherever it was desirable, as in the present case, to impress the beholder with a sense of awe and reverence, the Doric style of architecture was uniformly resorted to by the ancients. Its massive proportions, the simplicity of its outlines, and the stern baldness of its capitals, seem to be the natural expression of majesty and inflexible severity. It symbolizes reverence without affection. Accordingly the stately front of the Propylæa was composed of six stout Doric columns, each four feet and a half in diameter, and twenty-nine feet high. They have been sadly ill-used by father Time, who has spared little more than half their height. Behind this line, and before reaching the wall, is a space of forty feet and more, the roof of which was once supported by six Ionic columns. The reason for the adoption of another order here, was that the slender proportions of its pillars obstructed the view much less, and enabled the eye to gaze more freely on a ceiling adorned with sunken panels, all variegated with the most brilliant coloring.

The front vestibule of the Propylæa has been converted, for lack of some more convenient receptacle, into a sort of museum of antiquities. All the broken heads, fractured legs, mutilated arms, and fragmentary hands, dug up in every quarter of the Acropolis, are ranged on benches upon the strictest anatomical principles. This classification has at least the merit of enabling the visitor to gain a pretty complete acquaintance with the whole collection. My own attention was specially drawn to one or two large heads, in which the eye had been excavated, evidently for the purpose of filling the cavity with an eyeball of ivory, or some precious metal. We turned from the main building to our left, and entered a wing of the Propylæa, a square chamber with a narrow colonnade before it. This served in ancient times as a picture-gallery, or *pinacotheke*. True, it is difficult to suppose that many paintings could have been contained within the limits of a room about thirty feet square; but the merit of the pictures probably made up for their fewness. And if the space here allowed was but small, there were certainly much larger collections in the lower city, where they adorned the inner walls of the long porticoes with which the city abounded. It was doubtless the ambition of the young painter to hang his first production in some such public place, where the philosophers, as they walked to and fro, and the tradesmen, hurrying toward their shops, might pause a moment to admire its execution, and inquire the artist's name. The Battle of Marathon seems to have been a favorite subject at Athens, just as the brilliant victories of Napoleon abound in the galleries of Versailles, where you look in vain for any representation of Waterloo.

We crossed next to the right side of the entrance, where a smaller wing of the same building is for the most part concealed under the great square tower that occupies so prominent a place in every picture of the Acropolis. It is usually called a Turkish tower; but it was much more probably built by the Christian dukes of Athens in the thirteenth century. The Vandalism that has busied itself for the past thirty years in destroying every relic of the mediæval history of the country, has thus far spared this venerable monument. How long it will be permitted to stand is very doubtful. From a mistaken pride, the modern Greeks have thought it incumbent on them to signalize their admiration of antiquity, by obliterating every vestige of an age of barbarism and subjection. How different was the policy of those for whom they affect to entertain such enthusiastic admiration! Every work of their uncultivated forefathers was cherished with the most sedulous care; for it served as an index of their own progress in the arts of life. Even the traces of the Persian invasion were gladly preserved, that they might teach posterity the authenticity of achievements, which otherwise would have appeared too gigantic to be worthy of credit. The more powerful they could picture the Persian host, the more did they enhance their own prowess, since victory had crowned them in the unequal contest.

As I have said, the Propylæa was, until recently, encumbered with the remains of a dilapidated Turkish battery. In removing these ruins, a number of columns and bas-reliefs were discovered, belonging to a small temple of the Ionic order. It was then remembered that such an edifice had been described by travelers of the seventeenth century, as standing in advance of the Propylæa, on the southwestern corner of the wall. The exact spot was easily found by means of the remaining foundation. In 1835 its restoration was commenced; and so many pieces were found that scarcely a stone had to be supplied. The roof only is wanting, with the greater part of the continuous frieze that ran around the top of the building, sculptured with figures of the Persians. This was unfortunately discovered earlier, and shared the fate of Lord Elgin's spoliations. Though but twenty-seven feet long by eighteen broad, the temple of Victory had a double front, adorned with four Ionic fluted columns executed in the most

TEMPLE OF VICTORY WITHOUT WINGS.

finished style. It was Cimon who built it, in commemoration of glorious defeats inflicted upon the Persians, both by land and by sea. But the jealous eye of the republican Athenians would not suffer him to indulge in private ostentation; and prevented him from recording his own astonishing successes on the dwelling-house of a deity. He chose for its decoration the achievements of older generals, whose merits the populace could better endure to hear praised, since they had gone into a banishment whence no popular vote could recall them. Cimon dedicated this exquisite little temple to Victory; but fearing lest the fickle goddess should some day take it into her head to desert his native city, he robbed her of her wings. Perhaps he hoped in this way to fix her irrevocably to her present seat; but succeeding generations discovered to their cost, that if Victory had lost the power of soaring away on her airy pinions, she could, in a more prosaic manner, abandon her beautiful niche, and give them leg-bail.

We paused for a few minutes within the temple of *Victory without wings*, to admire the few sculptured slabs that have been collected there. They refer mostly to Victory, and originally formed a parapet around the platform of the temple. One was so exquisite that I could have stopped an hour before it without weariness. It represents the goddess just alighting on her favorite hill. She stoops to unbuckle her sandal, indicating the determination here to cease her wanderings and take up a perpetual abode. Nothing can be more elegant than the posture and the finish of the well-turned ankle. From the steps of the temple we obtained a delightful view of the sea, on the very spot whence Ægeus is said to have precipitated himself upon the rocks below, when he saw the black sails which Theseus, on his successful return from Crete, had forgotten to lower.

But we were impatient to visit the Parthenon, the grand object of attraction. So passing once more through the portal of the Propylæa, we stood in the presence of that majestic pile, which for beauty of proportion, excellence of material, and grace of ornament, is yet proclaimed by all who can appreciate the arts of architecture and sculpture, as unequaled by any fabric of more modern date. The first impression upon the mind is that of perfect symmetry and grandeur. Less august than when the dazzling brilliancy of its Pentelican marble was undimmed, it is perhaps more picturesque now. Its ruined pillars and tottering architraves are now laden with the traditionary interest of more than two thousand years. It is not the size alone that strikes the fancy; for the Olympium itself, though much larger, has never attained a tithe of its celebrity.

THE PARTHENON.

The summit of the Acropolis is not perfectly level, but is shaped into a number of distinct platforms, hewn out of the solid rock when Athens was confined to the limits of this hill. In after times temples took the place of dwelling-houses, and the inhabitants were compelled to descend into the valley. The entire area thus cleared is one thousand feet long and five hundred feet in its greatest width, containing about seven acres of ground. The greatest length is precisely east and west.

A modern architect, perhaps, would have placed the Parthenon directly in front of the entrance, so that only the western façade might be seen, thus preserving symmetry, or, rather, uniformity. Without doubt, however, the site was purposely chosen a little to the right upon the highest part of the citadel. This gives us the most favorable view of the temple, whose base is full forty feet above the ground on which we stand. The devotional feelings of an ancient pilgrim were deepened, too, as, in the long circuit he was obliged to make in order to reach the principal entrance at the opposite end, his eye could examine in detail the sculptured works upon its sides, products of the chisel of Phidias and his scholars.

As we walked up toward the Parthenon we met a small man, rather beyond the prime of life, who was introduced as Mr. Pittakes, the Inspector General of the antiquities within the kingdom of Greece. He is affable in conversation, and wholly absorbed in his favorite pursuit. His duty it is to see that the statuary and other works of art, discovered from year to year, are not carried from the country or broken up for lime by the ignorant peasantry. Of all the Greeks he is doubtless the best informed as to the topography of Athens, respecting which he has written a work of considerable merit. Notwithstanding his dry manner and a certain nasal indistinctness of utterance, there was no one whom we were more delighted to meet.

I do not know that a better idea of the Parthenon can be given, than by saying that its exterior is the prototype of the Madeleine at Paris, and the Bavarian Walhalla. Around the whole body of the edifice runs a continuous portico, sustained by seventeen Doric columns on either side, and eight in each front. The vestibule at either end of the temple was deepened by the addition of a second row of columns to support the roof. Such was the condition of the Parthenon a century and a half ago. Since that time it has incurred the severest losses. At one time a powder magazine was recklessly placed within the building by the Turks. During the bombardment by the Venetians under Francesco Morosini, in 1687, a bomb happened to fall into the very centre of the temple, and a fearful explosion was the result. A great part of the lateral walls was overturned, and more than half a dozen columns on either side fell prostrate to the ground. From that time the building, which at one period had served as a church dedicated to the Virgin, was almost deserted. During an attack of three days, the Venetians did more damage to the Parthenon than it had sustained since the year of its erection. They consummated their outrage by a robbery of the movable statuary which adorned the triangular pediments on the fronts. It is related of them, that, as their general was lowering the car and horses which were most prominent in the group, the ropes either broke or slipped, and the statues were shivered into a thousand fragments upon the pavement below.

The interior of the Parthenon was divided into two unequal parts. Rather more than two-thirds were taken up with the temple proper, while the remainder, toward the west, served as the treasury of the state, and went by the name of *Opisthodomus*. The great statue of Minerva, from whom the temple obtained its name of *Parthenon*, or the *Virgin's House*, occupied the centre, and drew the undivided attention of every visitor. It was the master-piece of Phidias, and was no less precious for its material than for its workmanship. The statue was all of the purest gold, except the face, hands, and feet, which were curiously wrought of ivory brought from the remote and almost unknown depths of India. It was not to be expected that a work of such intrinsic value should escape the rapacity of either Romans or barbarians.

We know comparatively little of the internal arrangements of the Parthenon; but we may be confident that they were embellished as lavishly as the exterior. Indeed the prodigal expenditure of ornament seems to have been one of the most

FRIEZE OF THE PARTHENON.

striking peculiarities of this temple. Although its length was only two hundred and twenty-eight feet, yet it was loaded with a profusion of sculpture such as would have been more than sufficient, according to the rules ordinarily followed, for an edifice of thrice that size. Not only were all the metopes immediately below the exterior cornice made to represent the single combats of centaurs and other fabulous monsters, but an uninterrupted frieze was placed on the walls of the body, or *cella*, within the colonnade. This inimitable work of art, when entire, was no less than five hundred and twenty feet long, with a width of more than a yard. It represented in high relief the yearly procession at the Panathenaic festival. In addition to these decorations, a group of statues filled each of the pediments, one representing the birth of Minerva, the other her contest with Neptune for the possession of Attica. What is more astonishing than even the quantity of statuary, is its quality. Slabs of marble intended to be seen at the height of thirty to fifty feet above the spectator, were finished with as much care as though designed for a close inspection. Of this I satisfied myself, not only from the pieces collected below, but by a nearer examination of those which remain in their places. In one of the walls of the Parthenon we found a narrow winding staircase, from which we emerged on the top of the front. Probably the same means of gaining a better view of the statues on the pediment was privately afforded of old to the artist and the more curious visitor.

Mr. Pittakes took us up to the eastern end of the edifice, and pointed out some excavations, undertaken within a few years, with the view of examining the substructure. The workmen have brought to light what a spirited writer has called the *work-shop* of the Parthenon. Huge heaps of chippings from the marbles, unfinished drums of columns, apparently abandoned on account of some defect in the stone, are mingled with traces of works made by all the nations who have ruled here in succession. Not least remarkable was the discovery of a quantity of *burnt wood* still lower down, at a depth of fifteen or twenty feet below the present surface of the ground. These timbers, from their position, must evidently have been older than the erection of the present Parthenon by Pericles, in the middle of the fifth century before Christ. According to the most probable hypothesis, they are traces of the conflagration kindled by Xerxes when the old Hecatompedon, the predecessor of the Parthenon, shared the common destruction of all that was most precious in Athens. Blocks of marble belonging to the same structure were also found, with a great variety of antique bronzes and vases.

Architects have been much interested of late in the results of some new and very accurate measurements of the Parthenon, which have revealed a number of startling facts. For instance, it has been found that of the apparently straight lines, few, if any, are strictly such, but, in reality, describe curves of a figure that may be calculated with the utmost precision. Thus, the platform and steps in front of the temple, though to all appearance perfectly level, have been shown to be three or four inches higher toward the middle than at either end. And as each side is similarly shaped, the base of the Parthenon slants in all directions toward the four corners. The same holds good, in some measure, with all the other lines, some of which actually curve in two directions. The columns, too, are found not to stand perfectly upright, but to slant inwardly, and so are some inches longer on the outer edge than on the inner. Nor do they taper uniformly toward the summit, but bulge out a little at the middle. Archæologists affirm that they have now discovered the secret of the undoubted superiority of all the ancient temples over even their most servile imitations in modern times. If such care was taken in the construction of the Parthenon and the Propylæa, we can no longer wonder that the enormous sum of a thousand talents, equivalent to $1,100,000, should have been expended upon the former of those buildings alone, at a time when that sum would command three times as much labor as at present.

We followed Mr. Pittakes from the Parthenon to a small ruinous frame-house, where, under lock and key, are preserved a number of antique vases and other remains. But in this department no Grecian collection can compare with the vast assortment of the British and Neapolitan museums. Descending the rotten stairs, I picked up a human skull, which I noticed bleaching in the sun close by: whether it belonged to some gallant defender of the Acropolis, or to a Turkish soldier, it was too late to inquire. The guard who accompanied us, and whose only duty was to see that we took away none of the antiquities, did not evince much surprise or feeling for the relic of one who may have been a former comrade in arms. Instead of giving it Christian burial, he threw it into a dark corner, and it rattled down into a hole, where it doubtless still lies. So much for the remains of the combatants in the revolution.

We next passed to the only other remaining group of ruins on the Acropolis, the curious cluster of temples that stand near the northern wall overlooking the modern town. I call it a cluster of temples, for the *Erechtheum* comprises several sanctuaries dedicated to various gods and fabulous personages.

THE ERECHTHEUM.

Its singularly irregular shape adds propriety to the expression, while it renders description the more difficult. It consists of an oblong edifice, which formed the most important part, and three dissimilar porches covering almost as much more ground. We approached it from the east, which, as in the case of all the more ancient temples, was the principal front. Passing through a portico of six Ionic columns, we jumped down some eight or ten feet, and found ourselves in the sanctuary of *Minerva Polias*, the defender of the city, a shrine at one time held in even greater esteem than its more pretending neighbor, the Parthenon. Clambering over stones and bushes, we came to a partition wall. Beyond it was the part dedicated to *Pandrosos*, one of the daughters of Cecrops, who was worshipped here with almost divine honors. Thence we reached a narrower space along the western end of the structure, which seems to have served as a mere passage between the northern and southern porticoes, the greatest ornaments of the Erechtheum. The former is a large and spacious porch of the Ionic order, which here is to be seen in its most perfect expression. Less grand, perhaps, than the stately Doric when gazed upon from a distance, the richness and chasteness of detail is calculated to make this order a more general favorite. The adjacent soil here is several feet lower than in front, and the columns are consequently much larger than those of the chief entrance.

A CARYATIS.

But the southern portico, that of the *Caryatides*, to which we next repaired, was an object of far greater curiosity and interest. Its dimensions are much smaller than those of the others; but here the place of ponderous columns has been assumed by six colossal damsels, whose marble heads support the ponderous roof. Some say that the statues represent the captive women of Carya, a town of Peloponnesus, destroyed by the Athenians for siding with the Persian invaders against their country. But I prefer the other story, which makes them portraits of the fairest and most distinguished of Athens' daughters, chosen on account of their beauty to sit for this honorable distinction. Theirs are no meretricious charms, but a dignified and devout expression, mingled with indescribable grace:

> "A group
> Of shrinking Caryatides, they muse
> Upon the ground, eyelids half-closed, . . .
> To linger out their penance in mute stone."
>
> ROBERT BROWNING.

Fitting guardians of the sacred olive-tree, which probably stood in this portico; the same tree that Minerva was fabled to have caused to grow, when she contended with Neptune for supremacy in Attica. The salt-spring, created by one stroke of the sea-god's potent trident, was also within the temple. Antiquarians will probably have a puzzling search before they find it.

I have spoken of six Caryatides: in reality there are but five; the sixth is replaced by a wooden effigy. Its prototype is far away in a museum, where, by foul means and fair, the plunder of the choicest monuments of antiquity has been collected. Lord Elgin, the spoiler of the Parthenon, in robbing that building, confined himself to taking away all the movable bas-reliefs. Here, with a more ruthless hand, he removed one of the statues that supported this graceful portico—as a *sample* of the thing, I presume. The consequence was, that the roof fell, but was recently restored, and a fictitious Caryatid has taken her place in the midst of the lovely sisterhood.

With the Erechtheum we terminated our survey of the Acropolis and its edifices. The whole area of the summit was once stocked with statues of benefactors and altars dedicated to the gods. Nearly all these have disappeared. The most precious and beautiful were undoubtedly carried away at a very early date, to grace the imperial palaces and private villas of Rome and Constantinople. A semicircular pedestal was, however, recently discovered by the side of the Propylæa, where we saw it, with an inscription "To Minerva the Health-

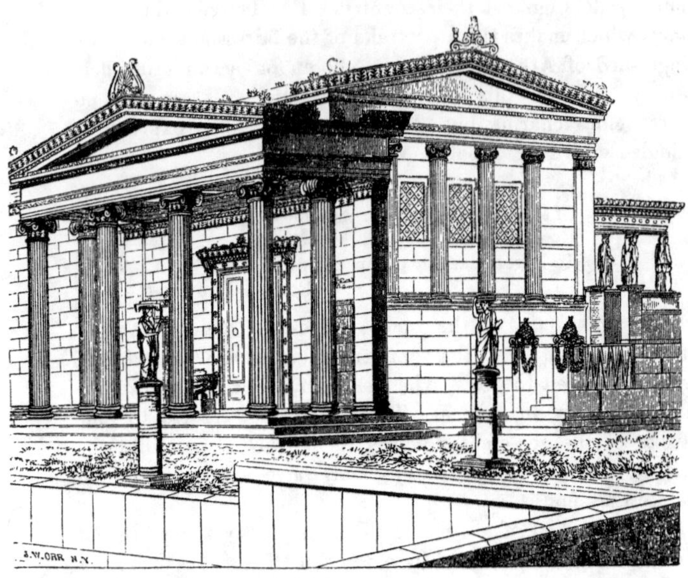

THE ERECHTHEUM RESTORED.

giver." It is said to have been erected in consequence of the following circumstance: A favorite workman of Pericles, while engaged in the construction of the magnificent portal, missed his foothold and fell to the ground. Strange to say, he was not killed by the fall, and his miraculous preservation, ascribed by his master to the guardianship of the goddess, was the occasion of the erection of this monument. But the most striking object that greeted the eye, as ancient travelers inform us, was a colossal statue of Minerva, standing between the Parthenon and the Erechtheum. It was surnamed *Promachus*, or "the Champion," from the threatening mien with which it confronted those who entered the sacred precincts. Armed with helmet and spear, it seemed about to take speedy vengeance on the audacious mortal who should dare to disturb, with sacrilegious hands, the consecrated temples on either side. The valiant warriors of Marathon had dedicated this statue, made of the spoils of battle, in token of their gratitude. Standing on a pedestal, the goddess was full seventy-five feet above the platform of the hill, and towered head and shoulders over all surrounding objects. The mariner, as he doubled Cape Sunium, caught a glimpse of the crested helmet and the spear-head, and shaped his course accordingly. It was a legend of the Middle Ages, that the conquering Alaric had advanced, in the fourth century of our era, to the city of Athens, and climbed the Acropolis, intending to rifle the time-honored localities of their accumulated treasures of gold, silver, and precious stones. But as the creaking gates of the Propylæa were thrown open at his command, he saw before him the gigantic statue of Pallas Minerva armed with spear and buckler. She seemed to threaten the trespasser with sudden destruction. The barbarian, who had feared neither God nor man, shrunk from what he deemed so unequal a combat, and retired from the place animated with mingled admiration and awe. Whether the story be true or apocryphal, the visitor is tempted to wish that our modern Vandals might have beheld some like vision, or at least, anticipating the universal execration of posterity, have been induced to withhold their hands from spoiling the most beautiful monuments of human skill.

We bade Mr. Pittakes good-evening, and retraced our steps toward the entrance, observing as we passed a lofty pedestal, standing opposite the temple of Victory, which was surmounted at first by the equestrian statues of the two sons of Xenophon. In later times, however, Agrippa, the favorite of Augustus, supplanted them, and now there is scarcely a trace of either of the statues. In descending the outer slope of the hill toward the town, we found the ground covered with a singular vine, which an old Greek servant who accompanied us called *picra angouria*, or bitter cucumbers. If the ripe fruit be merely touched the rind splits, like the common "touch-me-not," and the seeds are scattered in all directions. I found that it was the *momordica elaterium*, a powerful cathartic, and, in large doses, a virulent poison. It seems to abound most in the neighborhood of ancient ruins.

THE BEMA OF THE PNYX AT ATHENS.

CHAPTER IV.

ANTIQUITIES OF THE LOWER TOWN.

Having gratified my curiosity with a brief survey of the Acropolis, a visit often to be repeated during my sojourn in Athens, there remained to be seen the antiquities of the lower town. The buildings of the Acropolis have the advantage of belonging exclusively to a single age, and present us with the outlines of a picture of Athens in the time of Pericles: its lights and shades the imagination can easily supply. Those structures, on the contrary, whose ruins are scattered over the plain, date from various epochs. Some carry us back to the glorious times of liberty, when the name of Greek was synonymous with that of freeman. Others tell of foreign domination, when gold and tinsel could scarcely disguise the galling chains of the Roman Emperors. Though not so numerous as the ruins of the city of the Cæsars, nor spread over so extensive a surface, they are, on the whole, better preserved, and more interesting in themselves. They can scarcely be brought within the compass of a single excursion.

My first walk led me to that quarter of ancient Athens which the Emperor Hadrian took under his special protection, and was ambitious to have named from himself. Early one morning, issuing forth into the street upon which the Consulate faced, I followed it in the opposite direction from the Market, and in five minutes reached the open fields. Here, as on all sides of Athens, there stood formerly a low wall: but it has been destroyed since the time of the Turks, although the town has not spread at all in this direction. The view was quite unobstructed. But a few paces from me rose a light and airy gateway, through whose open arch appeared in the distance the remnant of a noble colonnade, on a platform overlooking the bed of the River Ilissus. Beyond the latter were some low hills lining the opposite bank, in which was embedded the stadium, or ancient race-course. The "Flowery hill Hymettus," a rugged mountain, formed the background of the tableau. Nearer on the left were the king's palace and the English church. Approaching the arch, I recognized in it the "Gate of Hadrian," marking the entrance into Hadrianopolis. Directly over the arch an inscription is cut in large letters, which in English would read thus:

"THIS IS ATHENS, THE ANCIENT CITY OF THESEUS."

But on the eastern side are the words,

"THIS IS THE CITY OF HADRIAN, NOT THAT OF THESEUS."

They indicate conclusively that the Emperor arrogated to himself the founding of this part of Athens, as Theseus had erected the older portion. But though the Emperor was a noble patron of the arts and sciences, and strove ineffectually to rekindle the half-extinguished embers of Grecian genius, we can only give him the credit of restoring and embellishing the dilapidated city. Over the archway there were columns of the Corinthian order, supporting a pediment of graceful proportions. Between the columns there were three compartments; the central one doubtless containing the statue of the royal benefactor, and the others statues of his favored friends.

All the great threshing-floors of Athens are situated near this gateway and the adjoining temple. From the fields for miles around the city, the wheat is brought on the backs of horses or asses to the public floor. This is generally a circular area of fifty feet in diameter, paved with common rough stones. Great heaps of sheaves are collected, until there is a sufficient quantity to give occupation to the threshers. Then the wheat is evenly distributed over the entire floor to the depth of several inches. Half a dozen horses with drags perform the operation of treading out the grain. The drag is furnished with iron teeth on its under side, and is rendered more effective by the weight of the driver, who stands on it with a rope to guide his horses, and a long stick in his hands.

The entire number of horses run abreast, and as they whirl around, considerable skill is necessary to prevent collision. The air, meanwhile, re-echoes with the merry shouts of the threshers. In a short time the grain is separated from the stalk, and the straw is removed with great wooden pitchforks. Should the wind be strong enough, the remaining wheat is winnowed by being thrown into the air by means of wooden shovels. Passing by these threshing-floors toward dusk one evening, I found that the grain not yet thoroughly cleansed of chaff had been piled up in various places in long low heaps. As we approached two or three peasants simultaneously shouted to us to take care not to touch the wheat. In seeking a cause for their solicitude, we found that the smooth surface of the heap had been stamped in various places, or, as they said, it had been sealed—"boulonetai." Impressions had been made by means of a board a foot long, with a few letters deeply cut into it, at intervals of a few inches, over the entire surface. The *object* was to prevent the owner from coming stealthily and removing any part of his produce, without paying the usual contribution of one tenth to the government. The owner is consequently obliged to lie down by the floor at night, and prevent any stray cattle from marring the impression of the seal. The custom is of Oriental origin, and it may be readily imagined how oppressive it is to the Greek farmer.

The archway is still a thoroughfare; for I met a long line of donkeys laden with brush, entering the town through it; while another string came, on their way from the market, with empty paniers on their backs. I walked to the columns that I had seen in the distance, belonging to the *Temple of Jupiter Olympius.* From afar some conception of their size could be formed, by comparing them with two or three wooden drinking-shops in their immediate neighborhood. But when I stood by the pedestal of one of these enormous piles, it seemed to tower almost to the skies. The square block on which one of them rested measured, I found, about eight feet and a half on each side. The base of the column was twenty-one feet in circumference, and it was more than sixty feet high. Of these immense pillars only sixteen were standing, and one of these has fallen since. They belonged to the southeastern corner of the edifice. Of the magnitude and appearance of the Olympium, the following particulars will convey some idea. It was 359 feet long and 173 broad. The whole was surrounded by a spacious portico, sustained on the sides by a double, and at the ends by a triple row of Corinthian columns. Twenty stood in each row on the sides, and ten formed the façade. There were, besides, a few columns in the entrance of the main body, or *cella* of the temple; so that the entire number employed in the adorning of the outside was no less than 120 or 122. The cost of quarrying such immense blocks of stone as make up these columns, must necessarily have been enormous; for they were brought with little or no mechanical assistance from the marble quarries of Mount Pentelicus. They have suffered less from the effects of earthquakes than the Parthenon; but the hand of man has dealt even more hardly with them. For ages the unfortunate Olympium has served as a marble mine for the inhabitants of Athens. As late as 1760 a seventeenth column was demolished by order of the Turkish governor, who used its materials in the construction of a new mosque in the bazar. Such also has doubtless been the fate of the whole interior of the temple, of which not a vestige has been left.

And yet

"Thou art not silent!—oracles are thine
Which the wind utters, and the spirit hears,
Lingering mid ruin'd fane and broken shrine,
O'er many a tale and trace of other years!
Bright as an ark, o'er all the flood of tears
That wraps thy cradle-land, thine earthly love,
Where hours of hope mid centuries of fears,
Have gleamed, like lightnings through the gloom above,
Stands, roofless to the sky, thy home, Olympian Jove!"

T. K. HERVEY.

The history of the Olympium adds interest to its ruins greater than the mere statement of their dimensions could give. No ancient structure in Greece has undergone such vicissitudes of fortune. About twenty-four centuries have rolled away since the first stone was laid, not far from a hundred years before Pericles commenced the Parthenon. To Pisistratus, about the year 530 B.C., may be ascribed the idea of erecting in Athens a temple to the Jupiter of Mount Olympus: but his plan was slowly executed during the period of the Athenian commonwealth. For ages the Olympium, like the shrines of Cologne and Milan, remained in an unfinished condition. The limited resources of the Athenian state could ill afford the vast sums needful for the completion of a temple, which, after that of Diana at Ephesus, was probably the greatest structure of the Greek world. All her own revenues, and those of her allies, were swallowed up in a rapid succession of useless civil wars, or lavished in the decoration of the smaller but more exquisite models of the Acropolis. To cap the climax of misfortune, when Sylla captured Athens with a Roman army, after an obstinate siege, he plundered the Olympium of all its newly-prepared columns, which he transported to Rome, and placed around the more potent Jupiter of the Capitol. After so severe a loss, more than two centuries elapsed before the Emperor Hadrian undertook to finish it. Those fine columns of Pentelican marble which we now see, were doubtless erected by this prince, and nothing older remains, but the massive stone walls supporting its platform, strengthened at regular intervals by strong buttresses.

An Athenian friend pointed out to me a piece of modern wall on the top of the architrave of one of the columns, between sixty and seventy feet above the ground. "That," said he, "was the cell of a solitary hermit, who many years ago took up his abode there for the remnant of his life. His superior sanctity soon became known throughout the town. Multitudes flocked out to see this new Simon Stylites, who spent his time, as was reported, solely in the exercise of meditation and devotion. Since, however, neither the one nor the other could satisfy his bodily wants, he was accustomed at stated intervals to lower a basket, which the devout old women were but too glad to fill with all necessary food. Unfortunately the old hermit has gone the way of all living; and no one has been found sufficiently devout or courageous to take his place, even in hope of living on the public during the term of his natural life."

Descending from the platform of the Olympium, I presently reached the bed of the Ilissus. It was as dry as the ground about it, except in one spot where there was a spring. At this spot the women were already busy washing clothes; while half a score of boys played about the water, and filled the air with their outcries. This, it is now well agreed, was the fountain Callirrhoë, or Enneacrunus, as it was called from the nine pipes that fed it. Its water was considered the purest, and maidens before their marriage, as well as priestesses, were wont to bathe in its mystic bosom. I followed the dry channel for some distance. In winter the rains swell the Ilissus to the size of a moderate creek; but it never deserves the name of a river, in our sense of the word. At present it was overgrown with shrubs. Among the rest, I noticed particularly the *agnus castus*, and the *oleander*, both of which flower in spring. They grow here in the greatest profusion.

A few steps brought me to the piers of an ancient bridge across the Ilissus: which was undoubtedly a much more constant, and, perhaps, a more abundant stream, when the country was more thoroughly cultivated, and the mountains were covered with dense forests. The bridge served as an approach to the *Stadium*, occupying a hollow between two low hills on the opposite, or southern bank. The ravine was naturally well adapted to the construction of a stadium, and it required comparatively little labor to give it the form required. This was done about the middle of the fourth century before Christ, for the celebration of the games annually observed during the Panathenaic festival. The hills on either side were crowded with benches for spectators, of whom twenty-five thousand might be accommodated with seats, besides the multitudes who could stand on the summit. The length of the level space at the bottom is 675 feet, and its width at the end toward the Ilissus is 137 feet. At the other, or rounded end, where the chariots were to turn, it is nearly twice as wide. Here the judges sat far aloft. The benches, which were originally of the common limestone, or else of wood, were replaced by the bounty of a single private citizen, Herodes Atticus, a subject of Hadrian, by marble seats; which, however, have been all taken away. The effect of those imposing games was further increased by two temples crowning the hill on both sides of the Stadium.

I made my way, through the clumps of bushes that cover the bottom of the Stadium, to the rounded end. Here I found a man busy at work, picking dandelion leaves, of which he was going to make a salad. This dish is said, by those who like salads, to be quite palatable; but I must confess that it was not to my taste. A little to the right of the judges' seat is a large opening in the side of the hill, which I explored. Following it a short distance, I found it nearly choked up in places by the falling of stone and earth from overhead. After a bend the passage comes out upon the opposite side of the hill. The object of this outlet was obvious enough. The charioteers who had been vanquished, drove, or rather sneaked out through it; while their victorious competitor proceeded to the city by the direct road, and received the loud acclamations of the multitude.

The heat was already growing oppressive, and I hastened to return. Beyond the Ilissus from the Stadium, a stone wall bounds a small inclosure which now serves as the English and American cemetery. Here are buried a number of our countrymen who have died far from home and native land. The whole is well laid out, and in time will be a cool and pleasant spot.

Upon another morning I went to visit the ruins on the southern side of the Acropolis. During the previous day there had sprung up a strong north wind, called by the Greeks *Meltempi.* While it continued the air was filled with sand and dust, raised in its course over the dry plain, upon which scarcely a drop of rain had fallen. It is said to continue at least three days; and during that time it is exceedingly disagreeable to venture out. It was quite impossible to make even the roughest sketch. Clouds of dust concealed the distant mountains from view. Not far below the southeastern corner of the Acropolis, I came to a half-ruined building, said to be part of the monastery where Lord Byron resided while at Athens. Just beyond it was the singular little structure that goes by the popular name of the Lantern of Demosthenes. More properly it is the *Choragic Monument of Lysicrates.* Its plan is quite unique. Upon a square foundation, now almost entirely buried beneath an accumulation of earth, rises a round building,

CHORAGIC MONUMENT OF LYSICRATES.

scarcely six feet in diameter. Six graceful Corinthian columns support an entablature, upon which are sculptured with exquisite skill, though on a small scale, the contests of Bacchus and the Tyrrhenian pirates. These criminals are seen fleeing before the wine-god and his attendant satyrs. In two or three places they are represented at the very moment when, by the mandate of Bacchus, their bodies are undergoing a transformation into dolphins. The fish's head already grows on the man's shoulders, and the unfortunate monster is about to plunge into ocean's depths. Elsewhere, Bacchus is seen relaxing from his toils, and playing with a huge lion, upon a lonely rock. On the top of the roof there is a triangular pedestal. This explains the use of the whole monument, or temple. Lysicrates, as indeed we learn from an inscription still legible on the architrave, was a wealthy citizen of Athens, and one of those who were expected to defray the expenses of training the orchestras, for the great musical performances in the neighboring Theatre of Bacchus. On one occasion, the same year that Alexander the Great invaded the Persian empire, his chorus gained the victory; and the prize, a highly ornamented brazen tripod, was adjudged to Lysicrates. This little temple was erected expressly to serve as a support for the honorable reward. The common people give it the name of Lantern of Demosthenes, because they have a tradition that the noble Athenian orator made it his study. The chief difficulty that naturally occurs to every one at first sight, is that the ancient worthy would have been at a loss to know how to enter the building, for the space between the columns was closed by curved slabs of marble, and there was no door. Besides, the dark interior of a monument scarce six feet in breadth, could not have furnished him a very pleasant place of meditation.

The modern town does not extend much further in this direction. The neighborhood can muster, however, a goodly number of boys; who, on another occasion, when I came to sketch the "lantern," or "*fanari*," gathered around me, to my no small amusement, and watched me as narrowly as they did my drawing. A friend of mine, an American artist, not long after, while engaged in the same occupation, was equally entertained in observing the interest that these urchins manifested in his proceedings. In fact, they came up closer than necessary; and on his return to the hotel he found that his handkerchief had been skillfully abstracted from his pocket.

Having turned the southeastern corner of the Acropolis, I

STREET OF THE TRIPODS.

reached a slope once occupied by the Theatre of Bacchus, of which scarcely a trace remains, except in the shape of the soil. The ancient approach to this celebrated edifice was by a thoroughfare running by the Monument of Lysicrates, and called the Street of the Tripods, from the number of those trophies displayed on every side. Directly above the theatre there is a natural cavern, which was formerly adorned with a façade by some successful leader in the orchestra; and two columns of unequal height standing at the very foot of the citadel's walls, were likewise surmounted by tripods. I climbed up to the cavern, which is now turned into a sort of chapel dedicated to the "*Panagia Speliotissa*," or the "Virgin of the Cave." A solitary lamp was burning in broad daylight before a rude picture; but not a soul was in sight. It is a pleasing feature of the Greek character, that even the vilest pay a sincere respect to religion. However mistaken their notions of morality and devotion in general, even the *kleft*, or professed robber, would never dream of touching with sacrilegious intent any thing belonging to the Church; though the unfortunate curate happening to fall in with him finds no pity at his hands. The churches and chapels in the most lonely places are left open without the least fear of desecration. Before the entrance of the cave lie one or two inscriptions bearing the name of Thrasyllus, the builder of the architectural part.

Following the base of the southern side of the Acropolis, I passed over the site of the Stoa or Porch of Eumenes, where the people used to take refuge, when a sudden shower of rain drove them from the roofless theatre. I noticed there several deep wells, and a bath made of stone, with an inscription difficult to be deciphered. I now entered the Odeum of Regilla, built by Herodes Atticus in honor of his wife. This private citizen was, next to his sovereign Hadrian, the greatest benefactor of Athens, where he left ample indications of his munificence. So great was his wealth, that the story was current that his father had unexpectedly discovered a treasure hidden under ground. According to law, it belonged to the crown; and Herodes wrote at once to the Emperor, to ask what he should do with it. "Use it," was Nerva's direction. The treasure was so considerable, that the Athenian replied he

ODEUM OF HERODES.

knew not how to use it. "Abuse it then," the generous monarch at once rejoined.* Accordingly the son lavished his money with a freedom that knew no parallel; but he had at least the merit of making it conduce to the public good.

I found the remains of the Odeum more extensive than I had anticipated. The spectators sat on marble benches on the side of the hill; but these have been carried away. The massive wall, however, behind the orchestra, rises to the height of three or four stories. The scene was formed by the receding of the wall toward the centre; and the windows behind it were closed, that the attention of the spectators might not be distracted by a sight of the landscape beyond. The other windows were large and arched, and plenty of light was obtained from overhead, since all the performances took place during the daytime. Lest, however, the people should be incommoded by the sun, a huge tent of canvas was stretched over the audience. It has been calculated that about six thousand people could be contained within the Odeum, whose diameter is about two hundred and forty feet; while the Theatre of Bacchus is stated to have been capable of holding twenty or even thirty thousand spectators. I climbed with ease to one of the windows, and sat there a while, enjoying an extended view reaching to the Saronic Gulf on the left. The hill of

* Gibbon, chap. II.

the Museum, which I intended to visit next, was directly in front. At the western end of the scene I found an ancient winding stairway by which I attained the exterior; and then ascended to the level of the ground by an ancient flight of steps.

A dry and dusty field stretched between the Odeum and the Museum. It was a veritable field of stones, mixed with fragments of broken pottery. A friend walking with me over the same ground, picked up the handle of a jar of common earthenware, with a stamp containing the name of the archon in whose time it was made. Such fragments are not unfrequently found, and seem to indicate, from the frequent occurrence of the names of Rhodes, Cos, etc., that most of the vessels were made in the islands of the Archipelago. Less fortunate, I discovered, nevertheless, two pieces of baked clay in the form of square truncated pyramids, above two inches high, and an inch and a half broad at the base. Dr. K. supposes them to have been used for plumb-lines, from their similarity to the weights now employed for that purpose; but Mr. Finlay inclines to think that they were weights used by weavers, or, perhaps, even registered weights. The two that I found had each a hole passing through near the top, for a string or handle, and were originally covered with glazing.

There were a number of men dressed in the common peasant's costume, with their wide baggy trowsers, engaged in collecting the stones into heaps—an endless task, as it seemed to me. How any thing can grow in so arid a soil passed my comprehension. Yet it is difficult to judge of the productiveness of the land, at a season when it has been parched during five or six months of uninterrupted drought; that is, since the middle of May.

The Museum is a hill of almost the same height as the Acropolis, though altogether different in shape, and presenting an easy ascent on this side. It is situated a few hundred yards to the south or southwest. The name is derived from a poet, Musæus, who is fabled to have sung his last songs here, and to have been buried on the spot. The chief object of interest is a very conspicuous ruin on the summit, which can be descried from afar on the plain. It is the *Monument of Philopappus*, the last descendant of the Seleucidæ, the ruling dy-

MONUMENT OF PHILOPAPPUS.

nasty of Syria until its conquest by the Romans. Semicircular in form, the concave portion is turned toward the city, and is adorned with sculptures of considerable merit, executed about A.D. 105, during the reign of Trajan. Originally there were three niches, separated by pilasters; but as the western third has fallen, there now remain but two niches. The principal one is filled by a mutilated statue of Philopappus himself, who seems to have become an Athenian citizen, and distinguished himself for his public liberality and munificence. This accounts for the permission granted him to erect his tomb within the walls by the Athenians, who were so much opposed to intermural interments. The niches on either side were smaller, and contained statues of Antiochus and Seleucus. Below them is a spirited bas-relief representing a triumphal procession—most probably that of the Emperor Trajan. As usual, not one of the heads of the figures has been preserved. The Turks, believing them to be the idols of the infidels, uniformly mutilated the countenances, that they might no longer be objects of adoration. The whole edifice seems to have been about thirty feet broad. The opposite or convex side was probably devoid of much ornament; and, indeed, any decoration would have been quite useless, since the city wall was directly in the rear.

On the Museum the fortifications of Athens joined the *Long Walls*, which served to keep up a safe and constant communication between it and Piræus. Standing on the top, I could readily trace the direction of the two walls, running parallel for nearly four miles, at the distance of five hundred and fifty feet apart. When they reached the heights above Piræus, these huge arms of the city opened and received the entire port within their embrace. The northern wall encompassed the principal harbor, while the other ran down to the seashore. Themistocles, who erected the powerful fortifications of Piræus, is said to have planned this immense undertaking; but it was executed by Pericles, and ranked among his greatest works. For the space between the walls not only offered a safe refuge to the villagers and country-people, but the walls were a long intrenchment defending all the fields to the south from armed invasion. The possession of so strong a system of fortification was naturally an object of envy to the Spartans; and when Athens fell into their hands, at the conclusion of the Peloponnesian War, they set about the work of destruction to the sound of joyous music, and crowned with festive chaplets.* It was fourteen years later that the Athenian admiral, Conon, supported by a Persian fleet, restored the walls to their original strength.

I walked down the western side of the hill, and in the hollow between it and the Pnyx I saw a curious tomb hewn out from the solid rock. Farther on I reached what goes by the name of the *Prison of Socrates*. There are three doors in the face of the rock. The left and middle one lead into a square chamber with rough walls. The other opens into an oblong room of small size, in the farther corner of which there is a doorway conducting to a third chamber, ten or fifteen feet in diameter. The ceiling is dome-shaped, and a round aperture lets in a flood of light from above. What these excavations

* Thirlwall's History of Greece, c. XXX.

served for, I was quite at a loss in settling to my own satisfaction. It seems improbable that they should have been used for a prison; and being inside of the walls, they can scarcely have been tombs. The notion has long prevailed among the Athenians that they were occupied by the Attic sage whose name they bear, and that he expired within their vaults.

Walking along the Pnyx, which is a ridge much lower than the Museum, I soon found myself on the level platform where the assemblies of the people were held. The ground seems to have been reduced to its present condition by artificial means. Its plan is semicircular; and the base, which appears to be straight, is in reality curved inwardly. Whether this was accidental, or answered the purpose of improving the acoustic effect, I am not informed. The arrangement, however, seems eminently to favor the conveyance of sound over a large area. The perpendicular face of rock, some ten feet in height, bounding the Pnyx on this side, is interrupted in the centre by a square stand projecting some feet out of the line. By means of steps on one side of it, I mounted to the top, and stood upon the *bema*, or rostrum, whence Demosthenes delivered some of his most stirring orations. On the crowded space before him were collected thousands of auditors who hung upon his words. Since no part of the area was occupied by seats, the number within reach of his voice must have been immense. Every voter could be accommodated with ease, for it contained no less than twelve thousand yards;* and six thousand hearers are mentioned as having been present on some particular occasions. The lower side of the platform is supported by a wall of stone drawn from the vicinity. These attracted my attention from their unusual size. One that I measured was twelve feet in length and six or seven high; its breadth I was unable to ascertain. The bulk of these blocks entitles them almost to be ranked among the Cyclopean constructions of the earlier period of Greek history.

Between the Pnyx and the Acropolis is a still lower hill, one of the same system of elevations, and I directed my steps thither as I returned to the consulate. It is a mere rock, rough and precipitous on three sides, especially toward the

* Wordsworth's Athens and Attica, p. 69.

Acropolis, where a large mass has broken off and fallen. This is the Areopagus, or Hill of Mars. Nothing in its external appearance would convey the least intimation that here was the seat of the most venerable court of Athens, or indeed of Greece, whose first duty is said to have been to try the god Mars on a charge of murder, while among its last scenes was the noble defence of the Apostle Paul. Here, in full view of the whole city, whose gorgeous temples, the resort of a devout and superstitious multitude, towered above the other buildings: the orator was called upon to defend the introduction of a new and strange religion. Unterrified by the fear of punishment for a crime that four centuries before had cost Socrates his life, St. Paul boldly preached a God, whom they ignorantly worshipped, and the resurrection of the dead, which they laughed to scorn. Of no site in Athens can there be less reason to distrust the identity. It has been proved beyond the shadow of a doubt. And though it be divested of all save these hallowed associations, the Christian can stand on no spot, even in this classic land, that calls up such thrilling recollections. It is well for us, perhaps, that besides some sixteen steps cut in the limestone rock, and a bench near the top, little remains to indicate the precise locality where the renowned court held its sessions. I felt that we might be induced to pay too much reverence to the scene of so great a transaction, and forget the truths the Apostle meant to inculcate. Strangely enough, the Greeks have built no chapel on the illustrious rock, though, until lately, there were the ruins of a small church of St. Dionysius the Areopagite at a short distance below.

I had now made most of the circuit of the Acropolis, and I brought my walk to a conclusion by strolling along the northern side until I entered a narrow lane, and found my way home.

To complete our survey of the antiquities of Athens, we must explore those that lie concealed in the modern town. Almost directly in front of the post-office is a singular octagonal building. The common name it goes by is the Temple of Æolus, or of the Winds, from the winged figures upon the sides. Each is the impersonation of the wind blowing from that particular point of the compass. Boreas looks northward down the principal thoroughfare of the city, toward the market-place. Zephyrus meets the mild western breezes that blow from the plains of Eleusis. A curious triton formerly adorned the top like a weather-cock, and the wand in his hand pointed out the wind that prevailed. This interesting monument, which was in reality a *Horologium*, or "clock-tower," built by a single public-spirited Athenian, Andronicus Cyrrhestes, served to keep time for the whole town. On the sides are to be traced as easily as ever the lines of the old sun-dials. A few years since new rods of iron were inserted as gnomons at each of the corners; and now the passer may read the time from the face of the marble, chiseled two thousand years ago. For cloudy weather a water-clock, the only time-piece the ancients were acquainted with, was placed for inspection in the interior of the edifice. This was, in fact, its principal design. An aqueduct, a few arches of which still remain, conducted the water of a small spring into a reservoir just behind the tower, and so supplied the clock. At present the Horologium stands in a hole full fifteen or twenty feet deep. This furnishes a pretty accurate standard to determine the accumulation of soil during the past twenty centuries. What treasures of art lie concealed beneath the rubbish it is now impossible to determine. The modern town has grown over it again since the revolution, and there are slender grounds for expecting that any thorough system of exploration will be undertaken in our day.

Walking down into the market-place our attention is immediately drawn to the gray stone walls overtopping the wooden shanties, and contrasting singularly with their weakness. I penetrated through the crowd of peddlers and buyers, and found myself within the inclosure of the *Stoa of Hadrian.* It was a great quadrangle, 376 feet long and 252 broad, with a stout wall of marble surrounding it. Externally the face was merely supported at intervals by massive buttresses, except on the west, where a stately row of Corinthian columns still shows that this was the principal entrance. Around the court on the inside ran a broad portico; and the court itself was perhaps cultivated as a garden. It contained a library and other buildings. But what a metamorphosis has the entire structure undergone! The whole interior, for I know not how long, has been used as a bazar. The quiet retreat of philosophers is the most noisy part of the city; the beautiful paintings of the walls are defaced; the costly marbles have disappeared. Where the library stood is seen an unsightly clock-tower erected by Lord Elgin himself, as a sort of indemnification, I presume, for his pilfering from the Parthenon. He has chronicled his own munificence in a long Latin inscription, which I have heard the more educated Greeks read with the greatest indignation. The government for a long time has been talking of procuring a more suitable place for the market, and clearing this whole area. This were a consummation much to be desired. As it was, in hunting out the spot where a few traces of the inner portico were said to remain, I was obliged to make my way through a butcher's shop, and past the heaps of new hides from a slaughter-house, to a place where, looking into a dilapidated hovel, I saw three or four columns supporting an architrave. How much more remains concealed, will only appear when the plan of the government is put into execution.

I left the busy scenes of the market, and a few minutes after found myself standing before a stately portal of four large marble columns of the Doric order. The precise object of this solitary monument is not, at first sight, quite evident; but it has been pretty well settled that it graced the entrance to the New Market, or Agora. This was not the space devoted to the purposes of trade in the palmy days of Athens; for *that* covered the ground south of the Acropolis and Areopagus. It was here, however, that St. Paul was in the habit of engaging in discussion, alike with the learned and the lowly. I found close by an upright slab of marble, on which were inscribed the prices of various commodities sold in the market, as regulated by an ordinance of the Emperor. One would think that with so strict precautions the hucksters could find few means of cheating their customers; but such does not seem to have been the fact. The maximum prices of many of the articles would furnish a striking contrast with their value in money at the present day.

I wished next to find my way to the Temple of Theseus; and for this purpose followed a westerly direction. Passing through what was once perhaps the most populous portion of the city, I could find but few remains. One of small extent is attributed to the *Stoa Pœcile*, the most famous of all the porticoes of which Athens could boast. A room in it, which I entered through a garden, was formerly used as a chapel; but has now been degraded into a store for all manner of rubbish. Further on there is another and more extensive collection of walls, which, from their construction with alternately wide and narrow layers of stone, are known to have been erected about the Macedonian epoch. In one obscure court I came across a statue of elegant workmanship, representing a Triton. His well-shaped body is terminated by a scaly tail twisted nearly up to his head. The general expression is one of suffering and despair. Hence Pittakes supposed the colossal effigy to have belonged to the monument of Phorbas, whom Erechtheus wished to slay.*

The *Theseum*, whose serene front soon appeared over the top of the mud walls in the vicinity, stands upon a slight eminence on the very outskirts of Athens toward the west. More perfect outwardly than any other temple extant, it gives a better notion of the imposing character of a Grecian shrine, executed according to the strictest requirements of art. It has undergone little change since the day of its foundation. The columns are intact; their sharp edges occasionally somewhat softened down by the wear of time, and a stray block in their lofty shafts moved slightly from its firm foundation, by the irresistible force of repeated earthquakes. The building was considerably smaller than the Parthenon. There are but six columns on the front and thirteen on the sides. Its length of one hundred and four feet scarcely exceeds the width of the Parthenon, and its breadth is but forty-five feet. Its antiquity, however, is greater than that of the shrine of the Acropolis, and dates as far back as 465 B.C. It is said to have been erected to cover the bones of the famous hero Theseus, which had been recently found on the island of Scyrus, and had been brought with superstitious care to this spot. In respect to sculpture, the The-

* L'Ancienne Athènes, p. 95 (1835).

seum presented a marked contrast to the richness of ornament that loaded every available part of the Parthenon. Of the square *metopes* on the architrave above the columns, merely those of the fronts were adorned with works of the chisel; on the sides they were quite plain, with the exception of those nearest either end. I found a porter at the side door ready to conduct me into the interior of the temple. In the present lack of a grand public museum, the government have suffered this edifice to be turned into a hall for the reception of a valuable collection of statues and inscriptions. Many of them are well worthy of protracted study. I was more particularly interested in a slab of marble carefully preserved under a glass cover. It was recently dug up on the site of a small temple at Marathon, and from the name of the artist chiseled upon it, has been supposed to have been wrought in the sixth or seventh century before Christ. The figure represented at full length is in low relief, and the execution is of that stiff and hard character which belongs to the infancy of art in every land. Its perfect preservation is indeed almost a miracle, considering the lapse of time.

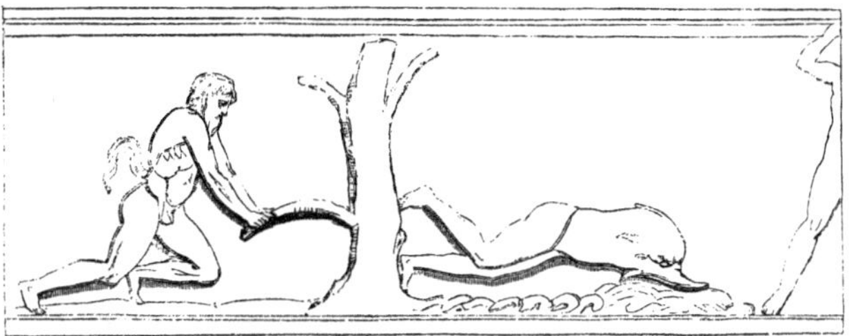

BAS-RELIEF FROM THE MONUMENT OF LYSICRATES.

HOROLOGIUM OF ANDRONICUS CYRRHESTES.

CHAPTER V.

WALKS ABOUT ATHENS.

On Sundays, and especially on the great feasts of the Church, the streets of Athens are thronged with men, women, and children, all intent upon recreation. At such times the shops are closed, and business transactions suspended. The early morning is spent in attendance on divine service; while the remainder of the day is devoted to visits or amusements.

The 26th of October (Old Style) was the festival of St. Demetrius—that holy man who acted the part of Lot with variations. So, at least, the legendaries would have us believe. Once upon a time, say they, the wickedness of Salonica had risen to such a pitch, as to render its destruction imperatively necessary. Angels were accordingly dispatched to bear intelligence to the saint, then sojourning in the doomed city, and bid him depart from its precincts. Demetrius, upon hearing the mandate, begins to remonstrate with the messengers, and endeavors to persuade them to spare Salonica. They answer that this is quite impossible: they have express commands. The holy man stops for a moment to reflect, and then exclaims, "I shall not depart. Go tell your Master that he must not destroy the city!" Notwithstanding the peremptory character of the instructions they have received, the angels dare not execute their commission. They return, and Salonica is spared! Such is the blasphemous history given of this highly-esteemed saint in the Greek legends.

All the Athenians who happen to be named after St. Demetrius, receive the visits of their acquaintance on his day; and these, in return, are honored in like manner on the festivals of their respective patrons in the calendar. Falling in with the custom, I walked out in the afternoon with a few friends, and called upon Mr. L. at his house in Hermes Street, not far from the solitary date-palm, so conspicuous an object in this part of the town. After passing through a narrow court-yard, we were ushered into a small but neatly-furnished parlor. Our host, a portly Greek of five-and-forty, rose to meet us, and received with smiling countenance our congratulations on his continued health and prosperity. We were invited to sit down, and were soon engaged in agreeable conversation. The ladies of the house contributed to our entertainment, and, before the termination of our short stay, brought in some refreshments. A favorite jar of sweetmeats—a curious preserve compounded solely of rose-leaves and sugar—was offered successively to each person, who helped himself to a single spoonful. By most persons the taste is considered very delicate and pleasant; while others think that the flavor of the flower is scarcely sufficiently smothered in quadruple the weight of sugar. Being forewarned, I limited myself to the usual supply, and thus avoided the mistake of some foreigners, who have committed the unpardonable offence of dipping the spoon a second time into the common jar. After tasting the rose preserves each guest took a very small glass of Samian wine, or a tumbler of water, as his inclination or his principles directed.

From the house of our Greek friend we proceeded to the public promenade, which, since the heat had diminished, was every evening crowded with the "élite" of Athens. The principal walk is on the road leading northward toward the village of Patissia—a continuation of Æolus Street. Pedestrians occupy the greater part of the hard and smooth surface of this road, scattering upon the approach of any vehicle. It is also a favorite resort of the king and queen, who may be seen almost any afternoon riding out on horseback in this direction, attended by a few guards. Their subjects on such occasions stop and do them homage as they pass, and receive a bow in return. A stranger need not be astonished, if, when he meets the royal party in some solitary place, he is honored with this mark of condescension on the part of their Hellenic majesties.

A more pleasant spot for recreation is the palace garden, to which I repeatedly gained access by permission of one of the king's adjutants. Its grounds are tastefully laid out with handsome walks and shrubbery, and the cultivated flowers are mostly the same as those that are favorites with us. In the midst of a labyrinth on the southern side is a small pond, whose surface is covered with the gigantic leaves of the *Victoria regina*—the monster water-lily of the tropics. The climate seems to be well adapted to its development; but I am not aware of its having flowered as yet. That this ground was once included within the populous portion of the city, is evident from the discovery of a number of antiquities. In one part of the garden a mosaic floor, by far the most perfect of its kind at Athens, was uncovered a few years ago, and is now protected by an arbor densely shaded by varieties of beautiful creepers. It is long and irregular in shape, and in an excellent state of preservation. Aquatic birds and other unmistakable symbols show that it was the floor of some elegant private bath attached to the villa of a rich Athenian citizen. Not far from this mosaic are the prostrate columns of a small temple, whose foundations are seen close by. Just beyond the fence on the east a long arched channel was found a few months after my arrival; but I have heard no satisfactory solution of its use. The land-owners in the vicinity of the royal grounds have every thing to fear from their gradual enlargement. It has even been proposed to extend their limits to the banks of the Ilissus, and take in the Temple of Jupiter Olympius itself; but as this would include one of the most popular resorts of the Athenians, the project was abandoned as infeasible.

The picturesque costumes of the Greeks—so different from those of other countries—give a strange liveliness to the scene on the promenade. Many of the gentlemen have adopted the common European dress; but the rest cling to that which their ancestors have worn for ages. The higher class usually wear the Albanian costume, consisting of a tight vest, and over this a short coat with the sleeves slit and hanging loosely from the elbow. From the waist, a white skirt, or *fustanella*, reaches to the knees, and is confined to its place by a wide sash or girdle. By the Greeks of the old school a very slender waist is esteemed the greatest point of beauty in a man; and some are said to draw the sash so tightly, that after the lapse of years it becomes painful to loosen it even at night.

Most of the lower class retain the nautical trowsers, differing from the Turkish in that, whereas the latter have a bag for each leg, in the former both legs are thrust through one large blue sack in such a way that the greater part remains flapping behind. With this dress, a thick girdle, or sometimes a broad leathern belt is substituted for the sash. The belt is made a general receptacle for pistols and daggers, whose projecting handles give the stranger an impression of insecurity, augmented by the fierce countenances of those that carry them. On the promenade, as well as in society, the Greek generally carries a string of beads, frequently of large size, which a stranger would naturally mistake for a rosary, until informed that it has no religious significance. In fact, it is only a plaything to occupy the fingers, while the mind and lips are busy with something else. When engaged in calm conversation, the beads pass slowly through the fingers; but as the speaker becomes more and more heated in debate, their motion increases in rapidity. Playing with his beads, which are apt to distract the attention of a foreigner, thus comes to facilitate the utterance of a Greek; and even a public speaker does not disdain to make use of them in his forensic efforts.

The ladies are gradually abandoning their peculiar provincial attire; and if now and then the graceful Smyrniote, or the odd Hydriote dress is met with, it is much more rare than the French fashion. Not unfrequently a lady will take a half-way course, and continue to wear the red *fezi*, or cap, such as is worn by the men. Set negligently on the head, with its long blue tassel hanging down on one side, it gives the female face too boyish a look to be becoming.

In the midst of the crowd, the priests may readily be detected by their long black robes reaching to the feet, and their large caps of the same color. Another distinctive mark of the order is their long hair, gathered up under their caps, and their long and flowing beards. A youth who contemplates embracing a monastic or priestly life, begins his preparation by allowing his hair to grow for a year or two.

It is said that in some portions of the peninsula of Maina, the southernmost part of Lacedæmonia, it was customary for the men to suffer their beards to grow, until they had revenged themselves for any injury they might have received. In the midst of the civil feuds which rent that unhappy district, this practice was adopted as a badge to indicate a thirst for revenge.* A singular, but I believe an authentic instance of this custom was seen in the following occurrence, some twenty years since. When the President, Capo d'Istria, on a certain visit to Maina, was entertained in one of the villages, he noticed an individual sitting at the further end of the same room; a man of gloomy and forbidding aspect, with long hair and unshaven face, who seemed to shun all intercourse with those around. Calling him, the President asked him whether he was a candidate for orders; and the man replied that he was not. "What are you then?"—"What you have made me," was the reply. The stranger proceeded to say that, a few months before, his son had been killed in a private quarrel. According to immemorial custom, it became his duty to

* This practice is the more interesting, from the fact that Herodotus tells us of a similar usage among the ancient Peloponnesians. In a battle between the Argives and Spartans, the former were routed, and lost the important town of Thyreæ. "From this time," says the historian, "the Argives cut their hair short (for formerly they wore long hair, according to fixed custom), and made a law, enforced by a curse, that no Argive should wear long hair, nor the women deck themselves with gold ornaments, until they should regain Thyreæ. But the Lacedæmonians, on the contrary, passed a law ordaining that, although previously it had not been their custom to wear long hair, they should do so thenceforth." (I. 82.)

slay the murderer; but from doing this he was prevented by the new laws introduced under the President's administration. He had, therefore, waited for justice to be done him; but months had elapsed, and yet the murderer was at large. "Now," added he, "if within forty days I am not avenged, I shall take the law into my own hands." The President promised to attend to the matter, even though much blood might be spilled in capturing the culprit. But after his departure, he forgot his promise, and so nothing was done. Two months after, the injured man went stealthily to his enemy's house, and killed, not only him, but four others of his family. He then sat down, and penned a letter to Count Capo d'Istria, somewhat to this effect: "I have waited not only forty, but sixty days, and no justice has been done me. I have now taken my revenge with interest." The perpetrator of the bloody deed was yet alive a few years since.

The influence of Oriental notions of propriety is observable in the restraints put upon the freedom of the gentler sex. A lady is thought to have broken all rules of decorum when she ventures out alone into the streets, even at mid-day. A stout man-servant must follow to protect her; or, at least, she must be accompanied by a trusty maid. There is much of the old Grecian feeling in this: for in Athens "no respectable lady thought of going out without a female slave; and the husband always assigned one to his wife. At a later date the number of these attendants was greatly increased."*

The dwelling-houses in Athens are of a character much superior to those of the rural districts and towns. True, the old portion surrounding the base of the Acropolis has been rebuilt on a plan very similar to that of the town before the Revolution; every wall that had not been ruined in that disastrous period was put to use by the returning citizens: and such was the scarcity of timber of suitable size, that the houses were necessarily constructed of a long and narrow shape. But the greater part of the city has since been erected in a more symmetrical manner. Unfortunately, three or four plans were successively submitted to the government, and in turn adopted. Any one of them would have made Athens a

* Becker's Charicles, p. 469.

finely laid-out city. Scarcely, however, had the Athenians begun to rebuild their houses in conformity with one plan, before it was replaced by another. The palace of the king was the single point whence all the principal avenues must radiate; and the palace, according to one plan, was to be situated on the high ground toward the Cephissus; and, according to another, at the northern end of the city. The citizens were ready to chant a *Jubilate*, when at length their doubts were removed, and the corner-stone of the regal mansion was laid with great pomp on a third site, near the banks of the River Ilissus.

All these adverse circumstances have not prevented the *New Town*, as it is called, from presenting a very comely appearance: and numbers of costly edifices, public and private, are continually rising. One of these gave the people a fine occasion for indulging in bitter sarcasm. The owner, a former member of the king's cabinet, had been noted for the peculiar facility with which an office could be obtained from him, by any one that was able to cross his hand with gold. To satisfy his vanity, the ex-minister inscribed his initials P. D. on the front of his palatial residence. But the people, supposing them to denote the source whence his wealth was obtained, chose to read them *proxenica dora*—that is, "consular bribes"—instead of simple Peter Deliannis.

In every house great precautions are adopted against robberies. These a few years since were frequently committed. A band of ten or fifteen robbers has been known to enter one of the largest houses in the city, by the connivance of the porter, and to plunder it of all its valuables. The poorer class of houses are entered with comparative ease. One of these —a small shop at the corner of the next street to my residence—was one morning found rifled of a small amount of money that had been left in the drawer. But instead of breaking through the thick door, the robber had effected an entrance by digging a hole in the wall, which he had found the easier task of the two. This little incident brought forcibly to my mind the passage of Holy Writ—"In the dark they dig through houses, which they had marked out in the daytime." Allusion to the same insecurity of earthen walls is made in the description of houses (as it reads in the original), "where thieves *dig through* and steal;" and in the remarkable passage where the prophet Ezekiel is represented as conveying his goods out, through a hole that he had made in the wall of his own house.

Our modern ideas of gallantry are greatly shocked by the open disparagement of the female sex, characteristic of Greek society. The birth of a daughter is as much a subject of condolence, as the birth of a son is one of congratulation. A foreign resident at Athens, the father of a large family of girls, is looked upon by his neighbors as the most unlucky of men. They wonder at his failure to appreciate their sympathy. A story is told of an Athenian, who had set his heart on obtaining a son to perpetuate his name. Upon learning the disappointment of his expectations, he endeavored to conceal his chagrin, and shame also, in the grove of the Cephissus; where he skulked for three days, before he could regain sufficient assurance to meet his acquaintance. The anecdote may be somewhat exaggerated; but the fact that such feelings exist can not be doubted.

This remarkable preference of the male sex is somewhat accounted for, by the prevalence of the custom of giving a large dowry with a daughter at marriage. In Maina alone the reverse is true: the husband purchases his bride at a heavy cost. Elsewhere a portion of the family estate must be sacrificed at the marriage of each daughter; and he who is able or willing to give most, is generally sure of seeing his daughters first established in life. Such is the mercenary light in which the marriage relation is regarded. Qualities of mind are but little taken into account. Nor is it considered an objection of any moment that the parties to the contract be totally unacquainted with each other's characters and tastes. Since the lady's consent is altogether unessential, her preferences are not necessarily consulted. The father's great concern is to marry off his daughter at as small a loss as possible; that of the suitor, to obtain the most advantageous match. Money being the chief object on either side, the unfortunate maiden is apt to fare badly between the two. Hence the frequency of ill-sorted marriages—a fruitful source of domestic misery.

The wife who has been forced into so unfortunate a union, is not free even from abuse and corporal chastisement; of the prevalence of which we need no stronger proof than is afforded by the frequent allusions to it in the proverbs most current among the people.

RUINS OF THE TEMPLE OF THE OLYMPIAN JOVE.

UNIVERSITY OF OTHO, AT ATHENS.

CHAPTER VI.

STUDENT-LIFE IN ATHENS.

"Let those that will believe it: I, for one,
Can not thus read the history of my kind:
Remembering all this little Greece has done
To raise the universal human mind."

MILNES.

IT may sound strange and incongruous to many an ear to talk of education and literature in connection with modern Greece. We have been wont to think of the Greeks as the most barbarous and illiterate nation of Europe. We began by ignoring the natural consequences of long ages of servitude, and expected them to emerge from the slime with a robe of unsullied brilliancy. Having been disappointed in our unreasonable anticipations, we have long since ceased to take any account of their struggles in the path of improvement. The wonderful development that popular education has undergone is unknown to most; and few are aware of the existence of any schools of learning that will favorably compare with our own. When, therefore, I say that the University of Otho at Athens possesses at least as many students, and twice as large a corps of professors, as the largest of our colleges, I am stating a fact that may excite some surprise.

Shortly after my arrival at Athens I was desirous of visiting the University, and making some inquiries as to the course of instruction. I had long intended to avail myself of the public lectures as the most convenient means of accustoming the ear to the sound of the modern language when spoken in its greatest purity. In company with Dr. King, who had promised to introduce me to some of the more distinguished professors, I walked thither one morning at about ten o'clock. The winter term had not yet commenced, after a long vacation of four months, from June to October. Although the regular day for opening was close at hand, only a few students were to be seen in the halls. The spell of summer continued as yet unbroken by a single refreshing shower; and neither professors nor students were in any way anxious to recommence their occupations until the oppressive heat should have somewhat abated.

The edifice is spacious, and by no means faulty in point of taste. Though built in the form of an **H**, only one of the two main portions is entirely finished and in use. The effect of the structure is good, but suffers in dignity from the lowness of the roof, contrasted with the size of the building. The principal front is said to be constructed in imitation of one of the galleries of the Erechtheum. A wide portico runs almost the entire length, and is supported by short pillars resting upon a high wall that half incloses it. The entrance is between two large Ionic columns of fine Pentelican marble presented by the king.

In the secretary's office we found the Secretary, Mr. Dokos, and one of the most distinguished professors, Constantine Asopius. He is an elderly man, some seventy years of age, I should judge. Born at Jannina, in Epirus, he studied there under the best teachers. Next he taught school for the Greek residents of Trieste. Lord Gilford—whose memory to this day is held in grateful honor by many Greeks, not only for his personal kindness, but on account of the lively interest he entertained in the whole nation—appreciated his fine abilities, and sent him at his own expense to perfect his education in Germany, France, and England. On his return he appointed him teacher of Greek philology in the Ionian Academy.*

* A. Soutsos, Panorama of Greece, Part II., p. 76.

When the University was founded at Athens, Asopius was called thither to fill a similar chair. He enjoys the reputation of being perhaps the best living philologist among the Greeks; and his learning is by no means confined to a single department. A fine intellectual head, and a face indicative of that rare attainment—a placid old age, ruffled by no impatient or peevish disposition—attract the admiration and affection of all the students. In their welfare Professor Asopius takes a warm interest; nor is there any one of whom the student is more ready to ask counsel. It may, indeed, be remarked that in general the coldness and hauteur which mark the relation of teacher and pupil in many of our institutions is here replaced by a friendly and even familiar intercourse. Professor Asopius was evidently pleased at the idea that an American had come to Athens to find out what facilities this city afforded to those who wished to gain a thorough knowledge of both ancient and modern Greek. He expressed the hope that I might be only the forerunner of a multitude of American scholars, and cordially invited me to his lecture-room. His lectures on the Odyssey, and on philology, and the history of the Greek poets, are held in high esteem. I began to attend them as soon as they commenced; but the indistinct utterance of the speaker is a difficulty which meets one at the very threshold.

The library was the only part of the building that was open to inspection. It took me quite by surprise. I had anticipated seeing at most a few thousand books. The librarian, Mr. G. Typaldus, informed me that there were not less than 70,000 volumes, and that the annual increase was six or eight thousand. Nor does it consist of works of small value or merit. As far as my subsequent observation went, the selection seemed to be excellent; while some works—such as Napoleon's *Expédition d'Egypte*—are rare and costly. In the English department, however, the library is singularly incomplete; and with the exception of the Smithsonian Institute's "Contributions to Knowledge" (of which the set is defective), there are no American publications of importance. This rapid rise of a collection of books which equals, if it does not exceed, any similar one in the United States, is the more astonishing as the outlay of money has been very small. Most of the additions have been by gifts of wealthy Greeks, and foreigners, among whom I am sorry not to be able to mention the names of any American benefactors.

From the library we walked a short distance to the house of Neophytus Bambas. An old woman answered our knock; and on asking for the *kyrios*, we were conducted through a corridor to a small back room, where we found Professor Bambas. He recognized Dr. King at once, and set about finding us chairs to sit down. A Greek student's room is not usually well provided with such furniture; but by the moving of a number of books and piles of manuscript, seats were provided, while the worthy Professor found a place for himself on the edge of a cot that occupied a corner of the room. One or two students, friends of his, who attended him as did the disciples of the ancient philosophers, stood just within the door, listening respectfully to our conversation. Professor Bambas was a short old man, with white hair, and long flowing beard, dressed in the monastic costume. His tone in conversation was distinct, but somewhat nasal. For the past thirty or forty years he had occupied a distinguished rank among the scholars of Greece, and he was a friend and contemporary of the great Coray. A native of Scio, so far back as 1816, after completing his studies at Paris, he taught in the Lyceum of his native city. In 1821 he joined the standard of Demetrius Ypsilantis, and for a single year followed a soldier's profession. But he soon abandoned an occupation so foreign to his inclinations, and retired to Cephallenia, and thence to Corfu, to occupy the chair of Philosophy. I was the more interested in him as having been associated with Rev. Mr. Lowndes and Mr. Nicolaides, of Philadelphia, in Asia Minor, in translating the Bible into modern Greek. The translation was made at the expense of the British and Foreign Bible Society. It was at first opposed by many natives on the ground that the language was so nearly the same as to render a version quite unnecessary. But the educated laity will now readily concede that the Scriptures must remain a dead letter to the people until they are supplied with it in an easier idiom than the original text, or the Septuagint. A second edition has, however, been greatly altered, so as to exclude many vulgarisms whose introduction seemed unavoidable in the first, and to meet the demands of the improved state of the language. It is to be regretted that of late years Professor Bambas has shown a disposition to stand aloof from the liberal movements both in Church and State. During the invasion of Turkish territory he was among the prominent advocates of that ill-starred measure.

While we were conversing a visitor was announced, who proved to be my friend the Sciote merchant, Mr. A. He had come to revive old reminiscences and forgotten acquaintance. He was once a pupil of Bambas in Scio, where he learned the first rudiments of knowledge, at a time when his native island was still the garden of the Archipelago. The master and pupil had not met since that fearful massacre which sent every family into mourning for the greater part of its members. Bambas did not know but that the boy had fallen a victim to the devouring sword, or lingered only to meet the more appalling doom of perpetual servitude. The scene was truly touching, when the old man learned from his own lips the merchant's name. He threw his arms affectionately around his former scholar's neck, and his flowing silvery locks mingled with the young man's darker hair as he kissed him, in true Oriental style, on either cheek. Then came a host of questions to be answered by each party—of friends long lost, of acquaintances in foreign lands, and of their own personal history. I felt that my presence would tend to mar the interest of the interview, and I rose to leave with a cordial invitation to come often to the Professor's sanctum. I regret to be obliged to chronicle the recent death of Neophytus Bambas—an event which deprived Greece of an honest and intelligent man whom she could ill spare, and of one who had always endeavored to serve his country to the best of his knowledge.

The number of students in attendance upon the University was daily increasing, and in about a week the various courses of lectures were successively commenced. Meanwhile I had formed the acquaintance of some more professors. Among them were Mr. Rangabes, who unites the apparently incompatible qualities necessary for the pursuit of archæology and the more graceful culture of the muse; Mr. Benthylus of the

Philosophical School; and Mr. Manousis, lecturer on Universal History. The latter, as I subsequently learned, is particularly obnoxious to the English, and to those who espouse their side, for the violence with which he attacked them during the differences between the British and Hellenic governments in 1850.

I found no difficulty in augmenting my circle of friends among the students, whose warm reception at once set me at ease with them. There are no dormitories within the University, or *Panepistemion;* the students consequently lodge in various quarters of the town. Their rooms are generally shared between two occupants; and as the most of them are in reduced circumstances, the stock of furniture and books is very small. This fact, however, attracts little notice at Athens, from the rarity of large fortunes, and the simple style of living. The salaries of the employés of the government are singularly low—so low, indeed, as to be utterly insufficient for the maintenance of a respectable appearance, without the means derived from peculation and bribery. Yet the professors of the University, most of whom are single men, without the exercise of any uncommon degree of frugality, contrive to live on salaries of six hundred dollars a year, and even to save some part of that sum: and even with such paltry emoluments, it is the highest ambition of numbers of young Greeks to occupy a chair in that institution.

The Athenian student always takes his meals at the eating-house, and his fare is simple and wholesome. The warmth of the climate reduces the necessity and relish for animal food, which rarely appears on the table in any considerable quantity, except at Easter. On that great festival, the most august of the year, it is a universal and immemorial custom to have a whole lamb roasted in every family. There is no one so poor within the realm as to be unable to have some part in the gayety and good cheer to which the day is devoted. On other occasions the only recreation that the student takes consists in a visit to the theatre, or a walk on the public promenade with a friend. He will then invariably insist upon accompanying him to the café to partake of the *rahat-lakoumi,* a Turkish sweetmeat deservedly popular throughout the East.

In imitation of the German plan, the University is composed of four distinct Schools—those of Theology, Law, Medicine, and Philosophy. The whole number of professors whose names appear on the programme of studies published soon after my arrival, was forty-six; of whom twenty-five were ordinary professors, and the remainder extraordinary, honorary, and adjunct; the distinction consisting merely in the difference of the emolument they enjoyed, and not in the character of their instruction. All these gentlemen are native Greeks, with the single exception of Professor Landerer, who has long resided in the country, and is a naturalized citizen. One of the faculty is annually elected by his associates as *Prytanis*, or President; but the powers attached to this honorable post are very limited, and extend little farther than the delivery of an oration at the yearly Commencement in June. The Prytanis of the previous year had been the Archimandrite Misael Apostolides of the Theological School, a man of talent and high attainments, but thoroughly wedded to the Russian party. He was now to be succeeded by Mr. Pellicas, one of the most prominent jurists and law professors of Greece.

The distribution of instructors in the several departments was exceedingly unequal; as likewise that of the hours devoted weekly to the branches of study. In Theology the three professors gave but fifteen hours of instruction; while in Law there were eleven professors and upward of forty lectures; in Medicine twelve professors and between sixty and seventy lectures; and in Philosophy and the kindred studies twenty professors and eighty-two lectures. The total number of lectures delivered within the compass of a week was, consequently, more than two hundred, embracing every department of science and art. There is a similar inequality with respect to the apportionment of students in attendance. Of 397 regularly matriculated students, during a previous year, 242 were studying medicine, 86 law, 62 philosophy, and only 7 theology. And though the number had now increased to 455, the same inequality was still observable. Besides these students who were inscribed on the books, and who expected to pursue a regular course of study (the *phœtetæ*), there were at least three hundred more attending certain branches with greater or less regularity for a year or two, who receive the designation of *acroatæ*, or "listeners." The number of students may, therefore, be safely set down at 750, without including those who occasionally frequent the lecture-room as they find time. It is a circumstance well worth the noticing, that rather more than one half of the matriculated students are from districts under the rule of the Sultan. Thus "Free Greece," as she is proudly styled, is furnishing to the millions of the same blood that are subject to the tyrant's sway, the benefits of a liberal education; and thus is she gradually preparing the way for their total emancipation from the shackles of ignorance and superstition.

As in Germany, instruction is given wholly by means of written lectures.* From the great lack of suitable text-books, the students labor under serious disadvantages, and are compelled to make the mere taking of notes an arduous undertaking, wasting in the manual exercise much time that might be far more profitably expended in reading on the subjects treated in the public discourses. It becomes the more indispensable to commit to paper the entire substance of the lectures, from the fact that the only examinations are those to which the candidate for a degree must submit. They embrace all the subjects comprehended within the course, and are so severe that comparatively few succeed in undergoing them. Their difficulty arises in part from the want of any prescribed order of study. Any lack of adequate preparation is consequently apt to remain undetected until the final trial.†

As the admission is entirely free, on a pleasant afternoon the lecture-room of a popular instructor will be crowded to overflowing. Step with me, for instance, into the hall where Professor Manousis daily holds forth, and you will find it thronged not only with regular students, but with others who eagerly seize the opportunity to hear an entertaining discourse

* The only recitation is one that is intended exclusively for those who expect to devote themselves to teaching.

† See the preface to "Directions to the students of each School, respecting the succession of the various sciences, and the preservation of Method and Order in the pursuit of the studies in the University"—a pamphlet published by the Prytanis in 1838, in order to diminish the danger of serious mistake.

on Universal History. Here is the soldier, off duty, in his gay uniform, and by his side the parish priest wearing his long black gown and large cap. The youth on another bench, who is distinguished by his long hair, is a candidate for deacon's orders. Here and there, mingled with these, is a fair representation of the townspeople who have escaped from their day's toils, and drop in for an hour or two before returning home. If the discourse be consecrated to Chemistry, the crowd of auditors will be still greater—the aisles crowded, and several standing even upon the lecturer's platform.

Connected with the University, there is on the hill of the Nymphs an excellent astronomical observatory, the munificent gift of a single wealthy Greek residing in Austria—the Baron Simas—who gave not less than $50,000 to build and furnish it with suitable instruments. Among these the chief is a refracting telescope, magnifying about five hundred diameters. On a clear evening the observatory is a favorite resort of the Athenians of all classes.

That an institution so well organized, presided over by men of the greatest distinction for talents and learning, and yearly attended by seven hundred and fifty youth, has been reared within the short space of twenty years, in spite of formidable obstacles from ignorance and prejudice, is a fact of which Greece may well be proud. But a yet higher claim to the respect of civilized Europe and America can be based on the completeness of her system of gratuitous and popular education, extending from the primary school to the very threshold of the University. It may be affirmed with confidence that none need be deprived of a respectable education, save in consequence of their own willfulness or want of industry. The whole area of Greece, containing, according to the official returns, 992,643 inhabitants, is divided into 272 *demi*, or townships. In these there were, in 1852, 325 common schools regularly organized, with 29,229 children, and in 1853, about 40,000. The studies are such as are most essential for the pursuits of ordinary life. It is not a little remarkable that over 4000 of these scholars are girls. Thirty years ago it was esteemed preposterous for a parent to teach his daughter any thing beyond reading and writing; and such a thing as a school for girls was unheard of. Yet, at present, there is a sort of female college under the care of Madame Mano, where several hundred young ladies are educated: it occupies an imposing edifice recently erected by the contributions of many, and the liberality of a few wealthy citizens. Of the school instituted many years since by our countryman, the Rev. Dr. Hill, and his estimable lady, mention is made in another place.

Next in rank above the common or *demotic* schools, are the *Hellenic* schools, eighty-five in number; and the six or seven gymnasia, corresponding to our grammar-schools, and, in part, to our colleges. Thence the transition is easy to the University, where the professional studies are first undertaken. These seminaries of learning are frequented by about 10,000 students.

Besides these institutions, there are a number of others more special in their character. The Rizarian School is a sort of theological seminary for the education of young men for the priesthood, founded by a wealthy Greek after whom it is named. Of the height of its standard in a literary point of view, I am unable to speak with certainty. It was brought prominently into notice during my stay in Athens by a rebellion of its sixty students. Their ostensible ground was the coarseness of the bread they were fed upon; but it was stated in the journals that the true reason was the dissatisfaction of the bigoted students with the more liberal views and practice of one or two of their professors. It was only by the intervention of the police, and the capture of a few of their number, that peace was restored among these bellicose theologians.

There is a Military School at Athens, a Naval School at Syra, and an Agricultural School situated but a few rods from the ruins of ancient Tiryns, in Argolis. But the latter, though possessing, it is said, some fifty students, is generally considered a failure. Perhaps the most singular institution is the Polytechnic School, "where on *feast days* and *Sundays* the mechanics of the capital resort to be taught chemistry applied to the arts, drawing, etc."*

* I am indebted for most of the statistical information respecting the schools of Greece, to a manuscript paper "On the State of Education

Such are a few of the data by which we may form an opinion of the present intellectual position of Greece. The system of education, though carefully planned on French, and especially German models, is doubtless capable of considerable improvement; but it is truly wonderful, considering the rapidity of its rise. In Athens alone there are five thousand souls, out of a population of about thirty thousand, engaged in study. Under such circumstances, no one can deny that the present condition of Greece is full of promise. Seed has been planted that must yield a plentiful harvest. Greece needs, however, a higher tone of morality, and a purer form of religion. This is the dark side of the picture. Would that clearer indications of a change so much to be desired could be presaged in the future. Then might we confidently abide the time, when, though insignificant in size beside the overgrown states of modern Europe, Greece would wield an influence disproportioned to the extent of her territory or the number of her inhabitants.

in Greece," procured from the Bureau of the Minister of Public Instruction, through my friend Mr. Pittakes. It has never been published, I understand.

THE ACROPOLIS RESTORED.

THE ACROPOLIS, FROM THE HILL OF THE MUSEUM.

CHAPTER VII.

MODERN GREEK CUSTOMS.

A WEDDING IN THE UPPER CIRCLES.

A MARRIAGE ceremony at Athens is a celebration very different from one in the country. In the former we find exhibited somewhat of European civilization and cultivation; while into the remote villages, the influence of foreign customs has not yet penetrated. There, people are married, as well as baptized and buried, according to the good old customs of their fathers. And yet, even in the city, so many characteristic peculiarities have been preserved, that they appear novel and interesting to a stranger. I was therefore greatly pleased upon receiving one day an invitation to the wedding of a young Greek couple, who were to be married a few evenings later.

The rite takes place generally at the house of the bridegroom, though in some provinces the parish church is resorted to. But in this respect, as in most others, each petty district has its own customs, immutable as the laws of the Medes and Persians. We went at an early hour to the scene of the evening's festivities. It was a mansion of the old style, built of stone and stucco, and facing upon one of the small streets that abound in the more ancient part of the town. A crowd of the lower classes, who, though not among the invited, made bold to collect in force around the door, seemed to preclude our entrance. A small company at a drinking-shop some distance down the street were keeping up their spirits with frequent potations, and made merry with the music of a stringed instrument, whose notes grated harshly upon our ears. This entertainment was every now and then interrupted by the jocose comments of the party upon the appearance of the guests, as they successively came into the light cast by a flaming torch fastened near the door. When at length we had worked our way up the thronged stairs, we found that some sixty or eighty persons were already assembled in the moderately large parlor, which though it seemed rather bare of ornament and furniture to one who had come from the West, had some pretensions in common with the drawing-rooms of Paris and London. The assembled company, composed as usual of a much greater proportion of ladies than of gentlemen, were mostly dressed in the latest style of Paris fashions. Yet there was a sprinkling of gentlemen clad in the genuine Albanian dress, comprising your free-and-easy people who wish to pass for the more independent class of society, and scorn to adopt the perpetually changing *mode*. There were not wanting a considerable number of pretty faces among the ladies (who, according to the common practice, congregated on one side of the room); but it was a beauty that consisted rather in freshness of color, and a good healthy look, than in delicacy of feature. If, however, fame speaks truly, some of the color is borrowed, and the belle of the ball-room makes but a sorry figure the next morning. All the tight lacing in the world could not give an Athenian young lady the wasp-like contour which is the admiration of French dressmakers and misses in their teens. Disguise it as they may, there is a tendency to *embonpoint* among the ladies, many of whom waddle about with a grace which would seem charming in the eyes of our Dutch progenitors. The men, on the other hand, are a lean, lank race, whose dark complexions acquire an additional touch of ferocity from the formidable mustaches which, when their hands are not otherwise employed, they may be seen twirling by the hour.

The company were all assembled, and on the tip-toe of expectation, when the bridegroom and the bride entered, and took their stand at the further extremity of the room. Each of them held a long, lighted waxen taper, and the groomsman and bridesmaid carried similar ones. The bride, arrayed in a white satin dress, covered with lace, and having for a head-dress a wreath of flowers, from behind which a long white veil hung down over her shoulders, looked charming—as what bride does not? She bore the classic name of Athena. The bridegroom was dressed entirely in Frank costume. The priests came in at the same time with the couple—or, more properly, there were present at the beginning of the service two priests, with a deacon and a young man who read the responses, and who corresponded to the *enfant de chœur* of the Latin Church.

There are two distinct services in the Greek Church pertaining to this ceremony; and the rite of marriage can not take place unless the parties have been previously betrothed. Sometimes, however, as in this instance, the one service takes place immediately before the other. The liturgy was read by one of the priests from an elegantly-bound service-book. In one part of the ceremony he stopped, and taking up a ring from the small table, on which were deposited the various utensils which the deacon had brought in, he thrice made the sign of the cross over the book. Then he touched it to the forehead of the bridegroom and to that of the bride. Last of all, he placed it successively upon the finger, first of one, and then of the other, after divers crossings performed in the air.

When the parties were thus lawfully betrothed, there was a short pause; and then the bishop, whom the relatives had invited to officiate, in order to give more brilliancy to the wedding, entered the room, and the priests hastened to do him homage. His ordinary episcopal costume consists of a black cloak and gown, and the clerical cap, over which a black veil hangs down behind as a distinguishing mark of his office. But on this occasion his head was covered with a crown, and he carried a heavy silver crozier, such as is only to be seen in the Greek Church—Roman Catholic bishops rarely appearing in public with it. The handsome dresses of the priests added to the singularity of the scene. The bishop now took a principal part in the services, reading from a book of solid silver binding, which one of the priests held before him. Whenever he found it necessary to lay aside his crozier, one of the attendant ecclesiastics took it, at the same time kissing his hand; and when he resumed it, the same ceremony was gone through, to the no small disgust of those of us who were not accustomed to such abject servility. The service was protracted, and we became rather weary of it; for it was chiefly made up of prayers, hurried through, and of passages of Scripture, mumbled over in such a manner as to be quite unintelligible. Some portions of the written form are in themselves so utterly senseless, that no one can have the least idea of what they mean.

The great and essential part of the rite was the *crowning* of the couple. The crowns were, in this case, merely wreaths of artificial flowers, numbers of which may be seen in the shops every day. The groomsman held one over the head of the bridegroom, and the bridesmaid held a similar one over the bride's head during the whole time, and they appeared quite fatigued before the end of the ceremony was reached. At last, the proper moment arriving, the bishop took one of the wreaths, touching it to the forehead of the bridegroom, and afterward to that of the bride, and made with it the sign of the cross between the couple. This he repeated three times, at the same time reciting the words that follow: "Thou, the servant of the Lord, Gregory, art crowned (or married) to the servant of the Lord, Athena, in the name of the Father, and of the Son, and of the Holy Ghost." He then crowned the bridegroom with this wreath, and with the other performed the same ceremony in respect to the bride. Subsequently, the groomsman, who is usually the godfather, or *nonnos* of the bridegroom, and is expected to be hereditary sponsor, exchanged the wreaths, and then replaced them on the heads of the couple. A cup was next handed by the bishop, first to the man, and then to the woman, and each of them drank a portion of the wine it contained. This very pleasing ceremony was symbolic of the obligation that both parties assume to participate equally in all the pleasures and sufferings of life, in its joys and its sorrows. I had heard it stated that a bitter ingredient is mingled with the wine; but those of whom I inquired assured me that nothing of the kind was customary. It was singular that so affecting an incident should be closely followed by another of a ludicrous character. The bishop took the hand of the priest; he, in turn, grasped that of the deacon; and so with the married couple, the singers, and all, a string was made, which the chief ecclesiastic led around the table in the centre of the room. The whole bore an amusing resemblance to some of the games that children play in America. With this the service ended, to the satisfaction of every one present. When the priests had retired, the company pressed around the bridegroom and bride to offer congratulations, some formal, and others affectionate. The guests remained but a few moments more. A servant came, bringing in a large waiter covered with candies, and each was expected to help himself plentifully to them, as well as to carry some home. A few of those present seemed to measure their kind feelings to the couple by the quantity they heaped together; and, judging by this criterion, their benevolent feelings were not small. Two or three drew out their handkerchiefs, and carried them away full. After this the company began to disperse, and we followed the general example.

It struck me as a very singular feature, that during the entire service I had been listening to, not a single response was made by the couple, nor had the consent of the parties been expressed, or any promise exacted of them. In fact, the bridegroom may arrange the whole matter with the parents or guardians of the lady, without her knowledge, and even against her will. And let not any one suppose that such an arrangement, while sanctioned by law, never actually occurs in point of fact. We must assure him that such things do happen, and not unfrequently. A case of this kind was related to me, as having taken place not long since at Smyrna; and the story was romantic enough, in its details, to form the subject of a tale of no ordinary interest. A wealthy inhabitant of that city, an old Greek subject, had an only daughter, named Theodosia. Her hand had been sought, and her affections had been gained by a respectable young English resident of the place. But the father was too proud to let his daughter marry a foreigner, and a heretic besides; and he commanded her to think no more of him. As an offset, he promised her in marriage to a boorish Greek from the East. But the affections, it is well known, are sometimes most unreasonably stubborn, and the young lady preferred an elopement. A rendezvous was fixed upon by the two lovers; but unfortunately there was a misunderstanding as to the spot, and Theodosia, after waiting for hours at the place agreed upon, was finally discovered and brought back to her father's house. Threats, and even chastisement were employed, ineffectually, with the hope of gaining her consent to the match. Notwithstanding this persistency, a day was appointed for the nuptials, the priests were called in to perform the rite, and the young girl was brought into the room by main force. While the service was being read Theodosia fainted, and the priests stopped until she recovered her senses, when they proceeded, and she was wedded to a man whom she loathed. This compulsion may appear the more remarkable from the fact, that at this time she was nineteen or twenty years of age. So inauspicious a wedding was not likely to introduce a happy union. It was not very long before she was forced to be separated from her husband, who treated her in a most cruel manner. Her father had been the strenuous advocate of the marriage; but for a long time he found himself utterly unable to persuade her to leave the man whom he had compelled her to wed.*

MARRIAGE AMONG THE LOWER ORDERS.

The customs that characterize a country are to be found in their purity chiefly in those remote portions where the manners of other nations have not as yet intruded. The increasing facilities of intercommunication, while they improve the condition of the poorer classes, so far as material interests are affected, destroy those striking contrasts in the mode of living

* Such is the story as related by one who had been a neighbor and intimate acquaintance of the parties; and it was confirmed by several esteemed Athenian friends.

which excite the curiosity of the stranger. An American walking the streets of Athens, hears at every turn the cry of the peddler, who, under the name of "pania Americanica," hawks the fabrics of the Lowell mills; and the Grecian mother finds it cheaper to clothe her daughters in these, than to occupy her leisure hours at the loom.

In secluded villages the ceremony of marriage, which in the capital has become gradually assimilated to the stereotyped form of other countries, includes a number of curious remnants of ancient usages. Every petty hamlet, or at least every small district, possesses its own customs, which entirely regulate the performance of the ceremony, and which none even of the more polished citizens attempt to abrogate. It would, therefore, be quite a hopeless task to describe *all* the different modes; and the customs that prevail in the province of Maina, at the southerly extremity of the country, may be taken as a fair specimen of the rest. The connection, long since projected, and fully discussed in family council on either side, has at length been approved, and the time for its consummation determined, by all the nearest relatives of the interested parties. Indeed, such a thing as a clandestine marriage, or one celebrated without the authorization of friends, is almost unheard of. Whoever should marry a young lady without first asking the consent of her relatives, would in Maina inevitably draw upon himself their fiercest animosity, and cause an irretrievable breach, sooner or later ending in revenge and bloodshed. We have heard the instance of one young man, who eloped with a girl of his acquaintance, and who, after forty years had passed, when surrounded by grown-up sons and daughters, fell a victim to the relentless hatred of those whom he had so long since offended.*

The more important preparations for the wedding uniformly commence on Thursday evening. Toward dusk, the young men who have been invited bring the wood necessary for cook-

* This incident is embodied in one of those pathetic *mœrologia*, or laments, which are repeated over the tombs of the deceased. In this poetic history the leading events of the man's life are related with considerable detail. Some persons have acquired a singular reputation for their skill in composing them.

ing purposes; while the young women meet to sift the coarse flour that is to be employed. On Friday, they again assemble to cleanse the wheat and to grind it in the hand-mill. The flour thus obtained is used that very evening, when the maidens gather round the kneading-trough to fashion several kinds of cake. One of the girls, who according to ancient custom must have both her parents living, begins the kneading; while the others, standing around, throw in various coins, and sing ditties which are mostly quite unintelligible, but have been handed down traditionally from dame to daughter for generations. The cakes made of this dough are sent to all the friends of the parties, as invitations to attend the wedding. Another large cake is prepared at the same time, to be cut on Sunday evening, at the house of the bridegroom, as a signal for the termination of the festivities.

The bridegroom and his intended father-in-law each invite their friends to their houses. If they live in the same village, this is accomplished in person; but if they live too far off, the invitation is equally well understood on the reception of the small cake, which in these hamlets takes the place of the gilt and crested envelope, and the "At home" card of our more refined countries. After its reception a person is in duty bound to go on the same day to the house to which he is bidden, where a convivial party is thus assembled. Its occupation for the afternoon consists in cleansing, and sometimes grinding the wheat, though this latter operation is often deferred for a day or two. While they perform these offices of friendship, the company enliven their labors by singing various songs, for the most part curious and characteristic, but few of which have ever yet been collected into a permanent form.

The remainder of the week is spent in a quiet manner, and it is not until the ensuing Saturday that the same parties reassemble, at the house of the bridegroom or bride, as the case may be, for no one is invited to both places. The bridegroom, who according to the custom of the district bears all the expenses, has agreed previously to provide a stipulated number of rams or sheep, which never number less than three, and rarely exceed a dozen. These he now sends to the house of his intended father-in-law, and with them, three times as many loaves of bread as there are sheep, and three times as many *okes* of wine* as there are loaves of bread. The men who are dispatched with these gifts—intended, of course, for immediate consumption—expect to be entertained and lodged at the house of the bride for the night. Such an addition to the domestic circle might terrify an American housekeeper; but as beds are a commodity unknown or unused, so far as the greater part of the population are concerned, even a large number of guests can be easily accommodated. The Greek peasant, provided that he finds plenty to eat, and especially to drink, lays himself down in perfect contentment, wrapped up in his huge *capote*, or shaggy cloak, by the side of the fire, kindled on a stone hearth, in the middle of the room; meanwhile the family, perhaps, occupy a small inclosed space at one of the ends of the house, to which access is gained by a ladder of two or three steps.

At about midnight another set of men are dispatched from the bridegroom's house. They carry a complete attire for the bride, who is dressed in it immediately. Then on Sunday morning, at about three or four o'clock, the bridegroom proceeds thither in person, accompanied by a few of his more intimate friends. And now the marriage ceremony, that is to say, the *stephanoma*, or crowning, takes place in the presence of all; the parish priest, who has quitted his slumbers at this early hour, officiating. Upon the conclusion of the service the priest retires to his home, and so does the bridegroom, leaving the lady at her father's house. But at perhaps nine o'clock, in broad daylight, he proceeds on horseback, attended by all his friends, to claim and carry home his newly-married wife. On either hand walk two of his nearest female relatives, on his father's and mother's side. When the procession reaches the house, the bridegroom does not enter, but, according to custom, stops in some part of the court, while the guests of the bride's father come severally to greet him. First his mother-in-law embraces him, at the same time placing about his neck a handkerchief, as a gift. All the women follow her

* Wine and oil are in Greece measured by weight, and an *oke* is nearly equal to three pounds of our standard.

example, and place a similar present on his shoulders, so that before they get through he finds himself loaded down with a pile of handkerchiefs. These, of course, he does not wish to keep, and within a few days disposes of, without compunction, by sale. As the custom is universal in that region, the matter is merely one of exchange, for each receives in the end about as much as he gives. And now the bridegroom and his friends may enter the house, where they are generously entertained, and for a while conviviality reigns.

But this must end. The father takes his daughter, and, committing her to the husband's care, gives him such advice and exhortation as he may think proper. Then, leading them both into the court, he makes them tread on some firm stone —a ceremony which, if it has any meaning at all, as, with regard to many of these more trifling particulars, seems rather improbable, is intended to convey the idea of the unanimity that should exist between them.* The parents now take leave of their daughter, and the friends accompany the newly-married couple to their home. The guests of the bridegroom as they go, divert themselves with songs of little poetical merit, indeed, but lively enough, in which they represent themselves as having "robbed a neighborhood, and spoiled a country, to carry off the bride whose praises thousands sing." This nettles the friends of the bride's father, who retort upon them by wishing that "the bride may shine upon them like the sun, or like the moon; that she may trample them under foot like the earth, and be in no way dependent on them for any thing."

The same ceremony that took place at the dwelling of the father-in-law is now repeated at that of the bridegroom; and the bride is not allowed to enter her new home before her husband's friends have all pressed around her to load her with presents, which consist of various little commodities, or of

* Strange to say, a custom very similar prevails among the Hindoos. "A stone being placed before her (the bride), she, with her hands joined in a hollow form, was made to tread upon it with the toes of her right foot during this address of the bridegroom: 'Ascend this stone—be firm like this stone—distress my foe, and be not subservient to my enemy.'" —*India and the Hindoos, by* F. DE W. WARD, p. 248.

money. All the assembled company then follow the couple into the house, where, after a few unimportant forms, they sit down to a collation, with which the entire ceremonial comes to an end.

Those acquainted with the customs of the ancient Greeks will scarcely fail to remark the very striking points of resemblance presented by these observances. The wedding, the bridal procession, the songs of the friends, and many of the inferior details preserve a similarity truly wonderful, when we take into consideration the varied circumstances, and the long space of time that has intervened. The fact must, however, be borne in mind, that the habits of the people in various districts are so extremely diverse, that the description of those which prevail in one place will by no means convey a correct idea of those of a village only a few miles distant.

A GREEK BAPTISM.

One of the tenants of a friend was about to have his child baptized, and we were included among those invited to witness the ceremony. The small cottage, which stood with its end to the street, was entered from the court on its side, and here a part of the family, in their gala dress, were awaiting the arrival of the priest who was to officiate. There is a large fund of kindness in the Greek heart, even among the poorest; and the inmates of the cottage received us with pleasure, and exerted themselves to the utmost to entertain us. The priest kept us waiting for him. When he came, I found that he was an acquaintance, and officiated in the neighboring church of St. Nicholas Rangaves, whose shrill little bell, ringing to call the people to their devotions, used to break in upon my morning slumbers. A good heart beats beneath that coarse black cloak, and a ruddy face beams with good-nature from under the priestly cap; but a plentiful use of the snuff-box does not improve its appearance as to cleanliness.

A large brass vessel, two feet in diameter, was brought in by a young man, and placed in the centre of the room, and several bucketfuls of warm and cold water were poured in until the temperature was judged to be suitable. But before the water was fit to be used, another operation was necessary; for the presence of any evil spirits or magic in the water would infallibly impair, if not destroy, the effect of the ordinance. If any such beings or influences lay concealed, they were surely dispelled by the manipulations of the priest, who, baring his arm, three times drew it through the water, making the sign of the cross. And if this had been ineffectual, they could scarcely remain after he had blown upon the surface, making on it the same sacred sign. The water being thus consecrated, the child was brought in, neatly dressed in white, and presented by its godfather for baptism. And now it was stripped of every article of clothing, and taken by the priest, who held it up before the whole company, in order, I presume, that all might be witnesses to the act. A small bottle of oil was taken, and with its contents the infant's entire body was rubbed. This is not considered part of the religious rite, but is merely intended to prevent any injurious effects of the application of cold water to its body at so tender an age, as is customary among the Greeks. And the precaution, if it be of any avail, is certainly needed. The common people consider the performance of the ceremony almost, if not quite, a *sine qua non* of salvation, believing fully in its regenerating influence. So, the more delicate the babe's constitution, the more anxious are the parents to have the rite performed as early as possible. Notwithstanding all their precautions, however, I have heard that great numbers of infants die yearly in consequence of the shock they receive.

The act of baptism itself consisted in three times entirely immersing the child. The priest managed this very adroitly, and prevented its strangling by covering its mouth and entire face with one of his hands. After this was done (the name being given at the same time), the priest returned the crying and shivering baby into the hands of the godfather and the others who stood by, who immediately wiped and dressed it. The baptism is completed by the application of a little of the "holy unguent" to the baby's forehead, ears, hands, and feet. This "holy unguent" is, or was until lately, compounded only by the Patriarch at Constantinople, and dispensed once a year to all the churches.* The child was now taken away, and the godfather distributed to each of the persons present a small, bright, silver coin, with the date of the current year, and a ribbon passed through a hole in it. The person who receives this piece of money is bound to keep it safely, that it may remind him of his having witnessed the baptism of that child. And this testimony he is expected to render, if necessary, before men, and also before the angels at the judgment day. The glittering coin that lies on the table before me as I write these lines, its neat knot of blue ribbon tied to it, recalls the image of that little departed innocent, who no longer needs here on earth a witness to its christening.

The godfather bears all the contingent expenses, which were in this case but small, though sometimes they amount to a considerable sum. Hence, it is esteemed quite a mark of friendship to be willing to stand sponsor for a neighbor's child. But the most important consideration, by far, is that the connection thus formed is no less binding than a natural relationship, and forever precludes all intermarriage between those who become so related to each other, to the same extent as with members of the same stock—that is, according to Greek law, as far as the ninth degree, I believe.

FUNERAL PROCESSIONS AND OFFERINGS TO THE DEAD.

Look with me for a moment at the procession which is slowly passing, on its way to the cemetery beyond the Ilissus.

During the summer months, while the fever is making its fearful ravages on the population of this unhealthy city,† many such may be counted every day.

* It has been the policy of the Patriarch and the "Holy Synod" to attach the Greeks to the "Mother Church" by making them dependent in this manner for the articles necessary for the celebration of the ordinances of religion.

† With a population of about 27,000 souls, Athens, in 1851, had 1105 deaths; while the births, according to the same official reports, were only 526. Evidently the population of Athens at this rate would soon become extinct, were it not for the great influx of strangers. It is stated that the previous year there were as many as 1400 deaths. The greater part of these were undoubtedly from Greek fever. It is a fact worthy of note, that of the 526 children born in 1851, only ten were illegitimate. The same year there were 122 marriages.—*Æon*, Jan. 30, 1852.

The melancholy nasal chant of the priests as they come along, betokens the approach of the train, and as it draws nearer, the litanies they recite become distinguishable. The corpse of the deceased is borne in a light wooden box or coffin; and the body, decorated with flowers, and clothed in white, is exposed to the gaze of all: for the lid has been removed, and is carried by a man or boy at head of the train. This lid has invariably a large cross painted upon it. As it approaches every by-stander reverently raises his hat, and stands uncovered until it has passed; but this mark of respect is paid not to the departed, but to the sign of the cross, as my Greek friends assure me. It must be confessed, there is something rather repulsive in this parading of death through the thronged streets of a city, especially when its subject has been chosen from among the aged, or bears the marks of great and recent suffering. Such is the manner in which the common people are borne to their last resting-place: but the death of a bishop occasions much more display of pomp. He is carried through the most public thoroughfares, dressed as in the discharge of his ecclesiastical functions, and placed in a sitting posture upon the bier. The place of burial being reached, he is interred in the same position, a distinction allowed to no one else.

The interest entertained by survivors for the memory and the souls of the dead, is evinced by the prayers that are said in their behalf, although the Greeks do not profess to believe in the existence of a purgatory. A singular practice calls up their remembrance yet more vividly. Several successive Fridays are set apart as especially devoted to the dead. The bell of the little church of Saint Nicholas Rangaves, situated at the very base of the Acropolis, attracted my attention on one of these occasions. Upon entering the church—a small edifice, scarce exceeding in size an ordinary room—I found a few persons waiting for the commencement of the services; the men and boys standing near the altar, while the women, as usual, remained somewhat farther off. Ever and anon some person would come in, carrying a small dish covered with a napkin, and after devoutly crossing himself, placed the dish upon the floor in front of the screen of the *hieron*, or holy place. These plates contained a peculiar sort of cake, which is called *Collyva.* It is, in fact, an offering made to the manes of the dead, and can certainly claim a pagan rather than a Christian origin. It is carefully made, the principal ingredients being boiled wheat and currants. The surface of the top is ornamented with various degrees of neatness, by means of the eatable red grains of the pomegranate, or almonds, or any thing of the kind. These cakes were sent by the relatives of those who had died within a year or two, and if handsome were allowed to remain before the chancel. If more commonly prepared, the contents were thrown together into a basket. In every plate of *collyva*, and in every basket, were stuck a number of little lighted waxen tapers, which burned during the service.

The notion of the common people respecting this usage was expressed to me by a person whom I asked to explain its purport. "The soul of the deceased," said he, "for whom the *collyva* is offered, comes down during the service, and eats a single grain of the wheat." But what manner of good this could do the disembodied spirit he was not able to explain; nor did he give me any satisfactory reason for offering so large a quantity, when the spirit is so moderate in its desires. The parish priest during the short service I attended took notice of the names of all those for whom *collyva* had been offered. At the conclusion he helped himself to his share of the cakes, after the spirits had enjoyed an ample opportunity of eating to their hearts' content. The rest was distributed by handfuls to every person present, to be carried away and eaten at home —a feast for the dead.

VIEW OF ATHENS.

CHAPTER VIII.

THE COURT AND POLITICS OF GREECE.

THE arrival of the American frigate *Cumberland* in the harbor of Piræus, followed shortly by the steamship *San Jacinto*, produced some commotion in the city of Athens. An intervention on the part of the United States in behalf of Dr. King had been threatened, but was not generally expected. No American vessel of war had done more than touch at Piræus for a number of years past; and multitudes had never even seen one of our frigates. The unusual circumstance was, therefore, set down at once as having some connection with the trial and imprisonment of the only representative of the United States within the boundaries of the kingdom.

The Hon. Mr. Marsh, American Minister to Constantinople, having been commissioned to investigate the heavy charges of injustice preferred against the courts of law by the joint testimony of all the Americans residing at Athens, was a passenger on board the *San Jacinto*. Though not accredited to the Court of Athens at this time, his official character rendered it imperatively necessary that there should be a formal presentation to the queen, who was regent during the temporary absence of King Otho in Germany. To arrange the preliminaries, Dr. King and myself called on Mr. Colocotroni, the master of ceremonies (*aularches*), whom we found living in very simple style, in the northern quarter of the town. He was a middle aged man, of slender form, and pleasing address. The interview was a short one, and we left, Mr. Colocotroni promising to send early notice of the time when it would suit the queen's convenience to receive the American Minister and officers.

Meanwhile an amusing incident occurred at Piræus. A young American lieutenant had long been desirous of procuring a block of genuine Pentelican marble, to serve as a pedestal for the bust of his father-in-law, a warm admirer of Greece. In the garden of a friend in Athens, he found a piece that exactly suited his purpose. The owner cheerfully presented him with it, and had it neatly inclosed in a box. One evening, after a call in the city, the officer placed it in his carriage and rode down to Piræus, expecting to find one of the ship's boats in waiting. It was late, however, and none were to be found; but there were other boats at hand, and he deposited himself and his prize in one of these. On reaching the frigate he stepped on board, telling the boatmen to bring his box on deck. Instead of doing so, they demanded an exorbitant fare; and when he refused to pay it, quietly shoved off, and put back to shore. The lieutenant, who was on deck and unarmed, was unable to stop the rogues; and retired to his state-room for the night, as may be imagined, considerably vexed at the occurrence. Early the next morning, application was made for the arrest of the dishonest boatmen. They were readily identified, and in their house was found the box, which they had conveyed thither with no little trouble, and had broken open to discover its contents. They had evidently been deceived by its great weight; and doubtless their chagrin was considerable, when instead of a small treasure in gold or silver, they found inside nothing but a worthless block of stone.

But for an unlucky discovery, the box would now have been restored to its owner. The marble had once been embedded in some church or chapel, as was manifest from a large Byzantine cross rudely carved on one face. The custom-house officers declared that this cross was old, and that the stone came under the category of antiquities, whose exportation is prohibited by law. There was no use in arguing the matter with them. The only resource was to send up to the city for Mr. Pittakes, the General Superintendent of Antiquities; who, on his arrival, laughed at the simplicity of the officials, and readily granted permission to export that block, and as many more such as could be procured.

On the day appointed by the queen, we rode to the palace, and were ushered into the waiting-chamber, upon the second story near the northeastern corner. Here we were met by Mr. Colocotroni, who was introduced to Mr. Marsh, Commodore Stringham, and fourteen other officers. Having been desired by Mr. M. to assist him in the translation of the various Greek documents relating to Dr. King's case, it was thought proper by Mr. Colocotroni, that I should be presented at the same time; which would otherwise have been out of order. The usual routine of commonplace remarks having been gone through on either side, Mr. Colocotroni seated himself by my side, and inquired privately respecting the rank and names of the several officers; for the purpose, as I afterward learned, of informing the queen on the subject, and furnishing her with appropriate staple of remark. He then retired; and after a brief interval returned and ushered us into the adjoining presentation-room.

Queen Amelia was standing near the centre of the room, which, though on no great scale of magnificence, was handsomely decorated and furnished. She was attired very tastefully: her dress was not remarkable for costliness; and she wore but little jewelry. Her height is good; and though well-formed, she is rather disposed to be fleshy. By most persons she is considered handsome. She is certainly better-looking than most of the crowned heads of Europe. At the age of thirty-two or three she had, however, naturally lost much of her former beauty. A few paces behind the queen was the *grande maîtresse,* Madame Pulsky, who during the entire ceremony of presentation stood in the same spot, immovable as a statue.

On entering the room each individual bowed profoundly, and then all ranged themselves in the form of a crescent, occupying positions corresponding to their official rank. Mr. Colocotroni first presented Mr. Marsh; and the queen having advanced, stood for some five or ten minutes engaged in conversation with him. Then Mr. Marsh accompanied her along the line, introducing each one in succession. To the superior officers a few questions were addressed, which had to be interpreted to those who were so unfortunate as not to know a single word of French—the language that the queen had chosen to make use of. The junior officers were, for the most part, honored with but a single interrogatory; and that related to their own department of naval service. The captain of the marines, for instance, was merely asked how many men he commanded, or some other similarly trivial question.

I have no doubt all were equally delighted when the awkward ceremony was dispatched, and a bow from the queen announced that we were at liberty to retire from the royal presence. If our entrance had been punctilious, our departure was still more so; and we literally bowed ourselves out of the room; for it would have been a gross violation of all courtly etiquette to turn our backs upon the queen. Although the retrograde motion was neither convenient nor graceful, we made good our retreat to the door. Most of the party seemed much pleased with the result of the interview, the consequence of which was an invitation sent to the American Minister, Commodore, and Captains, to dine at the palace on a specified day. Strange to say, only Mr. Marsh and one of the captains were forthcoming; the attractions of royalty not being sufficiently powerful to induce the Commodore to postpone his departure for Constantinople, where the presence of an American frigate was imperatively demanded to protect our citizens.

The king enjoys a far smaller share of personal popularity than Queen Amelia. Nor has it been on the increase of late years. Chosen by the three powers of England, France, and Russia, formerly in alliance to form a protectorate of Greece, he was elevated to the throne while a mere youth, after the assassination of the "Governor," Count Capo d'Istrias. The crown had previously been offered to the young Leopold, now King of Belgium; who was unwilling to accept it, unless certain of the hearty good-will of the people. Well would it have been for Greece had she been so fortunate as to receive such a ruler! Otho was the son of Louis, late King of Bavaria, and a younger brother of the present occupant of the throne. He was, consequently, educated a strict Roman Catholic, and entirely under the influence of the priesthood. From the date of his arrival in Greece until the first of June, 1835, his twentieth birth-day, the government was administered by a German Regency, whose conduct has been regarded in a very different light by those who have viewed it from opposite sides. The first eight years of King Otho's reign were a continuation of the same line of policy with that previously pursued. Within eighteen months after his accession, he gained the hand of the princess Amelia, of Oldenburg, who was some four years younger than himself, and a Protestant in point of religion. The Regency had filled most of the posts of honor and emolument with their own countrymen. Under the young monarch there was a German ministry: German generals commanded troops, many of whom were themselves Germans: and not a few professors in the university were of foreign birth.

The fact that both king and queen were strangers, as well in faith as in nationality, to the great mass of their subjects, was never palatable to the Greeks, who regard their religion as a precious heir-loom, and as the bond of union in the Hellenic state. But it was quite insupportable to the poor but proud revolutionary soldiers and klefts, to see a horde of foreigners reaping the rewards of their toils, and occupying the situations to which they considered themselves entitled. A constitution, too, had been promised from time to time; but it was a mere promise. The monarchy was in fact autocratic: the king's edict having the full force of law.

At length the people grew tired of waiting for the change that was to put an end to the disorders complained of. On one of the first days of September, 1843, a crowd gathered in front of the palace, gradually increasing by fresh arrivals from town and country, till the spacious square was one dense mass of human beings, all loudly demanding a constitution. It was now no time for delay, and promises could no longer avail. The troops themselves had caught the general enthusiasm, and siding with the citizens, were loudest in their vociferations. Cannon were even pointed at the palace, and Callerges, who sat on one of them, threatened to fire, if, at the expiration of a few hours, the king still refused to satisfy the popular desire. Otho was disposed to be obstinate. Nothing was farther from his wishes, than to be trammeled by a constitution, and to share his legislative functions with the representatives of the nation. His wife, though no less attached than himself to unlimited power, grasped the full consequences of resistance; and is said to have begged him with tears to bend, rather than break, before the approaching storm. Perceiving that the people were in no mood to be trifled with, Otho reluctantly yielded. The 3d of September (old style) is annually kept as a festival to commemorate the auspicious event. A representation of the people was at once called to draft a proper constitution; which, on the 18th of the next March, was solemnly sworn to by the king, in the presence of all the officers of the government.

In accordance with this instrument,* the legislative powers are vested in a Congress composed of two bodies, the Senate (*gerousia*), and the House of Representatives (*boule*). The former, which is intended to be the conservative branch, should be composed of not less then twenty-seven members, nor of more than one half the number of representatives in the other House, save with its own consent. The senators are chosen for life by the king; but the classes of individuals

* A Greek work entitled "Hippodamus; Principles of Constitutional Law, or the Greek Constitution Annotated, by N. Pappadoukas," contains a lucid and able commentary. The true author is reported to be the well-known Demetrius Kyriakou, some time Minister of Justice, one of the best lawyers of Athens.

from which they may be selected, are carefully enumerated. They are chiefly those who commanded the armies in the great revolutionary struggle, or have occupied high stations of honor and trust in the civil, judicial, and military departments for a specified period, varying from four to ten years.* The senator must be at least forty years of age. The other House is composed of the representatives of the people, one being elected for about ten thousand inhabitants. Their number can not be less than eighty. No male citizen above twenty-five years, with the exception of the clergy, is debarred from the right of voting; but none are eligible to office until they are thirty years old. The members of both houses are remunerated for their services, the senators receiving $83, and the representatives $43 per month, during the session. The intrusion of foreigners into office is effectually precluded by the provisions of the constitution, which expressly declare that no foreign army shall be allowed to pass through, or be maintained in Greece, unless permission be specially granted by law. To obviate future inconvenience from the anomaly of a king professing a religion different from that of the great mass of the inhabitants, the successor to the throne must embrace the Greek religion. The crowns of Greece and Bavaria, it is farther stipulated, shall never be united on the same head. The king's annual stipend is fixed by law at one million drachms ($166,000).

Such are some of the most important provisions of the Constitution, inaugurating a government theoretically perhaps the most liberal in Europe. All citizens are equal in the eye of the law; for the creation of titles of nobility is expressly forbidden, and there is no room for an hereditary aristocracy. And though the prevailing or established religion is declared to be the "Orthodox Oriental Church of Christ," yet one of the chief excellences of the Constitution is its liberality toward other creeds. "Every known religion is tolerated, and its worship conducted without hindrance under the protection of the law, proselytism and every other encroachment upon the dominant religion being forbidden." "Every one may publish his opinions orally, in writing, and by the press, ob-

* See Article 72 of the Constitution.

serving the laws of the State."* How these principles have been violated in Dr. King's condemnation I shall elsewhere narrate. Meanwhile, the checks upon the power of the crown are apparently as great as are compatible with the existence of the regal system. The budget is, of course, submitted by the ministry to the chambers. As the latter alone have the right to provide the revenue necessary for carrying on the government, by authorizing the levy of taxes and the collection of duties, the entire control of the Executive is apparently intrusted to their hands. The ministers are made personally responsible for their actions; and all members of the royal family are excluded from the cabinet, in order that they may not be liable to impeachment.

In practice, however, the throne may be said, under the present administration, to be almost unrestrained by the popular element in the accomplishment of the measures it has determined upon. It is notorious that the government of Otho is generally unpopular throughout the land, and yet it constantly succeeds in securing a majority in the chambers sufficient to attain its ends. The representatives are, it is true, chosen by the people at large, but the government is rarely at a loss for means to obtain a favorable result. Under the pretext of allowing the greatest freedom for voters, the election is made by ballot; but during the eight days of the election the ballot-boxes are left in the keeping of an election-committee.† In some cases the boxes are known to have contained a number of votes larger than the entire number of registered voters in the district. During the election, as well as before, the greatest exertions are made by all the government officers, in conjunction with the friends of the candidates, to influence the people to vote for those who are known to be most favorable to the measures of the king. But even in the House of Representatives there can not exist for any great length of time a numerous and determined opposition. Every method—bribes, offers of promotion, and of the patronage of friends, are employed, and most of those elected are soon induced to yield support to the government.

* Articles 1 and 10.

† Act to regulate the Election of Reoresentatives, tit. 3, arts. 18, 22.

An instance of the determination of the ministry to carry its plans at any cost was seen in the passage of a certain law in the summer of 1851. Its object was the creation of a large number of *ephori*, or officers for the collection of the revenue. Its introduction was the signal for opposition from those who were not attached to the courtly party, and saw no necessity for so considerable an increase of the places in the gift of the throne. It passed the Lower House, however; but on being brought up in the Senate, although the king had, in anticipation, created three or four new members, that body refused to concur in the proposed act. Thereupon the king prorogued both Houses for the space of some forty days. In the mean while ten or more additional senators were appointed, for the most part from the officers of the king's own household, or from the ministry, and all of them persons devoted to himself. The party thus reinforced was now enabled to reconsider the bill in the Senate, and it was passed in accordance with the desires of the ministry. In this manner, and by means of the most flagrant corruption, the throne is usually able to control with ease the deliberations of the legislative bodies. And this is much facilitated by the Constitution, which, although it declares that representatives cease to be such the moment they accept any post under the government, yet permits executive officers to be elected representatives.* Thus it happens that many military officers are at the same time members of one of the legislative bodies, where, as they retain their commissions merely during the sovereign's pleasure, they constitute the warmest adherents of the crown. A remarkable clause is, however, inserted in the Constitution, providing that in such a case the individual is not entitled to the emoluments of both offices, but only to those of the more lucrative of the two.†

In respect to foreign relations, the politicians of Greece may be divided into three parties—the Russian or Napist, the English, and the French: a result which the acute mind of Coray long since foresaw and deplored. For it was not, he argued, until Greece was divided into the Macedonian and anti-Macedonian parties that Philip found an entering wedge for

* Article 64.

† Article 68.

his ambition. The Russian party is undoubtedly the most numerous and influential. It stands forth the advocate of a close political and religious connection with Russia. Hence, almost the entire clergy are, from policy or conviction, among its adherents. Ambition to restore a Greek empire embracing all who profess the Greek creed and speak the Greek language, is its animating principle. Despairing of success in this vast undertaking with their own unaided resources, the Napists cast about them for some more powerful ally. France and England are unfortunately too much interested in the maintenance of the balance of power, to offer any hope of assistance, or even of countenance. The same policy that excluded from the map of the new state of Greece one half of the territory that had asserted and upheld its independence, restoring it once more to the Sublime Porte, would never help to weaken and destroy the Ottoman Empire. On the other hand, a community of religion naturally draws the Greeks to look to the great Russian empire for means to realize their ambitious projects. Some are simple enough to imagine that, after conquering Constantinople at his own expense, the Czar will be so generous as to make it over without equivalent to his friends the Greeks. While others assert that he will annex Asia Minor to the kingdom of Greece, and set one of his younger sons over the united empire.

The English and French parties are the advocates of democratic principles. To them belong the most liberal and intelligent statesmen, the Tricoupis, the Mavrocordatos, and, in general, the men of the largest patriotism. But they are in a minority, and their influence can scarcely be a positive one for good. They rather counteract the ill-advised measures of the dominant politicians.

The king, for his part, identifies himself with none of these sections, and strives, as far as possible, to employ them all as tools for the furtherance of his plans. The court is given to gayety and pleasure, and the revenue, which should be expended for the benefit of the nation, is lavished on balls and entertainments. The queen, Amelia, has the reputation of being the best rider and dancer at Athens. Her passion for the latter accomplishment is such, that whoever can dance well is a welcome guest at the public balls, and can readily secure her as a partner.

Meanwhile, the country is suffering for the want of attention paid by the government to the improvement of its natural resources. Probably the greatest obstacle to the prosperity of Greece is to be found in the difficulty of the interchange of commodities. No country in the world stands in more pressing need of good roads: in none are they more difficult of construction. Successive ranges of mountains, with their branching spurs, divide the cultivable ground into a thousand small valleys, each deprived of easy communication with its neighbors. From one township to the next nothing can be transported but by the horses and mules accustomed to climb the rugged mountain-paths, and tread firmly on the ladder-like ascents. The only carriage-roads in Greece are a few short ones about Athens, one, twelve or fifteen miles long, near Lamia, and others at Corinth, Chalcis, and a few other large towns. The ordinary mode of transportation is so expensive that it can not be much employed, nor is it available for any but the most valuable products. In this way it happens that Greece is often compelled to import wheat for its sea-board towns, whereas, at the distance of but a day's journey inland, there is, or might be produced enough to furnish an ample supply. With a revenue of twenty-one or two millions of drachms ($3,500,000), obtained from its million subjects, the government is unable, or unwilling, to expend even a million annually upon the most indispensable improvements. The *demi*, or towns, on the other hand, are too poor, too ignorant, or can not sufficiently combine their efforts to construct and maintain good roads.

Yet while such have been the shortcomings of the government, there are other respects in which it is entitled to the highest commendation. It can not be denied that it has succeeded in destroying many relics of a darker age. In Maina, particularly, it has broken up the tyrannical and lawless clans, whose perpetual wranglings and hereditary animosities among themselves, made the entire district the scene of oft-recurring deeds of bloodshed. To appreciate the value of the change, one should hear some of the sanguinary recitals that are yet current among the people. The *klefts*, or mountain robbers, from whose depredations no village was safe, have now been mostly brought to justice, or expelled. For years none have been heard of in Peloponnesus. The few that remain infest the mountains forming the boundary line of Turkey, or the sparsely inhabited districts of Acarnania and Ætolia. It is true that in reaching this end much needless suffering has been inflicted, by the rapacity and oppression of the soldiers and petty officers quartered upon the villages in the vicinity of the robbers; but this was to be expected, and it has been merely temporary in its duration. By far the greatest eulogium, however, that can with truth be conferred on the government of King Otho, is that it has spared no expense or efforts to diffuse education and intelligence among the people. Henceforth no one need remain in ignorance except from his own choice. To the diligent a free course of instruction is offered, extending from the primary school to the university. The present system of education promises to make Greece one of the most intelligent and well-informed nations of Europe; and the light of literature and science is again commencing to dawn upon its ancient seat of Athens.

Toward religion the government assumes rather an attitude of unconcern than of partiality. The king and queen have respectively their Roman Catholic and Protestant chaplains; but otherwise they appear quite indifferent to the subject. It is more to please the bigotry of the priesthood, than to gratify any preferences of their own, that any infringements upon the freedom of religious worship have been countenanced.

A GREEK CHURCH.

CHAPTER IX.

THE GREEK CHURCH.

A CIRCUMSTANCE that adds to the interest and importance of the consideration of the religious state of Greece, is the intimate connection which the prevalent faith has ever sustained with the national fortunes. To one even who should feel no concern in a subject most vital to the welfare of individuals, the consequence of its political bearings would commend it for careful scrutiny. There are few facts in history more striking than the tenacity with which the Eastern Churches have clung to their religious belief, through ages beset with temptations and perils: when they were exposed, not only to the seductive influences of power and wealth, but, at times also, to more open trials, under the form of political disfranchisement and persecution. This steadfast adherence to their ancient tenets it was, that alone preserved the nationality of the Greeks, during their subjection to the Mussulman power; this it was that rendered the resuscitation of their separate existence possible. It is even now the sole connecting link between the Hellenic kingdom and the provinces that are yet enslaved.

The Greek denomination, comprising a vast majority of the inhabitants of the Russian Empire, in addition to seven or eight millions in the Turkish dominions, embraces, probably, between sixty and seventy millions of souls. Compared, however, with the body of Protestants, whose numbers are but little superior, the Greek Church can scarcely be said to exert a sensible influence upon the intellect of the world. It is but just awaking from that lethargy in which the East has for centuries been plunged. It produces no theologians of any note, and it has made no contributions to current literature. The clergy, instead of being, as in the West, among the best-informed members of the community, have sunk to the common level; or, often, seem to be the enemies of learning and intelligence. It is this that adds so much to the singularity of the fact, that, tried by the test of purity of doctrine, the Greek Church is so far superior to the Roman Catholic.

In many respects the two Churches closely resemble each other; and in none more than in their hierarchical systems. Yet even here there are striking points of contrast, which point out the Oriental as by far the less corrupt. It has never allowed an ecclesiastical authority to arrogate supreme dominion in the Church. The four Archbishops of Constantinople, Alexandria, Antioch, and Jerusalem, have, it is true, obtained, under the title of Patriarchs, an acknowledged ascendency over the other bishops and archbishops. But the ground of this pre-eminence, as stated in the acts of Councils, is merely the existence of the custom of attributing to the prelates of those cities a great degree of honor. Consequently they have never claimed a more direct apostolic succession, an absolute power, or infallibility. The Patriarch, by his own confession, is simply a superior bishop, basing his pretensions, at farthest, upon the decrees of the Councils.

Until 1821, the Church of Greece retained a close connection with the "Holy Synod" of Constantinople. When, however, the Revolutionary War broke out, the Patriarch, who was suspected—no doubt with justice—of friendliness to the cause of freedom, fell a victim to the jealousy of the Porte; and another, a mere creature of the government, was installed in his place. The clergy of Greece, under the guidance of Germanos, Bishop of Patras, had taken a prominent part in the revolt. To reduce them to submission, the spiritual influence of the Patriarch was invoked. After having fulminated, near the commencement of the conflict, an edict of excommunication against all the belligerent Greeks, the Patriarch and his Synod, on the 20th of February (March 3d, N. S.), 1828, issued a second letter, addressed to "all Christians inhabiting Peloponnesus and the Ægean Sea." In this remarkable production they are reminded of "the submission and fidelity they owe to the *lawful Ottoman Empire watched over by God;*" and are warned not to lose precious moments in deceitful procrastination. They are allured by the prospect of a speedy restoration to the spiritual graces in the gift of the Church. "But if," it is added in conclusion, "we should again meet—which God forbid!—with stubbornness and disobedience, arising from the delusive ideas that lead you astray —*the ax is laid at the root of the tree. See you to that!*"*

A document of such a tenor, and issued at so inauspicious a juncture—when the exertions of seven years of continual warfare had been crowned with success for the Greek arms, in the decisive victory of Navarino—was not calculated, as may be imagined, to heal the breach. This injudicious measure too clearly proved, what had long been asserted—that the Patriarchate was but a tool in the hands of the Sultan. Every link that connected the Church in Greece to that in Turkey was sundered; and the former remained independent, though lying under interdict, until the year 1850. By the second article of the Constitution of 1843, now in force, it is expressly declared that "the Orthodox Church of Greece, acknowledging our Lord Jesus Christ as its head, is indivisibly united to the Great Church of Constantinople, and every other Church of Christ that holds the same faith; adhering, precisely as they do, to the holy canons of the apostles and councils, and to the holy traditions: yet it is independent, exercising its sovereign functions free from the control of any other Church."

Notwithstanding this declaration, the difficulties of the position of the Greek Church were felt in so lively a manner, that no new bishoprics were erected, and the vacancies created by the death of the incumbents were not filled. At

* The letter was republished in the form of a small pamphlet, at the office of the *Euterpe*, a literary periodical: Athens, 1852.

length the necessity of giving some more definite shape to the ecclesiastical affairs of the state, had become so evident, that the Ministry resolved to send a commission to the Church of Constantinople, with letters from the government and from the Synod of Greece, requesting them to "approve their ecclesiastical constitution; and, recognizing the Synod of the kingdom of Greece erected in accordance with it, to receive it as a sister-church holding the same doctrines, and equal in honor;" and to announce it as such to the other three Patriarchates.

The reply received to these letters was a master-piece of cunning. It was styled *The Synodical Tome*, and the Russian party in the state not only extolled it to the skies, but advocated its immediate ratification and adoption as an organic law of the realm. Such must have been the inevitable result, had not an antagonist appeared in the author of an anonymous work upon the subject, who was soon known to be the theologian Theophilus Pharmakides, a distinguished professor in the university. He stigmatized the entire movement as one which, if consummated, would lead to the virtual surrender of the established polity. The Patriarchal letter, instead of *recognizing* the Hellenic Church as already independent, proceeded, on *certain conditions*, to decree it such. This implied the right to revoke the privileges that were granted, if the terms of the contract should not be observed. The conditions were the following: The establishment of a perpetual Synod of bishops, to be the highest authority in matters of religion, and to exercise its functions independent of secular interference; the insertion of petitions for the Patriarch and his advisers in the public services; the procuring of the "Holy Myron," or anointing oil used after baptism, directly from Constantinople; the consultation of the Great Church on all important matters needing reflection. On these and other equally humiliating conditions, the Patriarch was pleased to remove the sentence of excommunication, and recognize the validity of the ordination of the Greek clergy.*

* The *Tome*, and all the documents relating to the discussion, may be found in the work of Professor Pharmakides, entitled *The Synodical Tome, or Of Truth:* Athens, 1852.

It was too evident that the *Tome* was but a fresh attempt to foist upon the Greeks the yoke of their ancient masters; and, when its impudent design was thus clearly exposed, no alternative remained but to reject it altogether. The only visible result it produced, was to awaken the jealousy of the nation, and call attention to many points in ecclesiastical history, of which the multitude had hitherto been entirely ignorant. How the Church insensibly passed from a democratic, representative form of government, to an arrogant oligarchy under the sway of the bishops and patriarchs, was fully discussed by Professor Pharmakides.

By a law framed in 1852, the ecclesiastical polity of the kingdom has been completely remodeled. It increased the episcopal sees to twenty-four—a large number, assuredly, for a population of scarce a million souls.* To each of these is annexed a salary payable by the government, and varying from seven hundred to a thousand dollars. The Bishop of Attica was, at the same time, promoted to be Metropolitan of Athens. Measures were at once taken to fill as many of the vacant episcopal chairs as possible. In order to allay the vexation naturally entertained by the Patriarch and his Synód, in consequence of the indignity offered to them in the rejection of the "Tome," a special messenger was dispatched by the king, with full power to confer on the mortified ecclesiastics as many decorations of the honorary Greek "Order of the Saviour" as might be found necessary; besides covering the insult with a profusion of empty compliments.

The differences between the Latin and Greek Churches, as already stated, are no less marked than their points of resemblance. It is not my intention to enter with minuteness upon a subject so strictly theological. It is rather my

* The Holy Synod of Greece was to be composed of one metropolitan, of Athens, the capital of the *nome* of Attica, and of Greece; ten archbishops, nine of them taking their titles from the capitals of the other nine *nomes* into which the kingdom is divided; the tenth from Corinth, "which, though not the capital of a *nome*, on account of the antiquity of the church founded there by Paul," is raised to the dignity of an archbishopric; and thirteen bishops complete the list of the hierarchy. The Synod nominates three candidates to fill every vacancy, and the king selects one from this number.—'Εφημερὶς τοῦ Λαοῦ, July 2, 1852.

aim to convey a general idea, that shall at the same time be a correct one, of the present attitude which the "Orthodox" Church, as it styles itself, assumes in relation to the great religious movements of the day. A fact lying on the surface is, that its doctrinal perversions, unlike those of its Latin sister, have never become part of a deliberately-formed system, ratified by successive generations, and codified, as it were, by a Council like that of Trent. Nor have its pretensions reached so daring a point. Its degeneracy arises rather from the ignorance of the Middle Ages than from a willful perversion of truth. It acknowledges but seven general Councils, whose authority is binding on Christians, the last in A. D. 786 being that which condemned the doctrines of the Iconoclasts. Yet, by the high esteem in which tradition is held, the multiplication of feast-days and of superstitious practices, the complication of the ritual, and a few cardinal errors of doctrine, a state of things has been induced, little superior to that existing in the West. On the other hand, the Greeks have never admitted the claims of the Pope to be the Vicar of God on earth. This, indeed, was the primary cause of the schism between the two Churches; the occasion was the insertion of the words *filioque* in the Nicene creed. The doctrine of the existence of a purgatory has never been admitted; although, practically, by offering prayers for the dead, such a notion is sanctioned. The Apocrypha has never been received into the canon of Scripture, "though containing many praiseworthy moral passages." Still, many intelligent men would be quite at a loss to discriminate between the books which their own fathers pronounce canonical, and those that are not. It ought also to be said, to the praise of the Eastern Church, that the reading of the Scriptures by the common people has never been forbidden by the Church; however individuals among the clergy may have endeavored, sometimes by open, and more frequently by secret opposition, to repress it.

The Catechism of Plato, Archbishop of Moscow, translated by Coray, and approved by the Holy Synod and the Minister of Public Instruction, is, I believe, required to be taught in all the higher schools of the kingdom. It is, therefore, a fair exponent of the doctrines of the Greek Church; while its completeness and orderly arrangement would entitle it, under any circumstances, to a careful perusal.* The Orthodox Christian, according to this catechism, recognizes Christ as sole Head of the Church, the clergy being shepherds of his flock; the bishops as first, and the priests as second in rank. The Church can follow no leader but Christ. The "power of the keys" committed to the Church, is the authority to reprove or exclude from its communion the unworthy participant. The Sacraments of the New Testament are seven: baptism, the Lord's Supper, chrism, confession, orders, marriage, and the anointing of the sick; but of these, the first two are superior in importance, and the last three are not binding on all Christians. The doctrines of baptismal regeneration, and the real presence in the Eucharist, are clearly set forth. The importance of the traditions and customs of the Fathers is insisted on, as an essential part of Christian doctrine and worship. The invocation of saints is defended, upon the usual grounds, against the imputation of violating the first commandment of the Decalogue. In the explanation of the second, the Greek Church discriminates between the graven image and the picture of a saint, declaring the former alone to be reprehensible. Yet it condemns as idolatrous "those that consider one picture more holy than another; that expect more benefit from one than from another; that bring into the Church a picture and will worship no other; that honor the picture with costly ornaments, more than that which is without, or the old one more than the new; or that are unwilling to worship in a place where there are no images."

To a Protestant there is, perhaps, no part of the Greek sys-

* The Catechism of Plato, translated from the German by the able hand of Coray, is a compend of Theology, rather than an elementary treatise, as its name would give us to expect. It is a volume of about 140 pages in 8vo. The first part, treating of Natural Theology, enters with detail into the examination of the proofs of God's existence, the nature and attributes of God, the natural estate of man, and his conscious ill-desert. The second and main division sets forth the Evangelical Faith, that is, Revealed Religion, with the exception of the Law of God, which forms the subject of the third part. The discussion of the particular doctrines is mostly full and satisfactory, while the notes of the translator are characterized by an evangelical spirit.

tem more shocking than the worship of the Virgin Mary, as it exists, and as it is countenanced by the standards now in use. To say that many of the common peasants are unable to make that distinction which the Church pretends to enjoin, and from mere veneration easily step over into the domain of a most culpable religious worship—is stating a fact which no intelligent eye-witness of their devotions can find reason to deny. It may not be so generally known that the prayer-books in common use, even more than the public service, abound with passages well calculated to mislead the worshipper, and induce him to look to the blessed Virgin for assistance which God alone can grant.*

* A single example of such a prayer may not be altogether out of place; and its completeness and elegance must atone for its length. It will be noticed that the several parts—adoration, confession, and supplication—are clearly marked and impressively conveyed. Yet so strong are the ascriptions of divine attributes, that were the prayer addressed to the Deity, no expression would be found inconsistent with His character. I translate from the *Hiera Synopsis*, a small volume of prayers intended for the use of private Christians (p. 44).

"*A Prayer to the Most Holy Mother of God.*

"O spotless, undefiled, uncorrupted, uncontaminated, pure Virgin, Queen, the Bride of God! Who didst unite God the Word to men, by thy wonderful conception; and join the alienated nature of our race to heavenly things. The only hope of the despairing, and help of them that be warred against; the ready defence of those that fly unto thee, and the refuge of all Christians. Do not abhor me a sinner and accursed; who, by base thoughts, words, and deeds, have rendered myself utterly vile. . . . But, as Mother of the compassionate God, kindly pity me a sinner and prodigal, and receive my prayer offered to thee by my polluted lips. And do thou, making use of thy motherly liberty, importune thy Son, and our Lord and Master, to open to me, too, the kind bowels of his goodness, and, passing by my numberless offences, turn me to repentance, and make me a tried doer of his precepts. And be present unto me alway merciful, compassionate, and good: both in this life as a warm protectress and helper, warding off the assaults of them that be against me, and leading me unto salvation; and in the time of my departure, caring for my miserable soul, and driving far from it dark visions of evil spirits. And in the fearful day of judgment, deliver me from everlasting punishment, and make me an heir of the unspeakable glory of thy Son and our God. Which may I attain unto, my Queen, all Holy Mother of God, through thy mediation and intercession; by the grace and compassion of thy only-begotten Son, our Lord, God, and Saviour," etc.

The condition of the clergy is an important topic for consideration. Like most other topics, to a general view it has a dark as well as a bright side. The priest, or *papas*, it is true, has not necessarily sundered, by a prescribed celibacy, all the ties that serve to unite him, in sympathy and affection, with his spiritual flock. In fact, many of the parish priests are married men; nor is this circumstance considered in the least discreditable. There is, however, this restriction: the aspirant for orders must marry, if at all, before becoming a deacon; and so it happens that while a priest may be a married man, yet a priest is prohibited from marrying.

Although the priest's tenure of office does not depend, as has been asserted, at least in Greece, upon the life of his wife, he can not marry a second time without forfeiting his priestly character. Happily, neither law nor public opinion place any obstacles in the way of his retiring. There are not a few curates who have renounced their sacerdotal functions from this cause; while a much larger number who took up arms in the Revolutionary War, and imbrued their hands in blood, are on that account incapacitated from officiating.

The ignorance and degradation of the clergy forms the gloomier aspect of the picture. Springing from the lowest class of society, they are notoriously illiterate and immoral. So deeply rooted has the notion of their debasement become in the popular mind, that when a boy is unruly, and his parents have failed in persuading him to learn some honest trade, they frequently consider the Church their last and only resource. This idea is embodied in a current proverb, which may be rendered in English by the couplet,

"Vicious and ignorant, gluttonous beast,
Nothing remains but to make him a priest."

But when the fact is known, that until lately there has been no provision for their education, beyond schools where they might learn to read and write, such a state of things will scarcely excite surprise. It is even asserted that a few ecclesiastics may still be found, unable to read their service, and consequently relying either upon their own memory or upon the assistance of others. I have myself met with several who gloried in the scantiness of the opportunities for instruction enjoyed by their order, asserting that a more liberal education had the effect of making atheists of the youth. Unfortunately this is not far from being the case in Greece. I have known several deacons and others in the University that were skeptics even as to the truth of religion, and would gladly cut off their long hair,* and lay aside their sacerdotal robes, could they be sure of gaining a livelihood by some other profession than that they had embraced. The monks are even more ignorant and degraded, while they display an inveterate hostility to every measure tending to enlighten and elevate the people.

Corruption is, unhappily, equally common in Church and State. It is notorious that no one can obtain the appointment of Greek Consul for the more frequented ports—such as Trieste, Marseilles, or Odessa—without first obtaining the influence and support of some important man near the king's person, by means of a costly present. A similar practice holds good with respect to the ordination of priests. So flagrant is this system of bribery in every department of the Church, that in a "letter-writer" published at Athens, not many years ago, and now lying before me, a number of forms are given for such occasions as the following. In one, the writer beseeches a bishop not to grant a divorce in the case of his daughter, and accompanies his petition with a present of 5000 piastres —a little more than $200. Another is an application to a prelate for a dispensation to permit a man to marry a third time. It will be remembered that a third marriage is an abomination in the eyes of the Greeks, and is considered criminal unless the previous permission of the Patriarch be obtained. The applicant states that the prelate's agent, to whom he had addressed himself, had demanded the sum of three thousand piastres; and he therefore begs not to be compelled to pay any thing more than that which is customary. The character of the transaction is more frequently veiled under the appearance of a gift. The Patriarch of Jerusalem grants plenary pardon to all that devoutly visit the Holy Places: but the pilgrim must first gratify his avarice by a present of some

* Letting the hair grow long is considered indispensable to the exercise of any of the priestly functions.

two hundred dollars.* Having satisfied his conscience at so cheap a price, the *Hadgi*, as he is now called, returns to his own country, with a store of acquired righteousness so ample, as to be quite sufficient, both in his own estimation and in that of his neighbors, to cover all his future sins. He rarely fails to make large drafts on this imaginary deposit. "As bad as a *Hadgi*," has become a proverbial expression to denote the most abandoned of characters.

On similar grounds, all who contribute twenty-five piastres to the treasury of the miracle-working church of the *Evangelista* at Tenos, have their names inscribed in a particular book, and receive the bishop's special benediction. The beatitude has been reversed, so as to become, "Blessed are the rich."

The Greek clergy may, like the laity, be divided into two parties, differing not on doctrinal points, but in their tendencies. The first is the Russian, or *Napist*, party—embracing by far the larger portion of the clergy—desirous of more intimate connection with Russia, in both Church and State. Opposed to liberal sentiments, jealous of religious liberty, and of English and French influence, it includes not only the few admirers of Russian despotism, but the more numerous class of those that hope, through the agency of Russian arms, to obtain Constantinople, and set up a new Greek empire. The other and less powerful party, on the other hand, expects more permanent advantage from the influence of Western letters, than from Oriental power. Here are found the friends of religious liberty—though opposed to proselytism—the patrons of education, the more consistent and strenuous enemies of every form of tyranny.

It requires no very great amount of penetration to discover, that one formidable obstacle to the success of missionary enterprises in Greece is the political ambition of the people. With the mass even of intelligent men, the contemplation of the future prospects of their country excludes from their minds all consideration of religion as a personal concern. To embrace a purer type of Christianity seems to them, not only to be forsaking the religion of their forefathers, but to be severing

* A translation of the certificate given to pilgrims was published a few years since in the *Missionary Herald*.

every tie that binds together the scattered members of the Hellenic race. "It will be time enough to consider the truth or falsity of our tenets," is a common remark; "when Constantinople has fallen into our hands." Meanwhile they are ready to regard every one that endeavors to disturb their ecclesiastical unity, as conspiring against the high and manifest destiny of Greece.

Three distinct missionary enterprises, undertaken by Evangelical Christians of America, have been prosecuted for a number of years. The earliest is that commenced about the year 1828 by Rev. Jonas King, D.D., under the auspices of the American Board. Shortly after, Rev. J. H. Hill, D.D., was sent out by the Protestant Episcopal Board. And the Baptist Missionary Union has until lately been represented on Greek soil by Rev. Messrs. Buel and Arnold—the latter having been for some years previous stationed on the island of Corfu.

Dr. King's labors were at first directed to the establishment of schools for the education of boys chiefly. But the American Board having deemed it inexpedient to continue the large appropriations requisite for prosecuting this enterprise, it became necessary to abandon it. As far as respects the mere intellectual education of boys, the necessity of private schools has been removed by the establishment of an extensive system of popular education, including higher seminaries of learning and a noble university. During the last few years, Dr. King has devoted himself to preaching and publishing useful religious books and tracts.*

Dr. Hill has long superintended a large female school, at one time containing several hundred girls, belonging to families that occupy the highest social position. Many of his former pupils are already exerting an extended, and, it is hoped, a very healthful influence in society. Mr. Buel—after having in vain attempted to establish schools at Piræus, in which the

* I am happy to learn that, since I left Greece, Dr. King has gathered a number of pious youth, chiefly, if not wholly, Greeks from Turkey, and has begun to give them systematic instruction in Theology. There are already ten of these students, and there is a prospect of farther accessions. These are the men, we trust, that are to become instruments of great good, in the reformation of the nineteenth century, among the Eastern Christian Churches.

Gospel might be taught without the introduction of the Greek Catechism, as prescribed by the government—now devotes himself (as did also Mr. Arnold, at Athens) to a work similar to that of Dr. King. Of the Rev. Mr. Hildner's schools at Syra, I shall speak in another connection.

It can not be denied that Greece has hitherto proved a difficult field of labor. To those that look for immediate results, and estimate success only by the abundance of present fruit, the seed may seem to have fallen upon a barren soil. But there are those who can not persuade themselves that more than a quarter of a century of incessant toils has been thrown away; that the multitudes that have heard the gospel preached in its purity will retain none of its elevating principles; that the child, who gained his first lessons of knowledge in an American school, has not been permanently benefited; above all, that thousands of copies of the Scriptures, scattered broadcast over the land, can fail, sooner or later, to be a potent element in the forces that shall bring about the reformation of the Greek Church. To such the progress of education and enlightenment, and the advance toward complete religious liberty, constitute a favorable omen of the approach of the time when the results of so much toil shall become manifest to all.

TEMPLE OF THESEUS AT ATHENS.

CHAPTER X.

CHURCH FESTIVALS AT ATHENS.

THE shops throughout Athens were kept closed all day on Good Friday. Their exterior was decorated with a profusion of waxen tapers, combined in a variety of ways, and giving them an appearance of considerable liveliness. At a number of stalls temporarily erected in the street of Æolus, crowds of citizens were seen providing themselves with torches—almost the only article exposed for sale—in anticipation of the great season of rejoicing so soon to succeed. Passing by this busy scene I walked on to the Church of St. Irene—the most important in the city as long as the Cathedral remains unfinished.

Last night, being "Great Thursday," as the Greeks call it, there was a service said in the various churches of the city lasting several hours. What are called the "Twelve Gospels"—that is, twelve selections of Scripture relating to the Passion of our Lord—were read at that time. During the protracted reading, or at its close, an image representing the blessed Saviour on the cross, was brought out by the priests, and laid in the midst of the church. It has been customary to produce, at the same time, an effigy of the apostate Judas, and to burn it in public. This immemorial practice has, however, of late years been abandoned, and is now prohibited by the government, in consequence, I understand, of the animosity that such a sight naturally revived in the breasts of the uneducated classes against the Israelitish population. The last outbreak of this feeling took place on the 4th of April, 1847, when a bigoted mob attacked the house of Mr. Pacifico, an unoffending Jewish resident. The doors were burst open; various members of his family were insulted or maltreated; while the more cunning took advantage of the opportunity to appropriate all that they could lay hands on. Happily for Mr. Pacifico, he was a British subject; and, since he found it impossible to obtain redress for his injuries, because of the inefficiency or partiality of the courts of justice, he appealed to his own government. It was only after a delay of three years, and the blockade of the port of Piræus by an English fleet, that the Greek ministry could be induced to pay the required indemnity.

There was no extraordinary service to-day at St. Irene's; but the image of our Lord was still lying in state beneath a rich canopy directly under the dome. An image, or ikon, in the Greek sense of the word, is nothing more than a simple painting; for, in the ecclesiastical works, a distinction is made, as we have stated, between images and statues: the worship of the latter being considered idolatrous, while the reverence given to the former is regarded as not only allowable, but even praiseworthy. The more devout, who seemed to consist chiefly of women and children, came in from time to time to say their prayers, and kiss the hands and feet of the image. An attendant sat near by at a table. As each worshipper was about to leave the church, he placed a piece or two of silver upon the waiter, or one of the holy *discs*, for the benefit of the church. In return he received a blessing, and a flower was handed to him from a pile that was doubtless consecrated.

In the evening I went again to St. Irene's, to hear the "Epitaphion," a sort of funeral service, in which every circumstance is carefully adapted to express sorrow and mourning, in commemoration of the burial of our Saviour. The ceremonies in the church being ended, a procession formed. Standing in the street at a distance, its coming was announced by the glare of a thousand torches borne by the throng that accompanied the funeral pageant. As it drew nearer I could catch more distinctly the mournful tones of the priests, as with measured chant they carried on a bier the image that I had seen in the church itself. It was preceded by a great wooden cross, before which the spectators crossed themselves repeatedly and bowed profoundly. The bier was followed by a number of distinguished persons, among whom was Mr. Païcos, Minister of Foreign Affairs, with other members of the government. Last year the ministers carried the pall. The convoy was accompanied by a military band, with muffled drums, playing a dead march, and followed by a large crowd, whose torches threw a dazzling brilliancy on every object as they passed.

Still more characteristic and impressive was the procession from a smaller church, which I met a few minutes later not far from the same spot. Without a band, or the presence of men of distinction, it advanced amidst a host of flitting lights. Instead of musicians it was preceded by a hundred or more children and youth, continually shouting rather than chanting that solemn petition so frequently occurring in their litany: "*Kyrie eleyson*"—"Lord have mercy!" But though there was a certain earnestness of manner, it was too evident that few in their boisterous shouts remembered the full import of the cry. Next came the priests, repeating portions of the service, and carrying, instead of the picture of Christ, a genuine coffin, covered with a black pall. Whenever the procession approached a church it paused, and did not proceed till a certain number of prayers were repeated.

Saturday is observed as a day of mourning rather than of festivity; but toward night the churches are crowded with worshippers. At about ten in the evening I took my station on a balcony opposite St. Irene's, to which I had been kindly invited by the occupants of the apartments. Until near midnight the time passed in agreeable conversation with our Greek host and hostess, and those of their acquaintance that had been invited to attend. A few minutes before twelve the king and queen, with their suite, drove up, and, preceded by the Bishop of Attica, ascended the platform erected in the centre of the square in front of the church. While they stood there facing the people, I could not but think of the feelings that must fill their breasts: the one as a Roman Catholic, probably abhorring the rites of an inimical faith; the other as a Protestant, grieved, if she reflected at all on the subject, at the superstitious observances in which she was compelled to act a studied part. For a quarter or half an hour the priests chanted the "Anastasis," a service commemorative of the resurrection of our Lord; but owing to the absurd practice of ringing the church bells incessantly, nothing could be understood. The number of tapers carried by the crowd being much greater, the effect was still more brilliant and pleasing than on Good Friday. This service was then transferred to the interior of St. Irene's, where it lasted a while longer.

To me the most interesting part of the occasion was at the conclusion of the exercises. Easter was now regarded as actually begun, commemorating the Saviour's resurrection. Each, as if animated by the joyful thought, turned to his neighbor, and kissing him, exclaimed, "*Christos aneste*"—"Christ is risen!" To which the other in turn responded: "*Alethos aneste*"—"He is risen indeed!" The salutation was first given by the ministers of state to each other, and from them it spread to the rest of the assembly. For weeks after I occasionally saw the same thing repeated; but it was only between acquaintances, when they met for the first time since Easter. Usage is said to limit the employment of this mode of address to the space of forty days.

After the termination of these ceremonies, all is mirth. The bells from all parts of the city send forth a joyful peal. Generally the Easter festivities have been accompanied by frequent discharges of fire-arms, after the manner of our "Fourth of July;" but this year the practice has been forbidden, and the prohibition strictly enforced. Various have been the surmises respecting the cause of this sudden rigor. The ostensible reason is the numerous accidents that have resulted from the use of balls. More probably the government feared lest the occasion should be seized by the discontented to make a revolution, or an attempt to assassinate the king. For months previous rumors had been circulated of an intention to overthrow the constitution of September, 1843; as was first alleged, by the king *à la Napoléon III.*, afterward by the people, or by some ambitious demagogues. An investigation was at this time in progress, conducted by committees of the Legislature. The whole matter seemed to be very much involved in obscurity.

A second service on Easter Sunday concluded the festivities of the Holy Week at Athens. It is styled the second *Anastasis*, and is chiefly remarkable for the recital of the gospel of the day in as many languages as the clergy can muster. It is currently reported that they "cram" for the occasion with whole pages of languages of which they do not understand a single word—a very natural result, since quantity, not quality, is the requisite for the occasion.

At the conclusion of Lent, whose fast has been kept with a strictness for which no parallel can be found in Western Europe, the rejoicings of the people are the greater, in proportion to their protracted abstinence. The fare of the peasant on Easter-day is the best of the whole year. There is no family so poor that, on this day at least, it does not have for dinner an entire lamb, roasted on the coals. Then the following Tuesday is kept as a general holiday. All business is suspended, and almost the entire population resorts to the fields about the Temple of Theseus, and the hills of Mars and the Nymphs, to join in dances, or to witness them. It is no exaggeration to say that on the occasion when I was present, there were thousands of men, women, and children assembled, all in their best attire. It was curious to notice the animated scene, so close upon the most venerable monument of Athenian art.

The *Romaic* dance, which can here be seen to great advantage, is quite peculiar to Greece. The dancers, who are always of the same sex, rarely number less than twenty or thirty. Having selected a leader, they form a sort of train, always preserving somewhat of a circular position, and often clinging to each other by means of a handkerchief passed around their neighbor's waist. Within this partial circle sits sometimes one musician, but oftener two or three. One plays discordantly on the pipe; a second laboriously endeavors to extract harmonious tones from an instrument not very much unlike a *banjo;* while a third, at measured intervals, thumps with a large stick upon a cracked drum. The music, however, seems to be of secondary importance. The motions of the dancers are slow and dignified, partaking of the nature of pantomime, in which the chief object of each is to reproduce the action and gestures of the leader. But at times the action becomes more violent, varying with the nature of the subject of song, and the temperament of the leader. It is a favorite idea among the learned Greeks with whom I have conversed respecting it, that the *Romaic* is but a modification of the *Pyrrhic* dance of the ancients, and its character, so utterly unlike the frivolous dances now in vogue, goes far toward establishing at least a connection between them. The *Romaic* resembles what I would fancy to be the war-dance of our Indians.

On the morning of the festival of Epiphany, a singular ceremony took place at Piræus, analogous to the marrying of the sea practised by the ancient doges of Venice. At an early hour the Archbishop of Athens, attended by a large company of ecclesiastics, repaired to the margin of the harbor. A vast throng, especially of boatmen, gathered around while he proceeded to bless the waters according to a formula provided for such occasions. At the same time he cast a small cross into the waves. By the contact, the waters of the bay are presumed to be hallowed, and the shipping in some measure insured from shipwreck and other perils of the deep. From the annual repetition, it would seem that the blessing is sufficient only for a single year; and were it not renewed, it would be almost impossible to persuade a Greek sailor to embark upon the unsanctified element. Scarcely had the cross disappeared from sight before a crowd of boatmen plunged in to find the glittering prize. And then began a strife in the deep water, until one, more fortunate than his competitors, emerged, clutching the cross in his hand. Amidst the congratulations of his friends, he now hastened home. Having equipped himself with his best suit of clothes, he next rode to Athens and presented himself with his cross at the palace. It is customary for the king to make the finder the handsome gift of one hundred or more drachms. The ministers of state, and then all others, follow the royal example; and, even before the day has closed, it not unfrequently happens that the boatman's gains amount to a hundred dollars.

The festival of the *Three Hierarchs* occurred on the eleventh of February, New Style; or twelve days sooner, according to the old method of computing time. It was observed in a special manner by the University. Not only were all exercises suspended, but most of the professors and students repaired early in the morning to the church of St. Irene, to attend a long and tedious service. The chief feature of interest was the delivery of a written discourse by the Archimandrite Misael, perpetual secretary of the Holy Synod. Preaching is of such rare occurrence in the Greek Church, that I was curious to know what a man holding so elevated a station in that communion would select for his theme. Taking for his text the sixteenth verse of the fifth chapter of St. Matthew, the archimandrite enjoined on his hearers the necessity of leading a good life, as well as professing the orthodox faith. And as suitable examples for imitation, he held forth the virtues of the three "Hierarchs," in honor of whom the day was observed: St. Gregory the Theologian, St. Basil the Great, and St. John Chrysostom. The discourse was a fair moral homily; but that was all. A pagan or a deist could have found little fault with its Christianity; for it ignored alike human inability and divine grace.

The churches in Greece are very numerous, but mostly small and inelegant. The village church is often no more than twenty or thirty feet long, without bell or belfry, and the exterior disfigured by a coating of whitewash. Some in Athens, even, are equally unpretending. On entering one of these humble structures, a narrow space at the farther end is found to be separated from the part occupied by the people by a highly-decorated wooden screen. It is adorned with several paintings, on canvas or wood, according to the wealth of the church. Those of our Saviour and the Virgin Mary occupy the most conspicuous places, on either side of the main entrance into the *hieron*, or "holy place," as the room behind the screen is called. One who is skilled in recognizing the saints by their appropriate symbols, can generally determine at first glance to whom the church is dedicated; for the picture of the patron is usually placed next to that of our Saviour. In the poorer chapels, instead of costly paintings, there are sometimes very mediocre engravings; but a curiously-wrought lamp of traditional shape invariably burns before them, and its flickering light is usually kept up all night.

In the larger churches there are three doors opening into the "hieron." Through the middle entrance appears the "sacred table," to which the name of *altar* is, I believe, never applied. It is there that the consecration of the elements employed in the Lord's Supper is performed; but this portion of the service is not witnessed by the people. When it takes place, the curtains are drawn over the door, and now only the low plaintive tones of the officiating priest are heard by the worshippers who stand with bowed heads without. The scene is certainly more impressive than the more gorgeous ceremonial of the Latin Church. As a reason for observing this secrecy, it is alleged that the solemnity of the service might otherwise be marred by the levity and irreverence of the audience. On either side of the principal entrance into the *hieron* are stalls in parallel rows facing each other. One, larger and handsomer than the rest, is set apart for the bishop, whenever he is present: the others are occupied by the men and boys that chant parts of the service. Women are not allowed to sing; nor, indeed, are they permitted to stand so near the "holy table." In St. Irene's they occupy the galleries; and elsewhere the sides or farther end of the nave is appropriated to them.

Still more singular, in the eyes of one who has often witnessed the devotions of Roman Catholic assemblies, and their numerous genuflexions, does it appear that a Greek auditory, no less reverent in their demeanor, should never prostrate themselves, but retain the primitive Christian custom of standing in prayer. Not only chairs, but kneeling-stools, even, are entirely wanting. The tottering bishop himself stands erect during a great part of the service. The stranger will, however, easily distinguish the more impressive portions of the mass, by the number of times that the sign of the cross is employed. The Greek rarely crosses himself less than three times in succession, and frequently does it nine times. In the use of this sign he is much more deliberate and reverential than the Latins, whom he regards as highly irregular in their practice; because, while he makes it from right to left, they make it in the opposite direction. With equal tenacity does he insist on the use of three fingers in pronouncing the benediction, thereby testifying his belief in the Holy Trinity. He likewise employs, in certain parts of the service, two bundles of waxen tapers. The first, composed of three, has the same symbolical sense as that just mentioned. The two tapers bound in the other, are used to set forth the two Natures in the one Person of our Saviour.

NAUPLIA, FROM THE BAY.

CHAPTER XI.

THREE DAYS IN ARGOLIS.

> "These massive walls,
> Whose date o'erawes tradition, gird the home
> Of a great race of kings, along whose line
> The eager mind lives aching, through the darkness
> Of ages else unstoried, till its shapes
> Of armed sovereigns spread to godlike port,
> And, frowning in the uncertain dawn of time,
> Strike awe, as powers who ruled an older world,
> In mute obedience."
>
> TALFOURD'S ION.

IT was between six and seven in the evening of one of the first days of April before I could make the necessary arrangements for a tour with a party intending to start on the morrow for Nauplia. Mr. Newton, late an antiquarian attached to the British Museum, but recently appointed Vice-Consul for the Island of Mitylene, and C., son of a prominent London publisher, were to be my companions, and we had engaged Demetrius, familiarly called Demetri, for our guide. By the time we had fully concluded to make the excursion, it was well-nigh dark; and yet neither Demetri nor I had procured our passes, without which we were liable to be stopped at any moment on our way, and perhaps subjected to considerable trouble in clearing ourselves from the suspicion of being either robbers or vagrants. The passport office was closed; but the timely disbursement of two or three drachms readily opened it for us. A fresh difficulty presented itself; for not a blank pass could be found in the office. The ingenuity of the clerk easily surmounted this obstacle. An old pass which had seen service was discovered; the name upon it was transmuted to what might be supposed to bear a slight resemblance to mine; and the words "with his man, Demetrius," were added. So were we permitted to visit Argolis.

The next morning saw us on our way to Piræus, by the Macadamized road, which for three-fourths of the distance runs in a direct line across the meadows. The German surveyors chose for its substruction the northern of the Long Walls of Themistocles, and every violent rain uncovers temporarily the upper course of stones. Our driver did himself credit, and we reached the harbor in three quarters of an hour, and in ample time for the little Austrian steamer upon which we took passage for Nauplia.

The weather was cloudy and dull when we started; but as we advanced the atmosphere grew clearer, and we saw with great distinctness the shores of the Saronic Gulf, upon which we entered. Just beyond the narrow entrance of the harbor, our attention was drawn to the simple monument of Miaulis; and only a few feet farther were the fragments of what popular tradition has dignified with the name of Themistocles' Tomb. Whether this be the exact spot of his sepulture or not, the bones of the great general of ancient times, and those of the most famous admiral of modern Greece, lie mouldering on the shores of the Ægean, within a few yards of each other. Themistocles, it is well known, was buried by the sea-side, in full view of the Straits of Salamis, the scene of his most splendid victory over the Persian fleet.

We altered our course as soon as we had cleared the promontory of Munychia, and, leaving on our right the island of Salamis, headed for the eastern cape of Argolis. This brought us within a very short distance of the Temple of Ægina, dedicated of old to Jupiter Panhellenius. Through the captain's glass we could distinguish without difficulty its standing columns. It is one of the most perfect edifices out of Athens itself; but we saw it to little advantage, and I reserved a visit for a future occasion.

There were quite a number of passengers on board our little steamer, and as the day was fair and mild, every body congregated on deck. Indeed, the trip being a short one, most of them were deck passengers. The Greeks are so talkative and so easy of access, that it is not difficult to make a number of acquaintances in a short time. Our company was a lively one, too. As they had nothing else to do, most of them amused themselves by playing cards. One party of eight or ten were seated in Turkish fashion near the helm, forming a circle around a cloth, on which figured a cold leg of mutton and several bottles of wine. The men helped themselves plentifully, and, disdaining the use of forks, cut the meat with their jack-knives, or tore it to pieces with their fingers. These were evidently all from the same neighborhood, and members of the same clan. Some had that free-and-easy look, united to a considerable share of fierceness, that distinguishes the old *kleft;* others, who were younger, belonged to the no less energetic, but more tractable class, that is now springing up to take the place of the mountain brigand. I fell into conversation with some students of the University that were returning home to spend the Easter Week vacation. Like all the rest of Greek students, they were poor, and evidently self-made men. Another set was collected around a musician, who afforded entertainment by playing on an instrument not unlike the banjo, and by singing some country songs.

There were but two cabin passengers besides ourselves, and they were members of the House of Representatives. One of them, Mr. Axelos, who represents the city of Nauplia, was disposed to be very communicative. He informed me that an election was about to be held at Argos the next day, or the day after, and that he was going thither to attend it. Being a partisan of the king, he seemed to be commissioned to procure as favorable a result for the ministry as he could. The officer to be chosen on this occasion was the *demarch,* or mayor of the city, the most important municipal authority. The mode of election, as Mr. Axelos described it, is a most curious one. The people choose twelve men as electors, and twelve more as substitutes. The first twelve choose from their own number four men with their substitutes; and finally three candidates are selected by these for the office of mayor. Their names are presented to the king or ministry, and these designate the one who shall be mayor. Out of the three candidates, I presume, the monarch may safely depend on finding one that will advocate the ministerial measures, for the sake of gaining office. And, of course, in so complicated a procedure, the government will find abundant opportunity for wielding an influence over the election. It would be too great a stretch of charity to believe that my friend, Mr. Axelos, had no part to take in the election at Argos, as he was furnished by the ministry with an order for an escort of soldiers through the dangerous pass from Argos to Corinth, of which he invited me to avail myself in returning to Athens.

By eleven o'clock we had crossed the Saronic Gulf, passing close to the island of Poros, remarkable of late years for the burning of the Greek fleet in its harbor; but more famous under the name of Calauria, as the scene of the death of Demosthenes. It is a bleak, barren rock, without the sign of a habitation on this side. We kept on our course, near to the main land, and inside of the island of Hydra, which rises high and rocky from the sea. The town itself is divided by a ridge, which, running out into the sea, forms two harbors, the smaller serving for quarantine. The house of Condurriotti, the famous Hydriote, stands on the narrow tongue of land between the two, and was pointed out to me. The commerce of Hydra has never recovered from the shock it received during the Revolutionary war. The prizes captured did not compensate for the great drains upon its resources. Since the Revolution, its neighbor, Spezzia, has regained some of its former importance; but Hydra has never sent forth such extensive fleets as those which it sent annually into the Black Sea. The privileges enjoyed by the islanders were so singular that they had little reason to complain of the tyranny of the Turks. Hydra was almost independent of the Porte, governing itself, permitting no infidel to set foot on its soil, and merely paying a small annual tribute. Commerce has usually the effect of removing national prejudice, and of making men more tolerant of the religion, manners, and customs of their neighbors; but at Hydra it seems to have had a result directly the reverse. A Smyrniote lady at Athens told me that her father once nearly lost his life for presuming to enter Hydra in Frank dress. So inveterate was the dislike entertained for the foreign costume, that he was pursued and hooted at in the streets, and compelled to take refuge in a house. It was a characteristic outburst of patriotism that led the admiral Tombazi to reply to one who exclaimed "What a spot you have chosen for your country!" "It was *liberty* that chose the spot, not we." But along with this noble sentiment, and with others distinguishing them above the rest of their countrymen, the Hydriotes possess a considerable measure of the sordid love of gain. It is said that there actually existed in their city, at the time of the Revolution, three mints for the manufacture of counterfeit Turkish coin, which was taken to Turkey, and there put in circulation.*

Our steamboat stopped but a few moments off Hydra, to land passengers, and then continued its course until, coming between Spezzia and the continent, we entered the Gulf of Argos. The town of Spezzia is less picturesquely situated than Hydra; but the island is lower and not so rocky. The harbor is long and narrow. The remainder of the afternoon was spent in steaming up the Gulf, with the bare rocks of the Argolic peninsula on the right, and the equally precipitous hills of Laconia on the other side, coming down to the very margin of the water. After turning a promontory, our steamer anchored directly between Nauplia and the little fort of St. Nicholas, or *Bourtzi*, on a small island opposite the city.

Nauplia is finely situated, and appears to great advantage from the water. The houses are generally built of white limestone, with tiled roofs but slightly inclined. They rise gradually one above another on the side of a hill that forms the end of the promontory, and is crowned by the fort of Itchkali. But these works are slight compared with those on the Palamede, a hill 740 feet in height, which commands the town

* Howe's Greek Revolution, p. 155, note *in fine*.

from the southeast, and renders Nauplia one of the three strongest places in the Morea—the Acrocorinthus and Monembasia being the other two. It is singular that so remarkable a situation as this should not have been occupied, in the times of the ancients, by a populous town. But Nauplia is scarcely mentioned by historians and geographers until a comparatively modern date. Even toward the bay the town is protected by a high wall, which rises from the water's edge, and allows the landing of boats only in a single place. It is said, also, that a double chain used to be stretched from the fort Bourtzi to the main land. It is no wonder that the Turks were foiled in the attempt to take this place by storm from the hands of the Greeks.

Although it was not late in the afternoon when we arrived off Nauplia, we were deterred from landing by a violent thunder-storm; and we concluded, following Demetri's advice, to spend the night on shipboard. The sun rose, on the morrow, in a clear sky, revealing all the features of the surrounding landscape. Northward we saw the low and level plain of Argos bounded by mountains; and on the west, at the base of the high hills that ran southward as far as the eye could distinguish them, was the low, marshy ground, where now stand the few houses of Myli. That was the ancient Lerne, the haunt of the famous Lernian Hydra, whose slaughter constituted one of the great achievements of Hercules. If the Hydra—as German critics pretend—was only symbolic of the pestilential vapors, which Hercules effectually removed by draining it, the monster is now as active as ever: for the neighborhood of Lerne, like all other low and boggy grounds in this warm country, is infested with fever and ague during nearly two-thirds of the year.

After waiting a long while impatiently for our guide, who had gone off to the shore, Demetri at last appeared; and we repaired in a boat to the landing-place, where we found the horses that had been procured for us. We set off at once, without stopping to look at Nauplia, for the old ruined cities of Tiryns, Mycenæ, and Argos. Through a number of narrow lanes we rode at full speed, brushing past the little open shops, and now and then drawing our beasts near the wall, in order to avoid a train of mules laden with sacks or baskets, or a row of donkeys carrying huge bundles of brushwood, under which they were almost hidden. As for foot-passengers, they shifted for themselves; and, in case the street was too narrow to allow more than a couple of horses to pass at the same time, they took refuge in some open doorway or shop. We left Nauplia through the only land gate, over which the old winged lion of St. Mark still exists sculptured on a slab of marble, a witness to the former supremacy of the Venetian Republic. We saw the same emblem, more or less entire, on various other portions of the wall. The Turks, when they gained possession of the city, after carefully destroying the head of the lion, which they supposed, doubtless, to be one of the idols of the Christians, cared little whether the remainder of the monument was still there or not. Passing the narrow strip of ground used as a promenade, at the foot of the Palamede, we came to the suburb of Pronia, which, when Nauplia was the capital of the government, as it was for many years after the Revolution, was crowded with country-seats of all the principal families. Pronia has witnessed some stormy scenes. The congress that assembled there was broken up by force of arms, and its deputies dispersed. On the cliffs that encircle the recess in which Pronia is situated, we noticed, in riding by, a lion cut out of the solid rock, in imitation of the famous monument at Lucerne. It commemorated the Bavarians who died in Greece.

We now turned northward, and entered the plain of Argos. A remarkable plain it is, indeed, and the scene of interesting historical events, from the time of Hercules, the Pelasgians, and the heroes of the Trojan war. The names of its celebrated cities, Mycenæ, Tiryns, and Argos, are mentioned as the seats of potent monarchs, at a time when proud Athens itself was mentioned by Homer as only a "demus," or town. The fertility of the soil, and its advantageous situation for commerce, led to its early selection for the principal kingdom of Greece; and it still enjoys the reputation of being superior in productiveness to any other part of the country, except Messenia. We certainly could not fail to be struck with the vast difference between this plain and that of Athens, than which a more rocky and arid district would be difficult to find. The Argolic valley, measuring, perhaps, a dozen miles in length—from Nauplia to Mycenæ—and not less than seven or eight in breadth at its southern end, gradually contracted as we rode on, until above Mycenæ it became a narrow defile. Fields of wheat, and vineyards of the Corinthian currant, occupied both sides of the road. The products of both are said to be excellent. But there are none of those fine old olive-groves that give such a light-green tinge to the landscape in Attica. No one that travels across it, as we were about to do, just after a heavy rain, and is obliged to wade through pools of waters covering the entire road, or to stem the current of the Inachus, would be likely to style the plain of Argos—as both ancients and moderns have done—"a thirsty land." Yet such it generally is, in consequence of the meagreness of the Inachus, the only torrent it possesses.

In half an hour we reached Tiryns. The long and narrow eminence is a striking object. Rising in the midst of a perfectly level country, it has been compared to a large ship upon the calm surface of the sea. The road runs parallel to its western side. Having turned into the fields on the right, we rode up to the principal entrance of this acropolis. We alighted at the walls, and, while our guide led the horses around the hill to the road, we explored the remains of Greek masonry. To reach the mouth of a passage running through the thickness of the wall on the eastern side of the place, it was necessary to thread our way through the mass of tangled vines and stinging nettles that had grown up luxuriantly during the rains of spring. The wall was built of large, rough, and apparently unwrought stones, heaped one upon another, with smaller ones frequently filling up the interstices. Some of the stones measured five or six, and others as much as ten feet in length. The passage-way was vaulted, not according to the principle of the

ARCH IN THE WALL OF TIRYNS.

arch, but with large stones projecting more and more, until the highest courses met entirely; their balance being preserved by their being proportionately longer, so that the centre of gravity should fall within the wall. We entered this curious gallery, and found it some eight or nine feet high, and stretching about one hundred feet in depth, when it comes to a sudden termination. A single stone at the end has fallen, and the light entering through the vacant space shows that the gallery never extended any farther. By the same dim light we could distinguish five or six openings, or doors, on the right, which served at some time or other as entrances leading from the exterior of the city. They have all since been walled up. What could their use have been? Perhaps for making sallies upon the enemy that might undertake to besiege the town.

We found another similar passage on the opposite, or western side of the great entrance; but it was less interesting. The vault was perfect for a short distance only, the remainder being quite destroyed. We passed on, and ascended to the top of the citadel, which appeared to be elevated some thirty to fifty feet above the plain—one part being much lower than the other, which was a sort of interior fortress. The summit is about seven or eight hundred feet long from north to south, and usually about one-fourth as wide, although it varies considerably. On these three or four acres of ground stood the city of Tiryns, one of the oldest cities in Greece, and principally famous for the wars with its neighbors. It is curious to see that in the time of that most invaluable of ancient topographers, Pausanias, sixteen or seventeen hundred years ago, it was in the same ruinous condition as at present. "The wall," he tells us, "the only part of the ruins that remains, is the work of the Cyclops; and built of unwrought stones, each of which is so large that a yoke of mules could not move even the smallest of them. Small stones have been of old fitted in with them, so as each to form a connection between the large stones."* Nothing but an earthquake could make much impression on these gigantic masses; and so most of the circuit of the wall remains quite perfect. The view over the vicinity is extensive. Near the hill a neat-looking building has been

* Pausanias, II., 25.

erected by the government for an agricultural college, which thus far has not met with much success. The Greek taste, I imagine, does not incline much to agriculture.

Demetri came to us before we had fully satisfied our curiosity, and reminded us of the long ride we had yet before us; but promised that if there were time, we should have the opportunity of spending half an hour more at Tiryns on our return. So mounting again, we rode toward the upper end of the valley, over a level district, abounding in villages and well cultivated, leaving the city of Argos far to the left. Near Mycenæ the soil became lighter, and the country less populous. At the little khan of Kharvati we diverged from the main road, and took a path which led us up to the village of the same name. Our arrival was greeted by some dozens of boys who came to beg, and by as many dogs that came to bark at us; but we set both at defiance, and pursued our way. We were struck with the miserable condition of the inhabitants, who live in low stone or mud hovels, thatched with brushwood and plants gathered in the vicinity.

A few rods beyond the village we reached the neighborhood of Mycenæ, and before entering the inclosure of the wall, descended into the far-famed *Treasury of Atreus.* An inclined plane, bordered on either side by massive stone walls, led us down to the building, which is excavated in the bowels of the hill. On advancing through the wide portal, we found ourselves in a great circular, vaulted chamber, about fifty feet in diameter, and forty in height. The walls gradually approach as they rise in a series of regular courses of squared stone, and form a conical dome—if I may be allowed the expression. Architecturally, the most remarkable feature of the construction is, that its solidity does not depend upon the vertical strength of the arch; but each successive circle of stones is so nicely adjusted, as not only to be firmly held together by its own weight, but also to support the pressure of the circles above it. A single stone—now displaced—capped the entire structure. The gateway, through which we had entered, was one of the most wonderful portions of the Treasury. Though scarcely more than eight feet wide, it is spanned by an enormous soffit twenty-eight feet long, nineteen feet broad, and three feet and nine inches in thickness! How that mass, weighing many tons, was brought to this spot, and raised to the height of twenty feet above the floor—and that, too, without the aid of modern improvements in machinery—is a mystery difficult of solution. Certainly the architects of Agamemnon's age possessed no mean skill. Above this ponderous slab there is a triangular window that serves to let a faint light into the building.

Leaving our horses here, we groped our way through a similar, but much smaller door, almost choked up with rubbish, into a lateral chamber. Demetri brought in an armful of brush, and kindled a fire, whose flame revealed to us the shape of a damp room some twenty feet square, by our measurement, and fourteen feet high, cut out of the hard rock, and left with rough walls. The use of this portion of the building is uncertain. Our guide persisted in calling it the Tomb of Agamemnon, while the rest he styled the Treasury of Atreus. The reverse, however, is the more reasonable supposition: the costly chamber may have been the monument of the illustrious monarch, while the rough chamber, protected by the inviolable sanctity that attached to the resting-places of the dead, may have served as a treasury for the living. Since the structure stood outside the walls of the city—the most ancient walls, at any rate—it is not impossible that this should have been a tomb; but some authors endeavor to prove, and with a show of plausibility too, that it was in some way connected with the worship of those early races that inhabited Greece before authentic history, and concerning whom the amount of knowledge we possess, notwithstanding the bulky tomes written about them, might be summed up in a few pages. Possibly the walls of this inner chamber were coated with marble, while those of the dome undoubtedly were covered with copper plates, as is evident from the abundant remains of copper nails studding their entire surface.

Riding along the crest of the hill, on which ran the more recent walls of the city, we came unexpectedly to a hole, through which the traces of a monument, precisely similar to that we had been visiting, were visible. The upper part of the dome had fallen in, disclosing some of the lower courses of masonry. Most of this "Treasury" is buried below the accumulated rubbish. There are two more outside the walls.

On reaching the acropolis of Mycenæ, we dismounted, and made a great part of the circuit on foot, observing the different kinds of construction that were here exhibited. Sometimes, as at Tiryns, there were great masses of stone heaped together, apparently without any attempt to give them a more symmetrical shape. In other places the masses, though scarcely smaller, were hewn into large and almost regular courses, the occasional crevices being filled with small fragments. In walls of a yet more recent date the stones were much smaller, but of a polygonal form, and generally so admirably fitted as hardly to leave a visible joint between. We entered the acropolis by a gate built, in the most simple manner, of three stones—two upright slabs covered by a third. On either jamb there were projections, against which the door rested, and on one side were two holes, in which was placed the heavy bar that secured it. From the elevated platform on which we stood we could look far and wide over the plain, where reigned "Agamemnon, king of men." This was the capital of the kingdom, while Tiryns to the south, and Argos, at the foot of that high hill almost as far toward the southwest, were the older and later capitals of the Atreidæ. The ground we stood on was perhaps occupied of old by the royal palace celebrated for the misdeeds of Clytæmnestra and Ægisthus, and where the victorious monarch, Agamemnon, was assassinated, with the laurel still fresh on his brow.*

We descended from the top of the hill to the object of greatest interest in the place—the *Gate of Lions*. Two enormous

* Agamemnon was sometimes styled King of Argos; but under this name was included not only the city of Argos—this being the capital of Diomede's dominions—but a large portion of the Peloponnesus, including particularly the cities of Mycenæ and Tiryns. (HEYNE, *Excurs.* 1, *ad Il.* 2.) The scene of the play of Æschylus was more probably laid at Argos, whose site certainly accords better with the description given by the poet, of the signal fires that transmitted to Clytæmnestra the news of the fall of Troy, and of her husband's speedy return. I have not deemed it necessary to enter upon this discussion. The reader may find some remarks upon it in a note by Professor Felton on LORD CARLISLE'S *Diary in Turkish and Greek Waters*, p. 252.

GATE OF LIONS AT MYCENÆ.

stones, standing on end, support a slab equally ponderous; and on the top of this is a triangular piece of gray limestone, ten feet long and nine high, upholding the only statuary to be found at Mycenæ. A couple of lions are represented in high relief erect on their hind legs, and facing each other. Their front feet rest on a low pedestal between them, which is, in fact, a short Doric column reversed. Unfortunately, the heads of the lions are entirely destroyed, and so, also, is any object that may have been upon the top of the column: thus every clew to the meaning of this curious monument has disappeared, and it is impossible to tell, with any degree of certainty, whether it was connected with the worship of the mysterious builders of Mycenæ. The artist who executed this work was not devoid of skill in portraying nature. Every muscle of the lion's body is expressed, and even exaggerated, though there is a certain stiffness about the whole that marks an early period of art. At a glance one is struck with the resemblance of the figures to Egyptian works; and no one that has seen the Assyrian monuments in the London and Parisian museums can fail to notice an equal likeness to their rigid outlines. It is a well-authenticated tradition that the Egyptians sent colonies to this part of Greece; but it seems very doubtful whether these monuments resemble each other any farther than as to the mere clumsiness that characterizes all works of remote antiquity.

The ruins of Mycenæ are the more interesting from the fact, that since the time of Pausanias they have undergone little or no change. "The inhabitants of Argos," says the historian, "destroyed Mycenæ out of envy; for while the Argives remained at rest during the invasion of the Medes, the Mycenians dispatched eight men to Thermopylæ, who took part in the contest with the Lacedæmonians. This brought destruction upon them, since it excited the emulation of the Argives. There remains, however, besides other portions of the inclosure, the gate with the lions standing over it. They say that these are the work of the Cyclopes, who constructed the wall at Tiryns for Prœtus." The great topographer also mentions the treasuries of Atreus and his children, his tomb, and those of Agamemnon and Clytæmnestra

We lingered for an hour or two among the ruins of Mycenæ, and then hurried back to Kharvati, to take our lunch at the khan. While we were partaking of such food as our guide had provided, some peasants brought us the ancient coins they had found in ploughing. Most of them were of the Byzantine period. They set an enormous value upon them, prizing especially all those that bore the impress of a Christian emperor. It is said that when a medal of Constantine is found, it is kept as an heir-loom in the family, and nothing can tempt the fortunate possessor to part with it. Some peasants at the same khan were taking their mid-day repast; but as it was still Lent, they rigidly abstained from meat and fish. They had before them a panful of snails, which they ate raw with their bread, seeming to regard them in the light of a delicacy. We were almost tempted to follow their example; but our prejudice against snails was too powerful to be overcome, and we confined ourselves to that which the more civilized Demetri had set before us.

In returning to Nauplia we took a longer road, which passes by Argos. This consumed more than two hours; for our horses were poor, and the road, though good in dry weather, led across the swollen stream Inachus, which is quite a respectable creek at this season of the year. We found Argos utterly unlike Nauplia in appearance. The houses are newer, and not so high; and many are surrounded by gardens and vineyards, forming a populous but straggling town. Nauplia is its rival, and for a long time entirely overshadowed it: but now Argos contains, if I am rightly informed, ten or twelve thousand souls, while Nauplia has only eight. Our object here was to see the remains of a Greek theatre. To reach it, we were obliged to traverse the greater part of Argos; and a crowd of boys seeing the *milordi* coming, quitted their games to follow our steps. We had seen enough of their character to know that nothing could be gained by commanding them to be gone. Each who had been loudest in his play but a moment before, pressed us in piteous tones to give him a penny; and when we alighted, half a dozen called us in different directions to show us the ruins. If we walked behind any one of them, he was satisfied that we had engaged him as guide; so that, by the time we were through, we found ourselves indebted to them, by their own calculation, in quite a considerable sum.

The theatre itself, however, was interesting enough, notwithstanding the disturbance of our clamorous attendants. The seats are cut out of the solid rock, and, rising one above the other, are divided by alleys into three divisions. Although the lower part of the theatre is covered over with soil, and a flourishing wheat field occupies the arena, some sixty-seven seats are still visible. In one or two places on the neighboring rocks, small bas-reliefs were rudely sculptured, of which we could make little. A friend of mine at Athens told me that he was a member of one of the chief congresses during the Greek revolution, which held its session in open air in this splendid monument of antiquity. Behind the theatre, which could seat about 20,000 persons, according to calculations made from the number of seats, rises the lofty Larissa, the castle of modern, and the acropolis of old Argos. Its name is sufficient evidence of a Pelasgian origin. It is covered by Venetian fortifications. The summit of the hill was probably the station of that watchman whom the Tragic poet represents as watching for ten long years, wet with the dews of every night, for the signal-fires that were to announce the capture of Troy by the Grecian troops.

From the theatre of Argos we returned to Nauplia. Our route led through the *agora*, or market-place of Argos. The name is not confined here to a building or an open square, but is applied to the portion of the town where provisions and other commodities are sold. There were few or no shops, every thing being exposed for sale on cloths and carpets spread upon the ground on either side of the way. Like the Turkish bazars, the place is noisy and crowded; every seller screams in your ear, extolling the quality of his wares, and you find yourself heartily glad when no longer within hearing. There were but few houses between Argos and Nauplia, a distance of six or seven miles; but the traffic and intercommunication was evidently considerable. We reached the harbor a few minutes prior to the departure of the steamer on its return to Athens, and my companions hastened on board. As for myself, I concluded to vary the excursion by crossing to Corinth by way of Nemea, and taking the steamer thence to Piræus. Since Demetri was to accompany the rest of the party, I had a new pass made out, and soon domiciled myself in the small old "Hotel of Peace," opposite the public square.

Mine host, who rejoiced in the name of Elias Giannopoulos, finding that we could converse in his own native language, was disposed to show me every attention. It was too late in the afternoon to procure permission of the mayor to visit the Palamede; but he volunteered to show me the other curiosities of the place. He took me to the Church of St. Spiridon, a small building in an obscure lane. "This," said he, "was the spot where Capo d'Istria, the first president of Greece, was slain by the sons of Petron Bey. The two Mavromichalis, the assassins, stood a few feet down the alley, and when the president, at the conclusion of divine service, issued from the door of the church, they gave him a mortal wound." My friend Elias, though he disapproved of the bloody deed, and admitted its utter uselessness, did not exhibit, I must confess, much sorrow for the murdered man, who was the head of the Russian party. He grew very animated in describing the abuses of the government at Nauplia, and the corruption introduced even into the municipal authority. My window at the inn looked out upon the monument erected to the memory of Ypsilanti, of whom Elias was a great admirer. He seemed very much interested in learning that a town in America had been named after the favorite hero of this part of Greece.

As Elias was about to send to Corinth to bring travelers to his hotel, I had no difficulty in procuring a horse and a guide to cross the Argolic isthmus. On rising the next morning, we found that the weather had undergone a sudden change during the night; and instead of a clear, bright day, such as we had enjoyed, the clouds hung threateningly upon the sides of the hills, offering but a poor prospect for our long day's journey. Again we traversed the plain of Argos, following the same road as on the previous day; and again we lunched at the khan of Kharvati, near the ruins of Mycenæ. Here the plain contracted into a valley, that shortly terminated in a narrow ravine. This was the entrance into the Pass of Trœtus, famous in antiquity for its difficulty. It was here that, in 1822, eight thousand Turks, under Drami Ali Pasha, after having ravaged the whole Argolic plain, and utterly destroyed Argos, attempted to cross the mountains into Corinthia. A handful of Greeks, with Nicetas at their head, were posted at the most defensible point in the pass, while sixteen hundred more occupied the heights about the entrance. For a time the Turks were permitted to advance unmolested; but when they had fairly entered on the intricacies of the defile, they were assailed from behind rocks and bushes with volleys of shot. In vain did the Turks attempt to dislodge their unseen enemies; they had to contend with mountaineers, trained in the rocky heights of Mount Taygetus. Drami Ali hoped, by pressing onward, to free himself from his perilous situation. But after two hours' march, with the enemy continually killing numbers of his men, he reached the narrowest part of the pass, where Nicetas had been impatiently awaiting his approach. Out of the entire army of the Turks, only two thousand succeeded in dashing through the opposing force. About as many more retreated to Nauplia; but between three and four thousand perished in the fearful conflict. Quarter was sued for by many; but the Greeks massacred to the last of their enemies. The spoil was very great, for the Turks were laden with the plunder of Argos and many Greek villages. How changed the scene now!

The pass was the picture of loneliness, and not a sound was to be heard. It is noted only for robbers, who have infested it until lately. It is even now considered the most likely place for their reappearance; although Peloponnesus is, at the present moment, entirely free from depredations.

The rain that had been threatening since morning now began to descend in torrents. In addition to this, the cold was excessive for the season of the year; and I found an overcoat and an umbrella poor protection. My guide, Sideri, wrapped in his great *capote* of camel's hair, fared much better. The Pass of Trœtus is long, and we sought for shelter, hoping that the rain would cease, or at least diminish. At length we reached a hut; but, upon opening the door, we found the dark interior crowded by a set of Greek peasants, who were endeavoring to console themselves with the bottle for the unpromising aspect of the weather without. Not relishing their society, we pressed onward, my guide and a fellow-traveler with whom we had fallen in amusing themselves by singing, in the nasal tone peculiar to this country, some Greek love ditties. Our new companion left us, and pursued his way to Corinth by the direct road, while we turned to the left, and proceeded to the little valley of Hagios Georgios, the ancient Nemea. I was determined to visit the ruins, whatever the chances of the continuation of the storm. Some caves were to be seen as we approached Nemea; they were those fancied by the poets of old to have been the haunts of the Nemean lion slain by Hercules. At length, from a small elevation, we saw before us the retired valley of Nemea—apparently about three or four miles long, and one mile broad—isolated among the high hills of Argolis. A few minutes more brought us to the Temple of Jupiter.

It was raining as hard as ever; but I dismounted and tramped through the high grass, to examine this famous structure. There are only three columns standing—two of which belong to the "pronaos," or chief entrance, and the third to the portico that ran before it. Yet the shape of the edifice can be made out with distinctness, from the lower course of stones belonging to the wall. All the columns of the portico that surrounded the temple lie strewn about the surface of the

TEMPLE OF JUPITER AT NEMEA.

ground. The numerous earthquakes with which this portion of the globe has been visited have thrown down one stone or one pillar after another; and where a whole column has fallen at once, its pieces lie on the ground beside each other in regular succession. The capital upon one of the remaining columns has, by the same convulsion of nature, been singularly shifted from its place; and a few more movements of the same kind will cause its fall. The inferiority of the coarse, gray limestone of which the temple was constructed, but especially the distance of Nemea from any modern Greek city, have saved the temple from spoliation. It seems very probable that there remain sufficient materials to reconstruct the greater part of the edifice. I sat down upon the wet stones, and, under the shelter of an umbrella, succeeded in transferring to paper a sketch of the ruins. The temple was of the Doric order, with a front of six columns. A ruined chapel near by was built of the ruins of this or some other ancient edifice of the same material. Instead of the busy scene which this valley must have presented two thousand years ago, when crowds of pleasure-loving Greeks thronged it, to behold the games celebrated here every third year in honor of Archemorus, not a single habitation stands within sight of the temple. The surrounding fields are partly sown in wheat; while a few shepherds tend their flocks of black sheep and goats on the neighboring hills.

We had entered the valley from its southern end: we left

it by crossing the hills on the eastern side, near a fountain, which was perhaps that of Adraste. Then we followed the course of a ravine, until, descending to the khan of Courtessa, we rested a while to dry ourselves and drink a cup of hot Turkish coffee. A *khan* is a cottage provided for the entertainment of the traveler, in which the farm-house and the hotel are combined under one roof. The khan of Courtessa is not very different from other khans throughout Greece, but as we sat warming and drying ourselves, I had a good opportunity of observing it. It is a small building, with a hard clay floor, in the centre of which a rude hearth is built, and the smoke must find its way out through the chinks of the roof, or the open doors and windows. At the farther end, a little room, or closet, is raised above the general level, with a boarded floor; while the other end is fitted up as a country store. The sides of the room are covered with the various products of the neighborhood. The floor is generally occupied at night as a sleeping-place, not only by the family, but by the countrymen who put up there.

At Courtessa, we entered upon a clayey country, where a torrent, now quite full on account of the recent rains, has cut itself out a deep channel. Our path crossed it very frequently, and sometimes we were obliged to wade for a considerable distance. At one place we crossed by means of a bridge, which, my companion informed me, had been the head-quarters of a celebrated *kleft* named Tambouris, who was accustomed to strip the passers-by, but was at last captured and put to death. The ancient city of Cleonæ occupied, it is supposed, an eminence very near Courtessa, commanding the passes. At intervals we saw, on the sides of the hills, caverns which had been converted into sheep-folds, by constructing a fence of brushwood around their mouths. The huts of the shepherds were built of the same fragile materials, and, being destitute of chimney and windows, were quite blackened with smoke.

It was after five o'clock when we began to descend into the plain of Corinthia. The rain had ceased, and we would have enjoyed a fine view of the Gulf, had not heavy clouds shut out the distance. As it was, a broad plain, partly covered with a flourishing olive-grove, was extended at our feet, stretching far beyond Sicyon toward the west. When we reached the small "Hôtel de Bretagne" at Corinth, the day was too near its close to allow of my ascending to the Acrocorinthus; besides, I hoped that the weather might become more propitious by morning.

I found that my friend, the deputy, who had so kindly invited me to come from Nauplia under the protection of his escort, had arrived before me, and occupied the only decent room in the establishment. My own was bad enough. Mine host, a red-faced Ionian, who spoke Italian better than Greek, came to know what I wished to eat. "What would you like," said he, "lamb, beef, or eggs, with bread and butter?" I expressed myself perfectly satisfied if I could procure some of either of the former. "I am really most sorry," replied he; "but there is not a particle of meat in the house." "Can you not procure some in the village?" I asked, quite alarmed at the idea that, after solacing myself all day with the prospect of a good dinner, I stood a fair chance of being starved. "It is quite impossible; there is not a bit to be found in town." "What in the world have you, then?" I demanded, with some repressed indignation. "Why, please your honor, there is nothing but some bread and eggs." So I dined on a piece of brown bread and two or three eggs, which, in absence of spoons, were dispatched as best might be. After which feast, I soon threw myself on my bed to await the morrow; and soliloquized—

"Non cuivis homini contingit adire Corinthum."

In the morning I found that the weather had not improved. Having an hour or two to spare, I concluded, nevertheless, to ascend the Acrocorinthus, the acropolis of ancient Corinth. It is a great hill, more than 1800 feet in height, lying south of the city. The Corinthians call it an hour's ride to the top; we accomplished the ascent in somewhat less time, I believe. From the Acropolis of Athens, it differs in every respect; being not only more lofty, but inclosing a far greater space within its walls. The summit, too, is not a level surface; but it could contain, as we know it has contained, a large town. Evidences of this fact are to be seen in the numerous cisterns, etc., of more ancient times. A ruinous mosque or two attest the rule of the Turks. We woke from his morning slumbers one of the six soldiers that formed the entire garrison, and he led us around the fortifications. These seemed strong enough; but one would say that, even without them, the rocky precipices below would render the position impregnable. Only five or six guns, I understood, were mounted. We lost all that extensive prospect for which the Acrocorinthus is celebrated; but had a good view of the two gulfs, and of the Bays of Cenchrea and Lecheum, with the adjacent country.

On our return to Corinth, we spent a short time in the examination of the only objects of interest that remain on the site of a city which once exceeded Athens for commerce and population—a temple in the very midst of the modern village, and an amphitheatre about three-fourths of a mile east of it. The former is a *hexastyle* Doric temple, of which only five columns belonging to the front, and two on one of the sides, are yet standing. Besides the noteworthy fact, that the only temple of which any trace exists at *Corinth* is of the *Doric* order, it is observable that the columns are "monoliths," or composed of a single block of stone. The temple could never, I think, have possessed much pretension to beauty, the proportions being too heavy. All the loose stones have been incorporated into the buildings of the village, to which they were so conveniently situated. The amphitheatre is small but interesting, with a subterranean passage under the seat of the presiding officers. Such are the only ruins of consequence on the site of one of the most remarkable cities of Greece. How familiar must every feature of the natural scenery have been to the Apostle Paul, who resided here upward of a year and a half (Acts 18: 11, 18), devoting himself to the sacred functions of his office! He seems, by implication, to have come to Corinth from Athens by land; and, when he departed, he sailed in a ship from Cenchrea for Ephesus. The village of Corinth barely contains a couple of thousand inhabitants. Its houses are low and poorly built; and Corinth, famous of old for its luxuries and pleasures, now presents the aspect of a miserable hamlet, with nothing but the ancient name to uphold its reputation.

The ride from Corinth to Kalamaki occupied about an

hour and a half. The distance is about seven miles. Until reaching the village of Hexamili, the road was covered with water from the continual rains. There the road to Cenchrea branched off to the right. In the vicinity of Kalamaki, we passed first the ruins of the ancient isthmic wall, and not long after the site of the great ship canal that was undertaken to unite the waters of the Saronic and Corinthian Gulfs. Here the width of the isthmus of Corinth is the least. It is to be hoped that the enterprise of the present day will soon construct a new canal, from which advantages so great would result to the commerce of the world. The isthmus is but three miles and a half wide in a direct line, and the utmost elevation is 250 feet above the sea. In this neighborhood the famous Isthmian games were celebrated once in four years. A theatre, situated on the hill above Kalamaki, can even now be recognized, and may have been connected with their celebration.

At Kalamaki I found the Austrian steamer waiting for the passengers and merchandise that had landed from the other steamer at Lutraki, on the Corinthian Gulf. At three o'clock we started for Piræus, which we reached at half past six that afternoon.

VIEW OF CORINTH AND THE ACROCORINTHUS.

TEMPLE OF JUPITER AT ÆGINA.

CHAPTER XII.

ÆGINA AND EPIDAURUS.

"And thence from Athens turn away our eyes,
To seek new friends and strange companies."
MIDSUMMER NIGHT'S DREAM.

THE months of April and May are the most pleasant of the year for traveling in Greece, and I had been waiting some time for agreeable companions only to commence my long-contemplated tour. By accident I fell in with two gentlemen—the one an Englishman, and the other a Frenchman—who proposed pursuing the same route, and who had reached Athens at the most suitable season. In other countries the traveler is left comparatively independent of the rest of mankind in forming his plans. Almost every where he will find good roads, regular conveyances, and tolerable hotels. He may spend at a given place just as much time as he shall find agreeable; and, on leaving, is certain of meeting fellow-travelers similar to those from whom he has parted. Not so in Greece. Here the tourist is tied down to the same party, from the time of departure until he once more sets foot in Athens—unless, indeed, he prefers proceeding in solitary glory, with no better company than an illiterate guide and one or two stupid peasants.

We found that the organizing of an expedition so extensive as that which we had planned was the work of some days. Guides there were in abundance willing to undertake, at a fixed rate *per diem*, to conduct us into any part of Greece. We put an end to their rival pretensions by a personal inspection of their equipments. The harness of the horses; the portable bedsteads, table, and chairs; the cooking utensils—all underwent a rigid scrutiny: the result of which was that we chose Nicholas Combotteca for our guide. I should not fail to mention, however, that the candidates for that honor were questioned as to their knowledge of the route, and we satisfied ourselves that Nicholas was better acquainted with the localities we were to visit than any of his competitors. Tuesday, April 27th, was fixed upon as the day for our departure, and our guide was empowered to engage a *caïque* at Piræus, as well as to send on horses to await our arrival at Epidaurus.

We did not forget to obtain the requisite passes for our whole company at the police-office; our passports were happily laid aside for the time, and we could travel with a simple order from one part of the country to the other. Without this we should have been subject, at every town or mountain pass, to be arrested as brigands—the only class that take the liberty of dispensing with this formality in Greece.

At an early hour on the appointed day a carriage was waiting at my door to carry my companions and myself to Piræus. Our luggage, in view of the fact that every thing was to be carried hereafter on horseback, was limited, by mutual consent, to a moderate carpet-bag, or something of equal bulk. In this bag we must, some way or other, find room to stow away our wearing apparel for more than a month, and sundry guide-books, which we severally contributed to the general stock. On the top of the carriage, and in another which had been sent on before, were piled baskets, mattresses—every thing, in short, that was to conduce to our future comfort. We had scarcely started, when my comrades discovered that I had brought a watch with me, at which they informed me that they had left theirs in the hotel-keeper's hands for fear of robbers, and were quite destitute of any jewelry to tempt the avarice of the *klefts*. Profiting by their example, I deposited mine in the safe-keeping of Mr. Buel at Piræus, and we then drove to the wharf. An unexpected delay awaited us here. The *caïque* we had engaged was at hand, and ready to sail; but the captain—whose crew consisted of two men and a boy—was missing. He had gone, we were informed, to get his clearance papers. The previous day had happened to be a holiday in honor of the French vessels lying in port, and as none of the public offices had been open, we were now obliged to wait till the necessary papers could be obtained. The consequence was the delay of an hour or more on the wharf, and great indignation on the part of Nicholas against the unoffending master, as well as against custom-houses in general.

Our order finally came, and we jumped into the small boat that was to take us to the *caïque*, lying in deeper water. Sails were soon set, but the breeze, though favorable, was light, and we advanced at a very slow rate. We left the harbor, and passed the ruined moles at its outlet, adorned during the Middle Ages by two lions* to guard the entrance, across which a chain was stretched with ease. We coasted for a time along the promontory of Munychia, and then struck into the Gulf, in a direct line toward Ægina. The Temple of Jupiter Panhellenius, the principal object we wished to see on the island, occupies the nearest, or northeastern corner, about twelve miles distant. We were hardly half way across before the favorable breeze gradually died away, and at noon a southerly wind sprang up. Our man Nicholas, with the assistance of the Arab cook, set us a table on the deck, around which we collected with the best of appetites; and the dinner, in truth, was not a bad one. Indeed, we never had the least reason to complain of our fare. The only inconvenience experienced at this time was an occasional roll of the boat; and once or twice we narrowly escaped having our viands precipitated into the sea by the shifting of the boom as the sail flapped to and fro. Meanwhile we were making little or no

* The lions, which were of marble, were carried away by the Venetians during their invasion of Greece, and now grace the entrance of their arsenal. Notwithstanding their loss, the harbor long continued to retain the name of Porte Leone.

progress. To console ourselves, I lay upon the deck of our *caïque* reading whatever books we had providently placed in our carpet-bags, and my companions solaced themselves by smoking their long *chebouks.*

We had a small cabin, for our craft was of twelve or fifteen tons burden; but as it was, we gave it as wide a berth as possible. The smell of the confined air and bilge-water was unendurable, and we would have preferred being thoroughly drenched on deck to taking refuge in the hold. On one side of this cabin was hung a small painting, or *icon*, of Saint Nicholas, before which the devout sailors lighted a small lamp in his honor. Beside it was another religious print, such as are found in abundance about here, but the subject we could not make out by the dim light. Every class of society in Greece has for its patron some one of the saints, or the Virgin Mary, who is presumed to look down with complacency upon his or her worshippers. The manufacture of these miserable engravings, or still more wretched daubs in oil-colors upon wood, is a lucrative employment. Every house must have one of the precious representations. It is a well-attested fact that even the burglar, who breaks into your house at midnight, and the pirate, who assassinates upon the high seas, are no less devout in this respect than their more honest neighbors. One of the modern saints has usurped the place of Mercury, the god of robbers. The shrine of this patron is enriched with the full tithe of the unholy gains of the avowed outlaw, who promises himself, in return, not only success and immunity in this world, but a bright crown and plenary forgiveness in the next. It is said that the visitor may have pointed out to him at one of the most celebrated shrines in the land—that of the Evangelista at Tenos—votive offerings well known to have been hung on its walls by the pirates in return for some fancied benefit received. Such ideas of common morality as this circumstance implies may well shock the sensibilities of those who have been educated in a more enlightened land; but they are the legitimate offspring of a system which elevates the ecclesiastical above the moral duties of man. Some saints appear to have a stronger hold upon the religious feelings or imaginations of the people than others. It may be doubted whether the faithful in Greece do not possess as many representations of St. George and the Dragon as does the whole island of Great Britain, while there is certainly more honor paid to St. Nicholas than even in the goodly city of the Manhattoes.

All day we enjoyed a very extensive and beautiful view. The eye ranged over the whole circuit of the Saronic Gulf, and the prospect included, besides the Acrocorinthus, the snow-capped summits of Cithæron, of Cyllene, and of Khelmos. The plain of Athens, too, was visible in almost its whole extent. On the right of it, Mount Hymettus, which, from Athens, appears to be one continuous ridge, was seen to be separated into two distinct masses.

By one o'clock in the afternoon we were lying almost becalmed within a mile or two of the island. Leaving the *caïque* to come on more leisurely, we got into the small boat and rowed to the nearest point of the shore. We reached an ancient landing-place, and proceeded by the shortest path to the temple. The island is high and rugged, measuring about eight miles on each of its three sides—its shape being that of an equilateral triangle. The soil is rocky and barren, and it can at the present time support but a small population. It was probably in consequence of this infertility of the soil that the Æginetans early turned their attention to commerce, and so became the rivals of Athens in the fifth and sixth centuries before the Christian era. The town of Ægina, however, was situated farther westward. We crossed in our walk a few cultivated fields, but for the greater part, the ground on either side was too rough to be tilled, and was very dry. It was, nevertheless, a very paradise of flowers, of those rich and varied hues that are characteristic of this climate. Before we regained our boat, we had gathered a variety of species, of which we were compelled, though with reluctance, to throw the larger part away.

The Temple of Jupiter Panhellenius, which some antiquarians suppose to be rather that of Minerva, occupies the summit of an eminence at the very northeastern corner of the island, and overlooks the sea on two sides. There were originally six columns on the fronts, and thirteen on each side of the temple, forming a portico that ran around the entire building. Most of these are yet standing, much corroded by the action of the storms that beat with resistless violence upon this unsheltered spot. They are of the Doric order, and are distinguished from those of the Parthenon and Theseum by their less slender shape. The inside of the inclosure is now an almost indiscriminate pile of blocks of stone, overgrown with ivy, and with small shrubs of prickly oak. No vestige remains of the numerous sculptured slabs which used to adorn the structure. The fragments of statuary found in the vicinity, in the year 1812, were purchased by the late King of Bavaria for the sum of £6000, and are now in the collection at Munich. Among the principal peculiarities of these representations is their strict adherence to nature; but they are less graceful than the subsequent works of Phidias on the Parthenon, and preserve more of the stiffness that characterizes the labors of an earlier age. It has sorely puzzled the learned to find upon them the traces of paint; from which it appears that the drapery, eyes, lips, and arms were colored. Many of the figures would seem to have been covered with armor of bronze fastened on by means of nails, the holes of which are to be seen. Some preconceived ideas of the taste of the ancients, too, have been sadly shocked by the discovery that the building itself was not suffered to retain its natural color. The *cella*, or body of the temple, was painted red, the tympanum sky-blue; the architrave, above the columns, was variegated with yellow and green foliage, the triglyphs, still higher up, being colored blue.*

While I sat down near by the southwestern corner of the temple to sketch it, J. was measuring the temple by means of the tape he carried with him—a practice to which he was very much addicted. The dimensions of the building, the size of the columns, and the proportions of the architectural details, were noted in a pocket-book. Thence they were transferred in the evening to a journal, after a careful comparison with those given by Leake and others, with as much satisfaction as

* See C. O. MÜLLER'S *Ancient Art and its Remains*, translated by Leitch, p. 48. The temple is supposed to have been erected near the same time with the Temple of Theseus, about B.C. 465.

a cockney experiences when, having read the description of the Apollo Belvidere in the Vatican, he pronounced Murray "all right." It is but justice to J. to add that he was much interested in architecture, and that his painstaking was not in reality so useless as it appeared.

We were loth to leave the charming site, with its extensive prospect over the island and the surrounding gulf; but we had to hurry back to our boat. I believe that we did not meet a single man on our way, so small is the population of this barren part of Ægina. On the distant left we saw the ruined town, which the inhabitants abandoned for the coast in the time of Capo d'Istria's rule. We passed no dwelling-houses at all, but several churches, one of them built on the summit of a hill. We found our captain had in the mean while succeeded finally in getting the *caïque* along shore. The place where we re-embarked was a miniature harbor of a nearly circular shape, cut out of the rock, which is almost level with the water's edge. It was evidently made by the ancients, to whom it probably served as the port of the Temple, which was completely isolated from the habitations of men. We noticed on its shores the foundations of a building or bath in a depression of the rock.

With a fair wind we sailed rapidly along the northern side of Ægina; then, as we turned southward, passed on our left the modern city of Ægina, a place of some note in the time of the Revolution, until the removal of the capital to Athens. In ancient times the Athenians laid the first foundations of their maritime supremacy on the ruins of the wealthy Æginetans, the inventors of the coining of silver money; and the same process has been repeated of late in a more pacific way. The museum, the gymnasium, and other public institutions, have been transferred to the new capital; and at the present hour the little town of Ægina is altogether devoid of interest. At about nine in the evening we reached the opening of the harbor of Epidaurus, which we entered with some difficulty, after tacking several times. It was full half past ten before we landed.

Nicholas led us to a house near by, half *khan*, and half private dwelling; but it was closed for the night, and the inmates were buried in their slumbers. Thereupon our worthy guide commenced a loud rapping at the door, and soon roused the owner, who loudly inquired from within the cause of this unseasonable interruption. The master of the house in vain pleaded, from within his bolted door, the old excuse that "his children were with him in bed;" we were pertinacious. A room was cleared with a little difficulty, by the removal of half a dozen drowsy heads. Our guide arranged our beds, and we retired to rest under the tutelary watch of St. George, whose image, lighted up by a flickering taper, adorned the wall of our chamber.

The next morning we rose at an early hour, having a good day's work before us; and after breakfast, while our attendants were loading the horses with our luggage, we went around the harbor of Epidaurus to see the ruins of the ancient Acropolis. The modern village, consisting of perhaps fifty houses, somewhat better built than the common dwellings of the peasantry, occupies one side of the bay. It bears the name of Pidauró or Pídaura, which is only a slight change from Epidauros, the ancient appellation. It would scarcely have appeared on the page of modern history, had not this, fortunately, been the spot chosen for the meeting of the first National Assembly. Here, on the 1st of January (old style), 1822, the following declaration of independence was framed and given to the world:

"The Greek nation, under the dreadful Othoman rule, unable to endure the most heavy and unparalleled yoke of tyranny, and casting it off with great sacrifices, proclaims this day, through its lawful Representatives, in National Assembly convened, and in the sight of God and of men, its political existence and independence."*

A foot-path led us around the head of the harbor, skirting a narrow marsh. A man who came along with us conducted us first to two statues lying hidden in the fields of wheat. They were much mutilated, and did not show many traces of fine chiseling. They were probably both recumbent figures on slabs of marble, serving as tops of monuments. Two or three of much superior execution have been taken to Athens

* Howe's Sketch of the Greek Revolution, p. 73.

or elsewhere. The ancient city occupied the high termination of a tongue of land that forms the southern side of the harbor. We were first led to a long line of ancient wall running along the southern side parallel to the shore; it seemed to have been the wall of the city. The stones it is composed of are polygonal, of that construction which goes under the name of Cyclopean, closely fitting one to another. Their size is not remarkable; there are few more than three feet, or three and a half in length, and most are much smaller. At another spot higher up there are remains of a wall built in regular courses, and with cement, which is a sure indication of its more recent date; for until the Romans conquered Greece there is no trace of any mortar having been employed in the building of walls. On the whole, however, we saw nothing of much interest on the site of the city, where we cleared our way through a tangled undergrowth of shrubs. To see the vegetation of Greece in all its glory, this is decidedly the most favorable time. Every spot where a plant can find room for its root is covered with a blooming profusion of wild beauties.

We returned to Epidaurus in season to find every thing ready for departure. It is time that I should give some account of our arrangements. Nicholas, who superintended the whole preparations, had sent on to Corinth to procure the horses, which had arrived at Epidaurus the previous day. These amounted to eight, all told. Besides the three which my companions and I rode, our guide had a fourth. The other four were pack-horses, upon whose patient backs were piled an indiscriminate mass of portable bedsteads, beds, table, and chairs, with every utensil that might be needed for a month to come. One horse was specially to be noted from the quantity of kettles and cooking apparatus dangling from its sides: above all which was perched our indispensable Arab. To attend the pack-horses we needed three more men, who served as *agoyates*.

Our company altogether must have presented rather a comical appearance as we defiled along the narrow path leading out of Epidaurus. The van was led by our guide, Nicholas Combotteca—a man of some thirty-five summers; thin, and clad in the common Albanian costume. A pretty good-humored man he is, but variable, and, for the most part, reserved. Nicholas, though possessed of little learning, is our leader. Next in importance comes Ianni, our cook. Though his face is black as coal, he holds his head as high as the best, and boasts of having been cook to the greatest folks in the kingdom. His father came from Arabia, I believe; but Ianni prides himself upon having been born on Grecian soil. No ill-will or dislike existed between Ianni and the drivers, for no prejudice against his color prevails in these parts. At any hour in the course of the day you might find him at his work, his face radiant with contentment. Ianni's importance commenced where that of Nicholas terminated. On reaching the end of our day's journey, the pack-horses were drawn up to the door of the khan, or, as was more frequently the case, of the private house; and Ianni was the first to enter, carrying a pair of saddle-bags on his arm. Every thing within reach was laid under contribution to furnish us with a dinner. Indeed it used to add no little relish to our meals to wonder where Ianni could have procured the materials for them.

The rear was brought up by the four *agoyates*. Panaghiotes, their leader, is an arrant hypocrite, but making great pretensions to strict honesty. He is chief proprietor of the beasts of burden; while the others are part owners. Two disputed among themselves the honor of being the "last man;" and they might often be seen far in the distance running to catch up with our caravan. Our own equipages were not of a very superior order. J.'s horse was unfortunately given to falling and losing his shoes in rocky places; and the other beasts were not much better.

Our baggage was sent on toward Nauplia, by the direct road passing through the village of Ligourio. We turned off to the left, to visit the ruins of the Hiero, or Sacred Inclosure, of Epidaurus. This ancient town obtained the whole of its celebrity from the sacred grove and temple of Æsculapius, situated at the distance of some four or five miles, in a secluded valley. The road thither followed for a while a ravine which ascends from Epidaurus; this, by-and-by, contracted into a mere mountain glen. The ascent was very slight at any point. The mountains on either side were rocky to the extreme, with rounded summits, and almost entirely bare of trees. One of them, by the name of Œta, seemed to be very lofty. We rode directly to the most interesting object remaining—the ruins of the theatre, one of the largest extant within the limits of Greece proper. We dismounted and climbed up the rows of marble seats to explore it. The form is finely preserved, and row after row of seats may be counted, to the number of fifty-six or seven, upon which it has been calculated that twelve thousand persons might be seated and witness the performances of the stage. As in most other ruins of modern Greece, the prickly oak has sprung up in the narrow flights of steps leading up the *cavea*, and has often torn away the marble benches of the spectators. Notwithstanding this, the theatre is undoubtedly the best preserved in Greece. The arrangements of such a building may be better learned by an examination of this edifice than by any other. From the orchestra ascended no fewer than twenty-four small staircases, dividing the audience, and giving ready access to every part of the theatre. As usual, the architect, in selecting the site, had taken advantage of a small recess or hollow, which with very little labor was made to assume the requisite shape. Some idea of the size of this theatre may be gained from the fact that its diameter was about three hundred and seventy feet.

Our guide led us next to the Stadium, which is to be recognized only by its outline, and by a few scattered seats. It appears to have been a very large one, though not to compare with that of Athens. In the very midst of the sacred inclosure are the few and uncertain remains of the famous Temple of Æsculapius, around which the other buildings were arranged as subordinate in importance. We could distinguish nothing but a mass of wrought stone, indicating the general form of the building. Near by are the more undoubted remains of ancient baths, built in Roman times for the reception of the health-giving waters of the place; for Epidaurus served the purpose of a fashionable watering-place; and the theatre proves that the frequenters of the baths were unwilling to forego even here their customary amusements. The cisterns, to which a small conduit leads, are extensive. One of those we passed was no less than one hundred and twenty or thirty feet long, the brick walls of the Roman structure being supported by what appeared to be an earlier Greek masonry. Among the confused remains of ancient temples, baths, and perhaps less considerable edifices, strewing the whole valley, it is difficult to recognize any one of those buildings whose splendor is portrayed in brilliant colors by the tourists who gazed, two thousand years ago, upon the same localities, with mingled curiosity and awe. In those days the sick of all kinds flocked to the fane of the wonder-working demigod, and whether it was the healing influence of the medicinal waters, or the effect of imagination, numbers returned to their homes, as they supposed, the subjects of marvelous cures. We may readily believe that it was esteemed more fashionable to be restored to health by the miraculous interposition of the god and his serpent, than by the more practical, but more ignoble, influence of drugs. The walls of the temple were crowded with tablets descriptive of cures, and rich with gifts suspended by the invalids who had been relieved; much as in some of the popular shrines of Italy at the present day. The sanctity of the inclosure, however, proved but a weak barrier to the cupidity of those who conquered the country, even before the Christian era.*

After an hour's delay we rode on, and, leaving the secluded valley of Hiero, reached a small village by the name of Ligourio. At the khan we sat down for a few minutes to lunch.

* The ordinary sacrifice to Æsculapius was of a cock, whose head was generally wrung off. The body, I presume, fell to the share of the priests. Such a sacrifice Socrates is represented as enjoining his friend to offer, while lying on his couch before his death; assuredly not in the so-called "prison of Socrates." The singularity of the matter is, that this custom, like many others in Modern Greece, has survived the lapse of so many centuries, and the fall of paganism. Dr. Röser, the king's physician—himself, therefore, a votary of Æsculapius—told me that, while at Calandri, a village some five or six miles distant from Athens, he saw a child to whose neck a dead pullet had been tied, as a sort of charm. In some parts of the country women often have a cock strangled to insure their safe confinement; and the interest of their attendants is consulted, since the fowl is afterward given to them. In Macedonia, on the other hand, the healthy teething of a child is supposed to be secured by its parents by means of cakes covered with sweets, distributed to other children.

This place, it is supposed, occupies the site of the ancient Lessa. The valley into which we had crossed was cultivated with considerable care, every available spot being planted with grain. As we were yet some distance from Nauplia, we rode rapidly forward, leaving our guide to come on more leisurely with one of the horses which had lost its shoe; nor, indeed, was there any thing of interest to detain us along the way. The mountains, barren and rocky on either side, presently left between them only an arid and stony glen, where the eye could scarcely rest upon a shrub or tree. Not a single hamlet did we pass, until at length, emerging from the hills, after a wearisome ride, we saw before us the Palamede of Nauplia, beneath which the quiet town nestles along the water's edge. Having overtaken our baggage train just before approaching the gates, we fell into single file, and threaded the somewhat intricate lanes of Nauplia. The "Hotel of Peace," of my quondam friend Elias, was again our rendezvous; and albeit remarkable neither for cleanliness nor for spaciousness, we long treasured, in our subsequent wanderings, the memory of its humble luxuries.

INTERIOR OF THE KHAN OF GEORGITZANA.

CHAPTER XIII.

MANTINEA—TRIPOLITZA—SPARTA.

On rising the next morning, we found the weather foul. It had been raining all night, and there were no indications of a respite. We debated the expediency of taking a carriage to make the tour of the plain of Argos; but, on inquiry, learned that the roads were too muddy for any wheeled vehicle. We sallied out, therefore, on horseback, at a little before eight, leaving our *agoyates* to proceed, with the baggage, along the direct road to Argos. As for ourselves, we set forth to visit the ruined cities of Tiryns and Mycenæ. I shall not detain the reader with a full description of these places, which have been mentioned elsewhere. The plain of Argos, always celebrated for its fertility, was now much more flourishing than it had been three or four weeks previous. The view of the mountains all around was, however, limited by the heavy clouds hanging over their sides. Late in the afternoon they began to break, and when we reached Argos we had ample time to climb the high and steep *Larissa* that overhangs the town toward the west. A winding path led us gradually around the hill, and presently we found ourselves on the summit, commanding an extensive prospect over the plain. About us were the dismantled towers and battlements of the Venetian or Frank fortifications, and in the middle of the castle we found a couple of large cisterns hewn out in the rock. During the late wars, the possession of this strong position was warmly contested by the Greeks and the Turks. Its almost impregnable strength commanded the passes to the south along the sea-shore, as well as the neighboring plain. But now the deserted walls are shattered and untenable. May the time never return when it shall become necessary to repair their ruins, and the sound of war shall again be heard in the depopulated valleys of Greece.

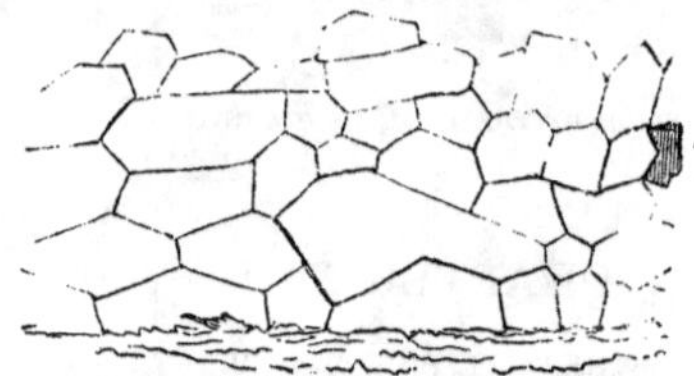

WALL OF THE CITADEL AT ARGOS.

On the morrow we rose early to accomplish the long day's journey before us. It was our purpose to reach Tripolitza that night, visiting on our way the site of ancient Mantinea. There is a steep mountain path, practicable only in the summer season, across the close range that bounds the plain on the west, separating it from the inland district of Arcadia. We soon discovered that the recent heavy fall of snow had formed a trackless waste, and we were compelled to turn considerably to the southward to reach an easier pass. In doing so, we skirted the Lernian marsh, or, rather, left it some distance on our left. This locality, so famous as the habitual resort of the Hydra, slain by the strong arm of Hercules, is at present haunted by a no less formidable and destructive monster, in the guise of the fever or "malaria." When another deliverer shall arise and free the country from its baleful influence, he will be quite as deserving of the remembrance of mankind as the deified hero.

Before leaving the plain of Argos, we came to the source of the Erasinus, a river which empties, after the course of a mile or two, into the Gulf. This is not a small spring, but an entire stream, that bursts out from the rock with great violence, and is evidently a subterraneous river. Both ancients and moderns have agreed in supposing it to be the outlet of Lake Stymphalus, full twenty-five miles distant. It is, in fact, such an opening as the modern Greeks call a *katavothron;* that is, a chasm, through which a stream worms its way beneath entire chains of mountains. In the high, mountainous country of Arcadia the rains fall more abundantly than in any other part of Greece, but, at the same time, there are fewer outlets for the streams. Huge and undivided ranges oppose themselves to the progress of the waters, which, collecting in the hollow valleys, form those pretty lakes that diversify that district, and present so striking a contrast to the aridity of the neighboring regions. The whole of Arcadia, however, would soon be converted into a single pond were there not some means of discharge for the superfluous waters. Fortunately the prevailing rocks are soft, and for the most part limestone. Through them, in the course of ages, the streams have gradually worn themselves a passage, and thus, after an underground channel of several miles, find egress into the lower lands, whence, in general, they easily take their way to the sea. But sometimes their farther progress is not unimpeded. A second, and even a third range, interposes; and again and again the river must delve through the rocky obstacle. Not a stream succeeds in breaking through the mountains, which separate Arcadia on all sides from the adjacent states, like a continuous wall, by a uniform course, except on the west, where the rapid Alpheus finds a narrow passage through a contracted gap. All the rest appear and disappear, as if disdaining to attempt an easier exit than that directly through the bowels of the earth itself.

Such are these *katavothra,* of which we met quite a number in our tour in Arcadia. Naturally these holes, in time, become partially, if not entirely, choked with the accumulation of sand, wood, stone, and other materials. Then the lakes, finding an insufficient discharge for their ever-accumulating contents, rise far above their usual banks, and flood the adjoining fields and villages. This has occurred periodically for centuries. Many extraordinary swellings are mentioned as occurring in ancient times, when, as the country was more densely inhabited, their devastations were still more extensive. Below the katavothron of Argos are situated several mills, which obtain ample motive power from the river, and directly above it is a large and curious cave, stretching back much farther than we had time to follow it. From the position it would seem very likely to have been the former channel of the stream below. The devotion of the neighboring peasants has turned a corner of the cavern into a diminutive church or chapel; it was, however, locked, so that we did not succeed in viewing its internal arrangements. Nicholas insisted on calling the cavern "the haunt of the Lernian hydra." We attempted to disabuse him of this topographical error by reminding him of the fact that Lerne lay several miles off, by the water's edge.

We now turned inland, and commenced a long and tedious ascent in a pass between the mountains, bearing the name of Ktenia and Roino, the former being nearly five thousand feet in height. The khan of Achladocampo ("Apricot Valley") was our resting-place at noon. This charming and retired spot was the site of the ancient town of *Hysiæ*. Its peaceful repose was once, at least, disturbed by the din of battle, when the inhabitants of Argos contested the field with the Spartans, and came off victors. The fortress of the town which was the reluctant spectator of this conflict has left some remains on the brow of one of the hills, but they seem to be of Roman construction. An upper room in the khan was soon cleared for us, and here we sat down upon a carpet spread out in the middle of the floor, to eat our mid-day meal. Several women were spinning around us. They used the antique spindle, which is twirled by being rubbed against the knee, and then left to twist the thread with the motion imparted to it. Occasionally the distaff was replenished from a large pile of cotton in one corner. Meanwhile, as we ate, we furnished them a fruitful theme of conversation, supposing, as they did, that we understood no more Greek than do most travelers from the west.

There awaited us, after leaving Hysiæ, an ascent yet more fatiguing over Mount Parthenius, which bounds the western side of the valley of Achladocampo. The road was for the most part a narrow ledge or shelf, now cut out of the solid rock, and now, again, paved with stone. Very little pains are usually taken to improve the state of the roads in these regions; but here, for the first time, we met an old man engaged in keeping the mountain path in repair. This he did, I presume, of his own accord, depending for his support on the contributions of passers-by. A collection of a few leptas secured to us his gratitude, and, if we might believe him, the protection of numberless saints of the calendar, whose names he glibly repeated. At length we reached the top of the hills, and suddenly obtained an extensive view of the plain of Tripolitza. The town itself was in full sight to the west. And now we commenced the descent. A village on our left furnished, in its vicinity, another example of the passage of a stream through one of those remarkable katavothra.

Leaving our baggage to proceed directly to Tripolitza under the charge of the Arab cook, we turned off toward Mantinea, some seven or eight miles northward. The prospect, as we approached, was quite alpine. On all sides we were shut in by mountains, of which Mount Khelmos stood out prominently in front, its snow-capped head with double its usual covering at present. The hills on either side approach at one spot, forming a separation between the parts of the plain. Our road led us along the right side of the valley, passing through a hamlet, where a troop of barking dogs came out to greet us. This is the invariable indication of approach to a village in the Morea, and it is an occurrence quite too uniform to be pleasant. Fortunately the courage of the curs was not equal to their zeal, and a few well-directed stones rarely failed to disperse the entire pack. We were not a little amused at the stratagem of one of our *agoyates*, who was accustomed to aim, first, a projectile, at which the dogs flew in a rage, affording him a good mark for his second missile. Not far from this village a peasant came running up, wishing to show and sell us a small coin he had found in ploughing. But his coin was too much defaced, and his price was too exorbitant, so that he failed to obtain a purchaser.

We reached the site of Mantinea, standing in the centre of

this part of the valley, in the midst of a marsh produced by a small creek, which shortly after buries itself, like its neighbors, in a katavothron near by. The ancient wall is the principal, or, indeed, the only object of interest beyond the mere position and natural features of this city, one of the most illustrious of Peloponnesus. This wall, it is true, rises at no place above three tiers of symmetrical courses of masonry; but the entire circuit of the fortifications is preserved. At regular intervals of sixty or eighty feet there are square towers projecting from the line of the wall, and numbering, it is said, near one hundred and twenty. The old moat is still filled with water, and we were compelled to ride around a great part of the wall before finding a spot which the horses could ford. Within the inclosure were some remains of a theatre, only its general outline and some scattered stones at its base being distinguishable. The most peculiar circumstance respecting Mantinea was its situation; for, unlike most Grecian towns, it possessed no acropolis or fortress. The lowness of its position suggested to the Spartan, Agesipolis, who in B.C. 385 laid siege to this city, a clever device for reducing it to terms. The walls at that time, it appears, were built of sun-dried bricks. By stopping the course of the stream, Agesipolis succeeded in inundating the vicinity of the walls, which soon began to crumble and fall. The inhabitants at once gave up the attempt to maintain themselves, and capitulated.

Perhaps no locality in the world can boast of an equal number of battles fought upon its soil. Besides several minor engagements, three great conflicts have been here described by three of the greatest Greek historians—Thucydides, Xenophon, and Polybius. In the first, fought B.C. 418, the Mantineans and their allies were routed, in a most decisive action, by the Spartans under Agis. Notwithstanding this success, however, the place was of ill omen for the Lacedæmonian arms. In the second of these great contests the Thebans, under Epaminondas, in the year B.C. 362, met and put to flight the Spartan army at the expense of their gallant commander's life. Carried almost lifeless to one of the adjoining eminences (the spur of the mountain which separates the valleys of Mantinea and Tripolitza), he beheld from thence the complete discomfiture of his enemies. Contented, he withdrew the hand with which he had closed the bleeding wound, and died in the full height of his glory. The third battle was fought between the Spartans and the Achæans under the generalship of Philopœmen, the "last of the Greeks," B.C. 207. It resulted in the defeat of the former, and the death of their king. This was one of the last and most deadly blows struck at the supremacy of Sparta.

No wonder, then, that a student of history should gaze with peculiar interest upon a field on which the destinies of states have been decided again and again, and whose soil has been stained with blood shed in civil wars. The plain is indeed one most suitable for such contests. Its fertility, so far superior to that of most of the neighboring valleys, gave to Mantinea its high rank among the independent cities in Arcadia. Yet nothing, it seemed to me, could better illustrate the diminutive size of these states, so famous in ancient story, than the mere circumstance that Tegea and Mantinea, those determined and implacable rivals, were separated from each other by an interval of only ten or twelve miles, which a horseman might easily traverse in little more than an hour. Had railroads been in use, the troops of one city might have been brought to the walls of the other in a quarter of that time. In view of the improvements of modern tactics, and especially the inventions of modern art, the misery arising from long-continued hostilities, or from their frequent recurrence, must necessarily come to an end. If the implements of warfare are more deadly, the aggregate of happiness is much greater than when the peaceful pursuits of industry and agriculture were continually disturbed by hostile inroads. Then the husbandman, who ventured out of sight of his native walls, fell into the hands of the predatory parties of the enemy. Battles, ordinarily resulting in the loss of but a few citizens on either side, were frequently the means, not so much of terminating the conflict as of engendering yet deeper hostility in the minds of the people who had been injured, but who had not lost the hope of retaliation. Such are the reflections that can not but force themselves a hundred times upon even the most enthusiastic lover of antiquity, whether he may read the history of Greece, or whether, like myself, he may have the good fortune to tread its classic soil.

The night overtook us on our way toward Tripolitza. Upon arriving, we found the town crowded with people from various neighboring villages, who had assembled to attend a fair on the morrow. They were collected in companies at the khans and drinking-shops, making merry with wine and music. Long after retiring for the night we heard their protracted carousals. The *panegyris*, as these periodical assemblages of people are styled, are occasions of great enjoyment among the inhabitants of the whole neighborhood. To them the blind bards, who occupy the place of the ancient rhapsodists, flock in considerable numbers. In a hospitable khan, or in the open street, a crowd hangs on the minstrel's lips; while he chants the heroic lay of some famous *kleft*, or recounts the actions of the no less courageous citizens of Souli, who ofttimes, from their mountain fastness, repulsed the Pasha's troops. Then, again, a more lively theme excites to the dance, accompanied by the inharmonious notes of a rude guitar. These simple ballads, constituting at once the most correct history of a nation's feelings, and the most entertaining and popular portion of its literature, are but short-lived at best. Few of them reach the ears of the educated; fewer still are ever committed to paper; and a score of years is often sufficient to obliterate the memory of those which have been most in vogue. A second generation of composers brings forth an entirely new series of poems on original topics.

Tripolitza contains little or nothing suited to interest a stranger. It is an overgrown village rather than a town. Standing on the site of an ancient Arcadian city, Pallantium, it is entirely destitute of any classical remains. Yet Tripolitza has played a most important part in the recent history of Greece. Even before the Revolution, its central situation in Peloponnesus, and the extraordinary salubrity and fertility of its environs, had induced the Pashas to make it the political capital of the province. It was said (but this, in all probability, was an overstatement) to contain at that time a population of twenty thousand souls. In 1821, when the "rayahs," after their lethargic submission of more than three centuries, had suddenly, by a single exertion of their unsuspected strength, broken asunder the slender cords with which the Sultan attempted to confine their vigorous limbs, the Turks fled in dismay to the open gates of Tripolitza. This city offered but a precarious defence. After a few months of negligent blockade, and one day of unremitted carnage, it fell a ready prey to an inferior Greek force. The streets swam with blood, and packs of half-famished dogs reveled upon the thirty thousand carcasses that choked the highways. The conquered were not spared by the sword; and few, besides the commandant, escaped by an appeal to the avarice of their captors.*

The scene was reversed in 1825, when Ibrahim Pasha invaded Greece with his Egyptian forces, and poured upon the wretched city the retribution to which he had long doomed it. The miserable inhabitants who escaped sought refuge in the mountains, where many perished of hunger. The rest for three long years from their haunts could espy the enemy in possession of their ancient homes. At length the treaty of pacification between Greece and Turkey put an end to their exile. The inhabitants once more gained possession of their deserted homes; but the wounds which a resolute enemy can inflict in a few days or weeks require assiduous treatment for years. The town of Tripolitza can scarcely yet be termed convalescent.

Our pack-horses were sent on by the direct road to Sparta, while we turned to the east, and crossed the Mantinean plain toward the ruins of Tegea, or, to speak more properly, toward its site. This place, like several others in the country, bears the name of Paleo Episcopi, from the only edifice in the vicinity, an old diocesan church. It appears to have been built in the early ages of Christianity, when the architects found an abundance of materials in the now forsaken temples of their heathen ancestors. Every thing from this convenient quarry came in good stead. A Corinthian pillar or a Doric column

* This scene is described, with all its details of horror, in the account of an eye-witness contained in Aldenhoven's *Itinéraire de l'Attique et du Péloponnèse* (*Athènes,* 1841), p. 271–4.

were equally acceptable. Whether plain or fluted, they were placed side by side. Bas-reliefs representing pagan subjects were embedded in the walls on the outside, or, laid upon the ground with their faces downward, formed a cheap and excellent floor. At Tegea the most important remains are some fragmentary inscriptions. Such are the few traces of a city, perhaps the most powerful in Arcadia, whose gallant warriors for six or seven generations withstood the famous troops of their neighboring and encroaching rivals, the Spartans. One of the expeditions of these restless enemies (about 580 B.C.) ended very disastrously for the invaders. The proud warriors who had so lately issued from their native city, flushed with the confident expectation of reducing the Tegeatans to peace and slavery, fell into the hands of those whom they had hoped to wrong. The Spartan, stripped of his burnished armor, was loaded with the very chains he had brought with him to fetter the enemy, and condemned, as a slave, to till for others the lands which he had too rashly expected to enjoy. The superstition of the age attributed this wonderful success to the possession of the bones of the ancient hero, Orestes, and subsequent reverses were ascribed to the loss of that palladium of Tegean liberties.

After satisfying our curiosity with all that was to be seen, or imagined to exist on the spot, we found a narrow road that was to lead us to the more direct route from Tripolitza to Sparta, which our baggage had taken. In a field on our right we observed a country *papas*, or priest, engaged in husbandry with some half a dozen men and boys of his spiritual flock. He had probably induced them to work for him by offering them a more tangible recompense than masses or absolution; for the Greek priesthood do not possess that almost unlimited influence which the Italian curate exercises over his ignorant and devout parishioners. They are usually attached to the people by the ties of fellow-feeling and intermarriage, and no despotism compels the unwilling service of the peasantry. The vicinity abounded with plantations of the *staphis*, or currant, as yet scarce in leaf; and the wheat-fields were full a month behind those of Attica. We shortly entered the ravine of the Sarandopotamos, a torrent which our guide averred was so called from the forty-times the road crosses it. In this wild district there were no bridges, and the horses were obliged every few minutes to wade through some branch, or the main stream itself. Hence a certain degree of judgment is necessary to select the most shallow parts of the stream; for the track is often quite undistinguishable on the gravelly banks of the creek. The whole ride was desolate, and rarely picturesque. The only living beings we met during the course of the day were a few *agoyates*, with their heavy-laden beasts, who carry on almost the whole internal trade of the country as far as there exists any trade at all. We lunched at noon, and rested our horses a while near a cool spring; then commenced a long, fatiguing, and uninteresting ascent of the mountainous country that divides Arcadia on the south from Laconia. Not only was the soil exceedingly barren and stony, but, from its height above the sea, the season was very backward. The oaks, of which there was a great abundance, had not yet put forth a single leaf.

As we began the descent into the valley of the Eurotas, our guide pointed out to us on the left, at some distance below, the small valley supposed to be that of Sellasia, in or near which was fought, B.C. 222, a battle, where the power of Sparta received a mortal wound. The united armies of the Macedonian, Antigonus Doson, and of Aratus, head of the Achæan league, defeated the Spartan king, Cleomenes, at this outpost of Laconia; and the ancient city of Leonidas and Pausanias never recovered its former influence. Wishing to ascertain how much my friend Nicholas knew of the historical incidents of the battle, I asked him to give me the best account of it he could. He confessed himself quite in the dark as to the matter, but thought that one of the warriors who distinguished himself in the engagement was that famous old hero Agamemnon, whose tomb we had entered a few days before at Mycenæ. On the whole, the tourist in either Greece or Italy may rely quite as much on the readiness of his guide's invention as on his historical accuracy.

The day was fast hastening to its close when we reached the crest of the hills, whence the valley of Sparta suddenly bursts on the eye with its broad expanse of green fields and

VIEW OF MOUNT TAYGETUS FROM THE SITE OF SPARTA.

pastures, relieved by the rugged, snow-capped cliffs of Mount Taygetus. We halted at the khan of Vourlia, intending to spend the night; for the few hours of light would not allow us time to descend into the lower country. Before dismounting, however, we found that a detachment of soldiers had taken possession of our quarters, having been sent here to watch for robbers, who always appear first along the difficult passes of the mountains. Making a virtue of necessity, we pursued our way farther to the village itself, and soon fixed on one of the most respectable houses of the place as our lodging. As usual, Nicholas overcame any reluctance of the inmates by the promise of a small gratuity on the morrow. But the necessary arrangements of the landlord and the unpacking of the baggage occupied considerable time, and allowed us to disperse through the village, and sit down a while to enjoy the extensive and delightful prospect. The old town of Mistra appeared in the distance, on the sides and top of a steep hill that seemed close upon Mount Taygetus. Thither it was that the inhabitants of Sparta betook themselves, leaving their ancient home to fall into ruin and desolation. But within some years a new town has risen on the old site, and threatens to eclipse its neighbor. The government has made new Sparta the capital of one of the nomes of the kingdom; and a number of white houses might be discerned somewhat to the left of Mistra, marking the new settlement. The aspect of the Vourliote women afforded us some amusement. Their dress was not very different from that which prevails in some other localities we had passed through; but they are accustomed to carry their infants in a sort of cradle upon their backs. The construction is very simple. A square piece of cloth, very thick and stiff, is supported by thongs inserted in the four corners, and these are made fast around the nurse's shoulders, much after the manner of a knapsack. In the *trough* thus formed the baby is laid, and the wonder is why it does not slip out. Whether such accidents are expected to occur from time to time, I was not informed. The mother, thus freed from all solicitude for her infant charge, moves about the house with activity, and engages with ease in her various occupations.

Our host proved to be a physician. A number of his medical books were lying about, being a nearer approach to a library than we had met with since leaving Athens. Our quarters, though of limited extent, were good. As for the *agoyates*, they generally slept wherever they could find a convenient spot. If the night was cool and the region elevated, they retreated within doors, and formed a ring around the hearth. But if, as to-night at Vourlia, the cold was not too severe, they preferred wrapping their shaggy capotes about them and lying down on the porch in the open air. No wonder that they do not catch cold, for their covering is intolerably thick, and no part of the face appears from beneath it. I have frequently stumbled over them unwittingly of an evening. Their horses, if they find no better place, are tied to some neighboring tree.

Before leaving Vourlia, we held a consultation as to our future course. We had intended, after visiting Sparta, to cross Taygetus to Calamas; but the mountain pass, we were assured, was at this season impracticable for our horses, though mules could take us over it. We should, therefore, be compelled to wait a day at Calamas, while the horses made a two days' circuit of the mountain. It was decided, accordingly, to forego this part of our tour, and turn northward instead, to see the ruins of Megalopolis, which had not entered into our original plan. The baggage at an early hour was sent off directly across the head of the valley of the Eurotas, to the small hamlet of Georgitzi, where it arrived within a few hours. The ride from Vourlia to Sparta occupied us little more than three hours. We first descended through the deep gorges of the mountains; but presently reached the large and clear stream Eurotas, coming from the northwest. At length we arrived at Sparta, on the right bank of the river. The northern part of the site is undulating, and the rest, where stands the modern town, quite level. On the opposite bank the ground rises in high, reddish hills, supposed to be the Menelæum. The view from this spot toward the west is one of the most beautiful that can be imagined, where Taygetus rises against the dark-blue sky. Below, five hills, less elevated, stand in a line, and receive, from their particular form and number, the collective designation of "Pentedactylon," or "the five fingers."

Few cities awaken at the very mention of their names so much interest as Sparta: a state whose predominance over its neighbors was secured by the courage of its well-disciplined and patriotic soldiers; whose gallant citizens were ever prompt to pour out their life's blood in defence of their country and their ancestral institutions; whose kings were not above labor for the common weal; whose chivalrous youth were a sufficient protection for their unfortified capital; whose women could boast that they had never descried the smoke of an enemy's camp-fires on the adjoining plain! Such a state must elicit the enthusiasm of mankind, so long as there exists a spark of the old martial spirit. It is natural, then, to feel disappointment when, after a pilgrimage of some days, the traveler finds little to mark the site of so important a city, and nothing to illustrate former greatness. We discovered a theatre of large size by the banks of the Eurotas; but, as in the case of similar remains elsewhere, it was only the general contour of the interior, and the walls supporting the base, that were visible. As for the seats of the spectators, they had long since disappeared, many of them incorporated in some modern building, and others burned into lime. The whole *cavea* was sown with wheat, in the midst of which, here and there, jutted forth some fragment of ancient statuary or defaced marble. We sat down to look about us, and identify, as far as might be, the various ruins laid down on the charts of preceding travelers. These were numerous enough, and of all kinds, but principally of Roman structure, mingled with those of the Middle Ages. Every where were to be seen great walls, many of them composed of ancient fragments imbedded among more recent materials. In one a row or two of the drums of columns supplied the place of some courses of masonry. I wandered over the hillocks and down to the river's edge. Along the bank stretches a level piece of ground, which, from the direction of the hills, takes very much the shape of a stadium or *dromos* of large size. It was here, probably, that the Spartan youth of yore were accustomed to practice all the exercises useful for a warlike education, and to engage in trials of speed.

On the whole, save a multitude of tottering walls, there is comparatively little of interest to distinguish the site of this famous city. These vestiges date only from the Roman period, when the glory of her ancient renown had forever departed from Sparta. It may be confidently asserted that little or nothing exists to remind one of the city of Pausanias and Leonidas. Of city walls there are none, the laws of Lycurgus having prohibited their erection. Of decorated buildings there are none, the Dorians having been early taught to repudiate all love of the beautiful, with whatever tends to polish and refine, and reckon every thing useless that did not pertain to the science of warfare. Their oligarchy, as a contemporary essayist has well remarked, was a perpetual ostracism of all merit that was not military. It never permitted the full and healthful development of the arts, the pursuit of war being esteemed the only honorable employment for a freeman.

Our guide, Nicholas, had an acquaintance in the modern village, and led us to his neat white house, where we lunched and spent an hour in the middle of the day. The weather was already very warm upon the plains, and it became not only unpleasant, but even perilous, to expose ourselves to the noonday sun. I bore a letter of introduction from Mr. Pieraches, the representative of this district, and a member of the extremely powerful Maniote family, Mavromichales, to a gentleman of the place; but as he was out, I failed to see him. Modern Sparta has been founded since the Revolution, and already, according to mine host, outnumbers its more ancient rival, Mistra. He gives to the former fifteen hundred, and to the latter only one thousand inhabitants. The central government, which has sought to rebuild all the more famous cities of Greece, as if their ancient renown could be restored by the mere erection of modern dwellings on the site, has determined that Sparta shall be symmetrically laid out, and has provided a public square for the promotion of the recreation of the inhabitants. Our host was an intelligent native of Patras, and Nicholas counted him a relation, as he had stood godfather to one of his children. The connection thus formed, he assured me, is as close as the relation of parent and offspring, and more sacred. The latter is only natural, while the other is holy and perpetual. It is a well-known fact, to which I have before alluded, that marriage between those who are bound to each other by such ties is forbidden by the canons of the "Orthodox" Church, as much as those coming within the interdicted degrees of consanguinity.

From Sparta we again bent our steps northward. Just outside the village we passed the so-called "Tomb of Leonidas," which seems to have been nothing more than a platform and a single course of stone belonging to a temple or other ancient edifice. The stones composing it measure, some of them, twelve or fourteen feet in length. Farther on, a small boy told us that a sarcophagus had within a fortnight been discovered in the vicinity, and led us to it. The upper part of the front, which alone had been exposed to view by the removal of the earth, sufficiently exhibited the excellent preservation of the whole. It was some ten feet long, adorned at the ends and in the middle with figures of bulls' heads, having crossed horns intertwined with curls and pine cones. The spaces between were occupied by two large rosettes. According to our informant, the owner of the vineyard where this sarcophagus was found, wished to incorporate the venerable relic in a new house which he was building. Fortunately, the law provides that several weeks shall elapse before any person shall so appropriate a discovery of the kind, in order that the superintendent of antiquities may have the opportunity of saving it from destruction if he deem it worthy of preservation.

Our road to Georgitzi wound along the banks of the Eurotas. Soon we left the plain of Sparta, entering a valley more narrow, and well covered with an undergrowth of small trees and shrubs. On the opposite side of the river there ran along the water's edge several tiers of hewn stone, forming a sort of wall or wharf—the only vestiges of *Pellana.* We passed through several plantations of thriving mulberry-trees set out in the midst of fields.

Janni, or Merdzianni, our Arab cook, following out the instructions he had received, had, as we found, established himself with our effects in the best cottage he could procure in the village of Georgitzi, and was busily engaged in preparations for our evening meal. Let me describe the house and its inmates. They will give a fair idea of the average dwellings and the lower class of the population of Greece.

The whole building, about thirty feet long and twelve or fifteen wide, was formed of rough stone, except the roof, constructed of boards, upon which the tiles reposed. A single room composed the interior. On the right of the door there had been built a square platform of boards, raised three or four feet above the clay floor, and attainable by means of a small rickety ladder. Upon this our beds had been spread out; and here we ate off the portable table that accompanied us every where. Meanwhile the culinary operations might be watched at the other end of the room, where a fire had been kindled on the large stone hearth. The smoke found its way out, partly through the interstices of the tiles, partly through the paneless windows and the door. Around the cook were grouped a goodly number of Greeks, men and women, eating and drinking, and making a very babel of the place as they waxed joyous over their wine. From time to time, a crowd of children, and grown people too, might be observed peering through the door, or even intruding into our small apartment, in order to have a look at the "Frank milords." Ever and anon Nicholas, by dint of threat or entreaty, would clear them from the door; but they speedily resumed their posts of observation, with such perfect nonchalance and good humor, that we were fain to permit the gratification of their curiosity.

Around the room, as usual, were to be seen some of the products of the neighborhood. Often there will be a large heap of cotton, whose picking provides ample employment for the women during the winter months. In autumn one corner is filled with golden ears of Indian corn. Over our heads were hanging from the rafters a number of wide and shallow wicker baskets, in which the silkworms were feeding. Already a chrysalis or two might be seen suspended by its delicate constructor from the lower sides of the tiles of the roof, through the intervals of which, when night fell, the moonbeams gleamed in upon us.

On the whole, I must say, the cottages of the Greek peasantry are remarkably wanting in the air of comfort which a few slight improvements might readily impart. No neat garden, with its wall-flowers garnishing the border, and the woodbine or honeysuckle climbing over a rustic porch, is to be seen, as in England, before the door of the most humble laborer. Few domestic animals are kept, except fierce watch-dogs for protection, who greet the traveler in packs as often as he has occasion to enter a village. Even to the rearing of the honey-bee, for which the country is admirably adapted, the people of Peloponnesus pay comparatively little attention; and a neat row of hives is rarely met with in that district. The few that you will find are made of osier baskets, merely plastered over with mud or clay and dried in the sun; and perhaps they answer the purpose well enough. This is one of not a few instances in which contrivances of a manufacture as simple as that of Homeric times are still commonly employed. Small, too, are the substantial comforts with which the laboring man's home is provided. Of furniture there is little except the mere utensils indispensable for cooking; and as the diet of the poor is simple and light, their number is restricted within a narrow compass. The articles we esteem as almost necessary to existence are wanting. Such a thing as a bedstead can not, I presume, be met with in a peasant's house from one end of Greece to the other. The poor consider themselves very fortunate if they can purchase some matting on which to lie. The greater part, so far as I know, are obliged to content themselves with the great shaggy coats, or *capotas*, in which they wrap themselves, and suffer little from the dampness of the bare ground. At the same time, the want of cleanliness pervading the houses makes them an object of disgust to every person who has not become accustomed to the sight.

THE GREAT GATE OF MESSENE.

CHAPTER XIV.

MEGALOPOLIS AND MESSENE.

Before leaving the retired hamlet of Georgitzana, we had ocular proof of the sensation excited by our arrival among the rustic population of this place, lying off from the usual lines of travel. At one time I counted no fewer than thirty-eight persons, chiefly women and children, all apparently intent upon seeing the strangers. The female part of this assemblage, engaged in spreading the news or scandal of the village, were scarcely less busy with the spindle and distaff, their never-failing resource in moments of leisure.

From Georgitzana our route lay in a northwesterly direction, across the hilly and undulating country separating Lacedæmonia from Arcadia, and kept Mount Taygetus on the left. A more frequented road leads to the pass of Leondari, which we did not visit. The country traversed was well wooded and picturesque, but sustains a very small population. The maple, the plane-tree, the wild olive, the oak, and the walnut abound. Cattle, though remarkably small, were more numerous than in any part of Greece I had hitherto crossed. We came to no khan on our way, and accordingly rested at noon under some large plane-trees near a cool spring of water, whose stream finds its way to the Eurotas. At about three in the afternoon we began our descent toward Megalopolis, which occupies the centre of a large valley toward the southwestern corner of Arcadia. It appeared exceedingly beautiful; the more so, perhaps, because the sterility of the rocky mountains that gird it is concealed by a growth of forest trees, in some places quite dense. The valley seemed to be some eight miles long by six wide. Its soil was very fertile, and cultivated with wheat. A single cypress, rising above the centre of Sinano, guided us thither; for during much of the time there was no road to follow. At an intermediate village we halted for a moment, while Nicholas accosted the Demark, and endeavored to obtain lodgings for ourselves and our suite. He was urgent in his claim, and supported it by representations of our fancied greatness and high rank in our respective countries. But it may be fairly questioned whether his success was attributable to any credit given by the Demark to our guide's high-sounding praises, or to the hospitable disposition which is common to all Greeks.

Riding about ten minutes to the north of the village of Sinano, we reached the site of Megalopolis. It occupied both banks of the Helisson, a small creek tributary to the Alpheus, which it joins a few miles to the westward. The ruins most distinctly traceable were those of the Theatre, the largest building of the kind, as Pausanias tells us, in Greece. It seems to have been not less than four hundred and eighty feet in diameter, and capable of seating some ten or fifteen thousand spectators. The opposite bank is covered with a confused mass of walls and rubbish, among which the site of the ancient forum has been sought. But it was sufficient for us to know that here it was that Epaminondas, that greatest of ancient statesmen, founded a city designed to act as a check on the overgrown power of Sparta. Within its walls were collected, by his advice, a great part of the inhabitants of almost every town in Arcadia, who gave to their new home the emphatic name of the "Great City."

While my companions were indulging in a bath in the cool waters of the Helisson, I was accosted by a couple of Greeks of the better class, who proved to be a justice of the peace, and the teacher of the public school. The latter, a fine-looking young man, told me that he had left the University at Athens only last year, and he appeared much interested in learning that I had been attending lectures there. Some of his scholars were with him, looking at the remains of ancient works, with which they had probably been familiar ever since infancy. They were unusually polite, and gave us considerable information about the place, whose name they pronounced as if it were written *Shinano*, by a corruption which in Greece, as in Italy, seems to be confined to certain localities. On hearing that I came from America, they plied me with geographical questions. They seemed especially pleased to find out that our continent was actually on the opposite side of the globe, as they had been taught at school, but had scarcely been able to believe. Accompanied by quite a number of our new friends, we retraced our steps to Sinano, where, meanwhile, suitable provision had been made for our entertainment. On the way thither, a shepherd-boy, who was feeding his flock near our path, ran up to offer some small copper coins for sale. They were scarcely legible; but he assured us he had picked them up himself, and so we took them. The consequence was, that within an hour the door of our lodging-place was besieged by a host of curiosity-mongers, bringing with them various articles of interest, which they begged us to purchase.

In starting from Megalopolis on the next day, we turned to the southwest; and after some miles' ride over the plain, came to the mountains that divide Arcadia from Messenia. The passage was long and difficult, the descent being very tedious into the plain. About half way, our progress was impeded by a procession, or what seemed to be such, coming up the mountain in the opposite direction. Women and children were generally huddled together on the backs of mules, which were besides overloaded with quantities of clothes, cooking utensils, fire-arms, and, in short, with every thing necessary to furnish the hut of a Moreote *tsimpanes*. It turned out that we had met one of those yearly migrations of the nomadic shepherds, who in the spring forsake their villages in the plain to pasture their flocks or cultivate the higher lands. On inquiry, we found that the caravan was composed of as many as fifty-six families, and that the next day was to be their great annual feast in honor of St. George, who may be considered their patron saint. These migrations take place more or less generally in all parts of the country; even the husbandmen leaving their villages in the spring, and spending a few days or weeks in ploughing and sowing their arable lands on the mountains. This done, they descend to the plains, and perhaps have no farther occasion to return until their fields are ready for harvesting. For their accommodation, they usually erect a summer village—a rude collection of stone hovels, given up more than three fourths of the year to the vermin, which, from the slovenly habits of the people, are sufficiently numerous to form a large, if not respectable, population.

The pass is called Dervenia—a Turkish word signifying a defile—and is guarded by an effective corps of five or six soldiers, whom we found fast asleep within the guard-house. In Peloponnesus the soldiery find little occupation; for of late years robberies have scarcely occurred there, except in the neighborhood of Calamas. In Northern Greece they are more busily employed; but, unfortunately, it is generally the case that when depredations are committed, the soldiers reach the scene of action just after the marauders have left; affording the villagers the poor consolation of a detachment quartered on them for several days.

Leaving the mountains, we entered upon the valley of Messenia, watered by the River Pamisus (now called Dipotamo), flowing into the Messenian Gulf. So well irrigated is this plain, and so fertile the soil, that it may doubtless be considered the garden of Greece, and almost every inch of ground is carefully cultivated. Mount Ithome forms the opposite side of the valley, but we found no road leading thither. Nicholas was not over anxious to look for one, but struck boldly at once through the fields in a "bee line" for the place of our destination. In spring, when the fields are ploughed, the farmer takes no pains to preserve the path of the preceding year, and expects that travelers will make a new one for themselves. No guide, therefore, can remember the location of the old road; and the common practice is to ride directly through the fields, whether they be wheat, barley, or any thing else, without the least compunction. At first I was quite solicitous about the injury our horses' hoofs would occasion to the young grain; but as the cultivators we passed seemed quite indifferent to the matter, I soon lost all concern. This morning, however, our progress was frequently interrupted by numerous ditches for draining or irrigating the country; and we were obliged to skirt them until we could reach a favorable spot for leaping or fording.

We passed a village bearing the name of Meligala, but saw little in the appearance of its inhabitants to indicate the prosperity alluded to in its appellation ("milk and honey"). Soon after, the ascent began. Our baggage-horses and their drivers had meanwhile taken a circuitous but much easier road around the northern side of the mountain of Ithome, and were to stop, if they could find lodgings, at the small village of Mavromati, within the walls of the ancient Messene. At the notch separating Mount Ithome from the pointed but somewhat lower head of Mount Evan on the south, and just above a monastery, we dismounted, and left our horses with the guide, to take them down to the village.

On the lower part of Mount Evan began the first traces of the walls, where we noticed particularly a window of shape somewhat peculiar, and overgrown with bushes and thorny shrubs. Thence we followed the line of the fortifications, interrupted occasionally by towers and gates, running up the crest of Mount Ithome. The ascent was very tedious. The path is steep, and the elevation very considerable. Over a stony ground covered with bushes of the prickly oak, which flourishes here, in connection with the yellow flowered broom, and under a burning sun, it was, perhaps, three quarters of an hour before we stood on the summit. This is occupied by an old ruined convent, whose ivy-grown walls we climbed to enjoy a view extending over the whole of Messenia. To the south and southeast lay the wide Gulf of Messenia or Coron, bounded on the east by the highlands of Maina, as far as Cape Grosso, by which all farther prospect was cut off. Nearer came the town of Calamas, on the shore of the gulf, and the intervening luxuriant plain watered by the Pamisus, which originates in a large marsh to the north. Toward the south and west the prospect was hemmed in by mountains, the intervening country being very hilly. Only to the northwest could we catch a glimpse of the Ionian Sea, and apparently of the island of Zante in the midst. Of the whole picture the snow-capped range of Taygetus was the most striking feature.

The monastery bears the same name as the more modern one below—Panagia of Vurcano. It is so called from a certain miraculous image of the blessed Virgin that used, as they say, to appear to shepherds in this neighborhood. Notwithstanding the sanctity of the spot, which was reputed to be so near to heaven, the old monks found the situation rather too airy; perhaps, also, the steep ascent was too difficult for their asthmatic corpulency. Hence the erection of the lower edifice. We entered the silent rooms and courts; but the most interesting part, the church, was closed. On the walls we found a curious tablet full of misspellings, and partly written in characters similar to inscriptions of an early date. But it was evidently the work of some illiterate monk.

There is no spot where the friend of freedom stands with a prouder feeling than on the summit of this rocky hill. Other localities have been noted for feats of valor, and have been the theatres of glorious successes. Greece may boast of her Thermopylæ and Marathon, and cover the graves of Leonidas the Spartan and Miltiades the Athenian with laurel wreaths and flowers. But Ithome was witness to a struggle all the more affecting because of its sad issue. It was the scene of a conflict in which a brave people, never despairing of their country's salvation, animated with indomitable courage and unexampled endurance, in cool blood made a choice of death to slavery. Three times, after long wars, were the inhabitants overcome by force of numbers or the treachery of their allies; and finally they were compelled to succumb to the ambition and rapacity of their grasping neighbors, the Spartans. Most of the fugitives emigrated; and some found a refuge in the city of Messana, in Sicily. But when the Thebans had by a single blow, at Leuctra, prostrated the long-established power of Lacedæmon, Epaminondas proved, from interest, a friend to the Messenians, as he had been to the Arcadians. He pursued in this instance the same shrewd policy, and showed himself the first master of the balance of power. To curb the strength of their overgrown neighbor, he surrounded Mantinea with new walls, levied contributions of colonists from every city in Arcadia for the new capital of Megalopolis, and reassembling the dispersed inhabitants of Messenia, built them a large and strongly fortified city on and about Ithome, to which now for the first time he gave the name of Messene. The existing remains date, almost without exception, from this period.

It was growing dark, and we hurried toward the village, making short cuts down the precipitous side of the mountain. On our way, and just before reaching the village, we were accosted by a lad who informed me that our whole caravan had gone up to the monastery, not having succeeded in finding accommodations in the village. "All the houses," said he, "are crowded with the peasantry of the neighborhood. All from far and near are coming to celebrate a *panegyri* in honor of St. George to-morrow." So we must needs wend our way back again, and it was late when we gained admittance to the cloister, after a number of vain attempts to make ourselves heard at the gate. Our guide made the best apology he could for not having let us know of the change in our destination; but his excuses were unanimously voted unsatisfactory, nor was any sort of good humor restored to one, at least, of our number, until we had partaken of our evening meal. The monastery was, as usual, built about a court, with galleries running around it, upon which the rooms opened. A chamber was assigned to us in an upper story, where we seated ourselves on a wide divan with two or three monks who came in to chat with us. As they knew no language but their own, I was obliged to act as interpreter for the company. Conversation naturally turned on the monastery and its inmates. They told me there were but fifteen monks all told, besides servants and novices, and that the revenues, which were but small, were yielded by several estates of land, or *metochia*, farmed for their benefit. The abbot was at the time absent superintending some of this property. Our farther inquiries were at length interrupted by the tardy arrival of our dinner, and our new friends would not accept an invitation to join us.

We were up on the morrow in time to step into the small church of the monastery, where morning prayers were being recited. It is a curious place, walls and ceiling being ornamented with odd fresco paintings, half effaced in many places, and full two or three hundred years old. The entrance is decorated with representations of the zodiac and of numerous saints. While the *agoyates* were loading the horses, my companions and I set out to see the existing ruins of Messene. On the way we passed the foundation of some temple, whose site is either not marked, or wrongly located in all the plans of the city we had examined. A number of persons came out to meet us with various coins found in the neighborhood, some of which, being in a good state of preservation, we took. On our descent we passed through the village of Mavromati, so called from its spring, the ancient Clepsydra, in which it was fabled that Jupiter bathed for the first time. The remains of the old theatre consisted chiefly of a great wall supporting its foundation, built in the same manner as the city walls we had examined yesterday on the mountain. The face of each stone, instead of presenting a flat and even surface, was rounded, so as to bulge out considerably toward the centre. Farther down we found several walls, and then the remnants of a double portico of columns three feet or more in diameter, which ran around three sides of the stadium or race-course. This, consequently, served for the reception of the crowds that flocked to see the games, and afforded an agreeable shelter in either rainy or very warm weather. Of the stadium itself there remain a considerable number of stone seats, with much of the walls, and the Doric capitals of the portico. A striking effect is produced by the small stream, which is now diverted from its ancient course, and pours directly down from the village into the stadium, where it runs over the seats and through the arena. Our explorations were diversified by the discovery and capture of a large, but, I believe, not a dangerous, snake, which I noticed creeping through the high grass. The reptile measured about four feet in length.

We returned through the fields to the village, where, after a peep into the old fountain, we mounted our horses, which were in waiting, and rode by the northern road along the side of Ithome nearly a mile, when we reached the famous *Gate of Megalopolis*. This unique specimen of Greek military architecture is not composed of a single portal, but of two gateways separated from each other by a circular court sixty-two feet across. Both were undoubtedly closed by ponderous brazen gates, and the exterior of these was flanked by projections of the walls, from the top of which the besieged could annoy those of their enemies who had the temerity to approach. But even should the outermost gate be forced, the assailants would find themselves inclosed in a small court, where a hundred unseen hands would be pouring down upon them a volley of stones, arrows, and other missiles; and the second portal would be no less difficult to break through than the first. The court is regularly built in courses of smooth stone; and the walls, still remaining about fifteen feet high, are adorned with two niches for statues. The lintel of the exterior gateway has been destroyed; that which surmounted the entrance from the city has merely fallen, from the giving way of the supports on one side. Strange to say, in this fall the huge mass of stone received no fracture, and now stands in an inclined position, with one end resting on the ground. On measuring it, we found this single block to be eighteen feet nine inches long, four feet wide, and two feet four inches thick—dimensions rivaling those of the far-famed Cyclopean works. This gate was undoubtedly built in the time of Epaminondas. An adjoining tower which we entered was very perfectly preserved. Its form was square, and twenty-two courses of masonry could be counted. We gained access to the interior by a door from the wall, and found, within, a room, fifteen or twenty feet square, of rough stone. There were two windows high up, and two *embrasures*, or openings, for the archers to shoot through, much resembling those now in use, being narrow on the outside and wider within, so as to allow greater freedom of action. Earthquakes have wrought sad mischief here, and trees and plants have grown up about the structure. Our guide would scarcely allow us the time to examine with care these ancient ruins and transfer their appearance to paper. So we pushed on with more regret at leaving Messene than perhaps any site we had visited since we left Athens.

We were to have gone on directly to Dragoi, or Tragoge; but, descending into the plain of the Pamisus, J.'s horse had the misfortune to wrench off one of his shoes and cut his foot badly. Nicholas knew nothing of horse-shoeing, and, indeed, prided himself on his ignorance. Our only resource was to deviate considerably from our track to the right, and hunt up the blacksmith of Meligala. This took some time; for it was St. George's Day, and the smith was reluctant to perform any work. Meanwhile, we sat in a neighboring khan, and soon beheld a crowd of gaping countrymen collected about the doors, to whom our coming furnished a rare staple of conversation. As they supposed us, like the generality of travelers, entirely ignorant of their dialect, their comments were quite free. In short, our whole equipment underwent a rigid review, and of each article of dress they expressed their approval or dislike. What most excited the interest of the spectators was a gutta-percha riding-whip, which H. carried and twisted into all pos-

ITHOME, FROM THE STADIUM OF MESSENE.

sible shapes, to the no small wonder of the peasants, who expected to see it break at every moment. They were a little disconcerted on discovering, as we were about to leave, that we could understand what they said. About one o'clock we got under way again, and, having yet seven hours of traveling, rode as fast as we could across the plain in a direct line to Constantino, a village with Turkish fortifications, by which we passed to the opposite side of the valley of the Pamisus, and commenced the ascent of a part of Mount Teffagi. The acclivity was very difficult and tiresome, as was the descent on the opposite side. It was already dark when we reached the bank of the Bouzi, the ancient Neda, and crossed it. Presently we overtook our baggage-horses and their drivers, like ourselves benighted on the mountains. They had lost much time on the way, not knowing the roads. We now came to a ravine, which, being a little difficult to cross, detained us an hour in the cold, while our guide went off to call a shepherd to show us the way. At length we reached the Khan of Dragoi.

TEMPLE OF APOLLO EPICURIUS AT BASSÆ.

CHAPTER XV.

PHIGALEA, OLYMPIA, AND ARCADIA.

OUR stay at the khan of Dragoi was somewhat longer than we had anticipated. We were all exhausted with yesterday's work, and felt reluctant to set out again. Indeed, J. was indignant that the guide should call us at four o'clock, and vowed that he for one would not get up. Seeing the rest of us nearly ready, however, he thought better of it, and concluded to terminate his slumbers. Still it was seven o'clock before we started.

The village of Dragoi, or Tragoge, is composed of scarce more than half a dozen houses or huts, in the best of which we lodged last night. The hill on which Phigalea was built we saw at a distance to the west. It is crowned with an acropolis of Cyclopean masonry. As it offered nothing of much interest, we began ascending the mountain on the east, and in about an hour and a half reached the temple we were in search of, situated a little below the summit, but commanding a very fine view southward to Mount Ithome, and westward toward the city of Arcadia on the sea-shore. To-day, however, the atmosphere was not at all clear, on account of the warm and disagreeable *Sirocco* wind, which had been blowing without intermission for the last three days. Though it does not produce the same bad effects as in Arabia and Africa, its presence is at once detected by the difficulty experienced in respiration, and by the very hazy and indistinct appearance it imparts to all distant objects, and especially to the mountains, without the intervention of any clouds.

The *Temple of Apollo Epicurius* of Bassæ we examined with much interest, both because it was built by Ictinus, architect of the Parthenon, and because its parts are more distinctly traceable than those of any other Grecian temple. It is an edifice of the Doric order, not of the largest size, being only one hundred and twenty-six feet long and forty-eight feet wide. The row of columns that ran around the building, and formed a continuous portico, is entire, with the exception of three that have fallen. Each front was supported by six columns. Behind these two more stood before the entrance to the body or *cella*, the position of whose walls is now marked only by a course or two of stones. The floor of the temple has an oblong depression, some thirty-three feet long, in the centre.* Here the great statue of Apollo must have stood, until it was removed to grace the city of Megalopolis, only seventy years after the foundation of the temple. Around this spot we noticed the lower parts of five half columns on either side. They formed the supports of a small interior portico; but the statue itself was uncovered. All the statuary of this beautiful temple has been removed to the British Museum, where the beauty of the sculpture, added to the remarkable purity of the Parian marble, make it conspicuous among the Greek antiquities. The lonely site of this structure, on this high and barren Arcadian mountain, remote even in ancient times from any large village, strikes one as very singular. It is, however, referable to the fact that this temple was erected by the inhabitants of Phigalea, a town some miles distant, to commemorate their deliverance, through the supposed intercession of Apollo, from a devastating pestilence. In an architectural point of view, its most salient peculiarity is

* Many archæologists suppose that these depressions were made for the purpose of retaining the liquids that were often poured over ivory statues, to prevent decomposition occasioned by exposure to the atmosphere in an open court.

the form of the columns, which taper perhaps more than those of any other Greek edifice, and closely resemble those at Pæstum.

Having satisfied our curiosity by this inspection, we returned a part of the way toward our last night's resting-place, and then commenced a fresh ascent. At the end of two or three hours we reached the large village of Andritzena, beautifully situated on the northern slope of a hill, facing the valley of the River Alpheus.* Though very straggling, it was certainly the largest and neatest place we had passed through since leaving Sparta. It is said to have been entirely destroyed by the Turks during the Revolution, when this part of Peloponnesus suffered most severely from the ravages of Ibrahim Pasha and his Egyptian troops. We sat in a private house to lunch, and while our horses were resting were accosted by a Roman exile, who had fled hither after the suppression of liberty in his native city. Few of these refugees have penetrated so far into the interior, though many are inhabitants of Athens.

The prospect as we commenced the descent was lovely; it extended for a considerable distance over the beautiful valley of the Alpheus to the hills beyond, surmounted by the snowy head of Olonus. In the valley we entered upon a paradise of flowers. No part of Greece is more plentifully clothed with vegetation, and almost none contains a smaller population in proportion to its natural resources. The fertile soil is covered with clumps of trees and shrubs of moderate size, that give it the aspect of a park. The laurel, lentisk, prickly oak, and thorn, just coming into blossom, lend variety to the landscape. To us the sight possessed peculiar charms, since, in the course of a few hours, we had passed from a region where winter had scarcely loosed its bands, into another climate, where the benignant reign of summer was already begun. Two hours more of riding among the hillocks of the plain, at no great distance from the Alpheus, brought us op-

* In crossing the mountains this morning, we noticed with regret the wantonness with which many forest trees of great size have been destroyed. The shepherds, it appears, are accustomed to light fires by night at the foot of the largest trees; and in this way about half of them remained only as blackened trunks, left to rot.

posite to the village of St. John, or Hagios Joannes. A fording-place was found without much difficulty. At other seasons of the year, or after heavy rains, the Alpheus is frequently much swollen. We had been by no means certain that it would not be necessary to ride farther up, and thus lose a day in crossing; or else go down as far as Agolonitza, near the mouth of the stream, where communication is kept up between the banks by a regular ferry-boat. We lodged in a house on the bluff overhanging the Alpheus, at a few minutes' walk from the principal part of the village.

Hagios Joannes is supposed to occupy the site of the important city of *Heræa,* of which no traces can be detected but a small piece of Roman brick-work, lying some distance back from the river. It is situated at the point where the Alpheus, forsaking its northwesterly course through the upper valley, turns and flows in the direction of the sea. Olympia, which we were next to visit, lies on the same side of the river, and the road thither follows the bank of the stream. The body of water is small, varying in breadth from 50 to 150 feet; but it is, nevertheless, the largest and widest river in Southern Greece. Its bed is at times much wider, and sometimes divided by two or three islands. Though the water is now shallow, scarcely reaching to the knee, the course changes exceedingly from year to year. There may frequently be seen dry tracts, which at some time or other doubtless formed part of the bed. This is peculiarly striking in the vale of Olympia, where the marks left on the alluvial soil have been mistaken by some antiquarians for the site of a stadium or hippodrome.

On our way we forded a couple of tributaries to the Alpheus. The first was the Rouphia or Ladon, a stream of considerable length, rising in the mountainous region of Northern Arcadia, and drawing most of its waters from the Lake of Phonia, through an underground channel or katavothron. The people of the neighborhood give the name of Rouphia to the united stream also, below its junction with the Alpheus. The other tributary, the Erymanthus, derives its appellation from the mountain where Hercules is fabled to have slain the Erymanthian boar. It is known at present as the Doana. There was nothing of antiquarian interest to entertain us on our way. At one spot, indeed, we passed a tumulus of considerable size: on riding up to it, however, I could perceive only traces of modern excavations. But the ride was charming, and the air balmy and spring-like. About an hour's distance from Olympia, we sat down under a clump of trees to our mid-day repast, and spent a part of the time allowed us in bathing in the Alpheus. The water was cool, but too shallow near the shore, and the current was very strong.

A little past noon we entered the small vale of Olympia, some two miles long and half as wide, surrounded on all sides by low and well-wooded hills, among which the river winds. Our guide first pointed out to us what he maintained was the ancient stadium; but we easily recognized in it one of the bends of the Alpheus laid bare by an alteration in its course. A few years since, the only vestiges that seemed to have survived the general wreck of ages to mark the ancient site of Olympia, were a few brick walls of Roman construction, and these scarcely sufficient to determine the precise locality. It is to the French scientific expedition in the Morea that we owe the discovery of the exact position, and considerable remains of one of the most famous temples of antiquity. At some period, perhaps, these ruins at the base of a hill, Mount Cronius, were overwhelmed by the Alpheus; or, at least, by some means or other were covered with several feet of alluvial soil, under which they lay as nicely concealed as ever was a mass of gold under the sands of some Californian creek. The fortunate discoverers have, of course, made way with all the portable statuary and bas-reliefs. The more ponderous columns lie scattered about in the excavation, just as when uncovered. The explorations were sufficient to show the general form of the temple, which was a great hexastyle building; that is, had six columns on each front. The columns are truly gigantic, measuring, as I found, over seven feet in diameter at the top of the first drum. As the style was the Doric, each fluting is over a foot in breadth. Their material is hard but ordinary porous limestone, abounding in petrifactions, and certainly incapable of receiving a high polish. This seems to necessitate the conviction that the entire edifice was covered with some sort of stucco, as, indeed, the discoveries have proved. The whole, we are told, presented to the eye the appearance of one of the most elegant structures in the galaxy of Grecian temples, and was dedicated to Jupiter, in whose honor the games were celebrated for nearly eight centuries before the Christian era. Its size varied little from that of the Parthenon at Athens; but as there were but six columns on the fronts, these must necessarily have been proportionately stouter and loftier. The surrounding space was occupied by the *Altis*, or sacred grove of the god; and the stadium was probably not far off, along the banks of the Alpheus. If so, we need not despair of its discovery at some future day, under ten or twelve feet of sand and mud. If any dikes were formed in this valley by the ancients, to ward off the encroachments of the treacherous stream, they have been long since swept away. The important variations in the course of the river within a few years, will be readily understood by any one who will take the trouble to compare the map in Stanhope's Travels with a more modern one.

Near the temple stands a ruined building of polygonal shape, said to be the stables for the horses used in the Olympian games; but we saw nothing to countenance the supposition. The situation of Olympia was celebrated in ancient times for the singular heat to which it was subject, sheltered as it is from every wind by the surrounding hills; and for the want of drinkable water, until supplied by means of an aqueduct built by Herodes Atticus, the benefactor of Athens. We experienced both of these inconveniences during the hour we spent on the spot, though we were yet in the beginning of May.

There flows into the Alpheus at Olympia a small brook, the Cladeus, at present called Stravo-kephali. We followed its ravine, through which, as was our uniform custom, our baggage had been sent on. The ride was pleasant, through pine woods and up a continuous ascent. About half past five we reached the elevated plateau, where stands the village of Lala, our stopping-place for the night. Our lodgings were at a pretty good house, which our attendants had been empowered to secure for our exclusive enjoyment, by turning the inmates out of their quarters, besides laying hands upon whatever they could find in the way of eatables and cooking utensils. But it is long since we have had the luxury of seeing panes of glass in our windows, or a roof destitute of crevices between the rows of tiles, furnishing a larger entrance to the pure air of heaven than is absolutely necessary for the purposes of ventilation.

The brief season of daylight that remained was spent in walking around Lala. It consists at present of only a few straggling huts, barely deserving the name of a hamlet. Thirty years ago it was a considerable village. Pouqueville in 1816 describes it as "a large straggling place, presenting vast palaces and detached groups of houses pierced with loopholes for musketry." It was inhabited by one of those Albanian colonies which it had been the policy of the Porte to transplant to Grecian soil, in order to check the growth, if they could not entirely destroy the being, of the old Hellenic inhabitants. Like most of their compatriots, they retained their national costume, their peculiar language, the Mohammedan religion, and an inveterate hatred to their Christian neighbors. When in 1820 the standard of revolt was unfurled, the Laliotes took part with the Turks, and for months ravaged the richer plains toward the sea. The Greeks in vain attempted to restrain them, till, reinforced by auxiliaries from the Ionian Isles, they were emboldened to lay siege to Lala, which, from its strength, offered them no prospect of capture but by a prolonged blockade. Meanwhile the Albanian Laliotes succeeded in procuring additional forces from Patras, whither they hoped to be enabled to remove their families for safety. Jousouf Pasha having thus collected an army of twenty-five hundred men or more, attacked the Christians, who numbered about fifteen hundred. After an obstinate conflict, lasting from morning to night, the Turks were worsted, but succeeded in making their retreat unmolested to Patras. On the following day the Greeks entered Lala, and, after plundering it, set fire to the village, which lay at too inconvenient a distance to supply with provisions. This was one of the first trials of valor between the Greeks and the Turks in the Morea, and tended greatly to inspire the insurgents with hope and courage.*

The only traces of the Turkish period now extant are two or three square inclosures or citadels, the remains, doubtless, of the "detached groups of houses" to which Pouqueville alludes; and although built in part of fragments of the Temple of Jupiter, at Olympia, they presented to us nothing of much interest.

It was late on the morrow before we set off from Lala. The plateau on which it stands is apparently quite extensive toward the east and west. In the neighborhood of the hamlet there are small cultivated fields, inclosed by fences neatly framed of interwoven brush so tightly put together as absolutely to prevent the intrusion of animals of any kind. On the northeastern side of the plain there stretches a remarkable line of hills, which, from their singular uniformity, strongly resemble a fortification composed of two embankments superimposed. Over the top of both towers the beautiful snowy summit of Mount Olonos, the ancient Erymanthus. We rode directly toward this range, and in the act of entering a narrow defile, caught on our left a clear view of the isle of Zante, far off on the Ionian Sea. Our day's ride, though a rough one, and consisting of alternate ascents and descents, was short. Passing near the village of Koumara, on the opposite side of the valley through which the River Erymanthus flows, we witnessed an interesting procession. To-morrow a couple of peasants are to be married, and then the regular ceremony is to be performed. But to-day the bridegroom and his attendants repair, with the music of a flute or bagpipe, to the house of the bride's parents, whence they bring back the young woman's dowry. Such a procession we noticed this afternoon, wend-

* The circumstances of this battle are given at length, and not very consistently, by Colonel Gordon (*Hist. of Gr. Rev.*, p. 212–14), Dr. Howe (*Sketch of the Gr. Rev.*, p. 23, 24), and Archbishop Germanos (*Hypomnemata*, p. 45–47). The number of the troops engaged, the disposition of the Greeks previous to the battle, and even the day of the month on which it occurred, are among the discordant points. The whole has been still farther complicated by an awkward typographical error in Gordon's work, from which it would naturally be inferred that all these occurrences happened a year sooner than they did.

ing its way along the side of the opposite mountain; but the distance was too great to allow us to see it with much distinctness. At a little past three we reached the lonely khan of Tripotamo—so named because it stands at the junction of three valleys, from each of which there pours down a stream going to swell the Erymanthus. The day was wet, and we were glad to gain a shelter, as well as to obtain time for writing up our memoranda, finishing sketches, attending to various specimens of natural history with which we had managed to store our traveling-bags to the no small detriment of books and clothing; and, in short, a variety of minor jobs, which, on account of our usual late hours, had accumulated on our hands. Still we had in the khan not only the discomforts of a windy chamber, but the apprehension of being kept awake all night by a number of sick children under the same roof, all of whom were afflicted with the hooping-cough.

The isolated conical hill, just eastward of the khan, was the supposed site of Psophis, or rather of the citadel of that town. Before we left Tripotamo we undertook the ascent, and were scarcely repaid for our walk through the moist grass by the sight of a few remnants of polygonal masonry. The place is one of the strongest that can be imagined, and even at present a few cannon placed on the summit of the hill would command all the passes. Yet we hear, I believe, of but one siege of this town, B.C. 219.

From Psophis we rode for two hours up the same winding valley of the Erymanthus, until we arrived at the small village of Dessino, where it seems to terminate. Thence we had intended following the road to Calavryta. Some of our party, however, entertained a great desire to see the Lake of Phonia and the surrounding scenery, said by many to be the most grand and picturesque mountain district in Greece. Nicholas maintained that, in order to accomplish this, we must inevitably proceed first to Calavryta, thence make an excursion of two or three days, and return thither again. To this we were averse, the time of my fellow-travellers' stay in Greece being quite limited. We had consequently examined our maps with care, and discovered what we imagined to be a practicable road leading over the mountains from the village of Dessino in precisely the required direction. Our guide still persisted in averring the impracticability of leading the horses (especially those that carried the baggage) over what could be nothing more than a mere foot-path. It was agreed to refer the matter to the inhabitants of Dessino, who might naturally be the best judges of the matter. These latter worthies gave us a ready audience. It was a feast-day; and after their morning devotions, all the wiseacres of the village were collected on the open common. Our arrival put an end for the time to their games and dances, and they gave us their advice with hearty good-will. But our perplexity was now to choose between the conflicting opinions. For while the old fogies smoked their pipes, and declared it was impossible with pack-horses to cross directly over to Cleitouras, "Young Greece" became exceedingly animated, and indignantly asserted that there was not a safer road in the town, as was proved by the fact that the marriage processions carrying the bride's dowry took that way when occasion required. The latter opinion corresponded with our inclinations, and so it was at once decided to undertake the ascent. We took the precaution, however, of engaging one of the youths, who had been the most zealous advocate of the scheme, as our guide. In half an hour we had reached the summit of the much-slandered pass, and sent back our lad well repaid for his trouble. The only difficulty we had encountered was that the path for a considerable distance ran along a narrow ledge of rock or sand, overhanging an ugly precipice. Once, however, it was necessary partially to unlade the pack-horses.

The descent on the opposite side was much longer. We passed on the way a monastery dedicated to St. Theodore or Theodosius, where there were some twenty-five monks, most of whom came out to see us. They were attired, not as ordinarily in long black gowns, but in garments of sheepskin, and wore conical caps. Below we found our way into a narrow but rather fertile valley, passing a couple of villages evidently of Albanian or Bulgarian origin, and thence into that of the ancient *Clitor*, whence we could distinctly see the hamlet where we were to lodge. J. went on with the baggage and our guide, while H. and I dismounted, in order to explore the ruins of the ancient city. This we did without difficulty; for, excepting the slight remains of one or two temples, and the half-obliterated site of a theatre, the sole interest is associated with the walls, which are preserved or traceable through almost their entire circuit. Being on a plain, they take advantage of a continuous hillock, along whose crest one side of the quadrangle runs, following its sinuosities. They are protected at distances of one hundred feet by round towers about twenty-three feet in diameter, almost half embedded in the walls. This construction, as far as we saw, was quite unique among ancient fortifications. We followed these walls, which are now rarely more than four or five feet high, for some distance through the cornfields, and over a soil abounding with fragments of broken pottery and building materials. Reaching the khan, we found our companion J. in vain attempting to explain to half a dozen boys, who were offering him a handful of old coins, that he wanted none of their treasures. We satisfied them by buying one or two; but I set more value upon a small copper piece that I had myself picked up on the site of the neighboring ruined city. Our khan was excellent. I am not sure that it possessed a single window-sash; but it was spacious. The whole house, some fifty feet long, consisted of one large room, and was provided with a plank floor. We occupied one end of it, and made no inquiries as to those who ensconced themselves in the other, after once putting an interdict upon all smoking and boisterous merriment, prolonged far into the night.

We were late in getting under way the next morning. The hamlet where we lodged is merely a summer village belonging to a place a few miles distant named Maza, and, I presume, is abandoned in winter. It stands on a small eminence in a very picturesque mountain valley, bounded toward the northeast by Mount Khelmos. We were still in Arcadia; and this morning as we rode, I heard for the first time the shepherds on the mountain sides playing on their pipes to collect their flocks about them. In the fields the farmers were just commencing to plough, and for this purpose employed the same rude instrument that is in common use throughout the East. This agricultural implement, which some, with a certain show of plausibility, maintain has undergone no improvement since the days of good old Homer, consists of a long pole with an iron point that serves as a coulter, while two bent boards on the sides represent the share. The labor of ploughing, which is done with oxen or cows, is not severe, as the plough merely *scratches* the ground to the depth of three or four inches.

Our monotonous rides are now and then diversified by the wranglings of the *agoyates*, or hostlers. Evidently our guide is no great favorite with them, as he has no manner of patience with their stupid blunderings or indolence. If they loiter on the way when separated from us, or are unnecessarily long in saddling and lading the horses, he shows his displeasure by such a volley of oaths as quite disconcerts the poor fellows. One of them, Athanasius by name, came to me and declared he never would travel again with Nicholas as long as he lived. The guide had been making use of a favorite oath of his, in which he wished that his Satanic majesty might take, not only him, but his father and his mother, including in the same category such of his more distant relatives as he went on to specify. No wonder that the *agoyates* felt aggrieved. As a general thing, however, the oaths employed by the Greeks are not by any means so shocking as those blasphemous expressions that greet our ears at every turn in America and England. In asseverations, too, the name of the Virgin or some one of the saints is commonly substituted for that of the Deity.

It took us a couple of hours to reach the eastern end of the valley, where the celebrated *katavothron*, or chasm, is situated, through which the waters of Lake Phonia, after having disappeared in a similar cavernous outlet, reappear as the principal source of the River Ladon. These form a small sheet of water, thirty or forty feet across, and of unknown depth in the middle, where the water comes up rapidly. As the surface, however, is placid, the appearance of this katavothron is altogether dissimilar to that of the Erasinus, the outlet of the neighboring Lake Stymphalus, which we saw near Argos.

At the end of three hours and a half of slow traveling we commenced the ascent of the pass toward the Lake of Phonia, from the village of Lycouria. The sides of Mount Saita were steep, and covered with a growth of pine-trees; but from the highest portion of our path we were rewarded with a magnificent view of the lake. This quiet sheet of water is about five miles long, and oval in its general shape, making, however, a considerable bay upon the west. On every side the lake is surrounded by high mountains cutting off all egress. Should the subterranean passages become entirely choked up, the waters would accumulate until they obtained sufficient force to break through, or attained the height of a pass opposite to that on which we now stood, and which, I believe, is the lowest point in the entire circuit of the mountains. In other words, they would have to rise over nine hundred feet before they would overflow this vast natural basin. The present surface of the lake is about twenty-two hundred feet above the level of the sea. The effect of this alpine scenery, and of the brilliant glassy surface of the water lighted up by the sun, was exceedingly striking, and contrasted favorably with the ordinary mountain landscapes in the midst of which we had been traveling.

During our descent toward the lake, the straggling clouds gradually collected on the mountain tops, and soon enveloped their sides. The moment we reached the water's edge, a most violent rain commenced, for which we were quite unprepared. Coverings were hastily thrown over the luggage, the *agoyates* drew themselves within their heavy capotas, and H. threw around him an impervious Scotch plaid. But our umbrellas furnished the rest of us little shelter, and the horses could not be induced to face the pelting storm. The rain, however, was as transient as it was heavy, and we soon proceeded along the margin of the lake toward the village of Phonia, over a ledge of rocks full of cracks and seams, which rendered it difficult even for a pedestrian to traverse it. Nicholas being behind, H. led the way, and, by some mischance, strayed from the path, until at length, urging his horse to mount a very high rock, the animal put one of his feet into a hole, from which he was unable to withdraw it. The horse struggled to get free, and must infallibly have broken his leg, had not H. held him near the feet, while I caught him by the head and prevented his rising. It was some minutes before the rest of the party came up, and after the horse had made several ineffectual struggles, which we had great trouble in subduing, they succeeded in extricating the unlucky foot. On regaining the path, we proceeded toward the village of Phonia, near which we turned aside through the fields to view the site of the ancient city of Pheneus. It is a peninsula, connected with the main land by a narrow isthmus, much resembling that of Epidaurus. A conical hill occupies the northern part, with remains of polygonal walls around the base. From the top the prospect was pleasing, and the snowy cap of Mount Cyllene, to the northeast, formed the most characteristic object.

We climbed up to the village, perched in a much higher situation, on the side and top of a hill, whence, after a slight lunch, we rode on for three-fourths of an hour to the Monastery of St. George, our quarters for the night. At the moment we entered, the few inmates were engaged in their afternoon devotions. Presently, however, their monotonous tones died away, and a fine old man came to greet us. The monastery was a large one, but not in very good repair. We were conducted to an upper chamber opening upon one of the galleries that ran around the court. The room was destitute of chairs; a carpet had been spread before the capacious fireplace, and there were a number of Turkish cushions for us to recline upon. We were more in want of a good fire to dry ourselves by than any thing else. Our monk soon had it kindled on the hearth, and we disposed ourselves to spend the hour, until our dinner should be ready, in chatting with our host.

As he himself informed me, our worthy friend was seventy-four or five years old, and had resided here ever since the age of ten. Clad in the ordinary monastic costume, with a black robe reaching to his feet, and a black cap on his head, he presented, with his long white hair and beard, altogether a patriarchal appearance. The monastery, he said, contained but twenty monks, besides ten novices; and he complained that it had been sadly impoverished of late. Its only property consists of lands, some of them bordering on the lake, a great part of which have been for years submerged. The three small channels through which the lake once found an outlet have been periodically choked with sand, wood, stone, and other materials. All efforts to clear them have failed, but the lake has ceased rising for the present. The monk says that there has been a sort of fatality about the matter. The very year that the Revolution commenced in Greece (1821) the waters began rising, and continued to do so until the coming of King Otho, when there ensued five years of prosperity.* The southern end of the lake is the deepest. Altogether the old man was very much inclined to repine at the dispensations of Providence, which, he said, had reduced the monastery to such straits as to render it too poor even to support an abbot.

* That faithful chronicler, Pausanias, assures us that of old the waters rose to such a height that they inundated the city of Pheneus, and that marks of the point they reached still remained on the sides of the mountains. The inhabitants attributed the construction of the subterranean canal to that convenient workman, Hercules, who had freed the neighboring Lake of Stymphalus from its horrid birds.

RUINS OF THE TEMPLE OF JUPITER AT OLYMPIA.

CHAPTER XVI.

STYX—MEGASPELION—VOSTITZA.

THE rain was falling without intermission when we rose on the morrow, and it seemed quite useless to undertake to proceed on our journey. Meanwhile, our friend the monk insisted on showing us the chapel, or church, standing quite detached from the rest of the buildings. It was one of the neatest in Greece; and the fresco paintings upon the walls, though executed in the last century, were still brilliant and pleasing. Our admiration was most excited by the sight of the shrine separating the holy place, where stands the "sacred table" (the Greeks do not call it an altar), from the body of the church. It was of gilt wood very highly ornamented and carved, and said by the monks to be the richest work of the kind in the country.* The conversation turning upon the priesthood, I elicited my cicerone's sentiments as to education. "Young priests," said he, "rarely go to the University to study. There are schools at Nauplia and some other

* From an inscription, it appears that the monastery was founded in a valley midway between its present site and Phonia in the year 1334, and was removed thence on occasion of a great overflow of the lake. The church was built in 1754 or 1768, I forget which. There are but few books in the establishment, and no regular library.

places, where they can obtain quite as much learning as they will need, and it is found advisable to give them no more. Philosophy *atheizes* them; and by the time they have completed their academic course, they are but too ready to abandon the sacred office."

Before long the rain held up, and we thought that we might with prudence venture out. We had wished to reward our attentive monk for his kindness, besides the remuneration given to the monastery for our entertainment. Out of motives of delicacy, my companions had insisted on giving it to him under the form of a contribution to the church he had been showing us. Just as we were leaving the gate, we were witness to an animated discussion between him and our Nicholas, from whom he was endeavoring to extort payment for some fire-wood. When he was told that we had already much more than canceled that score, he averred he could never think of touching a "lepton" of our donation, which must be strictly applied to sacred purposes.

It was out of the question for us to reach Calavryta that day. The best we could do was to make a short advance, and spend the night at the village of Solos. On our way, we enjoyed for a time a clear view of Mount Khelmos on the left, and of Cyllene, or Zyria, on the right, both of them thickly covered with recent snow. But the clouds were not long in collecting about the mountain tops, whence they rapidly descended and deluged us with rain. Altogether, we had a dismal afternoon of it. We were glad when, after passing the villages of St. Barbara and Zaroukla, we turned into a branch of the same valley, and entered one of three or four villages picturesquely perched on its sides. The small stream running through it is supplied by the Styx. We wandered through Solos for some time in quest of accommodation for the night, and, finding no suitable house, were quite at a loss what to do. Just at that moment, an officer of the army issued from his door close by, and, as soon as he heard there were some strangers hunting for quarters, pressed us with much cordiality to make our stay with him. His house was by far the best in the place. Our portable tables, beds, and chairs, were not put in requisition for the night, and we were favored with the presence of our host and a nephew of his at meal-time. The young man was able to give us important information respecting the condition and history of this district. He prided himself not a little upon the patriotic exploits of his father, whose name he pointed out to me in a recently-published work of Speliades on the Greek Revolution. Nicholas X. Soliotes was one of the original conspirators, to whose vigorous plans and no less energetic execution of them, the successful outbreak of popular vengeance was in great measure due. As soon as it was agreed to commence the momentous struggle, he was the first to draw his sword from the scabbard and fall upon the unsuspecting Turks. The first man slain in the Revolution fell under his hands; and he had increased the number of his victims to eleven before many days elapsed. When he rose to leave, our young friend invited us to pay him a visit at his own house; but, besides the fatigue we experienced, we were scarcely in trim for an evening call. Subsequently, our guide warmly censured us for declining; and assured us that we had missed a capital opportunity of seeing several very pretty Greek girls, the daughters of the revolutionary hero.

I was much struck with the simplicity of the lamps in ordinary use. The shape has scarcely varied from remote antiquity; if any thing, it is even more simple than formerly. One that I noticed here consisted of a small, oval tin saucer, with a short spout at one end. On this the wick rested, the greater part being coiled in the bottom of the saucer, which was half full of oil. At the other end, an upright strip of tin, bent above, served as a handle and support. This sort of lamp may be seen in almost every shop, except where a still more primitive method is resorted to. In the shoemakers' stalls, torches or tar lights are employed. No whale-oil is to be found in the kingdom. Olive-oil is universally burned in the lamps.

Our baggage left early in the morning for Calavryta by the direct route. We hired a guide to conduct us to the celebrated fall of the Styx; for Nicholas did not feel sufficiently familiar with the way to lead us thither. We followed up the same ravine in which Solos is situated, keeping far above its bottom, until we reached the foot of Mount Khelmos. The path generally ran on a ledge of earth that threatened every moment to give way under our feet. Our guide, a peasant from the valley, who should certainly have been accustomed to tramping through the snow, wished to lead us along an easy path, by which we could advance but a short distance, and then gain only a distant view of the Styx. He assured us most vehemently that the other road was quite impassable on account of the snow. The truth was, that, in consequence of the recent violent storms, it was difficult to get up high on the mountains, whose summits were covered with fresh and deep drifts. We insisted, however, on trying the more difficult path leading up the left bank of the Styx, whose fall is visible from below. After traversing a rugged tract, and surmounting the rocky hills at the base of the mountain, we commenced the ascent of the mountain itself. Leaving our horses, we proceeded about an hour, crossed several beds of snow of limited extent, and succeeded in reaching a spot whence we could gain an excellent view of the stream. Any nearer approach would have been exceedingly difficult at this season of the year, even had we possessed a guide worthy of the name of a mountaineer.

The far-famed "River Styx" is composed of two rills of water springing from the melting snows on the topmost level of Mount Khelmos, a few feet from each other. They run but a short distance before coming to the verge of a frightful precipice several hundred feet in height, over whose perpendicular face they leap at one bound into the chasm below. The amount of water they contain is very small, and long before they reach the ground they are transformed, as it were, into a thin spray by the resistance of the atmosphere. The cascade is surpassed in point of height and volume by many waterfalls in Switzerland; but various circumstances have combined to give it, both in ancient and modern times, the reputation of possessing supernatural qualities. The locality is wild and secluded, far from the dwellings of men. From the valley an indistinct view of it can be gained at one or two points only; its base, if accessible at all, is quite out of reach during three-fourths of the year, and the springs are covered with snow during an equal period, while the water at all seasons is of an icy coldness. The latter circumstance gave rise to the opinion that the water of the Styx was so deadly, not only that no man could drink it with impunity, but that even upon inorganic substances its influence was no less potent. It was imagined to be an almost universal solvent. "Vessels, whether of glass or crystal, or murrhine, or of earth, or of stone, are broken by this water," says Pausanias; "and vessels of horn, bone, iron, brass, lead, tin, silver, amber, and even of gold, are dissolved by it. But it can not injure the hoof of the horse: this material alone is not destroyed by the water." "It was natural enough that some difference of opinion should prevail as to the substance which had the virtue of resisting this terrible fluid," Colonel Leake remarks, "seeing that most certainly the experiment had never been fairly made. Plutarch gives his testimony in favor of the hoof of the ass. According to Pliny, it was the hoof of a female mule. Vitruvius seems to admit that of a mule of either gender. By Theophrastus the virtue was confined to vessels of horn, in which he is supported by another ancient author. It would appear, however, from Philo of Heraclea, Ælian, and the epigram at Delphi, that even among horns there was but one kind capable of resisting the Stygian water, and that was not very easily procured, being the *horn* of a Scythian *ass*."*

Some said that Alexander the Great was poisoned by means of the deadly water; but on this score the ancient world was not unanimous. It is, perhaps, the most singular circumstance of all, that the old superstition has survived all the changes of dynasties, and the wars and immigrations that have metamorphosed the aspect of society. Even our guide was unwilling to imitate our example, and drink of the pernicious stream. It is now called the Black Water, or Mavronero. Lower down, after its junction, the water is esteemed innocuous enough, and, indeed, it differs in no respect from the surrounding streams in taste or color.

Our peasant guide told us that during the Revolution, when the Turks invaded this district, the inhabitants of the villages took refuge here in large numbers on the rocks below the

* Travels in the Morea, iii., p. 164.

Styx, and were pursued a part of the way by the Turks. Of these refugees, three hundred, he said, lost their lives by being precipitated from the lofty and difficult rocks, to whose intricacies they were unaccustomed. The same statement was corroborated by another person; but precisely how much faith is to be attached to either the fact or the numbers, we were unable to determine.

We descended from the Styx, and, after rejoining Nicholas, dismissed our mountain guide, who readily confessed that he had told us that the path we had followed was impracticable only in order to spare himself a little fatigue. A new ascent awaited us in crossing one of the spurs of Mount Khelmos, which intervenes between this valley and the town of Calavryta. On the summit we came upon a high plateau, some 4000 to 4500 feet, I should judge, above the sea's level, where the snow lay scattered about in patches. On the uncovered spots a number of men were to be seen ploughing and preparing the ground for sowing wheat or barley, while the crocuses and a few other of the early spring plants were in full bloom on the very margin of the melting snow-banks. A few minutes' ride brought us in sight of Rumeli, or Northern Greece, with its long line of mountains retreating from Helicon and Parnassus, till, toward Patras on the west, it seemed to mingle with the heights of Peloponnesus. Before it lay extended the narrow Gulf of Corinth, without a sail to give its blue waters the appearance of life and activity. Behind us there was a confused mass of mountains and hills, among which a small lake lay embosomed.

After a long descent, we reached the town of Calavryta, the largest place in these parts, most interesting from the fact that here the first steps were taken to excite the outbreak of the late Revolution. The events of that contest are yet too recent in date to be invested with a romantic interest: the heroes who figured in it have not wholly passed off from the scene of contemporary history; and their actions, viewed too much in the mere connection of the events to which they naturally stand related in point of time, and too little in reference to the great results not yet terminated to which they conduced, have not yet been fully appreciated. Fifty years hence the world will do honor to the patriotism and self-sacrifice of the Greek revolutionary soldier; and travelers will make pilgrimages to the sites of the more illustrious conflicts between Christian and Infidel. On our way down the mountain, our guide had pointed out to us in the distance a large edifice about a couple of miles southward of Calavryta as the Monastery of St. Laura, where the plan of revolt already concocted at Patras was fully perfected by the original conspirators, who, headed by the archbishop of that city, had gone thither, upon the pretext of a journey to Tripolitza, to escape the narrow inspection to which the presence of the Turks subjected them. From this place, when the plot was quite ripe for execution, letters were sent throughout the breadth of the land to apprize all the patriots of the design.

Calavryta is quite an ordinary town, though better built than most of the interior places. The plain, some three or four miles long by three quarters of a mile wide, is fertile and well watered. Somewhere upon it stood the ancient city of Cynætha. On arriving, we found that our baggage had gone on toward the monastery of Megaspelion; but our horses were considerably jaded, and we were tired, and hungry enough to enjoy a lunch during the three quarters of an hour we staid at Calavryta. What time remained was profitably employed in making purchases of various articles, such as the more respectable shops were possessed of, and in replenishing J.'s tobacco-pouch, which had not been proof against the heavy drafts made upon it while we were traveling in the back districts of Arcadia. The streets, or rather lanes, are rarely more than a dozen feet wide; and the small shops, entirely destitute of windows, are thrown quite open to the street. A wide counter occupies almost the whole breadth of the front, upon which the greater part of the commodities are exposed for sale. Cobblers and tin-smiths alike sit cross-legged upon them, with their tools and wares by their sides. Thus situated, they keep a sharp look-out on every one that passes, and can gossip as much as they please with their neighbors.

Our presence among them aroused the curiosity of the talkative townsmen. Perhaps our laying in a store of straw hats, and of the Indian weed, augmented it. At any rate, a knot of idlers soon gathered about us while we were lounging around the khan waiting for our horses. They seemed determined to find out all they could about our destination, and we had as firmly made up our minds not to gratify them. A young fellow from the Ionian Isles accosted H. in Italian, and soon contrived to inquire whether "their excellencies were bound to Patras;" to which H. replied, that, though not impossible, it was yet doubtful whether we would go to that place. The questioner then mentioned a number of other towns to which he might suppose us *en route;* but, as the answers were somewhat enigmatical, he gained very little light in his search for information. Somewhat nettled at his poor success in eliciting that wherewith to satisfy his companions' curiosity, we heard him suggesting to them in Greek, as they beat a retreat, that most likely we were traveling without passports; but, whether our appearance did not justify them in setting us down as *klefts* or smugglers, or they did not care to make the inquiry, that was the last we heard of the matter.

From Calavryta we had before us a two hours' ride to Megaspelion, along the pleasant banks of the small river Buraicus, winding through a narrow valley toward the Corinthian Gulf. The monastery is by far the greatest, richest, and most famous in Greece proper. Imagine a vast cavern upward of a hundred feet in height, and much wider, as the niche in which this curious establishment is situated, and this on the steep side of a mountain at a considerable distance above the ravine. The approach is along the hill-side by a path winding gradually toward it, and which might easily be defended against a host of invaders. The steep land-slopes are cultivated in front of it in a succession of terraces, each presenting the appearance of a garden. As we drew near the building, there could be nothing more singular than its appearance. A single wall, one hundred and eighty feet long, and seventy or eighty high, closes up the lower part of the cave's aperture. It is no less than twelve feet thick, and offers little hope to the assailant of his being able to force his way within. Above, it is pierced with windows, and surmounted by seven or eight wooden houses of curious and diverse aspect, built more or less lofty, according to the irregularities of the cave's mouth, and leaning against the almost perpendicular rock that towers three or four hundred feet aloft. The light materials of which they are constructed contrast singularly with the massive proportions of the wall that supports them, and from which they project considerably in different places with staircases and covered galleries sustained by props.

MONASTERY OF MEGASPELION.

We rode around to the solitary portal situated at the southern end of the great wall; and here dismounting, we were welcomed by a number of monks, who were seated on a circular seat at the door, enjoying the shade and the evening breeze. Oriental custom required us to sit down and converse with them before entering the monastery, to which they welcomed us with much apparent cordiality. It devolved on me, as spokesman, to give the chief dignitaries some explanation of the nature of our tour, and to answer whatever interrogatories their curiosity might prompt them to make. As usual, these related principally to the affairs of the capital, but more especially to any new phase which the question of the possession of the Holy Sepulchre at Jerusalem had assumed since the last advices. As it was between two and three weeks since we had left Athens, we could give them little information that was new. H. had visited Megaspelion, when cruising in the Mediterranean in his own yacht, a couple of years since; but such is the number of strangers who from time to time come here to pass a night, that, naturally enough, the monks did not remember him. Profiting by a pause in the conversation, we excused ourselves on the ground of our day's travel, and betook ourselves to the room prepared for our reception, in one of those singular overhanging houses that crown the monastery wall. It seemed to be the best guest-chamber in the edifice. We were assured that we were but following in the footsteps of royalty, King Otho and Queen Amelia being uniformly entertained in this room whenever they come hither.

In the morning we were conducted through the building. The church, of course, was the part that the monks took most delight in exhibiting. Croziers and crosses, curiously carved, with other articles of solid silver, were proudly and admiringly displayed. But it was the holy "eikon," or picture of the Virgin, made, as we were informed, by the hands of St. Luke himself, and discovered during the Middle Ages by a princess of imperial blood, for which they expected the greatest veneration. The monks bowed profoundly and crossed themselves frequently before it, and reverently kissed the glass with which it is protected from the too rude salutations of the vulgar. This ugly portrait is, in fact, a bas-relief of poor execution, on a blackish wood, and does little credit to the skill of its reputed author. If authentic, it would seem to prove that St. Luke, besides being a wretched dauber, was a very inferior sculptor. Fortunately for the artistic reputation of the saint, there are tokens of its being a product of mediæval times, as evident as are to be found in any portrait ascribed to the same source in the Italian churches. The brazen gates of the church, made at Jannina in Epirus, some seventy or eighty years ago, are of elaborate workmanship.

From the church we were conducted, through intricate corridors and dark stairways, to the kitchens, the baking-rooms, the refectory, and the wine-cellars—each department being on a scale commensurate with the size of the monastery and the number of its inmates. There were a number of large casks of wine in the cellar, the two largest, *Stamato* and *Angelica*, being enormous. Their exact capacity I can not tell;

but the weight of the wine they could contain is estimated respectively at 40,000 and 60,000 pounds.* The wine kept here is all produced by the vineyards belonging to Megaspelion, and intended for home consumption. Not less than 160,000 or 170,000 pounds of wine are drunk at the monastery in the course of the year. Most of the revenues of the establishment are derived from the sale of the Corinthian currant, about 400,000 pounds of which are yearly sold by its agents. This year the crop has so signally failed, that the holy friars are in great trouble respecting their resources.

The library is contained in a small, dark room, and is kept perpetually under lock and key. There seemed to be about a thousand or fifteen hundred books and bound manuscripts; but in former times much larger and more valuable collections existed here. On two different occasions the library fell a prey to the conflagrations which reduced the monastery to ashes, notwithstanding the tutelar care of the sacred image of the "Panagia" in the chapel. The remaining manuscripts are principally transcripts of the Greek liturgical works and of the Gospels, and many of them are beautifully illuminated, after the manner of the Middle Ages. We could not examine the works critically in the short time at our disposal; but this had undoubtedly been done by others before us. It is a remarkable fact, that this small library is probably the largest collection of books to be found in any monastic institution in Greece; while the number contained in the monasteries of Mount Athos, in Turkey, though much larger, is not supposed to be very considerable. The incessant wars to which this fair but most unfortunate country has for ages been subject, the spoliations of western travelers, and the ignorance and carelessness of the inhabitants, all combined, are scarcely sufficient to account for such a total dearth of mediæval literature.

We strolled through the gardens and along the hill-side for a fine view of the monastery, to commit to paper, while the "hieromonachus," who had been our chief guide, pointed out to us the elements of its strength, and narrated the most striking incidents of its history. In 1770, during the revolt in which the Peloponnesians madly involved themselves by giv-

* 16,000 and 24,000 okes.

ing faith to the lying promises of Russian emissaries, the wary monks stood aloof, and, indeed, lent their aid to the Turkish captives, multitudes of whom they fed, lodged, and sent in safety to their own homes across the Corinthian Gulf. This kindness proved the salvation of Megaspelion, and was amply rewarded by the protection extended to the truly philanthropic monks.

Such a course was no longer practicable when the flames of the Revolution of 1821 burst out, and the conflict was a struggle, not for mere political supremacy, but for national and individual existence. The question now to be decided, was whether a single Greek should be permitted to breathe; for a deep scheme had been laid by the Sultan and his advisers to annihilate every vestige of the Hellenic race, and replace it by a barbarous horde of Albanians and Turks, that should render more implicit obedience to the Porte's commands. It was, consequently, one of the objects of the Turkish generals to reduce this fortress, commanding so important a passage between the Gulf and the interior. But the monk pointed out with pride the spot where the intruders were met and repulsed by the "Pallecaria," or braves, collected by the monastery. On a former occasion, we were informed, the enemy had climbed to the top of the cliff overhanging the cave, whence they hurled down huge fragments of rock, with the intention of overwhelming the building; but the projecting ledges themselves protected it from injury. With superstitious reverence our guide directed attention to one large boulder on the verge of the impending rock, which seems to be just about to fall. The invader had, with much toil, conveyed it to its present situation; but the Virgin, the patron of the monastery, interposed her power, and miraculously secured it fast just as it was about to descend.

There are altogether some two hundred monks at present in the building, besides fifty more attending to the cultivation of their farms in different parts of the Morea. Their life is an easy one, and their accommodations are much superior to those of the common people, by the sweat of whose brows they live.

Starting early this morning, we took the road for Vostitza.

At first it led along the small stream Buraicus, but presently diverged to the left. We lunched at a solitary khan in full view of the mountains of Northern Greece, and thence descended into a narrow plain bordering on the Gulf of Corinth. While the baggage proceeded at once toward Vostitza, we turned to the right, and rode half an hour or more, to visit the Cave of Hercules Buraicus; but it was scarcely worth our trouble. It contained nothing remarkable, with the exception of some niches, which may have been intended for the reception of votive offerings. We had wandered some distance from the public road, and we now took a more direct course across the plain, which was partly overgrown with myrtle, laurel, and oleander. The vicinity of Vostitza, however, is admirably watered, and almost marshy. It is cultivated chiefly with thriving vineyards of the Corinthian currant, of which Patras is the principal mart. Vostitza itself we found to be more handsome and well built than most Greek towns of its size, and with a population of only a few thousands, possessed of considerable commerce. It is built on the site of Ægium, the most prominent city of the famous Achæan league. Its ancient and modern pre-eminence it owes to a harbor or roadstead, on a coast where there is a great lack of safe anchorage. There are few or no remains of the ancient city, and the most interesting object we saw was a plane-tree of gigantic proportions, growing near the water's edge.*

We wished to cross the Corinthian Gulf at this place, and, as soon as we arrived, empowered Nicholas to make inquiries for a suitable *caïque* to transport us, with our luggage and beasts of burden, to the opposite shore. He soon returned, and reported that there was but one such boat in port, and

* Our guide Nicholas told me that at a small village called Pteri, a short distance northwest of Megaspelion, on the River Buphrasia, there is a much larger plane-tree. It is hollow, and in the cavity twenty-four persons can stand at once. This is pretty well for a country that has suffered so generally from the improvident destruction of the forests. The plane-tree, or *platanus*, is the largest that grows in these regions, and is probably as long-lived as any. There is one upon the banks of the Bosphorus, near Constantinople, which is believed to have been that under which Godfroi de Bouillon harangued the first Crusaders, at the close of the eleventh century of our era.

that the owner, having learned our situation, demanded the sum of one hundred and fifty drachms. The captain came to see us in person, and affirmed he would not abate a jot from the exorbitant price he asked. In reply, we offered him seventy drachms, and assured him that if he refused that price we should go on to Patras, where we were sure of finding an abundance of suitable boats. He left us no less than three or four times, and each time returned with a lower offer. He gradually fell to a hundred and twenty-five, ninety, eighty, and finally seventy, drachms, and agreed to start as soon as we desired.

INTERIOR OF THE ACROPOLIS OF ŒNOE.

CHAPTER XVII.

DELPHI—PARNASSUS—CHÆRONEA.

"Beneath the vintage moon's uncertain light,
And some faint stars that pierced the film of cloud,
Stood those Parnassian peaks before my sight,
Whose fame throughout the ancient world was loud."

Delphi, *An Elegy.*

It was late, however, before we were fairly under way. The chief cause of detention was the difficulty experienced in shipping our horses, which had to be hoisted into the *caïque.* To this unpleasant operation some submitted with very good grace, while others presented a sufficiently ridiculous appearance, by their plunges and struggles in mid air. H. and I had spent the morning in bathing in the Gulf, and visiting the chief shops of Vostitza.

At length we started, with a light but favorable breeze, heading almost directly eastward for Cape Andromachi. Had it blown fresher, we might without difficulty have made the Scala of Salona before nightfall. But the wind died away as we were rounding the Cape and entering the Crissæan Bay, at the bottom of which our destined harbor lay. We were becalmed, however, in the midst of a splendid panorama of mountains; Parnassus and Helicon being most conspicuous on the northern side, and Cyllene, Khelmos, and Olonos on the south. Our mattresses were spread on the deck, for the stench of the small cabin was quite intolerable.

In the morning at daybreak we found ourselves still becalmed, within a mile or two of last evening's position. Toward eight o'clock we passed the town of Galaxidi, and came to anchor opposite the Scala, or landing-place, of the large village of Salona, which lies a few miles in the interior. Here we experienced another delay of an hour or two before setting out for Delphi. We thought it not worth while to go on to Salona, the site of the ancient important town of Amphissa, and, accordingly, took a direct route through Crissa. The valley we were riding through was plentifully watered by streams descending from the hills, and covered with the most flourishing vineyards I had yet seen in Greece. It was not long before we entered a beautiful olive-grove. As usual, the trees are supplied with moisture by means of a system of canals, branching off into multitudes of shallow channels, one of which runs around each tree. Just beyond the grove, we rode by the village of Crissa, which shows some remains of remote antiquity in the way of polygonal walls. Delphi was situated in a valley beyond, and its walls ran along the crest of the hill back of Crissa, but a few hundred yards distant. For some minutes, as we approached them, we seemed to be traversing the cemetery of the city of the Pythian Apollo. Some of the sepulchres were mere sarcophagi cut in the solid rock, while others were chambers of more or less rude construction. We dismounted and entered one apparently the most perfect. It consisted of a single chamber, on three of whose sides were hewn receptacles for the dead, who had long since mouldered away. It is rare to find any traces of the covers of these sarcophagi. In the wall behind two of them were small niches, apparently designed for the reception of statues of infernal or tutelar deities, and perhaps of lamps kept burning there by the devotion of surviving friends. A second tomb we found quite similar to this, and beyond it a third excavation in the form of a semicircular seat, looking out upon the Delphic vale.

This celebrated valley opened upon our view suddenly as we rose rapidly toward the high and precipitous cliffs on the north. My first impression was a feeling of disappointment at its smallness, and I could scarce persuade myself that this was in reality the world-renowned seat of the oracle. Instead of any level piece of ground, Delphi was built on a steep slope, extending probably not over a mile in length, and certainly not half a mile wide from the rocks where we stood to the much more rugged heights on the opposite side. Down below runs the River Pleistus; beyond rises the bold face of Mount Cirphis; and above, on the northeast, are two remarkable crags, in a cleft between which springs the Castalian fountain. Evidently the vale could scarcely be cultivated without the construction of terraces. Accordingly, we find numerous walls of various periods, built as well for this purpose as to serve for the support of the platforms of the numerous edifices. They form one of the most striking features of the spot.

"Still could I dimly trace the terraced lines,
Diverging from the cliffs on either side;
A theatre whose steps were filled with shrines
And rich devices of Hellenic pride.

* * * * *

"The place whence Gods and worshippers had fled;
Only, and they too tenantless, remain
The hallowed chambers of the pious dead."

The rather neat-looking village of *Castri* occupies the very site of the celebrated shrine of Apollo, of which few traces remain. A church of St. Elias is built on the foundation of an antique structure, perhaps the "Palace of the Amphictyons"—a body which met alternately here and at Thermopylæ. On the highest portion of the slope we traced the stadium, so buried by the earth that continually washes down from the hills, that only two of the uppermost seats appear. The Delphic games were periodically celebrated here in honor of the god of divination and the oracle. The theatre was immediately below, but its form only is left imprinted on the soil; and near by is the fountain Cassotis. On the whole, the ruins of Delphi are unsatisfactory, with the exception of the famous fountain *Castalia*, which we visited next. It was of old a curious, open basin, of oblong shape, cut out of the solid rock at the foot of a perpendicular cliff, in which there are still to be seen three niches for statues. There was a secret channel behind, now laid open to view, the object of which was to draw off the superfluous water. In front of the fountain are three or four steps leading down into it. The side of the basin has been much broken, so that now the water runs through as a mere rill. Some Castriote women were washing clothes there, while others came from time to time to draw water. The whole interior, where the Pythia used to perform her ablutions before entering the temple, was filled with a thick growth of thrifty weeds and bushes, and bathing was entirely out of the question. We contented ourselves with tasting some of the sacred water.

This, then, was the famed seat of the oracle, where a frenzied girl, by her delirious exclamations, influenced the councils of distant monarchs, and decided the fates of the globe. Even in its desolation Delphi is beautiful, and no spot could be more appropriate for the shrine of a god than this secluded vale. But when its temples and princely palaces were in their pristine glory, few localities could have presented a more magnificent sight than burst upon the eye of the pagan pilgrims as, in solemn procession, they crossed the hills that seem to isolate Delphi from the rest of the world. The small village of Castri has succeeded to all this glory. Its houses are, perhaps, somewhat more respectable than those of the surrounding places, and its inhabitants lay claim to some sort of superiority over their neighbors, the Arachovites, who are probably of Albanian origin.

Having satisfied ourselves by a visit to each of the remains of antiquity, and examining the inscriptions whose discovery cost the distinguished Müller his life,* we proceeded to the

* Contrary to the advice of his friends and acquaintances at Athens, he attempted a tour through Bœotia and Phocis in midsummer. At Delphi he interested himself much in superintending some excavations on a part of the site of the Temple of Apollo, which were rewarded with the discovery of very valuable inscriptions. Such was his impatience to learn their contents, that, without waiting for the cool of the day, or until they should be transported to some shady place, he sat down in the sun to copy them. A violent fever was the result of this imprudent

private house where we were to lodge. Nicholas meanwhile had been making inquiries respecting the practicability of attempting the ascent of Mount Parnassus. The result was that he brought us two or three men who pretended to be experienced guides. They deterred us from undertaking it, and urged that the great quantity of snow that had fallen of late would render it impossible to reach the summit of the mountain. We scarcely knew how much faith to put in their representations, remembering our deceitful guide at the Styx, and were not too sure that Nicholas (who disliked all mountain excursions) had not persuaded them to tell us this story. The event showed that our surmises were incorrect; but we had concluded at any rate to visit the Corycian Cave, and we should lose no time by visiting Parnassus likewise.

It was a clear morning that we chose for the ascent. At four o'clock we were climbing the mountain behind Delphi, having left orders for our *agoyates* to proceed with our horses and luggage directly to Arachova, a small village some distance above Castri on the Pleistus, where we were to descend. The mules hired for the occasion were by no means remarkable for elegance, and too much inclined to weakness of the knees. The only check upon their propensity to fall was a halter, and, to guide them, it was necessary occasionally to administer a kick to one side or other of the head, as occasion required. With the exception, however, of finding ourselves once or twice landed on our feet over our mules' heads, we suffered no great inconvenience.

We shortly reached an elevated table-land, two thousand feet or more above the level of the sea, at whose extent I was somewhat astonished. We rode some distance over it, and then dismounted to clamber up to the entrance of the Corycian Cave. It is a large cavern, of no great beauty, but deserving a visit for its historical associations. When Xerxes invaded Greece, as Herodotus tells us, the Delphians sent their wives and children over into Achaia, and themselves retired, some to Amphissa, others to the summits of Parnassus and the Corycian Cave. There they lay concealed until

exposure, and he returned to Athens only to linger a few days, and be buried on the neighboring hill of Colonos.

VIEW OF DELPHI AND MOUNT PARNASSUS.

Apollo vindicated his honor by putting to rout the sacrilegious invaders, upon whom they fell and slew a considerable number.* We passed through several chambers with tapers in our hands, having taken off our shoes in order to walk more securely over the slippery floors. Our guides, for the purpose of expediting our visit as much as possible, wished us to restrict ourselves to the principal halls; but we explored the most considerable portion by creeping or crawling through one or more low passages. The Corycian Cave was dedicated to Pan and the Nymphs. At present the peasants call it "*Saranta Aulæ*," or the forty halls.

After leaving the cave, we rode across the plain to the *kalyvia*, or summer village, belonging to Arachova, where there was as yet not a soul to be seen. In the vicinity there was a large pond or mountain lake, whose only outlet is a subterranean one, giving rise, it is said, to the Castalian spring at Delphi. And now commenced the ascent of Mount Parnassus proper, which rises from this high plain. At first our path lay through a wood of pine and fir trees, reaching as far

* Herodotus, 8. 36–38.

as the place where the snow first appeared in considerable patches. There we were obliged to dismount, although usually it is possible to go much farther with mules. Now began our troubles. Our guide, as well as the peasant who accompanied us, was utterly unaccustomed to walking through the snow, and rather than trust himself upon it, even for a short distance, would lead us around twice or thrice as far. Presently, however, it was no longer possible to avoid the snow, and then loud were the complaints of the Greeks at the hardship they were undergoing. It would have been easy in fine weather to have reached the summit within an hour and a half; but at the end of a couple of hours, what with the depth of the snow, the circuitous route we had taken, and the slowness of our "mountaineers," we found ourselves yet a long distance below the highest peak, though high enough to gain a fine view. It would have been more extensive, had not the air been somewhat hazy toward the horizon. It was clearly impossible to reach the summit and return that day. H., who seemed most disappointed, proposed that we should bivouac for the night on the first bare spot of ground we came to, and make the ascent on the morrow. The rest did not relish so much the idea of an exposure to the night air in the vicinity of the snow, without more protection than an overcoat would afford us; but we had some difficulty in persuading H. to relinquish his scheme. In fact, it was rather tantalizing to be so near the top of Parnassus, and yet fail to reach it. As it turned out, it was well that we did not remain; for the next day the mountain tops were enveloped in clouds, which would effectually have deprived us of our desired prospect.

Very unwillingly we turned our faces toward Arachova; and the Greeks, who had positively refused to proceed farther, on the plea of fatigue, once more rose and led the way. Arriving at Arachova, we strolled through the village, which is picturesquely situated on the mountain side. The costume of the women was peculiar. They wore their hair long, and hanging down behind in a long cue; while their red flannel aprons and short dresses gave them quite a picturesque appearance. I had formerly known the "didascalos," or teacher, of the public school, who had studied in the University of Athens; but as the day was now well advanced, and our excursion had been a fatiguing one, we resolved not to seek him out.

From Arachova our plan had been to proceed to the town of Livadia, and thither we sent our luggage directly. For a couple of hours we accompanied it, until we reached the narrow pass of *Schiste*, between Mount Cirphis and the base of Mount Parnassus. At Schiste, in ancient as in modern times, three great roads met, leading respectively to Delphi, to Livadia and Thebes, and to Daulis. Here it was that, according to the tragic poets, Œdipus accidentally met his father, Laius, whom he unwittingly slew, and so fulfilled the prediction of the Delphic oracle. It is a lonely spot, upon which the frowning mountains look down in perfect harmony with such a deed of blood. But toward the east the defile opens, and discloses to the view a portion of the smiling plain of Bœotia, with the Copaic Lake in the midst.

There were three ruined cities, lying considerably to the north of the direct road to Livadia, which we desired to visit. We turned off here, and were not long in reaching the citadel of *Daulis*, overhanging a village of the same name. The fortifications, still remaining in good preservation, occupy the summit of a circular hill, near the western termination of a valley that lies on the eastern side of Parnassus, and opens into the great central plain of Bœotia. From the masonry of the wall, the stones of which are polygonal in form, but approach to regular courses, it would seem that the period of its erection must have been as early, at least, as the fifth century before Christ. But there are also indications of more recent constructions of Frank or Turkish origin.

It was the work of a few minutes to inspect all that remained of Daulis, and we hastily rode on for an hour to the second acropolis—that of *Panopeus*. Our mid-day repast was taken in the hamlet of Ai Vlasi, at its foot. The house that Nicholas chose chanced to have a board floor; but it could not boast a single chair. A broom was borrowed of the hostess; and, having cleared a spot to sit upon, we ate our lunch in peace, without disturbing the women, who, in another part of the same room, were busy picking cotton. The seeds were removed by means of a machine working with three or four rollers—a poor substitute for the American cotton-gin. The hill of Panopeus is lofty, and from its crest the eye takes in the entire plain of Chæronea. The remains of its walls we found to be the most interesting we had seen since leaving Messene, from their height and strength as well as their antiquity. But neither Daulis nor Panopeus have had the good fortune to occupy a prominent place on the page of history.

Not so with Chæronea, whose fortress, some two or three miles farther to the east, was the next object to be visited. Occupying a central position, in the neighborhood of a fertile district, and on the direct route between the monarchy of Macedon and the free republics of Greece, it enjoyed the unenviable distinction of three times furnishing a battle-field upon which the die of empire was cast. The first of these conflicts, in point of time, was of little moment, scarcely exceeding a skirmish between the Athenians and the aristocratic party of Bœotia (B.C. 447), and is lost sight of in the comparison with the fearful contest fought a hundred and nine years later.* Philip of Macedon had at length cast off his mask of dissimulation; for his specious arts, his seductive speeches, and his more potent gifts, had accomplished their full design. Before this, his aim had been merely to gain time, and to secure the undisturbed execution of his plans of aggrandizement. Among the measures taken for the furtherance of these, he counted as no lavish expenditure the bribes given to Æschines and others, whose names are consigned to the same infamy with his. The fault of the Athenians was not so much that they did not act, as that they were perpetually too late in their enterprises. They never moved a finger to save Olynthus or Potidæa, until those cities were ready to fall like ripe fruit into the mouth of the eater. The prophetic eye of Demosthenes had long detected the certainty of the impending struggle, whose scene it was in the power of the Greeks to choose. They might have met and crushed the infant monster upon his own soil, where a victory would have been

* The third and last battle of Chæronea was between the Romans, under Sylla, and the army of Mithridates, who was defeated (B.C. 85).

more decisive, or a defeat less disastrous. Their sloth induced them to neglect the propitious moment, and suffer the conflict to take place at their very gates, and to be no longer, as Demosthenes had long since foretold, one for supremacy and power abroad, but for their own liberty and the possession of Attica itself. Philip was suffered to advance to the banks of the Bœotian river, Cephissus (which flows through the valley we were in), and here upon its banks the matter was decided by force of arms. The exact spot on which the battle was fought can not now be recognized with perfect certainty, for the temple of Hercules that marked it has disappeared. But it is none the less positive that, before evening, this plain was covered with slain, and the hills with the fugitives. The Sacred Band of Thebes alone, to a single man, fell at their posts. From that day the light of freedom never dawned again upon Greece.

THE PLAIN OF CHÆRONEA.

We climbed the Acropolis of Chæronea with much greater alacrity than those we had previously inspected. The hill is loftier and more extensive; but we found the walls in a very poor state of preservation. They seem to have been double, and of great strength. At the base of the hill, on the edge of the plain, we examined a curious little theatre, resembling that of Argos, and, like it, cut out of the living rock. On the face of the rock separating the rows of seats I noticed a rude inscription in very large letters, purporting to be a dedication of the theatre to Apollo; but a part of it is at present scarcely legible. Near by is an ancient fountain, still serving for the neighboring village of Capurna, which is supplied by an old aqueduct. These are the only traces to be found of the city of Chæronea.

Mounting our horses again, we rode for five minutes across the plain to a tumulus opened some years ago. It had long been suspected of being an artificial mound, commemorative of one of the battles fought in the neighborhood. On digging, the revolutionary chief Odysseus discovered a colossal lion of white marble, and of good workmanship, which no doubt was the one described by Pausanias, as erected by the Bœotians over their countrymen who fell on that memorable day by the hand of the Macedonians. It is now in fragments, scattered about the trench, just as it lay twenty years ago. How its destruction was wrought, I can not state with certainty. I was informed by several persons that we owe it to the discoverer himself, who, suspecting that the statue contained some hidden treasure, deliberately blew it up with gunpowder. It need scarcely be added that his avarice was not rewarded with the object of his search. If the alleged circumstance be true, we shall have less reason to regret that such a barbarian met a tragical end in the Acropolis of Athens a few years later.

Leaving Chæronea, we now turned southward. The valley we were also quitting seemed fertile, and well watered by other streams, as well as by the Cephissus, which, entering it from the north, nearly opposite Panopeus, flows through the lower portion to join the Copaic Lake. But though susceptible of such general cultivation, we were struck with the fact that scarce a third or fourth part seems to be tilled. True, some allowance must be made for some of the crops, such as maize, cotton, and tobacco, which were yet to be planted during this and the ensuing months. Still it can not be denied that a very large portion of Greece is not cultivated at all, and of that portion reduced to some kind of cultivation there is little that is cared for as it should be. Covered as the country is with a network of mountains and hills, its valleys are most of them tolerably rich, some of them even exceedingly fertile;

and all the products of the temperate zones might be raised in abundance. There is not the slightest doubt that a much greater population could be sustained. Nicholas, with whom I was conversing on the subject this afternoon, said that, from what he had seen of the country (and there was scarcely a district that he had not traversed), he was certain that, instead of a million inhabitants, Greece should support three or four millions. And how can we doubt that, in Hellenic times, when the teeming population could not be nourished by the domestic produce, and recourse was had to the granaries of Pontus and Egypt, with a much higher degree of cultivation, Greece may have contained at least five or six million souls, exclusive of Thessaly and Epirus?

Our ride to Livadia was uninteresting, but was diversified by an accident which well nigh proved fatal to one of our party, who was precipitated, head foremost, from his horse, but providentially escaped uninjured. Livadia, or Lebadea, as the name is commonly written, is prettily situated, partly on the theatre-shaped hills, and partly in the plain, in the midst of which a smaller conical hill, crowned with a Turkish fortification, formed the ancient acropolis. Here, in a khan, and in the vicinity of an old Mohammedan minaret, we obtained lodgings for the night. While dinner was preparing, we sallied forth to view the modern town. It has certainly retrograded from the time of the Turkish dominion, when it was so important as to give its name to the whole of northern Greece, although even now it is by no means insignificant, with a population of perhaps three or four thousand souls. Finding little to interest, we walked up the narrow gorge behind the citadel, through which the river of Lebadea descends, visiting the probable site of the sacred grove, and of the famous oracle of Trophonius. The situation of the cave is not certain. It may have been one that we saw with its inner extremity blocked up with stones. There are numerous niches cut in the rocks on either side of the ravine, to receive such votive offerings as those who consulted the oracle chose to dedicate to the hero: but, though crevices and caves abound, there is none answering to the deep, mysterious cavern which the devotee used to enter with so much awe: nor have I heard that by entering any of these, a single Greek has lost his accustomed flippancy.*

There is a large fountain close by, the exact counterpart of the Castalian fount at Delphi, with similar niches behind it, and numerous passages in the adjoining rock; and the conjecture seems not improbable that these facilitated the pagan priests in deceiving the people who came to consult the noted oracle. From this and an adjoining spring, copious streams of water issue, which straightway form a respectable river, turning some mills in the town, and watering the plain.

The day that we were to leave Livadia, we found, on rising, that the rain was descending in torrents, and we were, consequently, delayed several hours in the khan, where, for the first time during our tour, there was presented to us that invariable attendant on a Swiss inn—the strangers' book—in which we were expected to inscribe our names. This mark of approaching civilization was due to the circumstance of our being but a couple of days' journey from the capital. The short excursions to which most travelers in Greece limit themselves, rarely extend farther in this direction than Thebes, Livadia, and perhaps Delphi.

About nine o'clock the rain ceased, and we pushed forward toward Scripu, on the margin of Lake Copais. The rain had swollen the torrents, and we were obliged to make a long circuit to avoid them. The Lebadean plain is exceedingly level, and so low that the lake can not be seen from it at all. Yet, though well watered, it is less fertile than that of Chæronea. There was an old monastery at Scripu, into whose large court we drove, and took possession of one of the monks' cells for our mid-day lunch. The church, standing on the opposite side of the square, is extraordinarily large for this retired region. The great quantity of ancient materials employed in its construction is supposed to indicate that this was the site of a temple dedicated to the Graces. Numerous inscriptions, apparently of the time of the Roman domination in Greece,

* Addison's Essay in the "Spectator" contains a livelier and more graphic account than any ancient author of the fabled properties of the Cave of Trophonius, the visitor to which was said never to smile again after his return.

are imbedded in the walls, and a statue or two have been recently dug up. Inside of the church there are several drums of columns of the same singular construction as those employed in the interior of the Phigalian Temple of Apollo, and a few small sculptured marbles fixed in the whitewashed walls, from which the old Byzantine paintings have been effaced.

Scripu occupies the site of the ancient *Orchomenus*, one of the most prominent towns in the Bœotian state, and a persevering enemy of the Theban power. The only ruin in the village itself is the so-called "Treasury of Minyas," originally an edifice similar to the Treasury of Atreus—the more interesting from its mention by Pausanias as among the most wonderful objects in Greece, and the earliest of the remarkable edifices of this construction. I was disappointed at finding so small a portion of the original structure standing, or at least visible (for there may remain a great part of it entire within the hill). In fact, there is nothing to be seen but a portion of the great portal, one of whose immense slabs remains, measuring sixteen feet long by eight wide, and over three in thickness. It presents to us, as it were, a first trial of the architectural skill that reared the monument of Atreus.

The remains of most interest and greatest extent, however, are those of the acropolis, built upon a ridge running up westward from the city, and at the farther end elevated and narrow. This point was occupied by the citadel, which was situated on a high rock, and was reached from within the fortifications by a stairway cut in the rock. Here the walls are in a better state of preservation than elsewhere, rising to some twenty-two courses of stone. The chief point of interest at Orchomenus is its eventful history. In the early ages it occupied the first rank among the Bœotian cities—long the rival, sometimes the superior, of Thebes itself. So limited a territory could contain but one mistress; and it was the lot of Orchomenus to succumb to the power and ambition of the city of Cadmus. Still, in every war Orchomenus was always to be found siding with the other independent cities of the district in defence of their common liberties. It was not till the year 368 B.C., that the project, long entertained, but opposed by the humanity and policy of Epaminondas himself, was, during his absence in the Peloponnesus, actually put in execution: Orchomenus was razed to the ground, and its inhabitants either slain or sold into slavery. At the time that this barbarous measure of policy was consummated, Orchomenus was at peace with the Thebans. Only a few years elapsed before the ruined walls were restored, though the new city never recovered its pristine influence, or a tithe of the wealth it was fabled to have possessed in the days of its old king, Minyas.

It is interesting to notice, in the fortifications now extant, the remains of walls, some of which evidently belong to the fourth century before the Christian era, while other parts are with equal certainty to be attributed to the more ancient city. The walls leading down the hill from the citadel, and inclosing the triangular space occupied by the city, are built of large and irregular masses of stone, such as were employed in primitive times. Hence it seems clear that the destruction of Orchomenus was not complete; but the Thebans were content with overthrowing so much of the walls as to render their restoration the work of months or years.

From the top of the tower, to which we climbed by about ninety steps, we obtained a wide view over the central plain of Bœotia, and extending from Mount Parnassus on the west to Parnes and the distant mountains of Eubœa eastward, with the hills of Locris to the north, and the snow-capped peaks of Cithæron and Helicon toward the south. Below us lay Lake Copais, into which the Cephissus and a number of smaller streams pour their waters. But, although the spring had been uncommonly wet, the lake seemed rather an extensive marsh, with large patches of water in its midst. It has no outlet above ground; but there are *katavothra*, or subterranean passages at the opposite extremity, near Thebes, through which it discharges into the channel of Eubœa, not far above Chalcis. We endeavored to trace out the plan of the citadel, but were not entirely successful, as the walls of which it is composed are somewhat intricate. In the centre was a large excavation, probably for a cistern. The walls from below run up almost contiguous to each other, and seem to have served merely to keep up a communication between the town and the fortress.

The vicinity of Orchomenus was the scene of a battle of considerable interest about the year A.D. 1310. The "Catalan Grand Company," a band of Spanish adventurers, had hired themselves to Walter de Brienne as auxiliary troops. When the Duke of Athens found them too dangerous and unruly subjects, and commanded them to depart, they refused to do so unless their arrears should be paid up, and they be permitted to march into the Morea. They consequently took up their station on the banks of the Cephissus, near Orchomenus, and awaited the attack of the duke, who soon appeared at the head of fifteen thousand men. The Catalans had well chosen their ground. They had turned the course of the Cephissus upon the low lands that intervened between them and the enemy; but the quagmire was concealed by the growth of grass clothing the fields. The first impetuous onset of the gallant knights in the train of the duke involved them in inextricable confusion. Horse and rider floundered and fell in the deceitful bog; retreat was cut off by the very numbers of the army; and all the cavalry fell an easy prey to the cunning Catalans. The rest of the Athenian host, deprived of their duke and generals, turned their backs and fled. Athens itself fell speedily into the hands of the strangers, who for seventy-five years enjoyed the possessions of their former masters. The good old chronicler, Muntaner, oberves that after the victory many a stout Catalan soldier received as wife a noble lady, for whom the day before he would have accounted it an honor to have been allowed to hold a wash-basin.*

We had climbed the hill on foot, leaving our caravan to proceed by the plain. We now detected it in the distance below, skirting the northeastern base of the hill, and engaged in following what is called in modern Greek parlance a "kake scala." The term is applied to any rough ascent, especially where the rock has been hewn out in steps. It is no uncommon thing for the traveler to proceed for a quarter of an hour over what is thus appropriately styled a "bad stair-

* Finlay, Mediæval Greece and Trebizond, p. 175.

ease." It is wonderful to see with what ease the beasts of burden, however heavily laden, ascend paths that would be difficult, if not impossible, for horses differently trained. This is owing in part to the manner in which they are shod, with irons covering the whole under surface of the foot. We soon rejoined our company, who had taken this bad road, as we learned, because of the lake which comes up to the very base of the hill.

We had now before us a ride of two hours and a quarter (not more than seven or eight miles, at the slow rate we were obliged to travel) to the village of Exarcho. The plain was well cultivated, but presented no objects of interest. Just before reaching the village we turned to the left to visit an ancient acropolis, that of *Abæ*. Here was the seat of another of those famous oracles whose responses obtained great renown; and the Apollo of Abæ was said to be more ancient than his namesake at Delphi. This was one of those upon whose predictions Crœsus relied, and misinterpreted or was deceived by it. Xerxes, with his fire-worshipping Persians, committed the temple to flames. The hill is defended on two sides by precipitous rocks, and elsewhere by a couple of parallel walls, about a hundred yards apart, covering the most accessible parts. Their construction is of the second style of Pelasgic masonry, in which the stones are beautifully fitted to one another. Near the principal gate, we noticed with curiosity and admiration a short detached wall, in which, as though for ornament's sake, the stones are large and accurately cut on the edges into circular arcs, and joined in the closest manner.

We retraced our steps to the road, and found our way to the khan of Exarcho, where our Arabian Janni had prepared for us a good dinner, turning to account all that the village could furnish in the way of eatables. When night came, a curtain, formed of H.'s Scotch plaid, was all that screened us from the rest of the household, who were quite numerous.

RUINED TOWER NEAR ŒNOE.

CHAPTER XVIII.

THERMOPYLÆ AND EUBŒA.

THE women of Exarcho and of some of the neighboring villages wear a singular and characteristic costume. Their hair, in general remarkably long and abundant, is braided, and hangs down behind in a cue. To the end of this is attached a long ribbon, and at the lower extremity of the ribbon a number of silver coins and medals dangle almost about the feet of the wearer. Every rare piece of money goes to augment the value of this costly head-dress, unless it be added to a corresponding ornament around the neck. The dress is a cotton gown reaching the ankles, over which is worn a short flannel dress without sleeves; both being confined by a wide belt around the waist. The head is covered with a handkerchief hanging down behind, and the feet are thrust into short, pointed slippers. Altogether, the appearance of a handsome Exarchiote woman is well set off by this costume, of which she is naturally proud. As for beauty, we have been disappointed, in our travels so far, in discovering so little of it. The hard domestic toils to which the Greek girl is subjected, almost from infancy, commonly destroy all traces of fine looks, and give the gait and form of old age to those in whom we look for the freshness and elasticity of youth. We certainly saw as many as ten handsome men, where we found one female whose face was above mediocrity: a fact that would lead us to infer much respecting the tyranny with which the feebler sex are treated in Greece, even if we did not know that they are considered the servants, rather than the companions and equals, of men.

PEASANT WOMAN OF EXARCHO.

Leaving Exarcho, which is a retired place, and somewhat remote from the direct road to Thessaly, we found our way in less than an hour to the ruins of Hyampolis, at Vogdana. The circuit of the walls incloses a small space—six or seven hundred feet long, and half as wide—on very level ground. We followed these walls through their whole extent, and found them to belong, like most of the ruined fortifications in this vicinity, to what may be called the third epoch of Greek masonry—that is, the period when the materials began to be laid in courses, though by no means regular or of uniform height.*

* The masonry of the Greeks, as exhibited in the remains of their fortified cities and tombs, may be conveniently referred to three styles or orders, only the third of which seems to have been employed in historic times. To the first, or Cyclopean order, are to be attributed those walls of Tiryns, for instance, and part of those of Mycenæ, which are built of ponderous masses of stone, scarcely fitted to one another by the chisel, and whose crevices are filled by the insertion of smaller stones. In the second, or Pelasgic, the walls are constructed of polygonal stones, their edges adapted to each other with wonderful precision, and often presenting a smoother and more beautiful face than those of either of the other classes. In the third order the stones become quadrangular, or nearly so, and are laid in regular courses. The second style is known

Soon after passing Hyampolis, the road emerged from the hills, and we entered a valley running westward, and situated along the northern base of Mount Parnassus, of which it commands at every point a magnificent view. At Drachmani, where we stopped at noon, we sent our pack-horses forward toward Pundonitza, while we rode, for a quarter of an hour, to the site of the important city of Elatea. The ruins are very insignificant; but, singularly enough, whereas in most cases the temples and public edifices alone have escaped entire ruin, and not a trace is to be seen of the private houses, here the area of the ancient city is covered with long lines of stones, forming, perhaps, the foundations of the dwellings of the people. In one place, however, there were remains of the pavement and cella of a small temple, whose interior seems to have been divided by a cross wall. The ground upon which the city stood is slightly inclined, and the position was not in itself a very strong one. Yet Elatea, placed on the great route leading from Thessaly into Bœotia, was, after Thermopylæ, the key of Greece.

Almost the first notice we have of Elatea, is the statement that in Xerxes' expedition into Greece it shared the fate of many other cities of Greece, and was destroyed with fire. But the most interesting incident in its history is connected with its seizure by Philip of Macedon in his advance upon Athens (B.C. 338). Although Demosthenes had not ceased to portray their danger, the Athenians seemed struck with judicial blindness, and could not be induced to believe that the wily king was endeavoring, by his intrigues, to compass their destruction. The potent spell, which even the enchantments of Demosthenes' eloquence was not sufficient to overcome, remained unbroken, till the blow that seemed to seal the fate of the Grecian republics fell suddenly upon the sleepers. Its as-

to have been generally discontinued previous to the fourth century before the Christian era, and polygonal masonry was in use at least as far back as the seventh or eighth centuries—perhaps much earlier. The Cyclopean mode of construction was employed, in all probability, for many ages anterior to that period, and is undoubtedly the oldest yet discovered in Greece. For a discussion of this subject, the reader may consult LEAKE, *Travels in the Morea*, i., 377, and C. O. MÜLLER, *Ancient Art and its Remains*, p. 20–22.

tounding effect—in a few moments changing the quiet of unconcern into terror and despair—is described by the orator in a passage which for ages has been cited for its graphic beauty. It was addressed to the people.

"It was evening when a messenger came and announced to the prytanes that Elatea was taken. Then some of them, rising up instantly in the midst of their supper,* drove out those that occupied booths in the market-place, and set fire to the sheds; and others sent for the generals, and called for the trumpeter; and the city was full of uproar. On the morrow, as soon as day dawned, the prytanes summoned the Senate to the council-chamber, while you proceeded to the place of public assembly, and, before the Senate had deliberated and framed its decree, all the people had taken their seats above. Afterward, when the Senate came in, and the prytanes announced what had been reported to them, and introduced the messenger, and he had spoken, the herald asked, 'Who wishes to harangue?' But no one came forward. And while the herald asked repeatedly, none the more did any one rise, though all the generals and all the orators were present, and the common voice of the country called upon whoever was capable of it to give counsel for its deliverance; although, if it had been necessary for those who desired the salvation of the city to come forward, all of you would have risen and mounted the platform."†

It was at this juncture that Demosthenes arose to encourage the dispirited people, and advised the fitting out of that expedition which was brought to so disastrous a termination at the Battle of Chæronea.

Having satisfied our curiosity, we returned to the village of Drachmani, and thence pursued our way toward Pundonitza, crossing Mount Cnemis near a hill of remarkable turret-like form, called Fontana. On reaching the top of the ridge, it became evident, from the absence of fresh tracks on the road, that our baggage-train and J., who accompanied it, though

* The prytanes were a committee of fifty members of the council, who presided in the assemblies of the people, and supped every day at the public expense in the prytaneum.

† Demosthenes de Coronâ, p. 284.

they started before us, had not passed that way. Some peasants whom we met also confirmed our surmises by saying that they had met no travelers. In such a predicament, we concluded to leave Nicholas in the pass until nightfall, while H. and I rode on alone to Pundonitza. The path, it is true, was not very distinct at all times, and it led through a district overgrown with bushes and trees; but, by following the general direction given to us, we descended the ridge in safety, and in a couple of hours found our way to the village.

Our first inquiry on arriving was for the *Papas*, or parish priest, at whose house we had been told we should find a welcome, and the best quarters. On either score we found no reason to complain. The priest seemed to welcome us with unfeigned cordiality, and was overjoyed on finding out who had sent us to his house, and that we could keep up a conversation with him in his own language. He introduced us to his *papadia* (for he was a married man), and as it was late in the afternoon, and we might well be hungry, insisted on setting before us his own simple fare—bread and cheese. We were particularly pleased with the manners and spirit of this poor and illiterate priest, who forcibly reminded me of Papa Trechas, whom all who have read Coray's introduction to Homer's Iliad will remember. In politics his views were liberal, free from the Russian tendencies that render the influence of the clergy so baneful to the country's welfare; while his religion seemed heartfelt, for the most part devoid of bigotry, and very evangelical.

The cool evening air tempted us to spend our leisure moments in strolling to the ruined fort, a short distance off. The village stands upon an extended plateau, on the very edge of the principal declivity of Mount Cnemis, which, on the east, falls abruptly toward the sea, but toward the north overlooks the plain of Lamia and Thessaly. Just at the commencement of the descent stood the ruined Turkish or Frank castle, to whose picturesque ruins we directed our steps, in order to gain the best glimpse of the country beyond. The hillock on which it stands must have been fortified even in the most remote antiquity, so important, in a military point of view, is the situation. Accordingly, we found some remnants of true Hellenic walls, which can be distinguished from all subsequent additions or repairs by the large and regular blocks of which they are composed, and the entire absence of mortar in the seams. Pundonitza was more prominent, however, in the Middle Ages than either before or afterward, and became the seat of a Marquis, who ruled over a large Frank territory, comprising a great part of ancient Locris and Phocis.* But of the Frank period nothing remains beyond a ruined chapel and a cistern or two of large size.

We had nearly given up all hope of seeing our companions before the next morning, when, between eight and nine o'clock, they drove into the court. Nicholas had succeeded in meeting them, and thus relieved us from the disagreeable necessity of losing another day at this place.

On the morrow, we commenced at an early hour to descend from our high position into the lower part of Locris. The eye could not weary of contemplating this extended prospect. The quiet Maliac Bay, or Gulf of Lamia, shut in by the island of Eubœa on the right, occupied the central portion. To the left was the fertile plain of Lamia, watered by the Sperchius, and beyond rose the high mountain range of Othrys, the northern boundary of modern Greece. We were approaching *Thermopylæ*, a couple of hours or more distant from Pundonitza. First, we saw on our left, between the high and precipitous hills above Thermopylæ and the higher Mount Callidromus, the pass—rough and difficult, it is true, but yet practicable—disclosed to Xerxes' army by the treachery and avarice of a neighboring peasant, Epialtes. Through it Hydarnes was sent, with a detachment of the Persian force, to turn the position of the Lacedæmonians, for whom nothing now remained but death or instant retreat. Descending farther, we passed a rivulet or two, one of which was doubtless the fountain where the Spartans were discovered by the Persian spies adorning their hair previous to the contest. Here, too, was the supposed tumulus of the Greeks, over which were inscribed those world-renowned lines:

"Go, stranger, tell the Spartans, here,
Obedient to their laws, we lie."

* Buchon, La Grèce Continentale et la Morée, p. 285.

Near this famous spot are yet seen the foundations of the first part of a great northern wall, built in a subsequent age, and stretching from this point to the shore of the Gulf of Corinth, beyond Delphi. The builders doubtless hoped, by this permanent construction, to preclude the possibility of any future barbarian inroads; but their posterity received a lesson, often taught, but rarely learned, except by bitter experience, that neither walls nor fortresses, be they ever so strong, are of much avail when they cease to be defended by the courage and intrepidity of patriots and freemen.

VIEW OF THERMOPYLÆ.

We reached Thermopylæ at length, and found the spot very different from our preconceived notions. But this disappointment was greatly owing to the changes which nature herself has effected. Thermopylæ is no longer the narrow pass where a few hundred brave Spartans could for days hold at bay the hundreds of thousands of the enemy. A wide strip of land now stretches three miles to the sea, where, as Herodotus tells us, the space between the mountain and the sea was once narrow, and there was but a single road.* In spring and winter a great part of this is rendered impassable by the

* Herodotus, 7. 200.

marshy character of the soil; but in midsummer an army might march through any part of it. This is the result of the long-continued action of the Sperchius and other smaller streams, whose waters are surcharged with alluvial matter, sand, and mud, which they deposit at their mouths. Thus, it is not only a well-ascertained fact that the plain of Lamia has extended itself very considerably toward the east and the island of Eubœa, but the same process is seen strikingly in present operation. The Sperchius, or rather each of its two mouths, has formed for itself a long and curved tongue of land, jutting out like a pier, through which it flows into the sea. Two such moles on opposite sides of the Maliac Gulf have stretched far toward each other, and may, in the course of centuries, unite and inclose a salt lake, which may some day be drained. It will be readily imagined that such a process, continued for a series of years, owing to the shifting of the beds of the rivers, would produce a remarkable change in the physical aspect of the country.

Here, then, it was that Leonidas, with his gallant band, met the overwhelming forces of the Persian king, and perished in the unsuccessful conflict. Here, too, the Roman legions were opposed by a less resolute people. And, last of all, the modern Greeks showed almost equal heroism in the defence of the pass, when the operations of nature, during long ages, had combined with the inventions of modern art to render ineffectual all valor and resolution. What has given to the spot such importance, both in ancient and in modern times, is the fact that the only road from the north, on the eastern side of the peninsula, must enter Greece at this point.

Next to the battle-scene itself, that which interested me most was the celebrated hot spring, from which the neighborhood derived its name of "Thermopylæ," or the "Warm Gates." There are, indeed, two springs; but the most remarkable, by far, is that which rises in the very midst of the ancient pass. Beyond a couple of small salt ponds we reached a plain composed of a white calcareous deposit, formed by the water flowing from the spring. Even twigs remaining a short time immersed in it, are incrusted as with stone; but it is brittle, and cracks to pieces when handled. As we rode over the crust, it gave forth a hollow sound. We tasted of the water, and found it medicinal, with a strong odor of sulphur. Its temperature is about 100° Fahrenheit. There was a company of peasants from the neighborhood, who had come to prove the healing powers of the water; but they informed us that the springs at Neo-Patras, the ancient Hypate, a few miles up the valley of the Sperchius, were in much better repute. If our time had permitted, we should have been glad to make a trip thither.

We now entered Thessaly Phthiotis, whose boundary is somewhere about Thermopylæ. Its principal town, Lamia, or Zeitun, as it was called till recently by the modern Greeks, stood on the opposite side of the plain, pleasantly situated at the foot of the mountains. Its acropolis occupied a hill to the southeast of it. Lamia is said to be a neat and well-built town; but we did not turn from our route to visit it. The vicinity has been the scene of a number of important engagements; and Lamia itself underwent a long siege shortly after the death of Alexander the Great. We rode on to the right, keeping as near to the head of the Gulf as was possible, in view of the marshy nature of the ground, the whole of which in winter becomes a perfect bog. In the vicinity of the village of Birbos, where we stopped for a while at noon, we found an encampment of soldiers, who were occupied in target-shooting. In this neighborhood, however, they see some real service from time to time; for we were now entering the land of robbers *par excellence*. True, all Rumeli, or Northern Greece, is more or less infested by them; but it is here that they may be said to abound. The Turkish frontier is so near, that they can with ease betake themselves thither when pursued; and it is even asserted that they receive encouragement and protection from the local Turkish authorities.

On the north side of the Gulf we fell in with the new road from Lamia to its port, Stylida, the village where we intended passing the night. This was the first carriage-road we had seen for weeks; for, throughout all the rural districts of Greece, all transportation must be effected by the means of beasts of burden. We reached Stylida at an early hour, and obtained good rooms. We had thought of attempting the ascent of Mount Othrys on the morrow; but the impossibility of finding mules, the troubled state of the country, and the reluctance of those who should have served as guides to incur the risk of falling into the banditti's hands, led us to forego the excursion, and spend the next day in a visit to the ruins of Larissa Cremaste.

Before leaving Stylida in the morning, we took care to secure a couple of *caïques*, which were, during the course of the day, to drop down the Gulf as far as the hamlet of Achladi. There we were to meet them, and be carried over to the opposite coast of Eubœa. We again fell into a common footpath, now leading through thickets of tangled bushes, and now through fields of wheat and barley. The soil appeared exceedingly rich, but less cultivated than almost any other portion of Greece—a circumstance, doubtless, due to the extreme insecurity of the entire region, and the impotence of the government to ward off from the unfortunate inhabitants the miseries of rapine and devastation. At a small village named Echinus we stopped to examine the remains of old Greek walls of regular masonry, and lunched at the village of Rachi.

We turned in at the house of the *Papas*, where a mat was spread for us; and, while we ate, he regaled us with a detailed account of an extensive robbery committed here a week before. Early in the morning, one of the band, in disguise, had found his way into the village as a spy, and made sure that almost the whole male population was dispersed in the distant fields, too far away to learn of the attack until it was too late. On his return, the miscreants, who, to the number of forty-five, had been prowling in the outskirts, being satisfied that the way was clear, entered Rachi at about nine o'clock A.M. The first direction of Semos, the captain of the band, was to seize all the fire-arms in the village, and to place the inmates of the fifty houses—women and children almost exclusively—in close confinement, while the robbers searched for all that was valuable and portable. Money, however, was what most moved their cupidity. The numerous silver coins forming the most showy part of the head-dress, and ornamenting the person of the women, were of course the first to be laid hold of. But the ruffians were not so easily satisfied; and, even after their search, they suspected that much property remained hidden. As in Turkey, the Greeks and other *rayahs* are accustomed to conceal their wealth from the rapacity of the Mussulman, under the garb of poverty, so has the unsettled condition of this border country compelled almost every peasant to use similar precautions. Every dollar that can be spared is added to the hoard concealed in some hole in the ground. The process resorted to by the robbers for discovering the whereabouts of these hidden repositories was a cruel, but, as we should judge, a pretty effectual one. A kettle full of oil was set on the fire. If the unfortunate woman, who protested that she was ignorant where her husband had hid his treasure, relented in view of the coming torture, she was not molested. But if she persisted in her obstinacy, or really did not know where it was, the scalding fluid was poured upon her neck, breast, and body. Five or six were subjected to this inhuman treatment; others were merely beaten; and one, whom we saw, boasted that, though the ruffians stabbed her in several places, she had not betrayed her husband's trust.

Notwithstanding all this suffering, strange to say, but one person was murdered, and that was a man against whom one of the robbers, himself a native of the place, entertained a personal grudge. A young man, who happened to be in the village, succeeded in creeping off to one of the neighboring hills, where he discharged his gun as a signal. The country people soon came to the rescue. The band were thus, after a stay of two hours, compelled to abandon the village, though they had not ransacked one half of the houses. The mustered peasants, with a few soldiers, pursued the robbers; but though, after journeying five hours beyond the Turkish line, they came up with them, they recovered only some of the heavier goods that were dropped in the flight.

Our host, the priest, complained with bitterness of his own misfortunes. He said that until lately he had been *ephemerius*, or curate, of Xerochori, in Eubœa; but he had been tempted to leave it, by the promise of a larger salary and a more healthy situation. Fortunately for himself, he was absent at the time of the inroad; but his wife, the *papadia*, was beaten and ill-used, like the rest of the women. The priest estimated his loss at three hundred and seventy-seven drachms, and that of the entire village, according to the schedule which the chief magistrate of the district had drawn up the day before our arrival, could not be less than twenty thousand drachms (about $3350). When we rose to take leave, the papas begged us to speak to his old parishioners about him, and let them know of his misfortune. We fulfilled the commission, a couple of days after, at Xerochori.

Achladi, the little hamlet where we had arranged to spend the night, was but twenty minutes' ride farther. Our pack-horses preceded us, while we dismissed our escort of two *gens-d'armes*, whom Nicholas had insisted on our taking in the morning from Stylida, with a small remuneration that perfectly satisfied them for their long walk. The last we saw of them, they were probably on the way for the nearest grog-shop, to take a glass of *raki* before retracing their steps. As for ourselves, we felt rather more secure without than with them, as two soldiers are little protection against a dozen banditti, even setting aside the chance of their passing over to the enemy, and coming in for a share of the spoils. Relieved from solicitude on this score, we now turned our horses' heads inland, and rode more rapidly toward Gardiki. The country was wild and picturesque, and we found the hill above Gardiki a lovely spot. Here were the ruins of *Larissa Cremaste*, originally an old Pelasgic town, as its first name indicates: the term Cremaste, or "hanging," is in allusion to its steep and lofty site. The summit must be five or six hundred feet above the village, and a thousand above the sea. We made the ascent by following the westernmost of the walls. These are of great interest in a military point of view. Built of large blocks of stone, laid in what approximates to regular courses, they seem to date from the very earliest historic period. The gates are peculiarly worthy of notice. They are set obliquely to the wall, and in such a manner as to follow that invariable rule in Greek military works, that the enemy should be compelled to expose his right side, which was unprotected by the shield, to the arrows and other missiles of those who occupied the walls. Having with me no plan of the fortifications, I attempted to commit to paper some sketch of their outline. This I soon gave up in despair; for to have traced all the complications of walls, running in so many different directions, would have been the work of a day. Had it been only for the superb view obtained from this remarkable spot, we would have been amply repaid for our ride through the sun, on a hot summer's day.

At Achladi we found half a dozen houses; the place is not even laid down on the maps. Our arrival was signalized by an outburst of wrath on the part of Nicholas, who looked in vain up and down the coast for any sign of the *caïques*, which were to have been here this morning. The poor *agoyates* came in for a part of the obloquy that was poured indiscriminately on every individual and object within reach. Even Janni, our inoffensive Arab, was surprised with a volley of oaths; to which, however, accustomed in a measure, he paid no more attention than turning to learn the cause of the sudden squall. Having vented all the expletives he could muster, our Greek rested satisfied, and for the next twenty-four hours exerted himself to prove that he was as proficient in the art of making himself agreeable as in savage passion and abuse.

Fortunately for his temper and ours, too, when we stepped to the window of our room early the next morning, we beheld the *caïques* leisurely coming up to the village. While the men were busy shipping the horses, and getting out the necessary papers, we had ample time for a bath and for scouring the neighborhood in search of antiquities. Our guide sent us on a fruitless excursion to the top of a hill, where we found nothing to compensate for a hot walk. On our return the men were not ready to start. Every petty harbor has a health-officer, or *hygeionomos;* and no craft is allowed to sail without clearance papers from him. The health-inspector of Achladi happened to be on a visit to Athens, and had left in his stead a substitute, who could neither read nor write; and he was off somewhere in the fields ploughing. His *secretary* was at Gardiki, and had to be sent for. When at length he arrived, he demanded as his fee a drachm for each person and beast, instead of one for each boat, to which he was entitled. Here was an opportunity for another storm on the part of Nicholas:

but on our announcing that we would certainly lodge a complaint at Athens, the extortionate official became more tractable, and allowed us to weigh anchor.

The wind was contrary. From noon to night we were tacking about from one side of the narrow strait to the other. At one time we hove to near a favorable spot for Janni to prepare our dinner; and we took advantage of the half hour to row ashore, and using the solitary drum of a column for a desk, we committed to paper some incidents of travel. The shore was wild, wooded, and picturesque. Not a house was to be seen, nor a trace of man's works, but in a ruined chapel near the strand. We had expected to arrive at Oreos before dark, in time to reach Xerochori, so as to have a quiet Sabbath at that place. But the head winds delayed us, and it was early on the morrow when we landed at the former hamlet, after a miserable night spent on the deck of one of our little *caïques*, without room even to stretch ourselves out to sleep. A sail of fifteen or twenty miles through the Straits of Artemisium had taken almost as many hours. The scene of the great naval contest between the Greek and Persian fleets, which took place at the very time that Leonidas was defending the Pass of Thermopylæ on the main land, we did not cross. It lies farther down, and nearer the sea. We saw it afterward very distinctly, on our way from Xerochori to Chalcis, when riding over the highlands.

Oreos is now a mere landing-place, though in ancient times one of the most important towns of Eubœa. Riding up to Xerochori, we passed an eminence lying back of it, surrounded by a wall of ancient materials. In early times the name of the town was Histiæa; but from the days of Demosthenes, who frequently mentions it, it has borne that of Oreos. About midway to Xerochori, we stopped a while, at the hamlet of St. John's, to allow J. time to visit the estate of a cousin of his, Mr. Mimon, who was absent. It is extensive, taking in a number of villages.

At Xerochori—which occupies any thing but a dry situation, as its name would import—we found poor accommodations for the Sabbath. As usual, our Sunday was the noisiest day of the week. After attending church early in the morning, the followers of the Greek persuasion give themselves up to diversions or traffic. It was market-day, and the peasantry of the district were assembled in great numbers. There was a public notary, whose little office, to our great annoyance, adjoined our rooms. He was busy all day reading and writing law documents, and his room was crowded until late in the evening.

Early on Monday morning we resumed our journey toward Chalcis. At first the ground was slightly undulating, but soon we commenced ascending, and found ourselves among those beautiful hills for which Eubœa is noted. It was pre-eminently a "rolling" country, with an alternation of round-topped eminences and fertile vales, both overgrown with pine-trees of a large size for this quarter of the globe. The scenery much resembles that of many regions in the United States. But as yet there is comparatively little cultivation to be seen. As we attained the highest portion of this end of the island, we began to enjoy a very extensive prospect, especially toward the north. There lay the Straits of Artemisium. Beyond the Gulf of Volo, or Pegasus, opened the landscape over the more distant plains of Thessaly. On their right, Mount Pelion raised its lofty peak; and far off in the distance could be plainly distinguished the snowy form of Mount Olympus itself, full eighty miles from us in a direct line. Toward the east the islands of Scopelos and Sciathos appeared in the Ægean.

At the close of a warm but pleasant day's journey, after spending full eleven hours in the saddle, we reached Achmet Aga, a pretty village situated in a hollow, about midway down the island to Chalcis. We had scarcely settled ourselves fairly at the khan, before a servant came to invite us to pass the night at the house of his master, Mr. Noel, who, in conjunction with Mr. Müller, a Swiss gentleman, possesses a large tract of country in the immediate vicinity. While we declined his invitation, from unwillingness to trouble him with the presence of so large a party, H. and I (notwithstanding that the state of our wardrobe, after an exposure to all sorts of weather, was scarcely respectable) went over for an hour or two. We found Mr. Noel, a well-informed and sociable Englishman, living in comparative solitude, and devoting himself to the management of his large farms. Of this independent life he appeared passionately fond, though far from the society of friends and from his native country.* With our circle at Athens he was, of course, well acquainted, especially with Dr. King and Mr. Hill, whose kindness to him when sick he gratefully acknowledged. Mr. Noel gave us much useful information respecting the island of Eubœa, whose long and slender outline, over against the coasts of Attica, Bœotia, and Phocis, every school-boy remembers. Though its dimensions are almost precisely those of Long Island, the population, according to Mr. N., is but seventy-five thousand. So sparse a population is insufficient to cultivate the island to any considerable extent with the agricultural implements now in use. The fields are said not to yield much more than a third as much grain as those of equal extent in England; and this, although Eubœa was once the granary of Athens! All the land is divided into two categories—one half being sown with wheat, and the other lying fallow, according to the popular notion—that is, cultivated with Indian corn or maize!

* I am not aware that Eubœa has ever been considered peculiarly unsafe as a residence for strangers. On the other hand, its natural advantages of position and fertility of soil, as well as the salubrity of its climate, have been lauded in England, as offering greater inducements to colonists than the remote dependencies of Great Britain. Many foreigners, too, have resided there with perfect impunity for twenty years. The sense of security thus engendered has lately received a fearful shock in the murder of Mr. and Mrs. Henry Leeves at their residence near Castaniotissa, not many miles south of Xerochori. The first accounts of this lamentable occurrence attributed it to the numerous banditti expelled from Thessaly by the Turkish troops in the spring of 1854. But I have since heard that it was effected by a band of peasants, headed by the son of the village priest, who had been befriended and educated in part by the benevolence of the deceased. Not content with murdering his benefactors for the sake of the property they had too imprudently brought with them, this fiend in human shape made use of the most cruel tortures to wring from them a disclosure of the place where they had secreted their valuables. When the neighbors entered the house after the sad catastrophe, they found the rooms spotted with the blood of the victims, and handfuls of their hair scattered over the floor. Only the infant son of Mr. Leeves escaped the malignity of the murderers.

The room in which we slept at the khan seemed to be used as a general repository. In one corner was a large heap of husked cotton, grown last year in the neighborhood. We had possession of the rest of the unfinished apartment. Our horses were accommodated in the stable directly below, while Nicholas and the *agoyates* lay down and wrapped themselves up in their huge capotas wherever they found space enough, whether in the entry or on the porch.

Leaving Achmet-Aga the following day, we rode along the little valley through fields of tall barley, until we soon began to ascend a rather difficult defile, which, like many others in Greece, goes by the Turkish name of "*Derveni*." In many places it was nothing but a continuous "scala," or staircase, to which our horses, though poor in other respects, were so well accustomed, that they mounted them with little apparent difficulty, and rarely, if ever, stumbled. In a few hours we gained the summit of the ridge, and then the full prospect burst upon our eyes, presenting us with one of those extensive views of the country which are scarcely less attractive than the sites of ruined cities, or the scenes of famous battles. The central part of the island of Eubœa lay before us. On the right, beyond the channel, was the Bœotian coast, with the summits of Cithæron, Helicon, Parnes, and Pentelicus, in the distance. At one place, along the border of the water, we distinguished the outlet of the katavothra, through which the Lake Copais discharges into the sea. We could discern Chalcis, too, before us, and the narrow Euripus on the other side. But the most striking object was the snow-capped head of Mount Delphi, whose ridge forms the backbone of Eubœa, rising full five thousand five hundred feet above the sea, and serving as a beacon to the country far and wide.

During the entire afternoon, we were crossing a sterile plain in the direction of Chalcis. Here once more we joined a road traveled by carts. As the road ran for a distance along the shore, we noticed the sand wet for a foot or more above the water, showing that it had fallen from the high-water mark. This is the only part of the Mediterranean where the phenomenon of the tides is perceptible, and it is due to the narrowness of the channel between Eubœa and the main land. We suffered much from the heat on the low, sandy plain, and were really glad to reach the gates of Chalcis. This town is situated on a low, sandy promontory. Its moat and wall have fallen into neglect, and only an embankment and a rude ditch now occupy their place. There is, however, an interior fortress, or *castro;* and much of the city used to be, and still is, inside of it. At a distance, Chalcis presents a picturesque appearance, by reason of two large domes of old Turkish mosques that have been suffered to remain. The modern aqueduct winds across the plain, and may readily be mistaken for the remains of some ancient work. As we rode through the streets, we could not but notice how much better Chalcis is built than the towns we had recently seen. The streets, bordered with shops and stands, forming the *agora* or bazar, presented a scene of considerable activity, and of much wrangling. Our ears were saluted by a variety of discordant cries from the country merchants; and we were obliged to jostle through the crowd, crying "varda" ("take care") to the pedestrians. Now and then a donkey, laden with a huge basket on either side, came brushing past us, compelling us to draw up our legs to prevent their being crushed between the beasts. Or, on turning a corner, we came suddenly upon a train of the same patient quadrupeds, down the narrow street in single file, each hidden beneath a towering mass of dry brush, like so many perambulating hay-stacks. Either a hasty retreat was necessary, or we found a convenient refuge in some adjoining portal until the way was clear. The cause of all this activity was, that Chalcis is the only important place on the island, the mart for its products, and the capital of one of the *nomes*, or districts, of Greece.

A curious discovery was made, a few years since, at Chalcis. A piece of the wall surrounding the citadel accidentally fell; and behind it there was perceived to be an opening. This being enlarged, proved to be a passage leading to a room, where were found a pile of coarse bags containing an enormous quantity of ancient armor. The articles were carefully transported to Athens by order of the king, and inspected by the historian Buchon. He pronounced them to belong to the first few years of the fourteenth century. He supposes that after the bloody battle fought at Scripu—the ancient Orchomenus in Bœotia—A.D. 1311, the defensive armor of those who had been slain was gathered together, and laid in this receptacle, from motives of reverence and curiosity. There it lay for five hundred and thirty years, until the casual falling of the wall brought it to light. This hypothesis, so interesting from its historical allusions, is fully confirmed by the variety noticeable in the style of the helmets, about one hundred in number. Some are of the kind worn by the Catalans; others resemble those of the Turcopole troops; while the majority seem to have belonged to the unfortunate Frank knights who fell in the marshy plain, and were overpowered by their opponents. All are rusty and battered, having evidently seen service; so that it does not appear that they were placed in this hidden chamber, as in an arsenal, for future use.*

* Buchon, La Grèce Continentale et la Morée, p. 134.

THE ACROPOLIS OF ŒNOE.

CHAPTER XIX.

THEBES AND ELEUSIS.

CLEAN beds, a tight roof, and windows provided with panes of glass—these were comforts not to be despised by a company of travelers who had been suffering from a continuous exposure to vermin, rain, and wind, in the rude huts of the peasants. With such inducements to tarry, we were reluctant to leave Chalcis when Nicholas came to inform us it was time to rise and renew our journey. We carried with us a pleasant remembrance of the place to Athens itself. At length, when the horses were once more laden, and all was ready, we sallied forth. To reach the bridge from Eubœa to Roumeli, it was necessary to traverse most of the town. On entering the inclosure of the *castro*, we noticed, in more than one place, the well-known winged lion of St. Mark, the emblem of the dominion of republican Venice. Within the fortifications there are many scattered fragments of sarcophagi, and other ancient works of art. We wished to see a large cannon that was said to exist here, similar to the famous one of the Bosphorus; but found, on inquiry, that it had been either broken up or melted into coin. We saw, however, some of its enormous balls, two feet or more in diameter, adorning the walls of the castle. There is nothing of particular interest in the city of Chalcis, which has a population of eight or ten thousand souls. The most striking fact is its position at the narrowest part of the long "sound," where communication between the main land and Eubœa is easiest and most natural.

On reaching the bridge from Chalcis to the main land, our first impression was of astonishment at the smallness of the passage. Toward the upper end of the island, it is at least seven or eight miles wide in some places; but here it contracts to a strait apparently not more than a hundred or a hundred and fifty feet in breadth. Here stands the celebrated *bridge of the Euripus*, a modern work, occupying the site of an ancient structure. It is built of stone, and is divided into two parts, by a fort standing in the midst of the passage. Upon paying toll, we were allowed to cross, and were once more in Bœotia. On this side of the strait there is a high hill, surmounted by a fortress of Turkish construction, which quite commands the city of Chalcis.

We took the ancient road, leading from Chalcis to Tanagra and Thebes, while following the shore of the bay of the Euripus, south of the bridge. Meanwhile our baggage-horses, diverging to the right, took the direct road southwestward to Thebes. The old Greek thoroughfares differed widely from the splendid Roman roads—those vast arteries connecting the whole body of the empire. Their construction was much more simple, and the outlay comparatively small. The story of Œdipus shows that frequently in the mountain passes—as at that of Schiste—the road was merely wide enough for a single chariot or wagon; and that when two chariots met, one of them was obliged to turn out in order to allow the other to pass. When the road ran over a ledge of rocks, as in the present instance, there appears to have been nothing but a mere track. The ruts of the wheels are still to be traced for a long distance, cut deep into the rocks. It is much more reasonable to suppose that they were purposely chiseled out, than that they were worn by the continual passage of vehicles over the hard limestone, according to the common notion. Between the two ruts, the rock is about as rough as it was by nature, so that it is difficult for horses to travel over it at any great speed.

The site of the town of Aulis is little more than half an hour's ride from Chalcis. It was here that the Greek fleet was gathered before the war of Troy, and was detained for long months by calms and adverse winds. To appease the wrath of the gods, whose displeasure the unpropitious weather was supposed to indicate, Agamemnon must slay his daughter; and hence arises the plot of the "Iphigenia in Aulis" of Euripides, the most pathetic, perhaps, of the tragedies of that great poet. Aulis is supposed to have stood on a rocky promontory projecting into the Euripus, on the left of the road; but the only trace of a city is that infallible one—the abundance of fragments of vases and pottery. On either side of the promontory there is a harbor; that on the north being shallow, and, as Strabo remarks, far too small to contain all Agamemnon's ships. The other is the true harbor, and still bears the name of "Bathys," or the "Deep." Upon the shore of this quiet sheet, took place—unless we are to look upon the whole Homeric story as a groundless fabrication—the bloody sacrifice of Iphigenia, a fitting representation of the surrender of every thing most dear in life to the demon Ambition.

Whatever may be the truth of these classic associations, the neighborhood of Aulis is now condemned to a death-like silence. Not a house is to be seen; and as we left the rocky coast, and turned into the level plain that extends to the Asopus, a similar desolation seemed to brood over that. There was no path to follow. We struck boldly across the uncultivated waste toward the point where we knew Tanagra to be situated. The ground was strewn with flowers, among which the Larkspur (*Delphinium*) of our gardens, growing in wild luxuriance, was the most striking object. Broom and other showy shrubs gave variety to the scene. Our ride of three or four hours over this barren country was warm and uninteresting, and we met not a single human being until we reached the ruins of Tanagra.

These consist chiefly of walls surrounding a rising, and by no means level site, a couple of miles in circumference. At one place, near the spot where we entered Tanagra, there is an old gate. We walked over a part of the area formerly occupied by the city, and discovered the ancient theatre and the foundation of a temple. The position is not a very strong one, but it commands a pleasant view southward over a wide valley to Mount Parnes and Mount Cithæron, the northern boundaries of Attica. The Asopus runs near its walls, and fertilizes its vicinity, the whole of which, at the time of our visit, was covered with waving fields of wheat. We were somewhat disappointed as to the extent of the remains of Tanagra; for they are by no means commensurate with the importance of a city whose circuit was so extensive, and which claimed to have given birth to the great poet Corinna. In its vicinity a bloody battle was fought in the time of Pericles, between the Athenians and Spartans.

Our horses were tired, and we ourselves were hungry. Finding, however, no shady spot to halt at, we rode on to a small village a mile or two distant, where we could rest and obtain good water to drink. It was at an Albanian house that we stopped for half an hour. Between the Greeks and Albanians, as a general thing, there is little love lost; for the Greek can never forget the hostile purposes with which the other race was encouraged by the Porte to settle within the limits of Greece. It is said that all the Albanians at present in the kingdom are Christians by profession; still, there seems to lurk a root of bitterness between them and the Greeks, and it is fostered by their difference of language and manners.

On the west of Tanagra the prospect of the interior of Bœotia is cut off by a mountainous ridge running parallel to the Asopus, and behind this lies Thebes. We followed the northern side during the whole afternoon, without seeing a house or a rill of water. We advanced at a rapid rate, not being detained by our customary train of pack-horses. We entered the valley of Thebes, and in a few minutes more reached the modern town.

No one can visit Thebes without a feeling of disappointment. However much he may have been forewarned to expect few or no traces of ancient palaces and temples, when the tourist comes to tread the streets, and is told that he must now fancy himself in the city of Epaminondas and Pelopidas, he instinctively casts his eye about for some vestiges of their times. But there is nothing to gratify curiosity. If we except a few scattered sarcophagi, and some fragments of ancient walls, nothing remains but the ground on which Thebes stood. The modern town spreads itself out in the Cadmeum, the old citadel, and is unable to fill the inclosure. Sallying out from our khan, we found the streets crowded with promenaders. Their costume might have been sufficient to indicate that we were approaching Athens and civilization. In the rural districts all the ladies wear the native costume; here probably one half have adopted the European, and ape the newest French fashions. Among the men, however, there is a pertinacious adherence to the native dress, which is certainly much the more picturesque of the two.

After a stroll through the main street, we reached a high spot toward the southern end of the hill, where we sat down and enjoyed, in the midst of a crowd of boys at their sports, a prospect of the Theban plain, on the west separated by a low ridge from Lake Copais, and from the part of Bœotia in which we had been a couple of weeks previous. Southward, the country becomes undulating; but beyond it the peaks of Cithæron, of Helicon, and, farther to the right, of Parnassus itself, were glowing in the last rays of a gorgeous sunset.

The sun had scarcely risen when we emerged the next day from the khan at Thebes, after strictly enjoining upon our *agoyates*, who were to proceed by the direct road toward Eleusis, not to tarry by the way. As for ourselves, abandoning the care of overseeing the lazy drivers—which had been one of our chief occupations on previous days—we rode for over two hours in a westerly direction to Thespiæ. It is singular that the town occupied the very midst of a valley, without any hill to serve as citadel. The numerous fountains were, doubtless, the chief attraction that led the inhabitants to choose a site so different from most of those we have seen. Nicholas could show us little in the way of ruins; and, after jumping over ditches, wading brooks, and exciting the astonishment of a bevy of girls, who, with skirts gathered knee-high, were rubbing and pounding the clothes at one of the fountains, we satisfied ourselves that Thespiæ has left us little more than a name. The shape of the city, however, is quite distinctly marked; and the lines of stones running in various directions would seem to be traces of the edifices of the valiant town, whose greatest distinction was that, while all the rest of Bœotia basely submitted to Xerxes, it stood by the gallant Platæans in refusing his messengers the customary homage of earth and water.

Ascending a hill north of the ancient town, we passed through the village of Eremo Castro, or "the deserted fortress." In its little church we found the finest and best preserved bas-reliefs that we had seen since leaving Athens. As we rode westward to the celebrated fountain of Aganippe, the country became undulating, and covered, even to the tops of the round hills, with flourishing vineyards. The fountain lies at the head of a long and narrow ravine, at the base of Mount Helicon. In size it is nothing more than a small spring of cool and limpid water, close by a ruined chapel of St. Nicholas. Its identity has been proved solely by an inscription found imbedded in the walls of the chapel. The former abode of the nymphs, to whom both the mountain and the spring were dedicated, is said to have been in a shady grove, where, amidst the gurgling of the stream, the warbling of the birds, and the dark thickness of the laurel and myrtle foliage, their votaries might fancy that the nymphs could assume a bodily form. Only a few old olive-trees have escaped the ravages of ruthless warriors and the improvidence of the Greek peasantry.

Turning once more, we took a zigzag course, and soon came to the vicinity of Leuctra, where, after passing an excavated monument and some remains of a small temple, we began to look about for some place for our mid-day halt. For this, a spot was generally selected where shade and fresh water could be obtained. Here a great willow, growing by the side of a rivulet, offered its shelter, and we seated ourselves upon the green grass to enjoy the lunch which Nicholas had provided, without minding the clamor of some women of the neighboring village of Parapungi, who were assembled near by. With these poor creatures life seems to be one continual "wash-day."

Nicholas tried to convince us that this was the plain of Leuctra, the scene of that battle so fatal to the influence of Sparta in the affairs of Greece. We asked him in vain for the tumulus said to have been erected over the bones of the fallen. He could show nothing of the kind, and fell back on the argument that this was the site he had always pointed out to travelers. If so, none of those who had heretofore employed him ever saw the field of Leuctra at all: those who come after us may be more fortunate. J. was disposed to give the battle-ground the go-by. H. and I were determined not to advance until we had ascertained the veritable locality. Suspecting that it lay beyond the northern ridge of the valley, we took our guide along *nolens volens*. Nor were we disappointed. In twenty minutes we had before us the tumulus, occupying the summit of the ridge overlooking the supposed scene of the battle.

The Lacedæmonians with their allies, in the spring of B.C. 371, occupied the part of the field on which we stood, toward the south and Platæa; the Thebans were encamped on the northern side, toward Thespiæ. The former army amounted to at least eleven thousand men; the latter could number little more than six or eight thousand. On the one side were numbers, discipline, and the confidence inspired by an uninterrupted series of victories; the others were flushed with hopes of success, and commanded by one who was the most perfect master of tactics the world had ever known. The result was one that could scarcely have been anticipated. For the first time, a Spartan army was routed in a regular pitched battle, and Epaminondas could claim by one blow to have destroyed the Lacedæmonian ascendency. The tumulus was reared by the vanquished over the bodies of a thousand of the allies, who had died on that memorable day. There are remains of ancient terraces, of monuments, and, as it seemed to us, of old walls, in the immediate vicinity.

There was one more site we had contemplated visiting before leaving the plains of Bœotia—Platæa, lying at the foot of Mount Cithæron, and somewhat out of our direct route. In a straight line it is not more than seven miles from Thebes or Thespiæ; but by our circuitous route, we had ridden quite three times that distance. It looks out upon the broad expanse of plain toward the north, abundantly diversified with hill and dale, and watered by streams, of which the nearest flows westward to the Corinthian Gulf, while the more distant Asopus runs in the opposite direction, to empty itself in the channel of Eubœa. We approached the inclosure of the walls from the west, where a copious fountain, still resorted to by the villagers of Kokla, springs forth close by the ancient cemetery. Here a number of sarcophagi, hollowed out from pieces of solid rock, stand tottering on the verge of the hill, or have fallen below. The city, whose circuit of wall remains almost entire, occupied a slight eminence of an oblong shape, stretching north and south. As its length is nearly a mile, we limited ourselves to inspecting the northern portion. Here the highest part is separated by a wall from the remainder, and forms a citadel; and another appears to have existed at the southern end of the inclosure. With the exception of the ruined foundation of a supposed Temple of Juno, there are absolutely no traces of any buildings.

With Leake's good map of Platæa and its environs, we attempted to gain a clear conception of the famous battle which took place here, the year after the battle of Salamis, in 479 B.C., when the Greeks completely discomfited the Persian army of Mardonius. The field of action, stretching from the camp of the Persians, and from the position of the Greeks before the battle, to the city, was five miles in extent; and, since the ground is undulating, with half a dozen ridges and intervening ravines, it is naturally somewhat difficult to recognize each detail. The engagement took place on the eastern side of the city. The Greeks originally were posted at the foot of Cithæron, some four or five miles distant, opposite the Persians, whose camp was on the other side of the Asopus. Fearing lest they might be circumvented, they retreated toward the city, the Lacedæmonians being on the right, the Athenians on the left wing, with the auxiliary troops in the centre. Before the battle commenced, they retired still farther, and the auxiliaries actually got quite behind Platæa. So the conflict came on. The Persians attacked the gallant Spartans; while the traitorous Thebans, and the inhabitants of the different Greek cities who fought under barbarian colors, fell upon the Athenian line. It was the Persians who first turned their backs and fled, and then the Thebans were repulsed and retreated to their own city. This was the last time that the Greeks were called upon to defend their country from that great power, whose numberless hosts seemed ready to destroy them from the face of the earth.

Platæa possesses much more interesting associations than Leuctra. It witnessed a noble contest for liberty and independence of foreign aggression; whereas the battle at Leuctra was only a strife of rival states for ascendency. The news of the battle of Platæa sent a thrill of joy through every true Greek heart; that of Leuctra shrouded the greater part of the Hellenic race in weeds of mourning. The name of Platæa has come down to us associated only with the glorious scenes of Grecian history; as the only state whose soldiers fought by the side of Miltiades and his followers at Marathon; as the steadfast opponent of Theban aggression and ambition; as the equally constant friend and ally of Athens; and last, but not least, as an active participant in the noble contest beneath its very walls.

We had tarried too long at Platæa, and now began the ascent of Mount Cithæron, fearing we should not reach our quarters for the night before dark. Gradually rising above the plain, we obtained one of those extensive panoramic views which are so useful in impressing the geographical positions of towns, rivers, and mountain ranges, upon the memory. At the top of the pass, whose ascent is easy, we fell in with the great road from Thebes to Athens. It is rather narrow, and, though Macadamized, is quite rough; but it pleased us as an evidence of our approach to the capital. It was a prospect, however, of mingled pleasure and regret: for it announced the speedy termination of our delightful tour, and a separation of those who had been close companions during a period, whose impressions the hand of time and the influence of other scenes will never efface. The road was sadly out of repair; bridges had been left to crumble, and a carriage could no longer proceed the whole distance from the capital. Still we rode gayly along, until the gray walls of an old Attic fortress, frowning upon us from a height commanding the pass, gave us warning of our approach to Casa, whither our *agoyates* had preceded us.

Committing our horses to the custody of our guide, we soon found ourselves at the entrance of the citadel, long and generally known as Eleutheræ, but conclusively shown by Leake to be that of Œnoe. The neighboring mountaineers know it now by the name of Gyphtocastro, or "the Gypsies' fortress," probably connecting it with some legend or story, which I did not learn. Whatever its name may have been, we found it the most perfect specimen of fortification we had seen during the course of our travels in Greece. Nothing seemed lacking to afford an accurate picture of a citadel, such as might withstand for months the most vehement assaults. On the northwestern side extends a long line of wall, looking toward Bœotia, with twelve or fourteen courses of stone rising one above the other. At regular intervals large square towers project from the walls, and furnish sufficient protection to

INTERIOR OF A TOWER AT ŒNOE.

two or three postern gates built close by. It was through one of these minor entrances that we gained admission to the inclosure, which was far too entire to admit of our climbing in elsewhere. We looked into one or two of the towers in the first place. There were three doors: one on the level of the ground on the interior, which was perhaps the ordinary entrance; the other two were on the sides of the tower, even with the top of the wall. Thus the soldiers could make the whole circuit of the walls behind an elevated breast-work, or parapet, with which the top was crowned, and pass through the second story of the towers. Here, too, were the embrasures, similar to those in the towers of Messene, through which the bowmen aimed and poured forth murderous discharges upon the assailants. Above these, again, were windows, intended, doubtless, for posts of observation.

This was the most exposed side of Œnoe; for on the other sides the ascent was more difficult, and, as attack was less to be apprehended, there was less need of defence. On the southern side, toward the khan, the walls descend lower, and are not in an equal state of preservation. The two chief gates were in the western wall. They appeared to me either to have been capped by a huge lintel, like the great gate of Messene, or to have been arched over with approaching stones. Like that gateway, each was double, and, between the two sets of doors, contained a small court. In every city whose walls are well preserved, the size of this open space varies, as well as its shape. At Messene it was a large circular court; at Panopeus it was small; at Larissa Cremaste there was merely a shallow recess on either side of the passage between the gates. Here the space is somewhat larger. In the centre of the inclosure of the walls is a small detached quadrangular structure, of which only the lower part is standing—probably an interior fort or watch-tower. It is chiefly remarkable for the mode of its construction: the stones are large, but instead of being rectangular, as in all the other walls, they are irregular polygons of various shapes, all closely fitted to each other. It seemed to me the most probable hypothesis, that this tower was contemporaneous in its erection with the remainder of Œnoe, and that the architect chose this style of building from motives of taste. It was an imitation of the old Pelasgian and Cyclopean works of Mycenæ, which were even then venerable for their age.

The shadows were deepening in the ravines, and slowly crept up the mountain sides. They warned us to bestir ourselves, and seek the khan, situated in the gorge far below us, by the side of a noisy brook. Janni had been ambitious to end off as well as he had commenced, and we sat down about eight o'clock to our last dinner, on which even more than ordinary pains had been expended. Then came a refreshing rest, which we relished after our ride of ten hours. Our attendants meanwhile stretched themselves on the ground outside the door wrapped in their impermeable capotas. Panagiotes came to me the next morning, complaining that he had not been able to sleep all night. At fifty paces there stood a guard-house for the protection of the pass, where a company of soldiers, abandoning all military discipline, had been carousing until dawn, interspersing their potations with the song and the Romaic dance.

We were all on our feet at an early hour. The conclusion of the journey was drawing near; and, though now beginning to regret the termination of the wandering life we had led for so many weeks, the magic name of Athens sounded like that of a familiar friend, and imparted spirit and energy to all. Our first intention had been to return by Eleusis; but neither of my comrades had visited the fortress of Phyle, and they therefore wished to return by that way. On the other hand, I preferred to go on with the *agoyates* to Eleusis. Accordingly, we separated for the day; but not until we had planned an excursion together for the next week to the Cape of Sunium and the Temple of Minerva.

This arrangement allowed me to visit a second time the lofty acropolis, and to sketch its most striking points. The interest of the locality, and the pure morning breeze sweeping through the quiet gorges of the mountains, made me forget the flight of time. When I regained the khan, I found that the *agoyates* were gone; but after saddling my horse, I soon overtook them as they were emerging from the mountain pass into a small valley, the whole of which was cultivated with wheat. We were not long in reaching a lonely Greek tower, an additional defence to the pass and the old road, and the only one of the kind I have seen. Only one corner is preserved in nearly its full height, with no less than thirty-three courses of stone. The ruin has thus assumed the form of a very acute pyramid when seen from a distance.

The road was excellent compared with those over which

we had been jogging; the *agoyates* were in the best of spirits in view of their speedy return home, and I had no reason to complain of a slow advance. For some time we crossed a monotonous succession of wooded hills, covered chiefly with the common pine of the country. Every tree had a notch near the ground, on the side of the trunk that was uppermost, to collect the resinous sap, which is principally used as an ingredient in the wine. At every important place my companions had commissioned Nicholas to obtain some of the "vins du pays;" but they had as uniformly declared them to be a beverage unfit for any but savages. The wines are in general very sour, and their pitchy taste is very disagreeable to all who are unaccustomed to it. Few travelers think even the far-famed Samian wine worthy of its world-wide reputation.

At the village of Mandra we entered upon the Eleusinian or Thriasian plain; and in an hour more we rode into the scattered village of Lepsina, or *Eleusis*. After satisfying myself with a hearty lunch in a hut that answered the threefold purpose of khan, drinking room, and shop, I made the rounds of the place. I had nothing to guide me but a plan of the site; but there were plenty of boys who volunteered to act the cicerone. The striking feature of Eleusis is its acropolis, a long, low hill, parallel to the sea, under the eastern end of which stands the village. I found few ruins of its wall, except at the foundation of a ruinous Turkish tower. Before reaching the hill, I came to a large collection of ancient remains, drums and capitals of columns, five or six feet in diameter. The use of one or two large masses of stone was puzzling. On one was carved a head of Minerva, with a medallion, or Medusa's head, hanging down in front. These were probably remains of the Propylæa. The Temple of Ceres, within whose inclosure the celebrated Eleusinian mysteries were celebrated, stood higher up on the rocky platform of the hill. I clambered to a small chapel at present occupying the spot, and gained a fine view of the whole plain. Toward the sea the prospect is cut off by the crags of the island of Salamis, and in the bay thus inclosed the water was of the deepest blue I had ever seen. Not even the Lake of Geneva could surpass it in this respect. Inland, the eye could trace a long row of arches belonging to the aqueduct, by which the Emperor Hadrian supplied the city with potable water.

From the citadel I walked down to the sea-shore, having first rid myself of the troup of urchins who had pestered me with their importunities for "backsheesh"—a cry well known in the East, even among the Greeks. They brought coins and other curiosities of doubtful antiquity; but I was incredulous, and refused to purchase. A walk of five or ten minutes brought me to the long semicircular pier, which was thrown out by the Eleusinians to render their harbor safe from the southern and eastern winds. Like every other work of the former inhabitants, it was built in the most solid fashion, although far from being on a large scale. A few boys were running over the loose stones, and a fishing-smack was moored to its end by a cable attached to one of the larger fragments. A number of sail were to be seen lazily flapping in the distance, off Mount Ægaleos, in whose neighborhood much of the fish for the Athenian market is caught. The air was sultry, and, as it was the last day of spring, gave premonitions of the approach of summer.

On my return to the village, I was glad to lie down in the shade before following the rest of my company, who had taken the road for Athens. A train of camels passing by, almost led me to imagine myself in a tropical climate—this being, I believe, the only place in Greece where that patient animal is found. The road from Eleusis to Athens is one of the best in the country. It follows an ancient highway, once lined with monuments, of which only one or two can now be recognized. The Eleusinian Cephissus, and one or two other streams, cross the road on their way to the bay, around which we wound for a time. Just at the base of Mount Corydallus, where the road enters the pass, we reached the two salt-springs called Rheiti, once dammed to turn some mills, but now left open. They formed the ancient frontier between Athens and Eleusis. The old thoroughfare is still evident, from its track cut deep in the rock. I rode on alone, and entered the picturesque pass of Daphne. At one place a number of small niches in the rock indicate that a heathen temple, probably of Venus, stood in the vicinity; and the inscriptions relate to the votive offerings placed within them by the piety of the devout worshippers. The foundations of the temple itself stand near by.

Farther on, upon "the Sacred Way," as the route was called which the great procession took when the mysteries were to be celebrated at Eleusis, I came to the Monastery of Daphne. Tying my horse outside the walls, I entered the courts, which were overgrown with grass, and seemed nearly deserted. The only living thing within was a dog whom I roused too suddenly from his slumbers, and who retaliated by a show of his teeth. There were many ruins around. The old Byzantine church, a curious specimen of architecture, stands on the site of an extensive temple dedicated to Apollo. M. Buchon, the indefatigable chronicler of the Frankish domination of Greece in the Middle Ages, made an interesting discovery here a few years ago. It appears that Daphne was called Delphina in the Middle Ages, and that this church was the burying-place of the Dukes of Athens. M. Buchon found their armorial bearings upon several of the tombstones on the floor.

Remounting my horse, I pressed forward to the brow of the hill, where the plain of Athens soon burst upon my eyes. The glorious Acropolis, with its russet-tinged temple, looked like the face of an old friend; and Athens itself wore a homelike air. Beyond it the long ridge of Hymettus, and the peak of Pentelicus, on the left, were purple in the rays of the setting sun. But I did not pause to contemplate the scene. In a few minutes more I had gained the plain. Then I passed through the olive-grove, that forms a wide belt of luxuriant green on either side of the Cephissus; and, before the close of day, was again threading the streets of Athens.

THE PLAIN OF MARATHON.

CHAPTER XX.

RAMBLES IN ATTICA.

See there the olive grove of Academe,
Plato's retirement, where the Attic bird
Trills her thick-warbled notes the summer long;
There flowery hill Hymettus, with the sound
Of bees' industrious murmur, oft invites
To studious musing; there Ilissus rolls
His whispering stream. MILTON.

MARATHON.

THE plain of Marathon lies about twenty-two miles distant from Athens, and, until lately, two days at least were required to visit it and return. Travelers from the West, however, are generally so pressed for time, that they have induced the guides, into whose hands they commit themselves, to devise a plan by which, with slightly increased expenditure, they may spare a day from the more numerous attractions of Athens, without at all affecting their "six months' tour in Europe."

Finding that the visit to Marathon could now—thanks to the exertions of those gentlemen—be accomplished as conveniently in one day as in two, I joined a couple of friends in undertaking the trip. The ride being a long one, we were obliged to rise early for departure. A guide came with a carriage to my lodgings before five o'clock in the morning. After rattling a while through the narrow and roughly paved streets of the city, we came to a tolerable road, which led out into the country by the great stuccoed palace of King Otho and the more tasteful gardens in its rear. On our left was Mount Lycabettus, a high hill overhanging Athens on the north-east, from whose summit I had many a time watched the last beams of the sun falling over the golden waves of the Saronic Gulf, as it set behind the mountains of Salamis. Centuries ago, how many an anxious eye must have been strained by those who, from the temple adorning that height, gazed upon the hostile fleets as they advanced to the engagement in yonder narrow strait of Salamis. From the stony plain at the base of the mountain, now just beginning to recover its verdure after a rainy spring, we took a northerly course toward the little village of Cephisia, at the very foot of Mount Pentelicus. The plain—at least the part that bordered the road—was barren, and seemed almost uncultivated. But, as we approached the village, it became more fertile; and now and then appeared a garden or vineyard, surrounded by walls of sun-dried bricks, thatched with straw or wild broom. Our carriage stopped at a small house, where we found the horses that had been sent forward the previous day awaiting us; for here, at the distance of nine or ten miles from Athens, the carriage road ceases, and the traveler must pursue his way over the mountains, upon the same rugged paths by which the natives have been content for centuries to keep up a communication with the neighboring villages.

The road wound about the northern side of Mount Pentelicus, into a valley which is a prolongation of the plain of Athens. The soil was still less fertile than before; not a village or hamlet was visible. To the north, the lofty range of Mount Parnes, which from Athens shuts off all prospect in this direction, gradually sank as we advanced eastward; and in one place displayed a narrow gap, one of the few openings between Attica and Bœotia. This was Deceleia, a famous pass in ancient times. It constituted the only communication through Parnes, with the exception of Phyle, and was therefore esteemed a most important post for defence. It was through this defile, which certainly does not appear to be a very easy one, that Mardonius, with his army of Persians, retreated to Platæa, after the fight at Salamis. Sixty or seventy years later, the Lacedæmonians, who seized it in the midst of the civil wars, made it the centre of their predatory incursions into Attica. And so strong is this position, that they could not be dislodged from their post, though in full sight of Athens, not twenty miles distant.

The valley we were in soon contracted into a narrow ravine covered with various shrubs. A succession of ascents brought us to the top of the pass, overlooking the village of Vrana. Another picturesque and more thickly wooded gorge led us down to the opening of the plain of Marathon, which was spread out in beauty before us. The background of this charming scene was filled up by the mountains of Eubœa, among which the rocky head of Zagoras overtopped the rest. The recent rains had given it, like some other peaks, a heavy cap of snow. Between the island and the main land was the Euripus, which is here seven or eight miles wide, and, in going northward, alternately contracts and expands, until, at Chalcis, the shores approach so near one another, that a stone might almost be thrown across the channel. The plain itself is perfectly level for five or six miles in length, and it can not be less than three miles to the nearest point of the beach. The water beyond it is quiet and glassy; for a long, low, and narrow tongue of land breaks the force of the eastern winds, and the bay thus formed is only exposed to the southern wind, or Sirocco. The ancients fancied a resemblance between this peninsula and a dog's tail; and therefore called it Cynosura. From the hillock on which we stood we could not see the tumulus. It lay hidden by the projecting spur of the mountain to our right; but the wide and shallow river of Marathona was visible in the distance, reaching the sea after a meandering course through the plain. A gap in the hills on our right was just wide enough to disclose Mount Pentelicus, covered with newly-fallen snow; and there was a ruined monastery with a single tall cypress in its garden, to serve as a foreground.

Vrana was a convenient spot for our morning meal. The sun was scarcely yet in the meridian, but a ride of several hours enabled us to do honor to the simple viands which our guide, George, drew from a capacious basket. The absence of chairs, or of any substitute which could be procured from the neighboring huts, compelled us to adopt the most common Oriental posture; and as we sat cross-legged on the turf, all the population of the hamlet collected at a short distance from us to make observations on our costume and habits. The urchins, albeit scarce a week passes without their seeing some of the "milordi," were vastly edified with our appearance. As for the women, with the distaff in one hand, and twirling the spindle with the other, they talked and spun, until it was hard to determine whether tongue or hands were most busy.

THE MOUND AT MARATHON.

We reached the mound raised over the slain of the battle of Marathon by pursuing an almost direct course across the fields. The roads, if mere beaten paths may be dignified with that name, are annually ploughed up in the spring; so that without any offence we could leap ditches, and dash over the fields of young wheat, as is, indeed, the universal practice in Greece. The hillock, or funeral mound, under which the hundred and ninety-two Athenians who perished in battle are buried, is perhaps thirty feet high. If its shape was ever angular, time has worn it down into a rounded form, except where the sacrilegious travelers of this century, in searching for brass and flint arrow-heads, have scraped away some earth from its sides. Unfortunately for these antiquarians, the latter sort has been found in abundance at places where no battle is known to have been fought with the Persians; for to those barbarians these primitive wedge-like missiles have been attributed. Geologists pronounce them to be of nature's own fashioning.

Standing upon the top of this monument of ancient glory, I could easily distinguish the positions most probably occupied by the belligerent parties twenty-three centuries ago. The Medes and Persians under Datis landed from their boats along the neighboring beach. The Athenians and Platæans, under Miltiades and his nine associates, had encamped the previous night in the neighborhood, at Marathon, a village occupying the site of the hamlet where we lunched. Thence they had descended to meet the Persians, and stationed themselves in such a manner as to have either wing protected by a high hill. The centre of their line was weak, either purposely or from necessity; while the extremities were made very strong. When the engagement commenced, the Persians were successful in the centre. But the victorious Athenians from the wings pouring in upon them, as it would appear, after a somewhat disputed combat, put to rout the whole multitude of the barbarians. The greater part ran to the sea, and saved themselves in boats, which they had drawn up on the sand; but many becoming entangled in the swamp, which was on their right, were cut off by the Athenians, or drowned.

Modern writers pretend to correct the numbers of the Persian host, as given by ancient historians. For they calculate that, instead of the half a million or more warriors, that were attributed to Darius by the later Latins and Greeks, the ships that brought them from Asia could not have contained two hundred thousand men. Of these, it is conjectured that not more than 30,000 were actually engaged in the battle, and opposed to 11,000 Greeks. So that, after all, the myriads of the "Great King" dwindle down to what would now be considered rather an insignificant armament for conquering a whole country. The glory of Miltiades would also be reduced to the skill employed in making one of his soldiers more effective than three of his antagonists. Be this as it may, Herodotus, the only historian who can claim the authority of a contemporary, contents himself with stating the number of the slain at nearly 200 on the side of the Athenians, and at 6400 on that of the Persians.

It was difficult for me to realize that the quiet plain I was looking upon had ever been the scene of so dreadful a conflict, and that here had been decided the fate not of Greece alone, but of all Europe. The quiet fields were occupied only by a few peasants engaged in ploughing. In the distance, to the northwest, could plainly be distinguished the marsh so fatal to the fugitives. It was not now so wet, however, as in the autumn, which was the season of the year when the battle took place.

From the mound we rode to the sea-shore, along which pursuing our way a mile southward, we reached the remains of a Temple of Minerva, which was surnamed Hellotis, just as an Italian church in a similar situation would, at the present day, be dedicated to "Our Lady of the Marsh." All that now remains of it is four or five plain, round columns, a foot in diameter, standing in the midst of a *mandra*, or sheep-fold, and an altar or pedestal in a neighboring field. An interesting circumstance connected with this temple was the discovery of one of the most ancient authentic pieces of sculpture that have, so far as I know, been found in Greece. It bears the name of the artist, and is thereby known to have been executed in the sixth century before our era. So perfect is every lineament of the face, and every fold of the drapery, that it has been thought worth while to place this large bas-relief in a glass case. It is now in the collection of antiques within the walls of the old Temple of Theseus at Athens, and might easily be mistaken at first sight for a fine slab from Nineveh or Thebes.

The day was by this time far advanced; and having now seen all that is most interesting at Marathon, we turned our faces westward. Instead of retracing our steps to Vrana, we directed them to the present village of Marathona, imbosomed in a small valley some distance to the north. From it a torrent issues and waters the plain. We reached it, after passing on our left the marble platform supposed to have been that of a monument erected in honor of Miltiades. There was no distinct road to the village; but our guide's knowledge was reliable enough as to the depth of the stream; and we avoided the bends by crossing alternately from one side of the river to the other. We did not tarry at the few houses, which, by a singular but not uncommon misnomer, have assumed the name of Marathon (whereas that village, doubtless, stood on the site of Vrana), but hurried on, by a difficult and rugged ascent, to reach the path by which we had come that morning. George preceded us, and, on one occasion, had advanced so far that he was hidden from us by a curve of the little gorge. Suddenly there was heard a noise of men apparently wrangling, and then the discharge of a gun, after which all was quiet again. It would have required no great stretch of imagination to fancy an encounter with brigands; for the northern part of Attica is from time to time infested with robbers, and our guide might have fallen a victim. The chances of such a catastrophe, however, were small. Besides, upon going forward, we were reassured by seeing George dismounted, and engaged in peaceable conversation with a couple of peasants. The sole sufferer was a large vulture, which, being gorged with food, could not fly off with the rest of the flock to which it belonged. It must have measured five feet or more from the tip of one wing to that of the other. The peasant who killed it, after cutting off the two wings, for the sake of the feathers, threw the rest away, and then accompanied our party most of the way to Cephisia.

Before we entered the carriage again on our return, we went to see a pretty water-fall of the principal branch of the famous Cephissus, where the shelving rocks, extending round in crescent shape, form a sort of cave. In summer time this "Grotto of the Nymphs" must be a delightful resort for the Athenians. And Cephisia, the only country place in the vicinity which abounds in water, was formerly a still more favorite site for the villas of the rich than it is now. There remained ample time for us, after seeing all the curiosities of the place, to return to Athens by daylight.

SUNIUM.

Sunium occupies the extreme southerly point of Attica, at the distance of thirty or forty miles from Athens. It has been customary to devote to the excursion the greater part of three days. The construction of new roads, however, and better arrangements have reduced the time required to a single day. We rose before dawn on the last morning of spring, and left Athens in a carriage, intending to ride as far as there existed any respectable road, which, fortunately for us, was the case for a longer distance than in any other direction from the capital of Greece.

If the reader will but cast his eye over a good map of this triangular peninsula of Attica, he will at once notice its singular conformation. A lofty ridge, bounding it on the north, forms the base of the triangle, while the sea-shore describes the other sides. From this central trunk, which bears in one place the name of Cithæron, and in another that of Parnes, two lesser branches run down to the Saronic Gulf, dividing Attica into three unequal plains. Of these, the plain of Athens is the largest, and is intermediate between that of Eleusis on the west, and Mesogæa toward the southeast. Mount Hymettus appears from Athens to cut off all communication with this small inland plain; but the road to Sunium finds an entrance into it through a wide gap at its upper end.

The country until we reached the village of Keratia, where the carriage road terminates, possessed little interest. Arid and stony, it is incredible that under any circumstances the soil should have supported a large population. Not a stream of running water, at this season of the year, greets the traveler's eye; scarcely a single tree throws its grateful shade upon the road-side. The parsimony of nature has in some degree been counterbalanced by the beneficence of man. Fountains have been constructed, and wells dug, at short intervals along the road. I asked a native how it happened that these wells should have been made at so great expense in lonely tracts, far from any human habitation. "Why," replied the Greek, "the erection of a fountain is regarded as a *psychicon*, or meritorious deed to aid in the salvation of one's soul. It is the same feeling that induces men to found churches or chapels, in fulfillment of vows made in sickness or danger." I could not but admire the benevolence thus displayed, notwithstanding its erroneous motive. Beggars in the streets of Athens (who are almost always either cripples or blind) are supported, on a similar principle, by the contributions of the passers-by. It is sometimes even ludicrous to see a representative, or some other well-known politician, slip a *lepton* (not quite two mills) into the hand of a poor man, and accompany it with the notice that it is "for his soul's sake." One is almost tempted to think that the coin is an indication of the value he sets upon the object in question.

We reached Keratia in about four hours from the time of leaving Athens, and waited in a large khan, which served at once as a country inn and store, until our horses were made ready. The men of the village being mostly busy at their work, we sat comparatively undisturbed by their impertinent curiosity. The remainder of our ride was the more difficult part. At first, the path led over a tolerably level district; but soon we came to the hills, which formerly went by the name of Mount Laurium, and which reach the very margin of the sea. The rock formerly abounded with veins of a lead ore containing a large proportion of silver. But this commodity, which enriched the Athenian commonwealth in its palmy days, had already grown scarce in later times. The ore was worked even a second time, in order to extract every particle of the precious metal. And now, it is said, not a trace of the silver can be found. The activity of the miners in days bygone is evinced by huge heaps of *scoria*, or dross, that surround the old shafts, and are of such size as to excite much surprise.*

We presently reached the sea-shore at a small bay, whence, for more than an hour, our path led us over rocks bordering

* It is certainly an interesting fact that the silver drawn from these mines was equally distributed among all the citizens, until Themistocles persuaded the people to apply this branch of their revenue to the building of ships for the Persian war. The silver extracted from the piece of stone you pick up on Mount Laurium may perchance have been used in equipping the fleet that served at Salamis.

the water. The tracks worn by those who have from time to time passed over them, follow all the contortions and fissures of the strata. Our horses would occasionally come to a narrow ledge, which, with all our confidence in their sure-footedness, seemed rather perilous. At length we beheld, on the crest of a neighboring hill, the remains of the ancient Temple of Minerva, which we had come so far to visit.

The view from the summit well repaid us for the difficulty of the ascent. We had reached the end of the Attic peninsula. The Ægean Sea, unruffled by a single breath of air, presented a glassy appearance, which the ocean never exhibits. Beyond were the islands of the Archipelago, seemingly but a few miles distant. But more impressive than all was the unbroken silence that reigned around us. Not a living thing had we encountered for nearly three hours. In fact, no one permanently inhabits this vicinity. The temple is better known by the seamen than by the natives; and the Italian sailors have given the promontory its present designation of *Cape Colonna.* Only twelve out of twenty-four columns remain. The order is that most commonly employed in the existing edifices of Greece—the simple and chaste Doric. Yet, in some respects, the Temple of Sunium differs from all other examples of this style. The flutings of the columns are wider and less numerous than in the Parthenon; while the shafts are so tall and slender as to present a marked contrast with those of the other temples, and especially with those of the Peloponnesus. At a short distance they appear to vie in lightness with pillars of the Ionic order. Sheltered by its situation from depredations on the part of the peasantry for building purposes, the temple is exposed to the full violence of every tempest that blows over it, and of every earthquake that rocks its foundations. But the more insidious agency of the saline exhalations from the sea has corroded its pillars, destroyed its sharp outlines, and obliterated every trace of its marble sculptures. The platform upon which the edifice stands is yet remaining entire. The walls of ancient Sunium may be traced through their whole circuit. It was evidently a place of some note as the chief town in the mining district of Mount Laurium.

Returning to Keratia, we pursued a route less rocky, passing by Thoricus, the modern Therico. The only objects of interest in this little hamlet are a gate of unusual construction, a ruined colonnade, and the remains of a small theatre. An hour later we were in the carriage returning to Athens. On our way we stopped for a few minutes in the vicinity of a chapel dedicated to St. John, to examine a marble lion of colossal size; but the execution was feeble, and the monument too much defaced to be worthy of notice.

PHYLE.

Professor B. was my companion on a pleasant excursion to the fortress of Phyle, situated in the very midst of Mount Parnes, which played a prominent part in Grecian story. Before we got under way, the sun was well up, and pouring his almost insupportable rays upon us. We were provided with books, maps, and provisions; and each carried, besides, an umbrella, without whose protection scarce any one ventures out during the warm season. The weather soon, however, underwent a favorable change; and the sky being over-

VIEW OF PHYLE.

cast, we were not long exposed to great heat. As we left the thoroughfares of the city, we struck upon an ill-defined road leading to the northwest; and, after making a slight descent, found ourselves approaching the little River Cephissus, which, in its course of twenty miles from the mountains, scatters fertility and verdure around. Great was the contrast between its banks and the rest of the plain, which in the month of October is dry, parched, and dusty. The whole valley, in its width of six miles, had been stripped of nearly every vestige of vegetation; for not a drop of water had fallen during the previous four or five months. The Cephissus, in truth, makes but a poor show as to extent. At no time does it equal a moderate creek. Its waters are drawn off by canals, and *let out* by the government to the neighboring land-owners in measured quantities, and at a fixed price. What is not absorbed by the ground, finds its way to the vicinity of the Bay of Phalerum, where it loses itself in the midst of the fields; and but little, after all, reaches the sea. The equally famous Ilissus, on the eastern side of Athens, is still more unfortunate, as, during the warm months, its bed becomes entirely dry.

The olive grove lining the banks of the Cephissus forms a belt of verdure for half a mile or more on either side, and is one of the most flourishing in all Greece. The trees are old, and twisted into the most fantastic shapes imaginable. The locality acquires additional interest from the fact that the *Academy* was situated in this vicinity, that garden where Plato was wont to teach his disciples, where the principles of a morality superior to that of the times were inculcated, and popular fallacies were refuted. But, alas for the reverence of the antiquarian, the precise spot can scarcely be determined with certainty. The two low hillocks of Colonos, a short distance to the right, are more certainly known. Here was the birthplace of the great poet Sophocles, who, in his tragedies, has represented Œdipus as on this spot lamenting his misfortunes. On one hillock stands the simple monument of Müller the Philhellene, who, after spending a lifetime in the study of Grecian history, begged that he might be buried here in sight of some of its most glorious monuments. Half an hour later we saw the Queen's Tower, a sort of country house, to which the royal couple may frequently be seen riding. Queen Amelia is passionately fond of equestrian exercises, and is esteemed the best rider in the kingdom. What with riding and dancing, her time is pretty fully occupied, and she finds little leisure to attend to the concerns of her subjects. Her non-interference, probably, quite as much as her reputed gentleness and beauty, has won the good-will of a people who certainly esteem themselves quite capable of managing their own affairs.

An hour or two more brought us opposite Mount Pentelicus and Cephisia, on the other side of the great plain of Athens. Here we turned into a valley between the hills, and began ascending to the village of Khassia. More properly the assemblage of houses we reached was merely the *calyvia*, or summer residence, of the inhabitants of Khassia. The real village lay out of sight. During the summer season the inhabitants abandon their villages, either because their position is unhealthy, or because they possess lands in a more elevated situation. These they must visit to plough and sow with grain during the early spring, and to reap the crops in the month of June, after the termination of harvest in the plains. Let not the reader imagine here one of those smiling villages of New England, whose regular streets are shaded by long rows of old elms, or adorned with lofty poplars; whose neat white houses testify alike to the industry and the success of the inhabitants. We found ourselves entering a confused mass of huts, built of stone or mud, and huddled together without regard to order or symmetry. The streets—often not eight feet wide—were unpaved and dirty. There did not seem to be a single tree or bush in the place. As we dismounted to rest our horses a while, some ragged boys in Albanian costume came to earn a few *lepta* by holding them; while three or four grown men, who might have been profitably employed in the cultivation of their fields, sat under an adjoining shed smoking their pipes and watching our movements. We walked a short distance through the neighboring lanes, but discovered nothing worthy of notice. Here and there the eye was met by the tottering wall of a cottage, whose tiled or thatched roof had fallen in. It was the very picture of desolation. We were heartily rejoiced when our horses had been sufficiently refreshed to allow of our proceeding. A few rods beyond the village there was a clear spring of water, where we found all the women of the village engaged in washing. This operation did not consist in *rubbing* the clothes with the hand or upon a board. Instead of this, the articles were alternately dipped in water, and pounded between two boards or two flat stones until they acquired the necessary degree of whiteness. What seemed to give the washers most trouble, however, was the *fustanella*, or white shirt, worn by the men, which any one who has ever seen an Athenian in native costume can not fail to remember. A strip of linen, a yard or three quarters of a yard wide, is wound in a loose manner, sometimes a dozen or more times about the body, and fastened by a long sash tightly drawn around the waist. This, too, gives the *pallecaris* a wasp-like figure, on which they are wont to pride themselves beyond measure. The white skirts, when stretched upon the grass, cover a great space. The whole female population paused for a moment in their occupation to reconnoitre us as we approached. Altogether they formed a picturesque group. With a freedom that might have shocked fastidious eyes, they had tucked up their dresses above the knee, and stood ankle deep in water.

From Khassia to Phyle the winding bridle path more than doubles the direct distance. We followed during much of the time the sides of a narrow ravine. At the bottom the dry bed of a torrent, which during the winter pours its waters into the plain of Eleusis, left no room for a road. Accordingly, we were obliged to make frequent ascents and descents before coming in sight of the fortress. The sides of the hills were covered with pine-trees wherever the rocky nature of the soil did not preclude their growth. The inhabitants put them in requisition, not only to furnish the fuel they need, but also to flavor their wines.

The fortress of Phyle at length came in sight. It occupies the summit of a somewhat isolated hill, that stands in the middle of the principal pass leading over Mount Parnes from Attica into Bœotia. On two sides it is protected by almost perpendicular rocks. There no walls were necessary, and none seem ever to have existed. On the other sides it was defended by strong fortifications, built of regular courses of masonry, of which I counted in some places sixteen yet remaining. The stones composing them seemed to be in general from three to six or eight feet in length, and about two feet high. We entered the precincts of the fortress, clambering over the rubbish formed by the fall of a portion of the wall, about midway between a square and a circular tower. From the platform, on which stood the barracks of the ancient garrison, no trace of antiquity could be descried. The only visible proof that the spot had been inhabited of old was the abundance of small fragments of vases and other pottery, which are found on antique sites when all other signs have disappeared.

The view from this position, which was a favorite one with Lord Byron, is almost unequaled. Not so panoramic as that from the summit of Mount Pentelicus, it presents in a more contracted space a *picture* of Athens and its vicinity. The wide notch in the mountain allows you to distinguish the city, and the Acropolis towering above it. Hymettus beyond constitutes a fine background—the plain, which is sunny and animated, in lively contrast with its sombre, deeply-furrowed side. To the right of this are the waters of the Saronic Gulf. If the day be clear, the faint outline of mountains in the Peloponnesus is perceptible to the eye.

But the attractions of the scenery do not equal the historic interest of this famous spot. The name of Phyle is honored as few others are, with an inscription upon the brightest page only of Grecian story, finding no mention in the records of the country's decline and fall. Its position under the old mode of warfare was almost impregnable, and commanded the passage between two rival states; but in modern days, the Acropolis of Phyle being much less important, has never, I believe, been occupied by a military force. The spot has been completely abandoned by men.

Thrasybulus, an Athenian patriot during the reign of the Thirty Tyrants, having escaped from Thebes, threw himself into Phyle, and with a handful of his countrymen set himself in opposition to the Spartans. It required but a short time to put the fortress in complete order for defence, so strong was its natural position, so perfect were the walls. From Athens the tyrants viewed with anxiety this invasion, and determined, by the help of their three thousand troops, to crush the incipient rebellion. But their first rash attack was repelled with ease; and the assailants were compelled to attempt the reduction of the place by cutting off supplies. This plan was frustrated without the interference of the besieged. A sudden fall of snow occurred, and the army decamped, as one may imagine, rather crest-fallen. The tyrants could not, however, suffer an enemy to remain intrenched so close upon the city, and therefore the following day sent a body of troops to encamp as a guard within a few furlongs of the fortress. Here was a fair opportunity for the exercise of the generalship of Thrasybulus, who succeeded in surprising them one morning about dawn. A second time he put the enemy to rout with considerable loss of men and arms.* But with Thrasybulus and his noble exploits the short drama of Phyle concluded, and its name even is scarcely heard again in history.† The ivy—that faithful attendant of fallen greatness—clings to the now deserted walls; but while its branches hang down in luxurious festoons in front, its roots are gradually loosening the massive stones, and contributing to the work of destruction. I plucked a leaf with greater reverence than from that which creeps over the ruins of the Palace of the Cæsars.

The return from Phyle was no less agreable than the ride thither. The heat was more moderate, and the sides of Hymettus and Pentelicus were bathed in a flood of golden light as the sun sank behind Mount Ægaleos.

THE MARBLE QUARRIES OF PENTELICUS.

The quarries of Mount Pentelicus are celebrated throughout the world for the spotless material they have furnished to ancient and modern art. The remaining edifices of antiquity

* Xenophon, Hell. ii., 4; 2–7.

† When it was supposed that Philip was about to invade Attica, a decree was passed that all not on duty should remove to Athens; and that all goods be brought in from the fields into Athens or Piræus, unless they were more than 120 stadia distant from Athens; in which case they were to be carried to Eleusis, Phyle, Aphidna, Rhamnus, and Sunium. (*Demosth. de Cor.*, 238.)

at Athens are mostly constructed of Pentelic marble; and the columns of the Parthenon, albeit time has not spared their immaculate whiteness, are all the more beautiful for the excellence of this far-famed stone. If there were, however, as great a demand for it in Greece as there is at present in Italy, we should probably see no less waste than in the quarries of Carrara. It is fortunate that these treasures are too remote from the capital to become an object of spoliation to the Athenians of our day; and the best wish we can make for posterity is that the citizens may remain ignorant of their value, or indifferent to their beauty, until some new Phidias may arise to make a proper use of them.

A winter's day is barely sufficient to go from Athens to Pentelicus and return. The quarries, being all the time in sight, serve as a goal to the traveler. I mistook them at first for patches of snow. Starting from Athens in the early part of December with a party of American travelers, we followed for a time the road to Marathon. Presently turning to the right, we reached the hamlet of Calandri, pleasantly situated in an olive grove at the distance of six miles from Athens. Not a house had we passed on our way. Independent of the fact that the Greeks are, like the French, a social people, the unsettled state of the country, until within a few years, rendered it scarcely safe to inhabit a lonely spot, even within gun-shot of the suburbs. The fields, which are stony and sandy, are but poorly cultivated in comparison with the more fertile parts of the country. A few miles beyond this insignificant village, we came to the foot of the mountain, and found here a new and unfinished country seat of the Duchess of Plaisance. This eccentric woman was a Philadelphian by birth, and was married to a Frenchman. But her oddities proving too much for the happiness of both parties, it was agreed that they should live apart, though on the most friendly terms. The amiable old lady now confined her attention to her buildings, and to half a dozen dogs of various kinds, which she took out on an airing every afternoon. She enjoyed among the inhabitants the reputation of being a millionaire, from having an income of fifteen or twenty thousand dollars, which was lavishly expended.

A few rods farther, we entered a grove of shady trees, with a rill of cool water passing through it, and came to the Monastery of Pentele, or Mendele, for which, as usual, the monks have selected the most lovely spot in the neighborhood. Intending to stop here on our return, we commenced the ascent, and were soon engaged in a steep and rocky ravine, through which, at first, the path winds. Around us we saw many of the shrubs of Greece; among them the oleander and the heather, with its copious bunches of flesh-colored blossoms. The arbutus, however, most attracted our attention. The branches were laden partly with clusters of bell-shaped flowers, and partly with the yellow or red fruit, which has somewhat the flavor of the strawberry. One of our party, after tasting sufficiently of the pleasant berries, was considerably alarmed when he found that the color of all was not similar, and that the leaves of some were remarkably like those of the laurel. His companions, for his edification, cited the famous incident from Xenophon about the soldiers who were poisoned by eating honey made from laurel flowers. Recourse to the guide dispelled these fears, and banished all thoughts of emetics. The suspected shrub turned out to be only a variety of the arbutus.

This ravine was evidently used in ancient times, for there are several quarries of considerable extent on either side; and in one place we found two large blocks of marble, hewn perhaps centuries ago, lying by the path. But the principal quarries are farther up. In themselves, as might be expected, they are not very remarkable; it is rather the immense quantity of the stone which has been removed at the cost of so much trouble, that strikes you with astonishment. Here, half way up a very steep and rugged mountain, at an elevation of fifteen hundred or two thousand feet above the plain, whose houses appear like so many dots in the distance, the industry of the extraordinary people that once occupied this land obtained the materials to beautify their city with temples and statuary. Directly in front of the quarries there are remains of an ancient inclined plane, in some parts still paved with stone, down which the huge blocks of marble were lowered to the base of the mountain. Thence they were laboriously carried to Athens, nearly ten miles distant. The marble, which is of a dazzling whiteness by nature, and, when highly polished, resembles the purest wax, is here discolored by the stains of time; and ivy thrives where the chisel and hammer are no longer heard. The mass of rock that has been removed must have been enormous; and yet there seems to remain a boundless store to be worked.

Adjoining the quarries was a large cave, which we entered. It was apparently about two or three hundred feet in depth; but passages branching off from the end run probably far into the interior of the mountain. It was just such a cave as the ancients used to dedicate to the Muses, or to some rural deity. The walls of the cavern were hung toward the entrance with tufts of delicate ferns and mosses; and farther on there descended from the roof large stalactites, which in some places had formed thick columns to support the vault.

Above the cave the mountain rises more than a thousand feet. We ascended to enjoy the finest view I ever saw in Attica. To reach the top was a somewhat wearisome undertaking. Our horses fell repeatedly; and we found it altogether more agreeable to perform the rest of the journey on foot. We left them a short distance below the summit, to which we climbed over rocks, and through clumps of the dwarf prickly oak, which abounds on these mountains. We were favored with a day than which none could be clearer. The eye ranged from Chalcis to the Peloponnesus, and to the snow-capped top of Parnassus. But it was the distinctness with which all Attica was laid out before our eyes that most struck us. The plain of Marathon seemed actually spread out at our feet on one side; and the city of Athens, ten miles distant in a direct line on the other, could have been seen distinctly but for the intervening hill, Lycabettus. There is a considerable heap of stones upon the very summit of the mountain. As the custom is, each traveler adds a new stone to it before he leaves.

On our return, after a tedious descent, the greater part of which we were compelled to accomplish on foot, we arrived at the monastery, where, by the providence of our good guide, Spiro, we found a lunch prepared, which we ate under the porch of the church. The monastery, which is evidently ancient, is surrounded by a wall, with numerous port-holes, through which the spiritual inmates have, doubtless, been enabled, in more troublous times, to defend themselves against the Turk or the *kleft*. At such periods the inclosure became a refuge for the peasants of the neighborhood. The dwellings within contain nothing worthy of attention, being constructed of wood or stone, very irregularly distributed around the open court; but the church, into which we stepped for a moment, is old and singular. The paintings on the walls are executed in the ordinary Byzantine style which prevailed a few centuries back; but the faces of the apostles in some of them have more than usual merit. The vestibule was covered with small fresco designs, half obliterated by time, in which the Old Testament history, ancient myths, and modern legends, are oddly jumbled together. Jonah, with a hideous sea monster, figures prominently in them. We saw no monks about; but a company of peasants were propping up the dilapidated trellises in the court. Leaving this interesting monastery, after having bestowed a trifle for hospitality's sake, we were soon coursing over the plain toward Athens.

HYMETTUS AND ITS BEES.

Hymettus is the nearest mountain to Athens, its base being scarcely two or three miles distant to the southeast. One day in January, I seized the opportunity of a fair sky to visit the lower parts of the mountain; and after an hour's walk across the plain, commenced the ascent. The dry season was scarcely over, for the first winter rain had fallen in December, after the annual drought of summer; but the fields already began to look green, and the ground was covered with the common anemones of every shade, from white and blue to red. An olive grove was the first sign of our approach to the Monastery of Syriani, or Cæsariani. It contains several buildings for the monks. As usual in the cloisters of Greece, the entrance to the rooms is by means of half-decayed verandas and staircases running up on the side of the building that faces the court. Here, also, is a church, over the door of which I noticed a painting of the Presentation of the Virgin at the

Temple, which was striking for its simplicity. Anna sits upon a step of the building representing the Temple of Jerusalem, toward whose entrance the child Mary advances; while the angels who are placed around proclaim the event to the universe. It is quite in contrast with Titian's grand conception of the same subject at Venice.

The monastery has sadly fallen from its pristine glory. The fraternity is represented by a single abbot, who lives here quite alone. I afterward learned that he is a man of hospitable disposition and agreeable manners, and regretted that I had not made his acquaintance. His is a remarkable history, and yet one that has been often paralleled in Greece. Previous to the Revolution he officiated as a parish priest; but having drawn the sword at the time of the war, and killed some Turks, the strict canons of his Church obliged him to cease from his ministrations. Under similar circumstances, many others of the clergy have become soldiers, lawyers, or politicians. This man, however, preferred a retired life, and settled down here. He came near losing his life subsequently by an act of imprudence. A noted *kleft*—this occurred but a few years since—had been infesting Hymettus, and levying contributions on the peasants even within sight of Athens. The abbot gave notice to the government of his lurking-place on the mountain; and the robber hearing of it, vowed to take revenge on the informer. At the same time, with that species of frankness which is not inconsistent in the breast of the brigand with the greatest amount of cunning, he sent a letter to his enemy apprising him of this intention. Fortunately for the latter, the *kleft* himself was murdered by an emissary of the government. A peasant was hired to join the robbers, and put himself under the command of the criminal, whom, on the first favorable opportunity, he shot. It is reported that this peasant, in his turn, became a *kleft*, and was killed in an affray with the soldiery.

One part of the worthy abbot's duties seems to be to watch over the miracle, which annually occurs on the festival of some one of the saints, and which twenty thousand persons congregate to witness. As the wonder consists in a sudden rise of the water in a certain fountain to an unusual height, and as the pipe that feeds it comes from within the inclosure, it must be allowed that his task can scarcely be considered very difficult.

I climbed a ridge which lies directly back of Syriani, whence, though it is not the actual summit of Hymettus, a view quite as striking as from Pentelicus or Phyle may be obtained. But it is not for its scenery alone that this mountain has gained celebrity, for it has lost much in picturesque appearance by the wanton destruction of the forest trees. The *honey* of Hymettus is as well known and as highly appreciated now as of yore. The delicate flavor it possesses is said to be derived from the thyme that grows wild in the greatest profusion, both on the mountain and in the plain. It may be that the bees gather the greater part of their honey on the former, but the hives are certainly all to be found in the little villages at its base.

I remember with pleasure a visit I made to the country house of a friend at the little village of Cara (the whole of which was attached to his grounds), and the pride with which he showed me a yard covered with hives, from which the honey had just been gathered. The hives were as rude as possible in form. A deep and narrow basket set on end, with the mouth covered over, is smeared with clay, rendering it perfectly tight. A hole is then made near the bottom of the basket, with which the bees seem quite content. Honey is thus obtained in such abundance, that it is sold at one-third of the price the most common kind commands in our markets.

THE STRAITS OF SALAMIS.

The country between Athens and the Straits of Salamis being very level, we determined to make a pedestrian excursion to the scene of the naval conflict of Xerxes. We started about half past nine o'clock A.M., and took the road to Piræus. Before reaching the town, at the distance of five miles from Athens, we turned to the right, and entered on a path leading westward, parallel to the upper end of the harbor. We passed near the modern cemetery, and, continuing our walk, traversed the sites of two ancient *demi*, which, from Leake's map, seem to be those of Echele, near Piræus, and

Thymœta, near the head of Port Phoron. The remains of walls inclosing the latter are quite distinct in courses of large stones. The harbor is small, but prettily situated. A *caïque* was taking on board some bread when we approached, and soon after set sail in the direction of Salamis. It struck me on the spot that this little bay is admirably adapted for smuggling; and so I find it was used in ancient times. This whole district is deserted; and from the time we left the outskirts of Piræus, we found no house at all, and met no persons but a few shepherds tending their flocks in solitude, and three or four peasants driving their loaded mules to the ferry of Salamis.

We soon reached the scene of action between the Greek and Persian squadrons. Not far from where we stood, the Great King had caused his throne to be erected in a conspicuous situation. Seated upon this elevation, his eye could glance over his fleet ranged in a triple line in front of him. Beyond it were the high hills of the island of Salamis; and at the bottom of a deep bay below them the town of the same name could be plainly distinguished. Across the mouth of this bay the Greek vessels were drawn up, between the easternmost promontory of Salamis and a small island that lies in the strait. The single line of the Greeks was opposed to the far more numerous vessels of Xerxes, which were arranged along the shore of the main land as far as Piræus. But few of the barbarians came into the combat. Their numbers only increased the confusion that arose, from the violence with which the enemy rushed forward to meet them. The two back lines of ships were more destructive to their own forces than to those of the Greeks, in a strait barely a mile in breadth. Fragments from the wreck of this proud armament are said to have been strewn along the shore for miles southward of Piræus. "The sea," says Æschylus, "was no longer to be seen for the broken ships and the bodies of the slain, which covered even the rocks and the shore. The remaining vessels of the Persians had recourse to a disorderly flight. Those disabled were surrounded by the Greeks; and the men, like a shoal of tunnies or a netful of other fish, were beaten to death with broken oars. Night alone put an end to the cries and groans that filled all the Pelasgian Sea; for never before was such a multitude of men slain in a single day."* Meanwhile the astonished and affrighted king, after witnessing the total extinction of his fond hopes of conquest, and the destruction of an expedition prepared at great pains, was happy to find relief from anxiety and danger in a precipitate and inglorious flight. This victory sealed the independence of Greece; and the battle of Platæa in the succeeding year (B.C. 479) freed her from all apprehension of fresh invasions.

As we sat on the sea-shore at the base of Mount Ægaleos, the modern Scaramanga, identifying the localities before us, and impressing their outline upon our memory, the unruffled strait wore that calm and placid aspect peculiar to the waters of this inland sea. There was nothing to disturb the stillness of the scene save the *caïque* we had recently seen, and two or three row-boats crossing at the ferry of Salamis. But for the sure testimony of history, we should have doubted that nature, here reposing so quietly, had ever been distracted by the din of warlike conflict, and the tumult of deadly passion.

* This translation is that of Colonel Leake, Attica, p. 253, 254.

TEMPLE OF MINERVA AT SUNIUM.

CHAPTER XXI.

THE MODERN GREEK LANGUAGE.

Graiis dedit ore rotundo
Musa loqui. *(Hor. de arte poet.)*

THE modern Greek holds an intermediate rank between the classic languages and those that have arisen on their basis in the other countries of Southern Europe. None of the latter have retained so close a resemblance to the Latin as the former bears to the ancient Greek. To this it is owing that scholars are divided in opinion with reference to its intrinsic character: some calling it an entirely new language, while others regard it as simply a dialect or corruption of the ancient. Hence the resemblance has hitherto proved rather an injury than an advantage to its reputation. Were the diversities of inflection and syntax as marked as in the case of the French or Italian, the modern Greek would claim to be judged exclusively upon its own merits; but closely related as it is to the ancient, there is room for invidious comparison. The superficial observer is apt to mistake the question, and is tempted to exclaim, "How far inferior to the tongue of Homer and Demosthenes!" instead of asking himself, "How does the language compare in richness, flexibility, and harmony with the Italian or Spanish?"

Much of the depreciation of the modern Greek, which it has become fashionable to indulge in, arises out of the difficulty experienced by foreign tourists, however well educated, in understanding the language in its strange pronunciation. The system introduced into Europe more than three centuries ago, and sanctioned by the name of Erasmus, is so unlike that which prevails in Greece, that the accomplished scholar, familiar with the writings of Plato and the tragic poets, can neither understand the language as now spoken, nor even those eminent authors themselves when read aloud by a native. It is natural enough, then, that he should regard the modern tongue as barbarous, and those that speak it as degenerate scions of a noble stock. On more profound examination, such a scholar would find the difference less in the language employed than in the pronunciation given to the words, and that this springs from two distinct sources. The more palpable is the different sound given to letters and diphthongs; the other, the following of the written accents as the sole guide in giving emphasis to syllables. In respect to both, the usage of the modern Greeks is perfectly systematic, and throughout consistent with itself. Each syllable is enunciated precisely as it is written, and every word emphasized according to certain fixed rules—the same that apply to the ancient text.

Most of the consonants have the same sounds as in our system of pronunciation. The letters Β, Δ, and Γ are softened, the first two being sounded like our *V* and soft *th* in *that*. Ξ is always pronounced like *X*, and Σ never like our *Z*, even at the close of a syllable, except when it precedes the letter M. X has a sound quite different from K, and not unlike the soft G of the Germans. It is, however, with the pronunciation of the vowels and diphthongs that most fault has been found. The Greeks will generally acknowledge that they have lost the distinction between *ο* and *ω*, which are now alike pronounced long. But not so with the rest. They insist that *αι* should be pronounced æ, and *αυ* and *ευ*, af or av, etc. No less than three letters and as many diphthongs receive in common the sound of our *e;* viz., *η*, *ι*, *υ*, *ει*, *οι*, and *υι*. It is urged by those who agree with Erasmus, that it can not be conceived that the ancients should have employed six different methods of expressing a single sound. In reply, the modern Greeks, with the disciples of Reuchlin, assert that the same inconsistency might be predicated with equal truth of any other language. They deny that the harmony of their language would be improved by the admission of such sounds as those introduced by Erasmus; and they fortify their position by bringing instances of proper names of Greek origin transferred into Latin in such a manner as to show that the combinations in question could not have been pronounced as Erasmus pretended. The use of the accents is an equally fruitful source of contention. Since, however, it is not my purpose to enter into the discussion of this intricate subject, which ever since the sixteenth century has divided the scholars of Europe into opposing parties, I shall only add that the system of accentuation has been rigidly adhered to; and, whether originally intended for use in pronunciation or not, has now become so thoroughly inwrought into the spirit of the language as to be followed out with scrupulous exactness in all its details.

Passing on to the acknowledged alterations of the language, it will be necessary to specify a few of the more important changes in the grammatical forms. In the declension of substantives, the most apparent one is the total loss of the dative case. The accusative is mostly employed in its place, preceded by a preposition. The dual has entirely disappeared. The verb has been greatly simplified by omitting in common discourse, except in a few conventional phrases, the optative mood, and the perfect, pluperfect, and future tenses. The auxiliary verb is introduced to express periphrastically the tenses that have thus been lost. The infinitive itself has become obsolete, and is clumsily replaced by the subjunctive with a conjunction indicative of purpose.

When we consider the long period of time during which the language has been exposed to the common vicissitudes of all human inventions, it appears more remarkable that so many words should have been retained with little or no alteration, than that some should have disappeared and been superseded by others of foreign origin. From the very nature of the case, in the continual intercourse, both peaceable and warlike, with the surrounding nations, many terms have been imported from Italy, Turkey, and Albania. But the most remarkable circumstance in respect to them is, that they have always, as far as possible, been changed so as to agree with the analogy of the Greek language. One of the most remarkable and characteristic alterations in words of undoubted Greek origin is the abundant use of diminutives—forms indicating, as has been somewhere remarked, as great a degeneracy in the people who introduce them as in their language itself.

A similar revolution has taken place in the syntax. It has become less involved, and more consonant with the spirit of other modern languages.

In this enumeration of the chief alterations which the noble tongue of the Greeks has undergone, I have described its condition at the commencement of this century rather than its present state. The past fifty years have wrought changes as wonderful, perhaps, as the world has ever witnessed in this branch of knowledge. It would not be extravagant to assert that there has been a greater improvement in the language of the people and the education of the masses, than even in the government and material prosperity of the country. This progress, as it naturally stands connected with the literary labors of Coray and his less gifted competitors, it seems more proper to associate with the consideration of the modern Greek literature. But it may not be out of place to repeat a few of its results, as they appear at the present day.

The emendation of the language has been begun by lopping off all unnecessary branches. Every word for which a native origin was not to be found has been proscribed with ruthless severity. Some of the least offensive, it is true, have been tolerated for a time, until suitable substitutes can be found; but their fate is none the less certain. Not that this reformation could be effected in a single day; for, as the departure of the language from its original purity has been gradual, so must the return be gradual. Yet it has been more rapid than the most sanguine could reasonably have expected. The press has been assiduous in its exertions for the improvement of the language. The university has wielded a potent influence toward the same end. The government has favored the movement by a return to classic usage in the language of its codes of law, and in its judicial terms, and even by restoring the ancient names of all the townships throughout Greece, where any such could be found. So great and so rapid has been the change, that, as is elsewhere remarked, even the professors in the University of Otho are compelled by it to remodel the diction of their discourses every few years. The contagion of this new epidemic has spread even to the common people of Athens and the other large towns. They are no longer content with speaking the same adulterated language as their immediate ancestors; and have consequently introduced words and phrases that are quite unintelligible to their less favored fellow-citizens, the inhabitants of the villages and rural districts.

What limits so singular and so radical a movement will reach, it is beyond the knowledge of any man living to foretell. The facility with which new words can still be introduced indicates that the language is yet in that plastic state in which a master hand may mould it as he pleases. At the same time, there is danger that the imitation of foreign, and especially of French, authors, may exert a deleterious influence on its purity and elegance, by the introduction of new and uncongenial idioms. On the other hand, a growing acquaintance with those classic models of composition which they already possess, will counteract the inclination of the Greeks to copy blindly from their foreign contemporaries.

The most serious inconvenience springing from the diversity of pronunciation that exists between the Greeks and the scholars of the West, is the formidable obstacle it offers to their intercourse with each other. The seven or eight millions that speak the modern Greek—a small portion within the bounds of the Hellenic kingdom, but the greater part outside of it—are every year advancing in intelligence, wealth, and influence. Their national literature is promising. The city of Athens already sustains a larger number of journals, for its size, than any other city in the world.* The language

* In 1852 there were fourteen political papers published at Athens; none, however, appeared more frequently than twice or three times a

has even now reached such a point, that to acquire a reasonable degree of facility in speaking it would be the work of but a few months, for one familiar with the ancient Greek, were it not for the dissimilarity of pronunciation. As the Greek people seems destined to exert an important influence among the nations of the globe, it were really desirable that this barrier to free intercourse might be wholly removed.

week. Since that date one or two dailies have been established. Syra had three newspapers, and Patras, Tripolitza, and Chalcis, each one. There were also three literary periodicals printed at Athens, with a total circulation of about 2000 copies. Now, as the population of Athens is estimated at 26,000 or 28,000 inhabitants, it is evident that the list of subscribers for each of these fourteen political journals must be very limited. We were assured by a prominent publisher that of none were there printed more than three or four hundred copies! Nor is the statement incredible, taking into consideration the cheapness of manual labor in the East, and the high subscription price demanded. Most Athenians read the papers at the *lesche*, or coffee-house.

FORTRESS OF PHYLE.

CHAPTER XXII.

THE MODERN GREEK LITERATURE.

THE intellectual development of a nation is a subject of inquiry even more interesting than its advance in material prosperity. In both cases, the causes that have given impulse to the activity of the people are often imperceptible in themselves, or, in the lapse of a few hundred years, have been irrecoverably lost sight of. Not unfrequently, after centuries of inaction, which, had they not been succeeded by a more vivacious period, might be mistaken for entire cessation of life, the popular energies have, without any apparent cause, sprung into new activity. Such was the fact respecting that nation, whose very name is associated in our minds with all that is brightest and most illustrious in remote antiquity. Its political course, indeed, brilliant and extraordinary as it was, lasted but a short time. Three or four centuries were the limits of its ascendency; after which it receded to the rank assigned by its contracted territory in the vast Roman empire. But for ages after its political importance, and even its independence, had been lost, Greece yet held the first place in literature, science, and art. Even this poor consolation, however, was at length withdrawn. The wave of barbarism rolled over it, and obliterated those marks of ancient greatness which had been spared by civil subjugation and oppression. At last the

Greeks reached that point of debasement to which we find them reduced at the time of the Turkish conquest. Every spark of patriotism was extinguished; and the people passed, without seeming to care for the change, from under the yoke of the Franks to that of the Turks. Schools of learning were nearly unknown. Their decline can be traced back to the age of Justinian, upon whose reign, otherwise brilliant, rests the reproach of having stopped the payment of the sums that for a long time had been applied to the support of teachers in the various cities of his empire. The means thus obtained were spent partly, we are told, in the erection of a new and splendid cathedral at Constantinople, to replace one destroyed by fire.*

Of a revival of learning in Greece, the first symptoms began to exhibit themselves in the last century. The very state of subjection in which the nation lay, was the occasion of the new impulse which both the material interests of the country and its learning now received. The Greeks were cut off from all hope of enriching themselves through the cultivation of the soil, by the continual presence and oppressions of the Turks, who, living among the people, were ready at any time to seize upon the avails of their industry. The fruits of years of hard labor were liable to be plundered in a moment; and, more than that, they were sure to involve the possessor in personal danger. The inhabitants of the maritime towns and of the islands possessed far greater advantages. The navy of their masters was manned almost exclusively by them. They enjoyed the right of carrying on commerce under the flags of several of the civilized nations of Europe; and they thus began to taste of various immunities, and of partial independence. They planted themselves in foreign cities, for the purpose of carrying on their trade to greater advantage; and many of the commercial houses that originated thus became wealthy. Meanwhile, though far from his native home, the Greek merchant preserved all his affection for his country, and retained the hope of some day returning, and spending his old age in comfort, with the wealth he had acquired abroad. It was impossible that such constant and intimate intercourse with the nations of Western Europe should be without profit

* Zonaras, iii., 52.

to a people who, whatever defects they possess, certainly show an extraordinary love for improvement.

Schools now began to be established in different cities of Greece and Asia Minor; and a high school was to be found at Jannina, in Albania.

The chief teachers of these academies of learning were drawn from Mount Athos, or the "Hagion Oros" of the natives, where some learning began to spread among the thousands of rich and idle monks who swarmed in the many monasteries. From schools such as these must have been, it was not to be expected that there should arise men remarkable for mental culture. Accordingly, among the authors who flourished up to the end of the last century, we find few or none, if we except Meletius, the geographer, who enjoyed a European reputation. Their scanty literature, as Lord Byron truly observed, was almost exclusively confined to works of a religious character. His remarks on the causes of this fact are just and forcible: "'Ay, but,' say the generous advocates of oppression, who, while they assert the ignorance of the Greeks, wish to prevent them from dispelling it; 'ay, but these are mostly, if not all, religious tracts, and consequently good for nothing.' Well, and pray what else can they write about? It is pleasant enough to hear a Frank, particularly an Englishman, who may abuse the government of his own country, or a Frenchman, who may abuse every government except his own, and who may range at will over every philosophical, religious, scientific, skeptical, or moral subject, sneering at the Greek legends. A Greek must not write on politics, and can not touch on science for want of instruction; if he doubts, he is excommunicated and damned; therefore his countrymen are not poisoned with modern philosophy; and as to morals, thanks to the Turks! there are no such things. What, then, is left him if he has a turn for scribbling? Religion and holy biography: and it is natural enough that those who have so little in this life should look to the next. It is no wonder, then, that in a catalogue now before me of fifty-five Greek writers, many of whom were lately living, not above fifteen should have touched on any thing but religion."*

* Lord Byron's remarks on the Romaic or Modern Greek Language.

The popular literature of the times, if that term may be so applied, comprised little more than the poetic legends of the saints, and a few paraphrases of Bible stories. Some of these are not wholly destitute of merit; and the quaintness of the style adds force to the narrative. We have seen a thick volume of such poems, containing sometimes as many as twelve hundred lines, called the "Cathreptes Gynaicon," or Mirror for Women. Though in extensive circulation toward the end of the last century, it is probable that the authorship of most of them dates farther back. To these must be added a large number of popular kleftic or banditti songs, as well as a few heroic hymns, such as that of Rigas, which were rarely committed to writing.

Commencing our retrospect with the beginning of the present century, our attention is naturally drawn first to Coray, at once the father of modern Greek literature, and the most distinguished writer it can yet boast of.

Adamantius Coray, or Coraes, was born at Smyrna, on the 27th of April, 1748. His father, John Coray, was, however, a native of Scio, and his son, in accordance with the notions of the Orientals, always considered that island as his fatherland. The history of his early days has been preserved to us in an autobiography, in which, within the compass of a few pages, he has attempted to note the more important events of his life. Like Franklin, he records mistakes and mishaps, as well as successes. He commences with the declaration that "whoever would write his own memoirs must note both the achievements and failures of his life with such accuracy as neither to magnify the former nor underrate the latter. A thing," he adds, "most difficult of accomplishment, on account of the selfishness and vanity that are implanted in each one of us." His father was a man of little education, but of great natural acuteness. His maternal grandfather was the most learned Greek philologist of his time, and had himself educated his four daughters, who were almost the only young ladies in the large city of Smyrna able to read and write.

Adamantius was early sent to a school recently established by a Sciote, which, he informs us, resembled all the other schools in Greece at that time; that is, the master gave very little instruction, accompanied with overmuch chastisement. So severe, indeed, was the latter, that his younger brother Andrew forsook his studies in disgust, contrary to his parents' advice. Besides the love of study and emulation, there was another motive that induced Adamantius to persevere. It was the provision contained in his grandfather's will, that his library should be adjudged to that one of his grandsons who should first leave the school possessed of as much knowledge as the teacher himself. This prize was the occasion of considerable rivalry between the grandchildren; but Adamantius was the successful candidate. The number of books it contained was small, but sufficient to convince the young student of the utter insignificance of the titles of "Most learned," and "Most wise and learned," which at that time were lavished upon all, without exception, who knew the declensions of nouns and the conjugations of verbs. The limited extent of his own acquirements, combined with the extreme difficulty of making progress in study in the illiterate city of Smyrna, instead of discouraging him, only roused him to more earnest efforts. He finally succeeded in obtaining masters to instruct him in Italian and French. These languages he wished to acquire, less for any direct advantage that he expected to reap from them, than for the assistance they would furnish him in the study of Latin. His teachers, he tells us, were superior in nothing to his former master, except that they imparted instruction without beating. But it was to his acquaintance with a Protestant clergyman that Coray used afterward to attribute, not only the progress he made in literature, but the moral principles that formed the basis of his excellent character. Bernard Keun, the chaplain of the Dutch consul at Smyrna, took interest in the young man, and instructed him in Latin and other languages. His name was never mentioned by his scholar but with love. Two years were subsequently spent by Coray in Holland, as an agent of the commercial house with which his father was connected.

It was not until 1782, when more than thirty-four years of age, that Coray succeeded in carrying out a long-cherished plan of going to Montpellier, in France, to study medicine—a profession best calculated to succeed among the Turks, who were compelled to be respectful at least to their physicians. For six years he remained at Montpellier, engaged principally in his studies; and in 1787 he commenced his literary career by the translation of the Catechism of the Russian monk Plato into the modern Greek language, and of several medical treatises into the French.

A year later Coray removed to Paris, which thenceforth became his permanent home. There almost all his works were published, and there he imagined that he could write with more freedom than in his native land, oppressed as it then was by barbarians, the very sight of whom was intolerable to him. It was at Paris that Coray first acquired reputation as one of the most excellent Greek scholars of Europe. The First Consul, Napoleon, desired that a translation of Strabo's Geography should be made into French, with copious annotations. This work was intrusted to Coray, in connection with two Frenchmen. The first volume was presented to the Emperor Napoleon in 1805, and with such favor was it received, that, besides the annual appropriation made to each of the authors during the continuance of their labors, a pension of 2000 francs was conferred upon them for life. At the same time, the Emperor made to each of them a present of a copy of the splendid and costly work on the Egyptian expedition published under his auspices. This translation, together with that of Hippocrates, which had been previously made, established the reputation of our Greek as a scholar.

But Coray desired no such empty and unprofitable distinctions as are acquired by the mere accumulation of knowledge. He longed to diffuse its beneficial influence, especially among his own countrymen. The difficulty, however, was to determine how their interests could be best promoted. The disastrous issue of successive attempts to liberate Greece, and more especially the bloody scenes which had occurred but a few years before, after the Russian invasion of the Morea, must have convinced him of the impracticability, even had he not been already persuaded of the inexpediency, of endeavors to render his native land independent. He deplored the state of ignorance, and intellectual and moral degradation into which it had fallen, still more than its weakness and political subjection. The fetters of the tyrant might by some unexpected means be broken; but the chains of ignorance which centuries had riveted could not be so easily cast off.

Coray's first enterprise was to furnish those of his countrymen who were desirous of learning—and he knew that there were many included in this class—with the means of instructing themselves. He therefore commenced in 1805 what he had long contemplated—the publication of the principal Greek authors, with copious notes. The utility of such a series can be estimated only by those who consider the rarity of books in Greece, and the still greater scarcity of dictionaries, works on classical antiquities, and annotated editions. Few presses were to be found in the country. All religious works were printed at Venice or Vienna, as many of them are to the present day. The zeal of Coray, however, would probably have fallen short of the accomplishment of his object, had it not been seconded by the liberality of the brothers Zosimades, rich Greek merchants living in Northern Europe, who furnished him with the funds requisite for the publication of his volumes, until the malevolent intrigues of the superstitious party induced them to withdraw their assistance.

The following works succeeded each other at short intervals: An edition of Isocrates was the first, and it raised yet higher the reputation of Coray as a critic. Next appeared Plutarch's Lives, Strabo's Geography, the Politics of Aristotle, his Nicomachean Ethics, the Memorabilia of Xenophon, Plato's Gorgias, and the speech of Lycurgus against Leochares. Then came the Strategics of Polyænus and of Onesander, Æsop, Xenocrates and Galen, Marcus Aurelius, Plutarch's Politics, Epictetus, Arrian, and several others, making in all thirty-nine volumes. In some respects the plan of these editions is quite peculiar. Each volume is preceded by a preface, now, at least, considered a most invaluable portion of the work. These prolegomena are partly introductory to the study of the author; and yet are made, at the same time, the vehicle for conveying such thoughts as, in the present state of the nation, the editor thought most likely to prove salutary. Often, indeed, their connection with the subject of the text is very slight; and, on the whole, the prolegomena must be viewed rather in the light of distinct tracts. Many of the more important have been collected and published in separate form.

Among the most attractive of these prolegomena are the series prefixed to the first four books of the Iliad. They are devoted to the imaginary history of an illiterate parish priest, a character of which, unfortunately, too many specimens are yet to be found in Greece. He is represented as officiating in his native village of Bolissos, on the island of Scio, which the author supposes to be the birth-place of Homer. This priest was surnamed Papa Trechas, from the rapidity with which he was accustomed to run over the church service—a feat upon which he prided himself exceedingly. He used to boast of his sixty-four journeys, and hence esteemed himself another Ulysses; from whom he differed only in this respect, that he made these visits to the sixty-four hamlets of the island, instead of the distant seas and regions visited by the Homeric wanderer. This furnishes a good opportunity for the exhibition of those errors in society which rendered the priesthood of the Greek Church, in general, at once the most ignorant and the most vicious portion of the community. For Papa Trechas had, in his youth, been so wild and unruly, that a council of his relatives had been called to decide what should be done with him. Various trades were proposed, but it was evident that the lad would not learn any of them. At length the wisest of the conclave said, "You see before you an ignorant, lazy, thriftless, and most vicious youth, and do you counsel to bind him out to some mechanic, as though he were capable of learning any trade? What else can you do with him than make him a priest?" The proposition was adopted by acclamation, every body wondering that the idea had never struck him before. And so the boy was set apart for the priesthood. But Papa Trechas is a character in many respects far superior to his fellows. Under his rough exterior is hidden a kindly nature; and his intellect needs only the first taste, in order to thirst for learning. The awakening of his conscience, and the regrets experienced in looking back on so many years of his life worse than wasted, are portrayed in a forcible manner. In short, Papa Trechas is a fair example both of what the priesthood are, and of what they may become.

His history exhibits, also, the influence they will exert when religion and education have fitted them for their sacred work.

We have selected this instance from the Prolegomena of Coray, as illustrating the method he took to enlighten the minds of his fellow Greeks on subjects which he thought to be of vital importance to their advancement. In his religious opinions, Coray was far superior to most of those with whom he was associated. Philosophy had not disturbed his convictions; but, on the contrary, had strengthened them. When the tares of a heathenish superstition were eradicated, the pure grain was left to strike its roots unobstructed in a soil well adapted for its growth. In his works the subject of religion is nowhere avoided, but is ever treated in an honest and manly way. After reading his treatises, no one can doubt that on almost, if not quite every important doctrine, his belief coincided with that of the Reformed Churches. It was with the object of opening the eyes of the Greeks to the fact that their superstitious observances were not an integral part of their religion, but a perversion which in the course of ages had crept in, that in 1820 he published a translation of the remarkable "Advice of Three Bishops to Pope Julius the Third."* "The publication of such a work," he informs us, "had for its object the improvement, and at the same time the justification, of the Eastern Church. It was impossible that long servitude, while it deprived the race of education, should not corrupt the clergy, and confuse our religious belief. Whatever, and however numerous, may have been the sins of the Eastern Christians, they are not to be compared with the frightful abuses of the Papal Court; they are but as drops to the ocean. * * * For any one to condemn all the Eastern priesthood on account of the luxury of a few Sardanapalus-like bishops at Constantinople, is as if one should

* This singular production, in the form of a letter of counsel written to the pope in 1553, by the three bishops of Brescia, Capri, and Thessalonica, was rescued from oblivion by the diligence of the scholar Llorente, and first published in his *Monumens historiques concernant les deux pragmatiques-sanctions de France*, etc., 1818. Llorente having been chief secretary of the Spanish Inquisition, and having had the principal documents in his hands, possessed an admirable opportunity of discovering the iniquities of the system with which he was connected.

liken all the laity to the Fanariots of Constantinople."* This little work, containing so many thrusts against the Eastern Church, under cover of the superstitions of the West, was, as may be readily imagined, very obnoxious to the hierarchy. Even the well-known fact that Coray was the author of the notes (though it was issued anonymously), would scarcely have saved it from the fulminations of the "Holy Synod," had not his friends managed to postpone the consideration of it until too late to arrest its circulation.

How devoted to his country's prosperity Coray was, we have already seen. Yet, strange as it may seem, no one was more grieved than he to hear tidings of the commencement of the Greek Revolution. During its continuance, he places the following words in the mouth of one of the persons in a dialogue: "They (the instigators of the Revolution) are scarcely deserving of forgiveness; since, with the blood of many myriads of men, with the disgrace of unnumbered women, with the conversion to Islam of multitudes of young men and maidens, with the destruction of whole cities, they have purchased freedom (or rather an image of freedom), which, after twenty, or, at most, thirty years, would have been surely and absolutely obtained, with incomparably fewer evils."† About the same time he thus writes to a friend:

"Contostavlos has brought me a sacred relic, a dry twig of a plant from the tomb of the founder of American blessedness, Washington. If our political revolution had been delayed but twenty years more, there would certainly have arisen among us also, if not some Washington, at least some *diminutive* Washington. But now, my friend, from the particulars they write me from Greece, our government is in a deplorable state. Ambition, covetousness, strife for power, complete infatuation, in a word, have taken possession of the heads of some few, who would long since have ruined their country had it not possessed Marathonian warriors, and an enemy to fight against still more stupid than themselves."‡

Coray lived to see his country freed from the domination of

* Βίος 'Α. Κοραῆ, σελ. 31–2.

† Προλεγόμενα εἰς τὰς 'Επικτ. Διατριβάς, I. 21.

‡ 'Επιστολαὶ 'Α. Κοραῆ. I. 92 (April 29, 1827).

the Turks. He died at Paris, in April, 1833, at the advanced age of eighty-five years.

Next, perhaps, to Coray, Neophytus Doukas (or, as the name may be anglicized, Ducas) was the best philologist among the Greeks. He was a younger man than the former, whom he survived about twelve years. Their minds were strikingly dissimilar. Both were enthusiastically bent on the improvement and elevation of their unfortunate fatherland; but they reasoned differently in respect to the means by which this end was to be obtained. Doukas, being a member of the clergy, had prejudices, which even liberal culture could not wholly eradicate. He perceived that the people had fallen much below their ancestors in all that constitutes the well-being of a nation; but he did not trace this as clearly as did Coray, to the perversion of the Church from its original character and mission. At the same time, Doukas was a blind admirer of antiquity.

In nothing, perhaps, did the two scholars differ more widely than in the views they adopted as to the direction that the modern language should take. The singular position which the Greek tongue occupied a half century ago, and occupies still, is this. In the midst of all its corruptions, it had been handed down from father to son, with so much resemblance to the original, that one might hesitate whether to consider it a modern language or a dialect of the ancient Greek. An immense number of words had been preserved almost unchanged. The conjugation of verbs and the declensions of nouns were identical, except in those forms which had been simplified or omitted, or where the auxiliary verb had been introduced, after the manner of the Western tongues. The pronunciation, too, whatever doubts were to be entertained as to its conformity with the ancient, had adhered with singular fidelity to the system of accentuation: an adherence quite peculiar in such forms, for example, as the passive aorists. But to this original element of the language, which was by far the predominating one, there had been added a host of foreign words, particularly Latin, Italian, and Turkish, with a smaller admixture from the Albanian and other dialects. Some insist that these words, having existed for centuries in the language, have become an integral part of it, and ought not to be lightly rejected. These persons warn the innovators, lest, by casting off such terms of foreign origin, they impoverish their mother tongue; while they fail to supply their place with others equally expressive, and more in accordance with analogy. Besides, they urge, and not without a show of reason, that in the course of twenty centuries elapsed since the commencement of the decline of letters in Greece, new ideas have been introduced, and circumstances have so changed, as to require similar alterations in the language of the people. It would, of course, be a useless task to turn over the pages of a lexicon to find the proper Hellenic word for a railroad, a steamboat, or a daguerreotype.

Doukas insisted on a rigid adherence to the ancient language, and struck out every word of foreign origin, or irreducible to a pure root. A more serious fault was to attempt the simultaneous re-introduction of a quantity of tenses, cases, and, worse yet, constructions which had fallen into disuse. The consequences of such a course are seen in the treatment his works have received. Written in a style which is itself entirely ancient, the paraphrases accompanying his editions of various classical writers are themselves as obscure as the original; and the modern Greek student, who refers to them to elucidate some particular passage, finds so much difficulty in interpreting them, that he at length prefers contenting himself with the meaning he can extract from the author. His notes are valued, but are not read. Yet it must be conceded that Doukas was a scholar of merit, and of great learning in his particular department. His industry and capacity appear more surprising when the fact is recalled that he wrote without assistance from any European editions; for it is said that he was scarcely acquainted with the Latin, or with any of the modern languages besides his own.*

* The works of Doukas with which we are acquainted—besides some volumes devoted to rhetoric, logic, physics, and general literature—consist of annotated editions of Sophocles, Euripides, Homer, Æschylus, Theocritus, Pindar, Anacreon, and Aristophanes. These editions, making in all twenty-four volumes, lie before us. They were published partly at Athens, and the earlier ones at Ægina, where Doukas was engaged in the instruction of the young. Of these various works we are told that about fifteen thousand copies were printed; a great part of

The views of the clear-sighted Coray, in respect to the direction which the development of the modern Greek language should take, were directly opposite to those of Doukas. With an ear as quick to the beauties of the classics, he united a better discernment of the difficulties to be encountered in restoring the common language to its original purity.

"As descendants of the Greeks, says the despiser of the common language, we ought to revive our ancestral tongue. That would be very well, assuredly, if we lived in those times when the dead were raised, and the gift of tongues was imparted without labor. But miracles do not occur every day."*

The obstacles that prevent a modern writer from ever attaining a perfectly pure and easy style, if he attempt to write like the ancients, seemed to Coray almost, if not quite, insurmountable. And even this difficulty overcome, a still greater discouragement presents itself, which we shall introduce in the critic's own words:

"Whoever writes in ancient Greek, after a few years (and frequently after a few days), will be forgotten, together with his works. And why should he be remembered? Because of the subjects on which he writes? But these, in process of time, will be more clearly and perfectly treated by our descendants. On account of his classical phraseology? And who is so foolish, or has such an abundance of time, as to leave the Homers, the Platos, the Xenophons, the Demosthenes, and so many other wonderful Greek writers, in order to read this new Hellenist? On the other hand, whoever exercises himself in the common language, if his industry be accompanied with judgment, it is possible that he may attain the rank, I do not say of a classic writer, but of those authors whom the coming generations will examine, in order to learn from them the present condition of the language."†

His description of an author who is too strict an imitator of the ancients is well drawn:

"Surrounded by lexicographers, by Atticists, by grammarians of every kind, he writes, erases, rewrites, and again

which were distributed gratuitously to the public schools and to poor students.

* Κοραῆ Προλεγόμενα, p. 42. † Id., p. 43.

erases; he is in doubt at every phrase, perplexed at every period. Now he takes counsel of one friend; now of another. At one time he throws away altogether the happy conceptions of his mind, because he knows not how to give them birth in an Attic shape; and at another he lops them, in order to make them correspond in length with some ancient phrase, the recalling of which he considers a most fortunate idea."*

But while thus ridiculing the thought of writing in "a language which the writer forms, in the first place, from his lexicon, and so gleans from the words and phrases of at least fifteen centuries, that is to say, from fifteen languages," Coray by no means advocated the retention of the imperfections and corruptions of the language as it is now spoken. On the contrary, he thought that the time for better things had arrived.

"What I term a reformation of the language, includes not only the alteration of different barbarously-formed words and constructions, but also the preservation of many others, which those who have not examined the nature of the language with attention are desirous of banishing from it as barbarous. Such a reformation was impossible in the time of Eustathius. The period of downfall is not the suitable time for rebuilding. The householder weeps when he beholds from afar the ruin of his dwelling; and as soon as the tottering walls have fallen, and the dust has blown away, he approaches and collects as many materials as he can from the ruins, in order to construct a new house. The moment, so long desired, for rebuilding, has at length arrived. * * * However much the language has been corrupted, it still retains many Greek words, and meanings of words, that one would vainly seek for in the dictionaries; many derivatives, of which only the primitives are found in the classics. In a word, it preserves many relics of the ancient language—venerable relics, the neglect of which has produced so many foolish grammatical rules, so many ridiculous etymologies, so many miserable interpretations of classical authors, so many ignorant teachers, and what is worse, has rendered so irksome the study of the Greek language."†

* Κοραῆ Προλεγόμενα, p. 45.

† Id., p. 36, et seq.

Such were the two schools that arose: the one, headed by Doukas, and more recently by Œconomus, desirous not only of restoring the language at once to its pristine purity, by the re-introduction of obsolete words, but also of employing the involved construction of sentences, which it is quite impossible for a modern ear to follow; the other school proposing to retain what is valuable in the modern language, yet gradually to restore it to the nearest practicable resemblance to its ancient form. It must be admitted that Coray sometimes erred in complying unnecessarily with popular errors—a defect the more conspicuous from the rapid progress which the process of purification has since made. Yet modern authors, especially those of the greatest reputation, have generally adhered to the school of Coray.

In Greece there has happened the reverse of what usually takes place in the progress of a nation toward a higher culture and civilization. While prose literature has prospered, and great progress has been made in science, poetry, on the other hand, has received little attention. Poems, it is true, have not been wanting; but, thus far, modern Greece has produced no Homer or Hesiod.

Panagiotes Soutsos is by many considered the best contemporary poet. The first volume of his "Hapanta," or "Complete Works," which is all that has yet been published, contains three tragedies, entitled "Blachabas," the "Traveler," and the "Messiah." The first treats of the resuscitation of the Greek race; the second is rather of the nature of a romance, "melancholy love being its chief subject." The character of the third is sufficiently indicated by its title. The style of these three poems is purely Hellenic, though the author has avoided the blunder of attempting to introduce the ancient syntax. The greatest fault we have to find with Soutsos is the inordinate vanity that disfigures his preface. In speaking of the various metres used in modern Greek, he employs quotations from his own poems as examples; and this may, perhaps, be excused on account of the paucity of specimens. But we can less easily pardon his egregious self-conceit, when he not only compares a number of lines from his tragedy of the "Messiah" to some of the most famous passages in Homer, and to one of Tasso (which he himself tells us is yet the boast of Italy), but even presumes to speak of them as "equally beautiful."*

The poems of Alexander Soutsos, brother of the author we have just mentioned, are of an entirely different stamp. Of his works that lie before us, one, entitled the "Periplanomenos, or Wanderer," is a poem in three parts, and contains reminiscences of a journey in Western Europe. Another, "Greece in conflict with the Turks,"† is descriptive, as its title implies, of various scenes in the history of the Revolution. A third small collection of poems, "The Panorama of Greece," was published in 1833, and was intended as a sort of mirror of the political state of the country, and the maladministration of the government during the Capodistrian period, as well as the condition of society at that time. The fourth is a *political* poem on the Revolution of September, 1843, by which the Athenians forced King Otho to grant them the constitution so long promised. From the subjects of these poems, the character of the composition in which the author delights may easily be inferred. His style accommodates itself to the matter. Making occasional use of language that is strictly Hellenic, he never sacrifices perspicuity to ornament, and willingly descends to the language of the market for the sake of being sprightly and entertaining. His poems, being eminently satirical, are read with avidity by all classes; and his songs are well calculated for popularity. Alexander Soutsos is at present as violently opposed to the government and ministry of Otho, as formerly to that of Capo d'Istria. The political tendencies of his various writings have rendered them extremely offensive to the government, and have on several occasions brought upon him no little trouble. Three or four years since, the police of Athens, having learned by some espionage that a political work of his was in the hands of the printer, seized both the printed sheets and the manuscript. This, of course, was done in utter defiance of that article of the constitution which guarantees the freedom of the press; for, even had the author been amenable to a charge of libel or

* Τῆς *αὐτῆς ὡραιότητος ἔπη* are his words: Πρόλογος *εἰς τὰ* Ἅπαντα Π. Σούτσου, p. 19.

† Ἡ Τουρκόμαχος Ἑλλάς.

treason on the publication of his poem, yet the laws of Greece provide no punishment for the writer until that moment, nor do they sanction the confiscation of his work.

There are few Greek poets of so great reputation as A. Rangabes, who is also well known as an elegant prose writer, and as professor of archæology in the University of Athens. We have read with considerable interest a dramatic poem of his, entitled "Phrosyne," referring to incidents in the history of Ali Pasha, of Epirus, at first the determined enemy of the liberties of Greece, which he was afterward, though unwillingly, instrumental in advancing. This production, it is true, is irregular in its composition, and extends to the immoderate length of four or five thousand lines, occupying more than half of a good-sized volume. But the "Phrosyne" is generally lively and interesting—the more so because the author chose a subject that acquires a romantic charm, from its association with the recovery of Greek freedom; while it is recent enough to be within the memory of the present generation. How far the loving character attributed to Mouctares, the Pasha's son, may be reconcilable with his subsequent bloody career, is open to some question. The poetical works of Rangabes have been collected in a couple of volumes, published at Athens in the years 1837 and 1840.

We have not space to say much of Salomos, whose poems have been highly commended, or of some of the younger poets, such as Coumanoudes, who have come more recently before the public. We can not, however, forbear mentioning the name of Athanasius Christopoulos, a more ancient author. This writer may be styled with truth a new Anacreon. We scarcely know whether his productions should be classed with the *literature* of modern Greece; for they are found rather in the mouths of the people, and in collections of popular songs, than in books. Confining himself almost exclusively to lyrical composition, he excelled immeasurably all his competitors. There is no pompous affectation of learning in his poems, but, written in language that all understand, and yet displeasing to none, they exhibit a pleasing freshness and simplicity. "His verses," to use the language of one of his fellow-poets, "inspired in the midst of flowery meads, and written by soft murmuring rivulets, have the fragrance of the rose and the myrtle, and glide naturally as streams of water."* Christopoulos has avoided the mistake into which a poet in his circumstances would be most likely to fall—we mean a servile imitation of the ancients, and a consequent degree of constraint. In this respect we know no other modern Greek poet who compares with him. His beautiful address to the sun is as pleasing to us for its *naïveté*, as almost any of the odes of Anacreon, some of which it resembles. This poem, and an ode to a nightingale, remind us of the song in Tennyson's "Princess," beginning with the words, "Oh, swallow, swallow, flying, flying south."

But we must leave the poets, and pay some attention to a few of the principal contemporary prose writers. The first place among these, in virtue of seniority, and a long sustained reputation, we give to Neophytus Bambas, the late venerable Professor of Rhetoric in the University of Athens. He was a man some seventy years of age, of small stature, with a benevolent face, and exceedingly agreeable manners. A monk by profession, he had few of the prejudices which disgrace that class in Greece; and received with cordiality every foreigner who came recommended to him as a friend to truth or to letters. His extensive learning, acquired partly in his native island of Scio, but perfected at Paris, pointed him out as a suitable person for undertaking the version of the Bible in modern Greek; and this task was confided to him by the British and Foreign Bible Society. The translation, which he accomplished with the assistance of two fellow-laborers, is acknowledged to possess great merit, and has been scattered far and wide over the country. Adhering, as it does, with fidelity to the Hebrew original, it varies in many places from the text of the Septuagint—a circumstance which the clergy have not failed, in many cases, to use as a handle for hindering the people from reading it. The style of the translation is very creditable, but the translators have not hesitated, where circum-

* Alexander Soutsos, in his poetical Ἐπιστολὴ πρὸς βασιλέα Ὄθωνα, l. 29, *et seq.* He informs us that Christopoulos was a Fanariote, a native of Constantinople, and consequently brought up in the midst of Byzantine luxury and folly.

stances required it, to sacrifice elegance to perspicuity. Such, however, have been the gigantic strides with which the language has advanced, during even the short space of ten or twelve years, that a new translation has become necessary. Considerable alterations have been made in the recent editions. This, indeed, is the case with all books of a popular kind.*

It is a fact of no common importance, and one that will be learned with pleasure by all well-wishers of Greece, that within a few months the Bible translated into the vernacular tongue has been made a text-book in all the public schools. The ministerial order which makes provision for its introduction, also requires that all the teachers shall henceforth attend at least one course of lectures of Professor Contogones of the Theological School of the University, on the subject of Hermeneutics. Greece owes this decree to the enlightened statesmanship of Mr. Psyllas.

Among the Greeks, Bambas is better known as a professor of distinguished talent, and as the author of several works on the Elements of Philosophy, Ethics, and Rhetoric, and of several Greek grammars. One of these contains a comparative view of the ancient and modern forms, and seems written in a truly philosophical manner. It would be very useful to any scholar who wishes to study the similarities and differences in the two languages. One of the most important works of Bambas is his volume of notes on several of the orations of Demosthenes, which are of an exegetical and historical nature.

It is to be regretted that the learned professor of late years attached himself more and more to the Russian or Napæan party, which is hostile to the reformation of the Church, and opposed to constitutional government, while it is willing to

* To instance but one out of many changes. Of all the variations of the modern dialect from the ancient, probably the most singular is the entire disuse of the infinitive mood, except in tenses formed by means of the auxiliary verb. The anomaly arose from the introduction of the subjunctive mood preceded by a conjunction, in places where the infinitive was more proper. In most cases of this kind, the new edition of the Bible in modern Greek has restored the ancient forms, which are assuredly well understood by Athenian readers, though less intelligible to the inhabitants of the provinces.

sacrifice every thing to the advancement of the national ambition. The weight of Bambas has thus been lost to the cause which at present needs the advocacy of every patriotic scholar. In the recent excitement at Athens among the students of the University, we understand that his pen was employed in inciting the people to the invasion of Turkish territory.

Professor Asopius, who occupies a chair of the Greek language in the University, is at present considered the best philologist at Athens. He is the author of several works on Syntax and on Classical Antiquities. In the thoroughness and variety of his acquirements, he resembles the lamented Coray; and he has been instrumental in counteracting, to some degree, the loose principles of morality which some professors, as well as the priesthood, have been engaged in propagating.

Among scholars, A. Radinos, now holding, we believe, a professorship in the Gymnasium of Patras, is much esteemed for his version of Herodotus, which stands high in public estimation, both for its accuracy and for the correctness of the style. The explanatory notes, also, are valuable for their clearness and ability.

To the department of antiquities, the investigation of the numerous ruins with which the country is studded, and the determination of ancient sites, the Greek mind has not yet applied itself with vigor and success. Up to the present moment, the best-informed archæologists and topographers have been foreigners: among whom Colonel Leake, the Englishman, stands pre-eminent. Few can be found in the country who have any tolerable knowledge of a branch of study which might be supposed to offer the greatest facilities for attaining distinction. At the same time, the government pretends to be most studiously careful of the ruins that remain, and has enacted severe penal laws against the exportation of ancient works of art; while the people manifest a patriotic indignation toward Lord Elgin, the spoiler of the sculptures of the Parthenon. Something has been done in the study of antiquities. Mr. Pittakes, who has devoted his life to this subject, has published all the inscriptions to be found about the capital, together with much antiquarian information, in a book entitled "L'Ancienne Athènes," and recently a more extensive work on the same subject. An Archæological Society has been established, having the same objects in view, and by its publications has contributed to enlarge our acquaintance with the ancient world. Its recent researches are unusually interesting. A certain plot of ground, along the base of the northern side of the Athenian Acropolis, was found to contain some inscriptions, from the tenor of which it came to be suspected that the senate-house, on whose walls the tables of laws were suspended, was situated there. Means were found by the society to purchase the ground, and to prosecute the excavations. The result has been the discovery of several interesting inscriptions, of which the most entire is a copy of a treaty of alliance, made in the year 378 B.C., between the Athenians and several of the islands, against Sparta. It affords a striking confirmation of the historical accuracy of Diodorus, who mentions the circumstance and the conditions of the treaty.* Similar investigations, if prosecuted with the requisite energy, would undoubtedly disclose records even more important.

To history greater attention has been paid than to archæology. But historical taste and accuracy are of slow growth in themselves, and require the possession of large and costly libraries. The distinguished historians of our own continent have been obliged to resort, for some of their most valuable sources, to the public libraries and archives of England, Spain, and Holland. It is not remarkable, then, that Greek writers, who, until within ten years, have had few opportunities of consulting even the most indispensable works, have not accomplished much in historical literature. They have, in fact, confined themselves to translating or compiling from the histories of their own ancestors, written by Goldsmith and Grote.† To modern history, and especially to that of their own revolutionary struggle, they have made more considerable contributions; but these have taken the form of personal narratives,

* Diod. xv., 27.

† Goldsmith's history is the ordinary text-book in all the common schools of the kingdom.

or contemporary chronicles, rather than of dignified history. They are not the less important, however, on this account. By their means, whoever will attempt to write a connected history of the Greek Revolution, will be furnished with ample materials. That event is yet too recent to be viewed with impartiality by a native, still less by one who was himself an actor in its scenes. Even a foreigner would need the utmost discrimination to discern the good from the evil, and to decide how far the Greek nation has disappointed any *just* expectations of progress in civilization and intelligence.

The "Memoirs of the Revolution," by Germanos, archbishop of Patras, are among the most authentic of the historical sketches that have yet appeared, but they embrace merely the first three years of the war. This prelate was one of the conspirators who met at the Monastery of Hagia Laura, near Calavryta, and was the first to raise the standard of rebellion—a fact that invests his account of the earlier events with considerable interest. He died in 1825, on his return from the West, whither he had been sent on a political mission. It was not until 1837 that the work of Germanos was published, under the editorial supervision of Kastorches, who assures us that it is given to the public precisely as it came from the hands of the author. Of the same class is the work commenced by Speliades, of which one large volume was published four years ago. A number of pamphlets have been written on the "Heteria" of conspirators, to whose efforts the outbreak of the Revolution was in part attributable. Mr. Tricoupes, the Greek minister at the court of St. James, has recently published a work which will probably afford to foreign readers the most reliable account of the war. We can speak of its merits only from the general commendation with which it has been received.*

There is another period, to which it seems remarkable that the learned men of Greece have not paid more attention. The age of Miltiades, Themistocles, and Cimon, was certainly the most glorious epoch of Greek history. It has long occupied

* All the constitutions and other official papers of Greece, from 1821 to 1832, have been collected in a few volumes by A. Z. Mamoukas, and constitute the documentary history of the Revolution.

the attention, and engrossed the study, of distinguished men throughout Europe; and nothing but merit of the highest order can hope to win laurels among so many competitors. Meanwhile, the history of mediæval Greece, or, to speak more accurately, of Greece from the time of its subjugation by the Romans, has until the present time been deemed unworthy of the merest epitome. And this neglect has, unfortunately, been intentional, arising from the prejudice entertained against the Middle Ages. The Greeks of the present day are keenly sensitive to the imputation of descent, not from Hellenus and Cecrops, but from a horde of Sclavonian settlers, who, it is said, took possession of their country during its ages of barbarism, precisely as the Albanians—a branch of the same stock—seized upon whole villages, both in Northern Greece and the Morea, within the last hundred and fifty years. They repel the charge, and regard its supporters with mingled indignation and contempt. The first place in their resentment is undoubtedly held by the German professor, Fallmeräyer, who, not without display of learning and ability, endeavored to prove that the modern Greeks are descended from the Goths and other barbarians, and that the ancient race has entirely disappeared from the face of the earth. A theory so startling, carrying with it so slight an air of probability, called forth numerous "refutations" and "answers" from the Athenian press. Of course, no definite conclusion has been reached, by the admission of both parties; but, while it were useless to deny that an admixture of a Sclavonic element has been introduced by successive colonizations and wars, it is yet more absurd to suppose that the greater part of the nation is not of Hellenic origin. Excepting the immediate investigation which this discussion has elicited, no attention has been paid to this interesting portion of their history by native writers. It has been abandoned almost exclusively to the distinguished historians, Buchon and Finlay.*

* M. Buchon, besides republishing the chronicle of the Frank conquest of the Morea, is the author of the "Nouvelles Recherches sur la Principauté Française de Morée," and other writings on the same subject. "La Grèce Continentale et la Morée," by the same author, is one of the best books of travels in Greece that we have seen. Mr. Finlay's

But while broad and inviting fields of investigation have been neglected, the Greeks have not been wholly unmindful of the glory to be acquired in some studies which have lately become popular in Western Europe. We refer to the examination of the treasures of literature, so long locked up in the Eastern languages. A young Athenian, who had already distinguished himself by his acquirements, resolved, in the year 1786, to leave the city of Constantinople for Calcutta, whither he had been invited, in order to instruct the children of some Greek merchants residing there. The opportunities thus afforded were not lost upon the studious youth; and besides the English, he acquired a good knowledge of the Sanscrit, Persian, and Hindoostanee. In the course of a few years more, Demetrius Galanos—such was his name—had obtained, by his assiduous labors, a competency, enabling him to devote himself entirely to the study of the Oriental languages. Having deposited his small fortune in the hands of some trustworthy merchants, he set off for the holy city of Benares. There he clothed himself like a Brahmin, as his biographer assures us, "and following their customs, and associating with the most holy and learned of their wise men, in the space of about forty years he not only acquired an extensive knowledge of Indian philology, but also was initiated by the most approved teachers into their highest theology. He made such attainments in their virtue and wisdom, as to be regarded by the English colonists, and the other Europeans, as well as by the most pious Brahmins and Indians generally, as a most holy and learned man." Whether by this language our biographer intends it to be understood that Galanos, while sojourning among the Brahmins, renounced Christianity, and feigned adherence to their creed, does not appear. At all events, during the time spent at Benares, he devoted himself in part to translating some Brahminical works. At his death, which occurred at that place in 1833, in the seventy-second year of his age, he left nearly half his estate, or about six

well-known "Greece under the Romans," "Mediæval Greece," etc., form a continuous history of the country, from the fall of Corinth to the end of the last independent duchy, to be concluded by a history of the subjugation by the Turks and of the late Revolution.

thousand dollars, to the principal academy of learning at Athens,* and also bequeathed to it all his manuscripts. The funds were employed in erecting the building of the University of Athens, where his manuscripts are preserved, the greater part of them having been published under the editorial supervision of Mr. Typaldos, the librarian, in six octavo volumes. They consist of translations of various poems, and collections of wise and moral sayings, some of which, according to the assertion of learned Europeans, were previously unknown in Europe, and were published for the first time through the Greek version. The accuracy of these translations is, we believe, undoubted; and if the originals are new to the literary world, the accomplishment of this work is an achievement highly creditable to the philology of young Greece. It is, however, hardly to be expected that any but domestic subjects should generally possess much interest for the Greeks, who can find in the investigation of their own annals, and those of their ancestors, and in the advancement of science and art in their own country, a more appropriate work for the present.

The novel attempt was made in the last century, by some members of the Society of Jesus, to introduce into the East the use of Roman letters in place of the old Greek character. The only book printed on this plan, so far as we know, is one that appeared first in 1746, and was republished at Constantinople in 1843. It is entitled "*The Rest of the Heart in the Holy Will of God, by Father Thomas Stanislas Velasti, of the Society of Jesus; a treatise compiled from the works of Father Rodriquez of the same Society.*" In this singular volume, otherwise offering little entertainment to the foreign reader, every analogy of the language has been neglected; and one unaccustomed to the modern Greek pronunciation will frequently be sadly perplexed in attempting to recognize under their strange disguise even the more common words. It is hardly

* Mad. la Comtesse de Gasparin, in her *Voyage au Levant*, i., p. 208, speaks of Galanos as a priest, and as having died at Athens. Whereas his biographer, Mr. Typaldos, expressly tells us that his uncle, then member of the Holy Synod of Constantinople, having proposed that he should enter the priesthood, he refused on account of his zeal for letters (p. 14). Galanos died at Benares, where there is a monument, with an English inscription, standing over his grave (p. 30).

necessary to add, that so absurd an innovation has found little favor with either the learned or the illiterate; and the book is regarded, by those who are aware of its existence, merely as a curiosity of literature.

The discussions arising from the ecclesiastical state of Greece, have been the occasion of the publication of a work by Pharmakides, which possesses more than ordinary interest. The circumstances that called it forth have been detailed on a previous page. This fearless author does not confine himself to a simple refutation of the dangerous principles contained in the "Tome" of the Holy Synod of Constantinople. He boldly attacks the whole system of prelacy, and declares the hierarchy to be the gradual outgrowth of the ambition and servility which early invaded the Church. "The mode of government," he says, "instituted in the Church by the holy apostles was democratic, and sacred history so acknowledges it. The churches gradually tended to form a community of federal, equal churches, independent of the secular power. * * After the death of the *democratic* disciples of Christ, political equality was for a while maintained between the numerous churches; and notwithstanding that there were enrolled in this federal league rich and populous cities, yet each formed, until the fourth century, an equal church, and consequently the bishops were all equal. But finally the episcopal hierarchy appeared, and in due time Popes and Patriarchs. From *democracy*, the Church passed to *aristocracy*." Again he observes, speaking of the primitive ages:

"At that time there existed no Archbishops, Exarchs, Patriarchs, or Popes. Every church, whether under the pastoral care of a bishop and elder or elders, or of an elder or elders only, was independent, and governed itself. The subjection of one church to another was unheard of. None had power over another. But equality and fraternity are not pleasing to human pride and ambition. Accordingly, the primitive democratic government was overthrown, and an aristocracy established in its stead."

The extracts we have given may suffice to indicate the general character of the work, which, in fact, does not relate so much to the doctrines as to the government of the Church.

Its influence upon the public mind at the time was sudden and powerful. The whole edition of two thousand copies was exhausted in four or five weeks, and the strength of its arguments may be inferred no less from the violence of the opposite party, than from the satisfaction of the liberals. The "tome" has been abandoned, and nothing more is now heard about the scheme of union. The style of Pharmakides is good, but, like that of many of the theological writers of the present day, somewhat patristic. His mind is vigorous, and his mode of thinking original. With most of his countrymen, he is much attached to his native land, and to the religion of his forefathers; which he reveres, not only as a divine revelation, but as a bond of concord between the now dissevered branches of the Greek race, and as the potent means of effecting their political union.

With reference to works of fiction, we do not know that any thing worthy of mention has issued from the Athenian press. The public are, however, abundantly supplied with translations of all the principal French novels, such as those of Eugène Sue, Dumas, and others of the same class. Less taste has been manifested for the classic works of Sir Walter Scott; and we doubt if any of Cooper's tales have ever appeared in Greek dress.

Before closing this brief survey of the progress of modern Greek literature, we can not forbear noting the marked influence which the judicial department, the bar, and the learned professions generally, have exercised over the rising taste for letters. In the term *learned professions* it is not intended to include the clergy. Whatever progress has been made in Greece has received but little assistance from them; though it must be allowed that this circumstance has been owing to their ignorance, rather than to any settled purpose of retarding the regeneration of their country. Some noble exceptions, too, will be found even among those whom we have mentioned. In jurisprudence, the greater part of the codes of laws have been drawn from those of the French, and, as we conceive, very unfortunately in some cases, as, for instance, those treating of religious liberty and toleration. The law terms have been borrowed, so far as practicable, from those that were in use in the Athenian courts two thousand years ago; and the legal nomenclature is quite intelligible to a classical scholar. The courts, rejecting technical words of foreign origin, have materially contributed to the restoration of the ancient language. Talents of a high order have already been exhibited at the bar of Athens. Indeed, the Greek mind seems to be peculiarly suited to excel in the legal profession. Acuteness, vivacity, and energy it possesses in a high degree; and we would recommend to the curious the perusal of the speeches of the counsel in the several trials of Dr. King, and in that of the followers of Kaïres, as favorable examples of forensic eloquence. We must not fail to allude more particularly to the defence made by Mr. Saripolos in the latter case, valuable not less for its eloquence than for its classic purity; and more interesting as containing a noble assertion of the great doctrine of religious liberty, both in respect to faith and worship. The first verdict in favor of the points contended for* was the result of this eloquent defence.

The University has, however, accomplished even more than

* Kaïres, a native of Andros, and a well-known friend to education, was, after a protracted struggle between his disciples and the fanatical party, tried by the Criminal Court of Syra, upon the accusation of having publicly taught atheistic doctrines. He was found guilty, and, with three of his followers, was thrown into prison, whence he made his appeal to the court of the Areopagus at Athens. Barely a week before the trial of the appeal, Kaïres died in his cell, of a disease contracted in the loathsome building in which he was confined. The appeal was tried in behalf of the three remaining appellants. We transcribe the first paragraph of the speech of Mr. Saripolos on this occasion, which may serve the curious as a specimen of the ordinary language used in the courts at Athens:

'Ο Καΐρης ἀπέθανε, καὶ ἀπέθανεν ἀθῶος. 'Ως πρὸς αὐτὸν κατηργήθη ἡ δίκη δυνάμει τοῦ νόμου. 'Αλλ' ὁποῖον μέγα μάθημα ἔδωκε πρὸς τὴν ἐπίγειον δικαιοσύνην αὐτὸς ὁ Θεὸς καλέσας ἐνώπιον τοῦ ἀναμαρτήτου δικαστηρίου του τὸν Θεόφιλον Καΐρην! 'Ο Ὕψιστος οἱονεὶ ἐκκαλέσας ἐνώπιον ἑαυτοῦ τὴν δίκην ὡς πρὸς τὸν κατηγορηθέντα ἐπὶ αἱρεσιαρχίᾳ Θεόφιλον Καΐρην, ἀπέδειξε προφανῶς, ὅτι αἱ τοιαῦται δίκαι ὑπεκφεύγουσι τὴν ἁρμοδιότητα παντὸς ἐπιγείου, παντὸς ἐξ ἀνθρώπων συγκεκροτημένου δικαστηρίου. Πᾶσα κατὰ τοῦ 'Υψίστου προσβολὴ ὑπὸ μόνου τοῦ 'Υψίστου ἁρμοδίως ἐκδικάζεται· τοῦτο δὲ, διότι μόνος ὁ Ὕψιστος εἶναι ἡ αὐταλήθεια, ἡ αὐτοδικαιοσύνη. Μόνος ὁ Ὕψιστος ὁ ἐτάζων νοῦν καὶ καρδίαν, μόνος αὐτὸς ὁ τὴν ἀλήθειαν ἀκριβῶς γινώσκων, μόνος αὐτὸς λέγω, εἶναι καὶ δικαστὴς ἐπὶ τῶν ἀποκλειστικῶς ἐνδιαφερόντων αὐτὸν ζητημάτων.

the bench or the bar in advancing the cause of science. The professors, being men of talents, many of whom have been educated in Western Europe, exert a strong influence upon the hundreds of students who daily congregate within their lecture-rooms; and through their instrumentality, more than through any other, the language has attained a degree of purity much higher than would have been deemed possible thirty years since. So that now, even among the common people of Athens, quite a different idiom is employed from that in use elsewhere.

We conclude by mentioning the principal dictionaries to be found in modern Greek: both to exhibit the point which lexicography has reached, and to indicate the facilities afforded for the study of a language and literature just beginning to attract, among western scholars, the attention which they merit. Among the lexicons for the study of the ancient Greek, the foremost rank is held by that of the Archimandrite Gazés, republished at Vienna in 1835, with numerous additions and emendations, drawn principally from the lexicons of Passow and others. It consists of three large quarto volumes, and contains a copious supplement of proper names. The various articles are exceedingly full; the meanings sufficiently numerous; and the examples cited abundant, and, in general, well selected. It is a convenient work for one who wishes to compare the variations of the modern language from the ancient. Smaller lexicons have been published by Koumas, and lately by Scarlatus Byzantinus, which are less fully illustrated by examples. We can do no more than enumerate a few of the dictionaries of the modern languages and the modern Greek. The Rev. Mr. Lowndes published many years ago, at Malta, an English-Greek and also a Greek-English lexicon. But besides being antiquated, they are meagre and defective; and when a word has many distinct significations, it is rare that all, or nearly all, are enumerated. Many words, too, in both languages, are altogether omitted. For the more common words of conversation, however, these works will be found very useful. A very good English-Greek lexicon was published in 1854, by George Polymeres, at Hermopolis, on the island of Syra. Although written especially to meet the wants of Greeks studying the English, it is a valuable manual for the acquisition of the Greek language. The Greek-French lexicon of Scarlatus Byzantinus is the most complete, as far as relates to the *higher* Greek especially; and hence it supplies the deficiencies of that of Lowndes. The French-Greek dictionary of Rangabes, Samourcases, and Nicolaides Lebadeus, is constructed upon the basis of that of the French Academy; it is, probably, the most satisfactory of the whole series. But in order to learn many of the words used by the people, and which rarely find their way into print, except in the collections of proverbs or popular songs, one must have recourse to more ancient works, such as the "Lexicon Triglosson," published some fifty or sixty years since. Even with the aid of this, the meaning of a popular word or phrase will often be sought in vain. This difficulty is enhanced by the differences of dialect prevailing in the several districts. It can be overcome only by the assistance of the oral explanations of a native. But an Athenian can by no means understand all the terms occurring in a Laconian lament or a Thessalian song. This, it will be remembered, is only true of the popular ballads.

The brief and necessarily imperfect view that we have taken of the present literature of Greece, may perhaps lead some to a more just appreciation of the richness of its contents. Its progress, we do not hesitate to say, has been unparalleled, if the short period during which the nation has had a political existence, and the difficulties, both moral and physical, attending every step of improvement, be taken into account. Twenty-five years of repose, after a war almost of extermination—and these years, too, disquieted by intestine commotion and foreign interference—are surely not a long period to allow for the regeneration of Greece, after the degrading influence of twenty centuries of subjection. An impartial mind will be rather surprised at the extent of what has been done, than disappointed at the failure of some perhaps too sanguine expectations.

THE STRAITS OF SALAMIS.

CHAPTER XXIII.

BALLAD POETRY.

"Religious, Martial, or Civil ditties; which, if wise men and prophets be not extremely out, have a great power over disposition and manners, to smoothe and make them gentle from rustic harshness and distempered passions." MILTON *on Education.*

A FORCIBLE writer has somewhere characterized the rich ballads of Spain as "Iliads without a Homer." The description is no less appropriate to those of modern Greece. Nowhere have warlike deeds been more frequent; nowhere have they been better appreciated. Under a poetic disguise is conveyed a faithful transcript of the social history of its population. Here we are to look for traces of ancient customs, and for superstitions half extinct. From the popular poetry of any nation we can judge with certainty of the prevailing tastes, and the grade of civilization. For in the ballad the individuality of the author is merged in the mass of those who appropriate not only his sentiments, but his expressions. The poet is merely the spokesman of the people; and the popularity of his production is a proof that it is consonant with their way of thinking. But the songs of Greece possess an additional claim to interest, in the fact that they contain the only record of many incidents of her history for several centuries preceding the hour of her resuscitation. An oppressed race naturally resorts to them to express without restraint the story of its sufferings, and to recount the exploits of its brave champions that foreshadow a coming deliverance. Unfortunately the record is but fragile, rarely or never committed to writing, and scarce outliving the generation that gave it birth. Twenty or thirty years is the ordinary span of even the most widely-known ballad. The valorous deeds or the misfortunes of a new hero engross the sympathies of all; and his no less noted predecessor must give way before his rising renown. Thus, doubtless, have a thousand fragments of historic lore been forever lost to the world. A writer,* through whose instrumentality attention was first drawn to modern Greek ballads, supposes that of near one hundred and fifty specimens contained in his collection, but one can be as old as the end of the sixteenth century, and that has been preserved ever since in writing. The others are handed down orally; and the most ancient ascertained is about one hundred and fifty years old. The majority relate to occurrences at the end of the last and the commencement of the present century.

The popular songs of Greece may be arranged in several distinct categories. The first comprises the large and varied class of *Heroic* or *Kleftic* poems, in which the adventures of the klefts are related at length, and with a general adherence to strict accuracy of fact, except in certain portions, which contain a conventional form of exaggeration. These pieces are the most interesting in a merely historical point of view. Next comes the class of Romantic poems, peculiar for the most part to the islands, where the imagination has received a different tinge, from contact with the Western European mind. More curious than these are those songs composed for special domestic events, forming in the minds of the people an essential accompaniment to the celebration of the marriage rite, or sung in mournful strains over the corpses of the dead. The former are, for the most part, handed down from generation to generation, with little deviation from a stereotype form, in each particular district. The latter have little in common, and are the spontaneous offspring of a lively imagination, excited by the sad emotions of the occasion.

* C. Fauriel, *Chants Populaires de la Grèce Moderne* (Paris, 1824), p. 99.

Before entering upon a more particular notice of these classes of poems, it is important to understand the principles on which they are composed. It is admitted by all that the rhythm of the Greek language has undergone a very considerable, if not a total, metamorphosis. The distinction between long and short syllables, which was the basis of the ancient poetry, having, with the lapse of ages, been completely lost in the common pronunciation, a new principle of versification was introduced, conforming to the highly scientific arrangement of the accents with which the language was provided. Who was the first to adapt himself to the alteration, it is, perhaps, too late to ascertain. In the middle of the twelfth century almost all poetical works were so written, even though their language might be completely ancient in character. The verse in most common use is the heroic, composed of fifteen syllables, and divided into two hemistichs, the former consisting of eight, and the latter of seven syllables. The fundamental foot is the iambus; and, consequently, the accent falls generally upon the even syllables. Some variation from this, however, is allowed; and trochees frequently appear, especially in the commencement of either half line. The principal accents must fall on either the sixth or the eighth syllable of the first, and on the sixth of the second hemistich. This is the metre employed in almost all kleftic songs, and in many of the lyrical productions. There are a variety of other metres more or less commonly used.

To appreciate that extensive collection of ballads which relate to the warlike exploits of the *klefts*, it is indispensable to have some acquaintance with their adventurous temperament and insecure mode of life. As the name—changed, by a mere aspiration, from the classic word for robber—sufficiently indicates, the *klefts* were a class of freebooters, supporting themselves by forced contributions levied upon the villages of the districts they infested. But their deeds of rapine did not subject them to that weight of indignation which so lawless a course of life might naturally call forth, as they were regarded in the light of a political party rather than as robbers and outlaws. Young men who could not endure the restrictions they suffered at home, and longed for freedom and repose; men in the prime of life, who through a succession of years had been the victims of oppression, and whom some outrageous act of arbitrary violence had rendered impatient of the yoke they had been meekly bearing: such were the materials from which Colocotroni, Liakos, and others formed their invincible bands. There were men of all ages, ranks, and conditions; but one feeling animated them all, and that was hatred to the Turks, and to those who patiently submitted to their tyranny. Retiring to the mountains, they led, under the generalship of some experienced captain, a life of independence, subject, nevertheless, to the greatest hardships and privations. Safety, or an opportunity of plunder, frequently necessitated the execution of marches of surprising length and difficulty. At times the stock of provisions was almost exhausted, and the *kleft* was compelled to put up with the scantiest fare, and subsist on the roots of such wild plants as would satisfy his hunger. But then, again, the elders of a village presented large sums, and furnished provisions to the band, to secure immunity from plunder. Occasionally, too, some rich bashaw fell into their hands, and was not released until he had paid a heavy ransom. The Greeks were generally exempted from these levies, except when want pressed heavily. The monks, however, were, from their indolence and wealth, special objects of dislike; and the *klefts* were not slow in turning to their own use the accumulated stores of the monastery; while the parish priest was rarely incommoded, farther than being forced to read prayers, or say the last offices for their dead.

At length, tired of the constant annoyance which a band of resolute men could inflict upon their provinces, the Pashas would send proposals of peace, and engage to employ the *klefts* as a body of hired troops. With the change of occupation, their name was changed to *Armatoloi*, or militia-men. An opportunity was now afforded the Turks of compassing by treachery the destruction of their new and formidable allies. It was rarely lost. Those who escaped the massacre of their chiefs, joined by fresh recruits, were soon again wild *klefts* upon the mountains, inflicting deeper wounds upon their enemies, and animated by hatred yet more deadly against the

Turks. This alternation from resistance to peace, and from peace again to rapine and plunder, was of continual recurrence in the western and northern portions of Greece, where the *klefts* were most numerous. The plains of Thessaly and Epirus suffered most from their ravages. Mount Olympus and Kissabos (the ancient Ossa) are frequently mentioned in the ballads as the head-quarters of these bands.

Such were the *klefts*, whose history might furnish matter for a volume of romantic interest. Regarded less in the light of robbers than as brave opposers of Turkish tyranny and champions of Greek independence, their praises were in the mouths of those even who were too timid to imitate their valor. To confound the *klefts* of the period anterior to the Revolution with the class that now infest some portions of Greece, would be entirely to mistake their character, the principles for which they contended, and their importance in a historical point of view.

The ballads rarely contain a reference to more than a single incident in the life of a brave. It may be a signal victory gained over a vastly superior force of the enemy; or some almost miraculous escape from their hands. More frequently the entire poem is a poetic lament over the disastrous fate of the warrior-chief, who has fallen into the snare set for him by a wily Pasha, or by the treacherous elders of some village, who would court favor with the ruler by surrendering into his hands the *klefts* that have taken refuge in their midst. One relates the fortunes of a brave named Diakos, who has seen all his men cut down about him, and, after losing both gun and sword, has fallen alive into the enemy's hands. Although life and promotion are promised him, if he will but apostatize, he chooses to be impaled, rather than deny his faith and the religion of his forefathers.

From the great abundance of kleftic ballads, it is scarcely possible to select any that will convey a correct notion of their general character; and the difficulty is yet more sensibly felt, when the attempt is made to render into foreign prose the flowing verses of one of the most sonorous of modern languages. The following poem I have chosen, to give an idea of the generality, less for any peculiar merit than because of its brevity. It is the lament of a wounded chief, who feels that his end is fast approaching:

"The Sun is setting, and Demetrius commands his men:
'Go, my braves, to the water, that ye may eat bread this night;
And thou, Lamprakes, dear nephew, sit near me here.
Put on my arms, and see that thou do them honor.
And ye, my braves, take my poor sword;
Cut me green boughs, and spread them for my bed.
Bring me a priest to hear all my confession,
That I may tell him all my sins that I have done.
Thirty years an Armatolos, and five-and-twenty a Kleft;
And now Death has come to me, and I must die.
Make my tomb wide, and let it be high;
That I may stand erect to fight, and have room to load.
And on the right side do you leave a window;
That the swallows may come to bring the spring,
And the dear nightingales warble in the good month of May.' "*

The following is a record of the death of Theodore Metros:

"In the hall of Theodore, at the palace of Metros,
Much people is gathered; many are assembled together.
'Is not a marriage taking place, or is it a festival?'
Neither is it a marriage nor a festival:
But Metros is ill, grievously, and like to die.
Physicians come and go; but of cure there is none.
His comrades weep for him, and weeps his sister;
His mother weeps for him, and his sad father too.
'Dost thou wish for marriage, Metros, that I may give thee a wife?'
'I wish no marriage, mother. Stoop, that I may kiss thee.
Care for my children, my poor boys.
Bring me my dear sword, mother, that I may kiss it;
And bring my gun, that I may bid it farewell.
Charon has betrothed me, he has betrothed me:
He has given me the stone for a mother-in-law, the monument for wife;
And the worms themselves for brothers and cousins.' "

A striking peculiarity of this species of poetry is the abundant employment of *parallelisms;* the second clause being frequently a counterpart of the first, though it may convey the same idea in a somewhat varied dress. No less remarkable is the structure of the introduction to the ballad. Sometimes all Nature, by a forcible hyperbole, is represented as plunged in mourning at the disaster that has befallen the

* In the collection of popular ballads by Zambelius, No 13, p. 607.

hero. "Wherefore do the mountains grow black, and the meadows wither away?" exclaims the bard as he commences his narration. Or else a bird may be represented as singing, from the wall of some adjoining fortress, the funeral dirge of the *klefts*. Often, as in the following piece, the auditor is supposed to break forth in an inquiry as to the cause of the fearful sound that is heard afar; in answering which the poet gives an account of the battle, where the Greeks are fighting against fearful odds. It is worthy of special note that many such phrases are conventional expressions, appearing in numerous songs, and designed to call the hearer's attention, and lead, in a natural manner, to the subject of the ballad.

"'What can be the sound that is heard, and the great tumult!
Are not bullocks being slain, or is it beasts that roar?'
'Neither are bullocks being slain, nor is it beasts that roar:
Boucovallas is engaged in fight with fifteen hundred men,
In the midst of Kerasobos, and in Kænouria.
The balls fall like rain; they fall like hail.'
And a fair maiden cried from out the window:
'Cease, John, from battle, cause the firing to stop,
That the dust may settle, that it may be clear,
That thy band may be numbered, to see how many are lacking.'
The Turks are numbered thrice, and there lack five hundred;
The *kleft* boys are numbered, and three braves are missing.
One went for water, and another to bring bread;
The third and best stands at his gun."*

The fact that these kleftic songs are not confined to one locality, but disseminated far from the mountainous districts that gave them birth, is due to the "*panegyris*," public festivals and fairs, at which great multitudes from the surrounding country gather, not only for purposes of trade, but also for recreation. Dances abound on these occasions; and crowds gather around the blind musicians, who sing the ballads they have composed themselves, or learned from others. These perambulating musicians perform the part of the ancient rhapsodists, and, being possessed of extraordinary memories, the number of pieces which they can recite and sing is quite remarkable. For each of these poems they compose a new tune;

* Song of *John Boucovallas*, in the collection of Zambelius, No. 39, p. 629.

and when it meets with a good reception, they are well rewarded for their pains. It is said that a minstrel, who was likewise possessed of considerable talent as an improvisatore, was in a few years enabled to lay by so large a sum as to settle down at his ease at Ampelakia, in Thessaly. The only accompaniment to the voice is a sort of lyre, with but two or three strings.

The day of the true *klefts* has probably passed away forever. In the Revolution they contributed not a little to the deliverance of their country. Those who had been the leaders of a few desperadoes, became the captains of large detachments of troops capable of meeting and repulsing the Turkish armies. Being thoroughly acquainted with the country, and inured from long experience to all the labors and difficulties of a guerrilla warfare, they were formidable opponents on a soil so mountainous as that of Greece. Since the Revolution, many of the more distinguished chiefs have risen to honorable posts under the government, while the rest have resumed more peaceable occupations. As the exploits of the *klefts* have now ceased, it must necessarily follow that this branch of the popular literature, which has been devoted to them, will become extinct, or undergo at least very essential modifications. Even now, among the collections of kleftic poems, there are to be found many that relate properly to revolutionary heroes, though framed upon the model of the more ancient class of ballads.

Turning to the peaceful plains and villages, we find in their songs a perceptible resemblance to those of former times. Athenæus and other ancient authors tell us that the return of the swallow was hailed by the Greeks as the harbinger of spring. Special hymns were composed in its honor; and those who sang them claimed a slight present from their auditors. A similar practice still obtains. On the first day of March, troops of children may be seen tripping forth from the village school-house in holiday attire, and carrying a branch or rod, on which a rough wooden figure of a swallow is perched. At every door the juvenile procession stops, to sing a welcome to the swallow, whose coming they represent as introducing joy into the household, and hastening the festivities of Easter. From the praises of the swallow, they next turn to beg a present of money or eggs, some for themselves, and the greater part for their master.*

On St. Basil's day, the first of the new year, similar parties of children wander from house to house. On this occasion their songs are not unlike those of the first of March. They consist chiefly of addresses to the family, each one of whom receives the honor of a separate song; and they conclude with an ode to St. Basil. In lyric pieces of this description but slight literary merit may be expected. Naturalness and a striking similarity to the popular songs of the ancients, as far as they have come down to us, are often combined with great homeliness of diction.

How much poetry connects itself with the most ordinary occurrences of life, is evident from the multitude of poems framed for such occasions. When, for instance, a peasant intends to leave his native place, whether his departure be final, or merely for a time, he invites his friends to partake with him of a farewell meal. During the feast, or at its conclusion, his departure is made the burden of song; some of the guests describing in general terms the bitterness of separation, while others enter with minuteness into the circumstances of the present case. These regrets are generally thrown into poetic shape on the spur of the occasion. Other farewell songs are recited in mournful tones, as the traveler is accompanied by his friends and neighbors to the limits of the town.

The nuptial customs, so complicated and yet so picturesque, differing in every district, yet invariable there, furnish a copious subject for the rustic muse. There are verses for the maidens to sing when they sit grinding the flour for the wedding-cakes; others when they sift it; and still others when they knead and bake. Snatches of poetry are sung by the youths as they help to attire the groom, and by the maidens

* A specimen of these modern songs may be compared with one of the ancient ones still extant; both are contained in a pamphlet entitled "A Refutation of those that have thought, written, and published, that none of those who now inhabit Greece are descended from the ancient Greeks, by Anastasius G. Leucias." Athens, 1843. (In Latin and Greek, p. 110.)

that wait on the bride. Every part of the marriage ceremony is thus viewed in a poetic light.†

It would be difficult to find a more curious class of lyric poems than the *mœrologia*, or laments sung over the corpses of the dead. Unlike the verses repeated at nuptial festivities, which are nearly always of a stereotype form, the *mœrologia* are the spontaneous product of the imagination in each particular case. The name seems to mean a lament over the fate of an individual. When the body of the deceased has been decently laid out upon a bed, ready to be carried to its last resting-place, the relatives and friends assemble round the lifeless remains, to take a last farewell of what they lately held so dear. Now they pour out their vain regrets. But the *mœrologia* are not mere expressions of feeling; they are chiefly made up of a history of the departed. If it be a woman, the survivors relate her fortunes, and dwell upon her beauty, her virtues, or her wealth. If a man, they celebrate his strength and courage, and the stratagems or treachery of his enemy. The wife not unfrequently reverts to the time of her betrothal, and tells the story of her married life. In one, when a husband had been basely murdered by those whom he had entertained under his own roof, the indignant widow exclaims: "Fire and poison may that bread and wine become which they ate and drank; for instead of bread they gave him a ball, and the wine became like powder."

In this recital, the faults of the dead are not unfrequently set forth as prominently as his excellences. The speakers are mostly of the female sex, while the men are passive spectators. Some women have enjoyed a great reputation for their wonderful facility in this sort of improvising. The heartless practice of hiring mourners is, however, I believe, confined to Asiatic Greece. Yet it is no uncommon occurrence for a perfect stranger to step into the sad circle of friends, and, addressing the corpse as if he could hear, beg him to carry some message to departed friends. The tidings thus intrusted to the soul, which, it is imagined, has not yet

* In a pamphlet giving an account of the forms accompanying the marriage rite, I find no less than twenty-six pieces of poetry, to be repeated at as many different stages of the ceremony.

commenced its journey to the nether world, relate to those matters which here interested it most—to family events, or to the success or reverses of domestic feuds. So important has the recital of the *mœrologia* come to be regarded, that in some places, when a person has died in a foreign land, these songs are addressed to a figure that personates him, extended on a funeral bed.

Of a character entirely different are the religious poems, in which the most striking historical passages of Holy Writ are represented in dramatic form. The "Mirror for Women" is a thick volume containing a large number of these pieces, wherein various Scriptural characters are held up as models for imitation, or as warnings to the female sex. More celebrated than any of these is the "Sacrifice of Abraham"—a drama, as has been truly remarked, "full of touches of most natural pathos." The style is easy, and the language makes no pretension to classic elegance. It is, indeed, just such a composition as the most illiterate can read with entertainment and profit. Although written no later, certainly, than the last century, it has retained its hold on the people, and has been reprinted within a few years.

In this brief description of some of the kinds of popular poetry, allusion has been made to prevalent superstitions whose existence they indicate. There are others equally curious. Charon no longer appears as the ancient ferryman of the Styx; but has usurped the place of Mercury, and figures as conductor of the dead. Every object, both animate and inanimate, is supposed to be guarded by a spirit. The plague is personified as a blind old woman, groping along the sides of walls. The small-pox, that fearful curse of the poor man's hovel, is represented as a fury: but the same fear that led the ancients to forbear uttering words of ill omen, lest they should provoke the ire of evil spirits, induces the modern peasant to call her "eulogia"—*the blessing*.

It is a noteworthy fact that, while the attention of the modern Greeks has naturally been bestowed mainly on those treasures of ancient lore which constitute their lawful patrimony, it has not been altogether withdrawn from their own popular ballads, in which so much of recent history, and of customs that are fast becoming extinct, is recorded. Mr. Fauriel's work, in the French language, was the first to awaken general interest on the subject. His preliminary remarks upon the habits of the *klefts*, and the nature of the ballads relating to their exploits, are as yet unsurpassed. Since then there have been published numerous collections, and now not a year passes without fresh additions to this interesting department of literature.*

* Four collections of ballads are before me, published in Athens alone, between 1835 and 1848; and there are doubtless many more. A young writer, Mr. Lelekos, commenced in 1852 a serial containing a considerable number of interesting pieces connected with the manners and customs of the people. More recently, a native of Laconia, in a pamphlet of 40 pages, published a metrical description of his country written at the close of the 18th century, and ten interesting *mœrologia*, a species of poetry which, from its ephemeral character, has until now seldom found its way into print. Perhaps the best collection of kleftic songs is to be found in the "Demotic Songs" of S. Zampelios of Corfu, who has prefixed six hundred pages of learned disquisition on the state of the Greek race in the Middle Ages.

HOUSE OF JONAS KING, D.D.

CHAPTER XXIV.

THE TRIAL OF DR. KING.

FRIDAY, the 5th of March (New Style) 1852, was the day set for the trial of Dr. King, before the Criminal Court of Athens, on the charge of reviling the Greek Church. The incessant clamors of the newspaper Æon, the organ of the Russian party, had finally induced the king's attorney to institute a prosecution against the foreign missionary: and the opponents of religious liberty already exulted in view of their approaching triumph. On the preceding day, a friend of Dr. King had brought to him a small printed hand-bill, which, he said, was being industriously circulated through the city, and posted along the streets, with the evident purpose of inciting the people to acts of violence toward Dr. King. It read as follows:

"To-morrow, Friday, the 22d of February (Old Style), the famous false apostle, *Jonas King*, will at last be tried before the Criminal Court of Athens. Accordingly, as many Christ-loving people as desire to be present at this curious trial may attend the said court at ten o'clock A.M., and hear the false apostle convicted of the foolish babblings he has uttered against the Mother of God, the Saints, the Images, and, in a word, all the Sacraments, Doctrines, and Traditions of our Holy Church."

In consequence of this notice, a demand was made of the police for additional protection on the day of the trial. The first token of the requisition was the appearance of a detachment of four police-officers at the gate of the Consulate early on Friday morning. They had come to attend and protect Dr. King on his way to the court-room. After a short season of prayer with his family, he expressed his readiness to go. I walked with him, while his young son followed, under the care of the faithful man-servant, old Barba Constantinos. Two of the most prominent lawyers of Athens had been retained as counsel. We took the house of one of them on our way. Mr. Pelicas was waiting to escort us. He was a small man, with fine features and an intellectual countenance, esteemed to be one of the most upright members of the Athenian bar, and at this time professor of law, and Prytanis (or President) of the University of Otho.

The king's attorney had proposed to Mr. Pelicas that Dr. King should wait at his house until sent for; but the missionary determined to be present, at all events, at the appointed time. The Criminal Court held its sessions in an old building at the corner of Athena Street and a small lane. The lane, from which access was gained by a broad flight of steps to the court-room, was already crowded with old and young; but no disturbance occurred on our arrival. The chief of police, who was rather friendly to Dr. King, had detached a number of policemen, armed with musket and bayonet; and presently that individual came in person. The more fanatical part of the assemblage had already found their way into the court-room, and were impatiently awaiting the process. The space allotted to the audience was crowded to its utmost capacity, and here and there appeared the black coat and cap of a priest.

By the courtesy of some officials, I was permitted to take a seat within the bar, in a position whence I could see and hear every thing that was said and done. It was a curious spectacle, that array of animated faces that crowded the farther end of the room, all intent on hearing the trial of one of the most interesting and important cases that had ever come up for decision before a Grecian tribunal.

The judges chosen to try the accused appeared very punctually, entering the court-room from a small chamber in the rear. As the accusation related not to a *crime*, but to an offence of secondary grade, the legislation of Greece, in imitation of the French practice, makes the bench sole judges both of the law and of the fact. Trial by jury is only resorted to in cases of murder, treason, and other felonious deeds. The five judges, Messrs Nicolopoulus, Papaspirides, Kallisperes, Boniseres, and Œconomides, took their seats on a platform facing the audience: the first-named, as president, occupying the middle seat. At opposite ends of the table before them, and on the same platform, sat Mr. Typaldus, the attorney general, and Mr. Matakides, the clerk.

The first duty of the clerk was to call over the names of the witnesses. The prosecution had cited twelve witnesses, of whom nine answered to their names; and the defence twenty-one, out of whom only ten ventured to appear—a striking disparity, which tended to show how strong was the fear of popular or priestly violence entertained by those who should have borne testimony to the good character of the defendant. Dr. King perceived that there was no ground for expecting any more favorable occasion, and readily consented to the proposal of the attorney general, that both sides should mutually abandon the absentees. The trial accordingly proceeded.

I have stated that the accusation against Dr. King was that he had, in public discourse, during the years 1850 and 1851, reviled the Greek religion. To this was originally added the utterly gratuitous accusation of reviling religion in general. But the Areopagus, on appeal, had judged the latter imputation too ridiculous to be sustained, and had ordered its erasure. It was, therefore, to prove the former part of the indictment alone that the witnesses were summoned.

It would be tedious to describe, or even enumerate, the various witnesses, as they were successively brought up to the open space in front of the president, and sworn. They merely repeated what they had previously testified in the secret inquest, which always precedes the finding of a bill of indictment. In the main, the testimony seemed to be true; but a Protestant would have found it difficult to imagine in what respect the language attributed to Dr. King was objectionable, or tended in the least to constitute a reviling of the Greek Church: unless, indeed, it be reviling to state personal opinions when they happen to be diametrically opposed to those of an auditor. In short, the testimony proved only that Dr. King held the doctrines generally received by the religious communion to which he belonged in America.

The witnesses were nearly all young men. Some were students in the medical school, and others candidates for the priesthood. Besides the usual animation that characterizes the Greek, they seemed moved by strong partisan feeling. I remember, in particular, a youth called Kyriakoules, whose expressions of enmity against the defendant were so strong, that the presiding judge himself was obliged to interrupt him, and exclaim, "You are here as a witness, not as an accuser!" He held in his hand a paper, from which he attempted several times to read extracts; but desisted on being told that his business was merely to answer the questions put to him. Persons who stood near him when he was not testifying have assured me that he was armed with a dagger, and that he incited the boys around him to hoot when any thing favorable to Dr. King was elicited.

A lawyer would have noticed one striking peculiarity in the testimony, as well as in the indictment. Although several of the witnesses pretended to have heard Dr. King use language disrespectful to the Greek religion, they never mentioned the exact words, nor specified the time or occasion of their utterance. Hence the defence was utterly unable to bring proof that such language had never been made use of, since no witness could depose any thing more than that no abuse had been indulged in upon the occasions when he was present. No testimony, however, was more flagrantly unfair than that of a half-crazed old man, who was permitted to give in his evidence against Dr. King, although, by his own confession, he had not entered the missionary's house for seven years. Yet the term stated in the indictment embraced only the years 1850 and 1851!

In the examination of the witnesses, the president of the court displayed the most obvious prepossession in favor of the testimony adverse to Dr. King, and of those who so testified, whether their evidence was pertinent or not. On the other hand, he seemed determined to browbeat the numerous and respectable witnesses for the defence—a course which, combined with the tumultuous applause, or the equally pronounced disapproval of the audience, to a great extent encouraged by the supineness of the court, disturbed not a little the self-possession of the witnesses. The presiding judge even went so far as to reprimand one of the criers of the court for ordering some noisy priests to be silent, and deprived him for that day of the badge of office.

The king's attorney now rose, and argued the case for an hour and a half, or two hours. In order to prove that the accused was guilty of reviling the Greek religion during the two years mentioned in the indictment, he brought forward some books written by Dr. King, and showed what his creed was. One of these, entitled "A Defence," was published many years since; and the other, "An Exposition of an Apostolic Church," was published in the United States. He did not attempt to prove that these pamphlets were written by Dr. King; but taking this for granted, he inferred, from passages which the court permitted him to read, that Dr. King believed, and therefore taught, doctrines at variance with the standards of the Orthodox Church. And this, he maintained, constituted the crime of reviling the Greek religion, as contemplated in the law.

At the end of the lengthy theological discourse of the king's attorney, Mr. Triantaphyllos, one of Dr. King's lawyers, began by alluding to the contrast presented by the scene now witnessed with that beheld twenty-three years before, when his client had come, intrusted by the liberality of the American people, with provisions to feed the famishing Greeks. He then proceeded to answer the arguments of the king's attorney; and said that that officer had wrongly sought to introduce a religious discussion. (Here he was interrupted by the court, and told to abstain from such language—as if the king's attorney were a privileged character.) If such a discussion were to come off, Dr. King should have employed Protestant counsel to defend his religious tenets. In conclusion, he urged that, by the constitution and laws of Greece, religious toleration and the right of discussion were guaranteed.

Mr. Pelicas followed, with a clear and logical speech, in which he exhibited the inapplicability of the law to the case of Dr. King. The mere expression of opinions adverse to those of the Greek Church could not fairly be construed as a reviling of, or even an indication of malevolence toward, that Church; much less as an insult to religion in general—an accusation which the king's attorney had sought illegally to reintroduce into the indictment, and for which not a particle of evidence had been shown.

When the king's attorney had made a brief rejoinder, Dr. King arose, holding some documents in his hands, and wished to say a few words in his own defence. The papers contained proof that the prosecution was of the nature of a conspiracy against him, and that some of the witnesses were principals in the plot. The judges had already risen, and were about to retire. Mr. Nicolopoulus said that opportunity had already been given to the defendant to speak; but that he might, if he chose, hand in the documents that he held, and the court would take them into consideration. Dr. King stated some facts in explanation of their contents; and then, seeing the uselessness of attempting to convince an impatient court, handed the papers to the president, and sat down. The judges, most of whom had remained standing, immediately left the room, to confer as to their verdict.

About half an hour elapsed before the door opened, and the judges resumed their seats. Mr. Nicolopoulus proceeded to pronounce a decision, which was afterward reduced to writing, with considerable alterations. In the court-room, it was stated that the accused was found guilty of reviling the Greek Church; in the recorded verdict, that his offence was the less heinous one of using malevolent expressions against it. Only two such expressions are singled out from all the mass of testimony, and from the articles of the indictment, as the ground of the finding of the court. This is what the court says: "The calling the Mother of God simply a woman, and affirming that she bare also other children, and saying that the Communion, that is, the body and blood of our Lord Jesus Christ, is bread and wine, are incontestably malevolent expressions."

The defendant being thus found guilty, the king's attorney moved that he be sentenced to three months' imprisonment, according to the law in this case provided; and that, on the expiration of that term, he be banished from the country, in accordance with another article, as a person convicted of a crime, and "pre-eminently dangerous to the common safety and to morals, by his manner of life, character, and conduct." The defendant's counsel opposed the motion, averring that the latter portion of the penalty was utterly unsuitable, since there was nothing in the history of the defendant that rendered him obnoxious to any of these charges.

The court now retired a second time, and shortly returned. They sentenced "the said Jonas King, convicted as aforesaid, to fifteen days' imprisonment, to the costs of the trial, and the duty on the stamps, to be collected by the committal of his person," and ordered "his exile from the territory of Greece, after the execution of the sentence of imprisonment."*

Thus was concluded this judicial farce. The judges, who had come instructed to convict Dr. King, withdrew, and the audience, who had come to see him convicted, after expressing their joy by prolonged applause, hastened down to the street to see the missionary carried away to prison. The king's attorney, however, who, as it subsequently appeared, was in no

* One of the judges that sat on this trial, with whom I had some slight acquaintance, was in the habit of saying that he wholly disapproved of the verdict and sentence, and that he had voted against their adoption in the private deliberations of the court. Since, however, he manifested no disapprobation of the extraordinary conduct of the presiding judge, and did not exercise his right of withholding his signature from the record, I am at a loss to know how much credit is due to the assertion.

hurry to incarcerate Dr. King, at once acceded to the request of his lawyers, that he might be permitted to return to his house, in order to make preparations for his imprisonment and exile. A large mob had meanwhile collected around the building. The friendly officer, to whose interest in Dr. King the detachment of so many policemen had been due, begged us to tarry until the tumultuous crowd dispersed, lest it should undertake to commit some violence. Accordingly, we remained a while in the deserted court-room; but the people below showed no sign of retiring. Finally, it was thought best to lead Dr. King by a private passage, and through an unoccupied shop, to the front of the building, on Athena Street, where a carriage was in waiting. The officer entered it with us; a couple of armed policemen mounted the carriage—one taking his seat on the box, and the other standing up behind. The fanatical mob that lingered about the entrance on the lane, seeing themselves thus outwitted, ran toward the carriage with loud yells, but were driven back at the point of the bayonet by some soldiers stationed in the vicinity.

Saturday, Sunday, and Monday passed, but no order was sent for Dr. King's arrest. The design of the king's attorney then became evident. No one can appeal from the decision of the Criminal Court unless his exceptions are filed within five days after the rendering of the verdict, and unless the prisoner is undergoing the infliction of his sentence. It was the policy of the State to defer Dr. King's imprisonment until the expiration of these five days, in order to preclude an appeal. Had he allowed himself to be thus beguiled, his negligence would have furnished a specious pretext for refusing redress. Strange as it may seem, the missionary was thus compelled to demand the partial execution of his own sentence. After a confinement of a few hours in the loathsome *Medresé*, of which I have elsewhere spoken, he was taken to the police-office, where he underwent imprisonment until he fell sick and was carried home. The expulsion of Dr. King being the real object of the prosecution, nobody cared for his incarceration, and nothing would have been more pleasant to the government than to hear that he had escaped of his own accord.

Seventeen days elapsed before the appeal came up for discussion in the Areopagus, the Supreme Court of Greece. That tribunal can only review the points of law contained in the record; and it was on these that exceptions were taken. The highest court was called on to pronounce whether the mere statement of opinions at variance with the doctrines of the Greek Church constituted a malevolent expression against that Church, and whether such an offence rendered a man dangerous to the common safety and to morals. The Areopagus, in manifest violation of common sense and equity, replied that the Criminal Court was competent to decide as to what were malevolent expressions, and what rendered a man dangerous to society. At the same time, it reversed all that part of the verdict which found Dr. King guilty of reviling religion in general. It is difficult to perceive where the court drew the line of demarcation between its own jurisdiction and that of the Criminal Court. Instead of ordering a new trial, the Areopagus affirmed the sentence of the lower court, with the trivial alteration of the term of confinement from *fifteen* to *fourteen* days.

Dr. King was now at the mercy of the government. As a last resource, he drew up, in his character of Consular Agent of the United States, a protest "against the unjust decisions of the Criminal Court of Athens and of the Areopagus, and against any execution whatever of them." This he forwarded at once to Mr. Paicos, Minister of Foreign Affairs. It was probably this movement that arrested the hands of the Greek government. The possible interest of the American nation in the sufferings of its distant citizen had never entered the heads of those who were so eager to drive the missionary away. But whatever may have been the cause, Dr. King was allowed to remain unmolested in his own house until the arrival of the American vessels of war.

Meanwhile the public press of Athens was loud in its condemnation of the whole of this fanatical affair: stigmatizing it as unjust and ill-timed; as a violation of the sacred right of religious liberty guaranteed by the Constitution and the laws of the realm. "The introduction of this case into court," said one paper, "was, in our opinion, a foolish measure, for religious discussions can not be carried on in a tribunal of justice.

But when the matter is considered in its political aspect, that, at the very moment when our government is endeavoring to obtain the importation of the Greek currant into America free of duty, the attorney general should bring Mr. King, who is an agent of America, to trial, and that the court should order his expulsion from Greece—all this seems to us, to say the least, a political solecism."

"Mr. King," it added, "has been prosecuted and condemned to expulsion, for teaching every Sunday, in his own house, the tenets of the denomination to which he belongs. Don Constantine, the parish priest of the Catholics, who preaches, not in his private house, but in the Catholic church, doctrines contrary to our holy religion, should, therefore, also be prosecuted, if the king's attorney wishes to be consistent. Consequently, we must destroy the article in the Constitution respecting toleration, and proclaim that every religion, indeed, is tolerated, and its rites may be celebrated without hinderance; but that the priests of the foreign religion will be prosecuted penally, unless they profess the doctrines of the Orthodox Church."

Nor did the conduct of the judges escape the animadversion it richly deserved. All intelligent men were shocked to find that the most sacred provisions of law had been violated. Even papers that could not be suspected of sympathy with Dr. King or his work, joined in denouncing a trial in which "the legal tribunals of Greece"—to use the forcible language of Mr. Marsh—"had been guilty of an abuse of the principles of justice, and a perversion of the rules of law, as flagitious as any that ever disgraced the records of the Star Chamber."

"We can not forbear to mark with reprobation," said the *Courier of Athens*, "all that occurred in the court-room. The evening before the trial of Mr. King, some pious individuals had distributed a profusion of printed cards of invitation. On the day of the discussion, a crowd of the lovers of scandal repaired to the rendezvous with a determination to exercise a pressure on the court. The lawyers were at every moment interrupted by vociferations, while the remarks of the prosecuting attorney were greeted with loud applause. Could not a little more, we will not say severity, but impartiality, have repressed such manifestations, so contrary to our manners, to the dignity of justice, and to the spirit of toleration that characterizes and does honor to the Greek people? We are grieved to be compelled to announce that the liberty of defence, and the gravity which should preside at the deliberations of justice, have been greatly compromised. Especially are we pained when we think of the long echo which this trial can not fail to have through the United States—that country, so great in its present, so immense in its future, and which showed itself so sympathetic, so enthusiastic even, for the cause of our independence."

The subsequent history of Dr. King's case may be summed up in few words. Besides the unjust trial to which he had been subjected, there were other grievances of longer standing. He was proprietor of a considerable plot of ground on the outskirts of Athens, which he had originally bought of the Turks for a mere pittance. As the city increased, it became exceedingly valuable. But the government, in 1835, announced the intention of taking a part of it for a public square; and though this plan was never put into execution, Dr. King was debarred from building upon it himself, and, of course, could find no purchaser. Thus the matter stood for seventeen years; the government neither taking, nor allowing him to make use of the land. The former American consul at Athens had, of his own accord, laid the case before Mr. Webster, and sent on for the documents relative to it.

With characteristic promptitude, Mr. Webster, then Secretary of State, on the 29th of April—just one month and four days after the publication of the decision of the Areopagus—instructed Mr. George P. Marsh, our minister resident at Constantinople, to proceed to Athens, and investigate the facts relating to the alleged grievances of Dr. King. Mr. Marsh arrived at Athens August 1st, 1852, and, after completing his inquiries, left on the 21st of the same month. His able reports, since published by the American government, exhibit the injustice of the treatment Dr. King has received at the hands of the Greeks in the clearest manner. On the 5th of February, 1853, Mr. Everett, who had succeeded to the Department of State, on the death of Mr. Webster, directed Mr. Marsh to return to Athens, and demand of the Greek government an entire remission of the sentence passed upon Dr. King, and a pecuniary indemnification for the land he had been deprived of. The opinion entertained by the American government may be inferred from the following passage: "The whole character of the proceedings, as minutely detailed by you, is such as to place the character of the Greek tribunals and the administration of justice in an unfavorable light. Either the sound and safe maxims of criminal jurisprudence, which prevail in this country, are unknown to the jurisprudence of Greece, or her tribunals were presided over by persons who entertained very false notions of the judicial character, or there are prejudices against Dr. King which, in his case, at least, corrupted the fountains of justice. It is not in the power of this government, at so great a distance, to form a confident opinion to which of the above-mentioned causes the result of Dr. King's trial is to be ascribed. It may have been in part produced by all three, and there is reason to suppose that such is the case. This state of things unavoidably destroys all confidence in the Greek courts, so far as Dr. King is concerned, and compels the president to regard their decision in this case as unjust and oppressive."

The conduct of the Greek government in answer to the demands of Mr. Marsh was not such as the American government had a right to expect. The printed correspondence reveals a variety of subterfuges to avoid compliance with the dictates of justice and an enlightened policy, an avoidance of the points in issue, and other evasions such as cunning would readily suggest to obstinacy, for the sake of gaining time. Mr. Marsh left Athens without having succeeded in persuading the Greek cabinet. During the following winter the government, of its own accord, granted to Dr. King a full remission of the sentence of imprisonment and exile. At length Mr. Pryor, specially commissioned by the president, in the summer of 1855, to procure an indemnification from the Greek government, succeeded in obtaining precisely what had been so obstinately refused two years previous—that is to say, if I am rightly informed, the sum of $25,000 for the land taken away from Dr. King by the opening of the public square.

Such have been the consequences of a trial unequaled in importance by any that have come before a Greek tribunal since the establishment of national independence. It was instituted by the fanaticism of the priestly party, with the purpose of crushing all religious discussion. It has resulted in the firm establishment of toleration as guaranteed to all known religions by the first article of the Constitution. And while convincing the Greek government that the United States stands ready to espouse the cause of any of its citizens in distress, it has strengthened the hands of the American missionaries in Greece, by evidencing the interest which American Christians feel in those who are battling for their holy faith at distant points of the globe.

GATE OF THE NEW AGORA.

CHAPTER XXV.

DEPARTURE FROM ATHENS—SYRA—CORFU.

After bidding adieu to the good friends whose kind offices had contributed so much to render my stay at Athens both agreeable and advantageous, I rode down to Piræus on the day before the steamer left, and spent some hours in taking leave of my acquaintances there. One of the number was Madame Caratzas, daughter of the famous Marco Bozzaris, and formerly one of the maids of honor to Queen Amelia. She is a fine-looking woman; but scarcely impresses one with the idea that she was ever so beautiful as she is said to have been by those who saw her ten years ago. She has several young children. The name of Marco Bozzaris, though never mentioned but with profound gratitude by the Greeks, is not so much in the mouths of the people as a stranger would expect. This is to be accounted for by the fact that, cut off in the midst of his course, his influence upon the issue of the Revolution was unimportant, save in a moral point of view, as he afforded a glorious example to his countrymen. He is, moreover, represented by many of the Greeks as an illiterate man, little distinguished above most of the combatants, who would probably never have emerged from an obscure sphere, had not his magnanimous death been immortalized by the pen of Halleck and of others, and by the enthusiasm of Christian Europe. I am loth, however, to give credit to any statement that detracts from the traditional honor in which the name of Marco Bozzaris is held.

The country seat of Mr. Contostaulos, to which I next repaired, lies out of Piræus, and his house is surrounded by a garden of ten acres reduced to profitable cultivation. Mr. C., who speaks English well, was one of the agents that came to the United States during the late revolution to attend to the construction of a frigate or two for the Greek navy. Although, in the progress of the negotiations to secure this object, much money was, without doubt, squandered uselessly, the character of Mr. Contostaulos has been triumphantly vindicated from all aspersion. In the neighborhood of this villa, I entered an establishment lately erected by a Mr. Rallis for the unwinding of silk from the cocoon. I was informed that upward of forty operatives were employed, and that the daily produce is one hundred and forty large hanks of silk, weighing more than twenty pounds. The investment is, probably, a profitable one; for the wages of operatives vary from sixteen to twenty-five cents a day.

The famous "Maid of Athens," whose memory will endure so long as Lord Byron is remembered, besides exchanging her name of Theresa Macri for the more prosaic Mrs. Black, has transferred her residence to Piræus. That she was fascinating once, no one can doubt that has read the glowing descriptions not only of Byron, but also of other travelers. It may be readily imagined, however, that forty-two years have not passed since the poet saw her without producing considerable changes in her personal appearance. Her children have inherited a large share of her beauty. Travelers have frequently remarked that they never beheld a more noble frame than that of her eldest son, whose premature death since my departure has thrown a gloom over a once happy family, and over a large circle of acquaintance. Mr. Black is Professor of English in one of the two Athenian Gymnasia, and holds at the same time the post of British Vice-consul.

Modern Piræus covers only a small portion of the site of the ancient town. The houses are mostly collected on the eastern side of the largest of three harbors, all of which were once used for commercial purposes. Old Piræus, which is supposed to have equaled in size, or even surpassed Athens itself, seems to have extended over the rocky peninsula of Munychia, as well as the more populous districts of Piræus proper and Phalerum. A lofty wall, whose circuit can be easily traced, ran around the entire town, constituting as strong a defence from the sea-board as on the land side; and the entrances to the harbors, which were rendered narrow by strong piers projecting from the opposite sides, in time of danger were further guarded by heavy chains extended between their abutments.

Very few traces of public and private edifices remain. Near the port of Munychia, the principal bathing-place of the present inhabitants, there is the foundation of a temple dedicated to Diana. Not far from the same spot a theatre seems to have existed. Tradition points out, on the heights of Phalerum, the locality where St. Paul saw the altar dedicated to the "Unknown God," of which he made such happy use in his speech on Mars' Hill. The altar is a rude detached rock, six or eight feet in height, one side of which has been cut into a regular façade, with a niche between two imperfect pilasters. The hypothesis that this was the altar referred to by the Apostle, rests on the slender basis of a passage in Pausanias, which says that there were altars to unknown gods at Phalerum, without specifying their precise locality. It is exceedingly doubtful whether the rock served as an altar at all. On another part of the same hill, an opening in the ground leads downward by a stairway to a great depth. Its use appears to be unknown, unless it may have been to gain access to a secret well.

On the 28th of September, bidding farewell to Rev. Mr. and Mrs. Buel, at whose hospitable mansion I had spent the previous night, and to a number of my Athenian friends, who had ridden down to see me leave, I went on board the small Austrian steamer *Archiduca Ludovico*, bound for Syra. By a singular and unforeseen coincidence, it was the anniversary of my arrival at the same port.

Our steamer should have started at six o'clock P.M.; but it was full an hour later before we got under way. A short distance from us lay a government sloop at anchor. A stout man dressed in gaudy costume, who stood on its deck, monopolized the attention of all the Greek passengers. This was the public executioner. Such is the repugnance entertained by the modern Greeks for the infliction of capital punishment, that the greatest difficulty is experienced in obtaining any one willing to execute the sentence of the law. The executioner is certain of falling a victim to the revenge of the friends of the culprit, unless extraordinary measures are taken for his protection. The individual that was on board the sloop-of-war had been successively carried to Chalcis and other places, where executions took place.

It was already quite dark when we started; and in making our way out of the harbor, we barely escaped sinking a small pleasure-boat. We reached the island of Syra early the next morning, and anchored off the city of Hermopolis. A few hours only were allowed the passengers to pass to the larger steamers, that were to convey them, according to their destination, either to Trieste, or to Smyrna and Constantinople. I improved the little time thus afforded me in looking about the town.

A boatman whom I engaged to convey me to the shore promised to conduct me to the house of Rev. Mr. Hildner. The city is entirely modern; for the old village of Syra before the Revolution covered only the top of a lofty hill. Hermopolis extends over the lower portion of the same hill; and between the two towns there intervenes a considerable space of open ground. Syra proper was constructed at a time when, on account of the depredations of pirates, the most inaccessible spots were chosen for the sites of towns and villages. The lower town is probably by far the most commercial place in Greece, not even excepting Patras.* The population is about

* According to the statements of a Greek journal, it had in 1852

eighteen thousand, of whom twenty-five hundred live in the upper town. The inhabitants of this quarter are almost exclusively Roman Catholics, and the hill is crowned by a monastery belonging to that denomination. As we ascended the hill to Mr. Hildner's house, we found the streets so steep that I was not astonished that no carriages or conveyances of any kind were to be seen. Indeed, I do not know that any are employed.

Mr. Hildner received me very kindly, and insisted on my going with him to see the schools under his charge, connected with the "Church Missionary Society" of England. They contain at present about two hundred and fifty scholars; and the number would undoubtedly be much larger, were it not for the opposition of the government and clergy, excited by the determination he has evinced not to introduce the Catechism of the prevailing church. The method of instruction is partly Lancasterian. A Greek gentleman, Mr. Evangelides, who was educated in the United States, has established a flourishing academy in Syra. I had only time to call on him for a few moments, as the steamer for Trieste left at noon.

Our new steamer, the *Forward*, sailed the whole afternoon among the Cyclades. When I came on deck the next morning, we were off the southern coast of Messenia, near the island of Sapienza. Passing by the old Turkish town of Modon, whose walls reach to the water's edge, we pursued our way northward, keeping close to the shore. This gave us an admirable opportunity for seeing the Bay of Navarino, so famous both in ancient and modern times. It is of a semicircular shape, and the long and narrow island of Sphacteria, or Sphagia, nearly incloses it, leaving a single narrow entrance at the southern end. The old town of Navarino, or Neo-castro, as it is universally called by the Greeks, occupies very nearly the site of Pylus, the home of Nestor, mentioned in the first

six hundred and eighty-four vessels of all kinds, with a capacity of about eighty-eight thousand tons, and manned by near five thousand sailors. The greater part of these are, of course, small vessels; there were one hundred and fifty-three of between three and four hundred tons, and only nine between four and five hundred. The value of the whole shipping was estimated at $1,760,000.

books of the Odyssey. The island of Sphacteria is celebrated for the defeat and capture of a Lacedæmonian detachment in the seventh year of the Peloponnesian war; in which the boast of the braggart Cleon met so unexpected a fulfillment. The bay itself was signalized by the conflict between the Allied and Turco-Egyptian fleets, on October 20th, 1827, an action which arose from what would seem to have been a casual occurrence, and ended in the total annihilation of the Turkish fleet. In the course of three hours, two hundred and fourteen ships were sunk, disabled, or captured; and from that time the independence of Greece was established.

That afternoon about four o'clock we entered the harbor of Zante. The city is situated at the foot of a high ridge, on whose summit is a fort occupied by the British garrison. We stopped merely to take in and land passengers. The next morning at five we were entering the harbor of Corfu, the ancient Corcyra, the chief island of the Ionian Confederacy, and the residence of the English lord high commissioner.

Having a few hours to spend in this place, where several days could be occupied to advantage, I landed with an Ionian lawyer, whose acquaintance I made at Athens, and who was returning from a visit to Zante. By special favor, we were permitted to take our seats in the boat of the health-officer. As it was yet early, I walked with my friend first of all to the famous shrine of St. Spyridon, the patron saint of the island. His bones, which are reputed to be possessed of miraculous properties, and which, doubtless, exhale that singular sweetness peculiar, according to the legendaries, to saintly relics, are encased in a silver sarcophagus, and deposited in a corner of the chancel. My companion told me that thousands of the laboring classes visit the church every morning before going about their daily work, in order to kiss the silver coffin, and expect by this pious act to insure good success in all their occupations.

A recent occurrence has tended to raise to a still higher pitch the awe in which the relics are held. A lawyer, as the story goes, not long since brought suit against a former client for about one hundred dollars, due as a remuneration for his services. The respondent averred that he had paid the money some months previous; but confessed that, relying on his lawyer's honesty, he had taken no receipt. This the plaintiff stoutly denied, and confirmed his denial by an oath taken on the Gospel. The judges having long since perceived that the people are more afraid of perjuring themselves when sworn on the relics of St. Spyridon than when they merely kiss the Scriptures, resorted to this expedient in order to extort the truth. The lawyer, however, still persisted in his demand, and invoked upon himself the vengeance of St. Spyridon if a word of what he said was false. Thus he gained his suit. Not long afterward, his right hand, with which he had touched the silver sarcophagus, began to mortify; and the gangrene spread so rapidly that it could only be checked by the amputation of his arm. The superstitious immediately inferred his guilt, and attributed his misfortune to the efficiency of the relics. The incident has very sensibly augmented the veneration of the common people; and this feeling is fostered by the ecclesiastics, who profit by the increased amount of contributions to the funds of the church.

I called at Corfu on the Rev. Mr. Chartres, chaplain of one of the Scotch regiments, and a missionary of the English Presbyterian Church among the Jews, of whom there are great numbers here. While walking with me to the summit of the citadel, he gave me some account of his labors, and the difficulties he had encountered in imparting instruction to the Jews, and particularly in overcoming the prejudice entertained by that people against the education of girls. From the citadel there was an excellent view not only of the city, but of the surrounding country. The ancient Corcyra is supposed to have stood considerably south of the present city, which is crowded into a narrow space by two heights, each crowned with fortifications. There are two mountains in sight, Monte Decca on the south, and Monte San Salvadore on the north, at a greater distance. There is a bay just in sight below Mount Decca, at whose mouth is said to be situated the rock called the "Sail of Ulysses." In the same direction are the "*Gardens of Alcinoüs*," and the fountain where the poet tells us Ulysses surprised Nausicaä and her maids.

The city of Corfu contains about twenty thousand inhabitants, and is very compactly built, from the nature of its situation. The Jewish quarter is large, and the synagogues, though with an unpretending exterior, are well furnished. As usual, several congregations worship in different stories of the same edifice. Two or three British regiments are stationed here, and there are altogether five in the Ionian Confederation. The English rule here more as masters than as protectors. From the tone of public sentiment, as expressed in the Legislature and by the press, there appears to be little sympathy felt by the Ionians for the English. The attempt to cause the heterogeneous elements to coalesce, has thus far proved abortive. The inhabitants of the "Seven Islands," claiming a common origin with the Greeks, are already anxious to effect a union with the kingdom of Otho. Italian has until lately been the official language; but recently the Legislature has decreed that all speeches must be made in Greek. The rule is very inconvenient for those who are accustomed to make use of the Italian alone; but it will draw yet closer the bonds that unite the Ionian Confederation to the Hellenic kingdom. The young men will henceforth be obliged to complete their education at the University of Athens, instead of resorting to the schools of Pisa, Bologna, or Rome.

At eleven o'clock our steamer weighed anchor, and we were once more under way for Trieste. We kept close to the high coast of Albania, and before night had reached the Dalmatian frontier.

INDEX.

THE END.

www.ingramcontent.com/pod-product-compliance
Lightning Source LLC
LaVergne TN
LVHW020127110826
845151LV00001B/297

* 9 7 8 1 4 2 5 5 4 0 8 5 2 *